PERGAMON INTERNATIONAL LIBRARY
of Science, Technology, Engineering and Social Studies

*The 1000-volume original paperback library in aid of education,
industrial training and the enjoyment of leisure*

Publisher: Robert Maxwell, M.C.

Preserving the Environment
(PGPS-102)

THE PERGAMON TEXTBOOK
INSPECTION COPY SERVICE

An inspection copy of any book published in the Pergamon International Library
will gladly be sent to academic staff without obligation for their consideration for
course adoption or recommendation. Copies may be retained for a period of 60 days
from receipt and returned if not suitable. When a particular title is adopted or
recommended for adoption for class use and the recommendation results in a sale
of 12 or more copies the inspection copy may be retained with our compliments.
The Publishers will be pleased to receive suggestions for revised editions and new
titles to be published in this important international Library.

Pergamon Titles of Related Interest

Preserving the Environment
New Strategies for Behavior Change

E. Scott Geller
Virginia Polytechnic Institute

Richard A. Winett
Virginia Polytechnic Institute

Peter B. Everett
Pennsylvania State University

**With an invited chapter on Water Conservation by
Robin C. Winkler**
University of Western Australia

PERGAMON PRESS
New York   Oxford   Toronto   Sydney   Paris   Frankfurt

Pergamon Press Offices:

U.S.A.   Pergamon Press Inc., Maxwell House, Fairview Park,
                     Elmsford, New York 10523, U.S.A.

U.K.   Pergamon Press Ltd., Headington Hill Hall,
                     Oxford OX3 0BW, England

CANADA   Pergamon Press Canada Ltd., Suite 104, 150 Consumers Road,
                     Willowdale, Ontario M2J 1P9, Canada

AUSTRALIA   Pergamon Press (Aust.) Pty. Ltd., P.O. Box 544,
                     Potts Point, NSW 2011, Australia

FRANCE   Pergamon Press SARL, 24 rue des Ecoles,
                     75240 Paris, Cedex 05, France

FEDERAL REPUBLIC Pergamon Press GmbH, Hammerweg 6
OF GERMANY   6242 Kronberg/Taunus, Federal Republic of Germany

Library of Congress Cataloging in Publication Data

Geller, E. Scott, 1942-

   Preserving the environment.

   (Pergamon general psychology series ; 102)
   Includes indexes.
   1. Energy conservation--Psychological aspects.
2. Environmental protection--Psychological aspects.
I. Winett, Richard A. (Richard Allen), 1945-
II. Everett, Peter B. (Peter Ben), 1943-
III. Title. IV. Series.
TJ163.3.G44   1982   333.79'16'019   81-11906
ISBN 0-08-024615-X   AACR2
ISBN 0-08-024614-1 (pbk.)

Printed in the United States of America

To our children
Krista Scott and Karly Scott-Hillis Geller
Emily Anna Winett
Holly Jean and Benjamin Peter Everett

whose future quality of life
depends on present efforts to
preserve the environment

Natural Bridge of Virginia. Photo by Philip C. Lederach.

Contents

Preface

Each of us has been frequently asked questions such as, "What does psychology have to do with recycling? with energy conservation? with litter control? with mass transit?" These questions have been directed to us by individuals from all walks of life, including professionals involved in different aspects of environmental protection and resource management and, indeed, even by fellow psychologists. Today it seems that virtually everyone believes, or at least wants to believe, that our environmental problems can only be solved through breakthroughs in physical technology and by the natural workings of the marketplace. While we readily acknowledge the important roles of increased production, innovative technologies, and price levers in solving environmental problems, all too often behavior change strategies for environment preservation are either ignored or little understood by the public and policymakers. If behavioral technologies to promote conservation and resource recovery are accepted, they are often viewed as short-term, stop-gap measures, usable until new physical technologies are available.

Behavioral and what are sometimes called "low" technology approaches (e.g., passive solar in homes, use of bikes for transportation, recycling paper) require changes in human behaviors—sometimes entire life styles. But for many, even the simplest behavior changes can seem inconvenient and risky. It appears safe and easy to continue current activities and life styles and hope that an innovative physical solution will work. Indeed, they have in the past. Physical technologies have shortened some wars, diminished many of the drudgeries of household duties, and given us tremendous mobility. But will physical technology continue to work? Physical technology tends to be expensive and long range. Also, if behaviors are not changed, will physical technology alone solve our environmental problems?

In our opinion the answer to this question is obvious. In fact, the use of physical technologies without behavioral technologies is partly responsible for some of the environmental problems discussed in this book. For example, innovations in heating and cooling systems have eliminated for most people the problems of extreme temperatures, but as typically used, these systems consume too much energy. Modern packaging has provided us with a wide variety of fresh foods but has also created a throwaway, wasteful society. And, of course, the automobile gives us great individual freedom and mobility but also air pollution, urban blight, endless highway billboards and strips, and dependence on OPEC. These unfortunate side effects of physical technology may have been lessened if their introduction had been accompanied by behavioral technology.

In addition, even when a safe and inexpensive physical technology is developed, its adoption clearly depends on behavioral technology. For example, there are many physical technologies (e.g., retrofitting) for drastically reducing home energy use. The major problem has been, and still is, developing effective marketing strategies to assure widescale adoption of diverse retrofitting techniques.

The major purpose of this book is to show the potential of behavioral technology for alleviating environmental problems, by coordinating in one text over 150 studies that have been conducted during the last decade on environmental problems from a behavioral perspective. We discuss recent studies that have demonstrated the application of the principles and methodology of behavior science to the systematic change of behaviors related to environmental problems, such as waste reduction and resource recovery in communities; electricity, gas, and water consumption in the home; and transportation in private and public vehicles. Although the field is relatively young and many ideas suggested by the behavioral perspective have yet to be validated, we believe that the studies in this text clearly make the case that a behavioral focus has much to offer as a basis for assessing and solving environmental problems. If this book makes this case convincingly, then we hope to have the following effects on policy, paradigms, and disciplines (including our own):

• Environmental and resource problems have typically been approached from the perspective of engineering, architecture, other physical-technical perspectives, and economics. For example, the production of more fuel-efficient cars has been emphasized as a major solution to gasoline shortages. Residential energy conservation is most frequently approached through innovative design in new homes and redesign (retrofitting) of existing homes. The public has been frequently informed through the media of great potentials in solar and wind energy, in nuclear fusion, and in other inventive and exotic sources of energy. And the promotion of environment preservation is so often portrayed as simply a matter of deregulation and pricing strategies. We certainly do not dispute the relevance of these approaches to the solution of environmental problems. We do, however, question the apparent *sole reliance* on these traditional approaches and paradigms as the basis for environmental policy. We show in this book that there exists an established framework and set of strategies for modifying behavior which are increasingly being applied to environmental problem solving. At the very least, these strategies are an important adjunct to existing paradigms and policies and, in some instances, offer entirely different conceptualizations, data sources, interventions, and policy directions. One of our objectives is to influence the development and application of environmental policies in ways more consistent with a behavioral perspective.

• We frequently point out, contrary to current public and political opinion, that pursuing conservation via behavioral technologies does not mean individual sacrifice or a reduction in the quality of life. For example, if fewer people drove automobiles there would be less air pollution, more freedom to walk about, and less drain on our economy from the importation of foreign oil. A society that valued recycling would decrease our wasteful, useless "conspicuous consumption" and preserve our resources for future generations. Community-based conservation programs may renew neighborhoods by focusing on local human resources and the development of common goals. We believe that it is neither romantic nor utopian to believe that both a higher quality of life and environment preservation can be achieved through large-scale changes in environment-related responses. It is hoped that this book will encourage realistic behavior change policies that balance physical and behavioral technology.

• The emerging discipline of environmental psychology has not paid enough attention to the environmental topics of this text. Environmental psychologists have too often failed to consider the reciprocal relationship between environment and behavior. They have researched the impact of environmental factors on behavior to the exclusion of studying the contrary question—How does behavior affect the environment? For example, it is important to understand how contemporary urban patterns influence environmental perceptions, cognitions, attitudes, and even specific behaviors such as personnel interactions and shopping practices. However, from a humanistic and policy perspective, it may be even more important to understand how individual and group behaviors affect urban environments, and then to intervene in order to influence patterns of human behavior in directions that optimize the quality of life for all of us. Thus, we hope to direct the attention of environmental psychologists toward behavior change strategies and influence a more balanced, reciprocal perspective in the study of environment-behavior relationships.

• As psychologists we have often been dismayed at our profession's apparent lack of interest in environmental problems. It appears as if psychologists, like other citizens, believe the solution to environmental problems rests outside of their domain, i.e., through physical-technical breakthroughs. Indeed, as a result of a number of indifferent receptions from fellow psychologists, one of the authors (PE) rarely attends any psychological conferences or conventions. Two of us (SG and RW) continue to frequent psychology conventions annually, but have been continually disappointed in meager audiences at our environment and behavior presentations. We hope that this book serves as a catalyst for our colleagues and their students to realize that potential solutions for environmental problems rest within their knowledge base and that their active participation is urgently needed and potentially rewarding.

Besides trying to meet these hopes and objectives, organizing, writing, and editing this text has provided us with additional opportunities. We believe that the text has been a vehicle for sharpening and focusing our values with regard to environmental problems. At times, organizing the text has provoked in each of us a questioning of our basic commitments to behavioral technology and conservation. Yet, these doubts and challenges have culminated in, perhaps, more seasoned but firmer convictions.

The text has also provided a means to review and reassess some of our own career directions. Since each of the authors has been involved in the field for a decade or so—our entire professional careers— the text is in many ways a review of our careers. It is unusual in a technical book to have such intimate knowledge of so many of the studies, our own and those of others, and to have the opportunity to assess their strengths, weaknesses and overall contribution to the field, while trying to develop a synthesis to refocus ourselves and the field.

Organizing the book has also provided a formal way for us to expand our conceptualizations and methodologies. Actually, the focus of our research and teaching has changed rather drastically in the last decade, having been modified by the behavioral principles covered in this text. Two of us (SG and PE) started as experimental, laboratory-based psychologists, while one (RW) was a beginning clinical researcher and behavior therapist. Clearly, we have expanded the content and scope of our work. As represented in this book, we have focused our professional attention toward conceptualizations in diverse fields, including marketing, architecture, community planning, communications, and economics, and have worked closely with experts in these and other disciplines. We feel that this interdisciplinary, eclectic position is an essential framework for environmental problem solving. This book has provided a way to try to organize these different inputs, although the integration is admittedly not always apparent, coherent, nor complete.

Our interest in different theories and frameworks has illustrated an important feature of applied research. Rather than being atheoretical, applied research needs to have theoretical underpinnings. The application of theory then serves the important function of empirical feedback for theory modification. Thus, we feel the work in environmental problem solving serves as a testing ground for theory and principles and is a vehicle for developing and expanding paradigms and behavior change strategies.

It has also been with a sense of urgency that we have written this book. When we first discussed writing this book in 1977, there was still much public doubt about the reality and importance of environmental problems and the energy crisis. Since that time events have moved quickly, but we fear not always in the best direction. At the time of this writing (summer 1981), the lessons of gasoline lines, Three Mile Island, and soaring energy prices seem to have been quickly forgotten. A current oil glut is seen not as another manipulation of our energy policies by OPEC and other countries, but as a sign that there is no immediate problem. Once again, we have been influenced by consequences (or the lack thereof) and public attention (and faith) has shifted toward technical fixes, physical technology, and unleashing the oil companies. Our fear, as many others have pointed out, is that once we proceed too far along certain paths, there is no turning back.

Our basic message in this book is that many of our environmental problems can be alleviated, albeit not completely solved, by the appropriate mix of behavioral and physical technologies. Physical technology alone is not sufficient. We believe that the quality of life for present and future generations depends on following a balanced policy of behavioral and physical technology.

We hope this book will be considered for adoption as the primary or supplemental text in a variety of both undergraduate and graduate courses across several disciplines, including psychology, sociology, economics, education, urban planning, public health and administration, marketing, architecture and environmental design, business management, and public policy. Specific graduate and advanced undergraduate courses within the social sciences for which this text is directly relevant are: behavior modification, environmental psychology, social ecology, behavioral community psychology, resource management and administration, consumer behavior, community planning and development, social economics, and other courses which deal with relationships between the environment and human behavior.

A significant portion of this text offers practical advice for developing and evaluating programs to improve the quality of environment-behavior relationships, and therefore the text should be a valuable resource for those who develop, implement, or evaluate public policy. Furthermore, we are hopeful that the book will be of interest and use to the increasing numbers of citizens who are seriously concerned about the present and future quality of life and who perhaps have already contributed toward finding solutions to environmental problems. Our text offers action strategies which these individuals can apply to preserve the environment, to assess the impact of their efforts, and to recruit the additional human support needed for large-scale intervention and impact.

Acknowledgments

Since financial support for researching behavioral approaches to environmental problem solving has been *under*whelming over the past decade, we are especially grateful for the grant support we have received for our work in this area. Without such support many of our studies would not have been completed, although we hasten to add that an increase (rather than the current, drastic decrease) in funding for research in the behavioral and social sciences is absolutely essential if the potential of the research findings presented in this text is ever to reach fruition. The National Science Foundation has supported our research in residential energy and water conservation (Grant DAR-7910256 to RW and Grant SPI-800 3981 to SG). Other energy and water conservation research by SG was funded by the Virginia Department of Energy and the U.S. Department of Energy. Litter control research by SG was supported by the Virginia Division of Litter Control, the Jackson Company in Pomona, California, and the Center for Environmental Studies and the College of Arts and Sciences at Virginia Polytechnic Institute and State University. Much of the research in transportation conservation by PE was supported by grants from the College of Human Development and the Pennsylvania Transportation Institute at the Pennsylvania State University, Urban Mass Transportation Administration Contract No. PA-06-0047, and the Urban Mass Transportation Administration Cooperation Agreement No. PA-06-0056. Much of RW's research in energy feedback was supported by Grant 5507-RR05636-11 from the Division of Research Resources of the National Institutes of Health. His work in the effects of flexitime on family and community life was supported by Grant MH-30585 from the Center for the Study of Metropolitan Problems of the National Institute of Mental Health. The interdisciplinary efforts of SG toward developing community education and community action models for energy conservation were funded by Title I grants for Community Service and Continuing Education in Virginia.

Many friends, colleagues, and students have provided invaluable support, insight, and hard work over the years in helping us with numerous projects and professional activities. Without their effort and consideration our environmental projects and this book would not have been completed. Indeed, it would take several pages to list all of the individuals who have influenced our behavioral research and writing, but we would like to express sincere gratitude for the special support of the following students and colleagues:

Mark Albert	Dick Johnson
Mark Augustine	John Kagel
Jon Bailey	Jerard Kehoe
Lee Barnett	Eleanor Kingsley
Larry Becker	Karen Larson
Ruth Becker	Ingrid Leckliter
Sam Bowen	Brenda Buttram Lederach
Bill Brasted	Suzie Love
Kathy Brehony	Udit Makranczy
Larry Bruwelheide	Joni Mayer
Jamie Carlyle	Andy Meyers
Bob Chiang	Nancy Miller
Steve Churchill	Mike Neale
John Cone	Charles Noblin
John Cope	Mac Parsons
Kim Cuddihy	Lisa Paterson
Brian Deslauriers	Susan Pelton
Jeff Erickson	Dave Post
Peter Ester	Dave Reichel
John Farris	Anne Riley
John Ferguson	Alice Rowan
Jim Filipczak	Holly Sazima
Fred Fishback	Bob Schubert
Rick Fort	Clive Seligman
Haller Gilmer	Jeff Shilling
Dave Glenwick	John Slater
Mark Gurtler	Betsy Talbott
Victoria Anderson Gussman	Peggy Tuso
Joe Hatcher	Barry Watson
Steve Hayes	Harold Wheeler
Scott Hayward	Merrie Wilent
Ken Hearn	Ken Williams
Mark Hildebrand	Jill Witmer
Richard Ingram	Ruth Wylie
Lenny Jason	Jim Yokley
Elizabeth Jenkins	

We also gratefully acknowledge the craft and dedication of Jolene Downs who typed several versions of the text, and we have certainly appreciated the advice and encouragement of Jerry Frank, the Senior Editor of the Behavioral Sciences Division at Pergamon Press, who waited so patiently since 1978 for us to complete this text.

Last, but certainly not least, we gratefully acknowledge the inspiration and support from our families, especially our wives—Carol, Sheila, and Carol. They perseveringly covered for our many absences from family events, not only throughout the preparation of this text but also during the decade of our behavioral research and writing, which is reviewed herein. Ever since our professional careers began, the rate of the verbal response "but I've got so much to do" has been a high probability behavior following opportunities for family togetherness. We sincerely thank our families for dealing with the "time out" that inevitably followed such verbalization.

Chapter 1

Energy Intensive and Energy Efficient Behaviors: Home, Work, Transportation

John and Barbara Noblin and Robert and Susan Gilmer are typical middle-class couples who live in a suburban community located near a mid-sized city. Both the Noblins and the Gilmers are in their late 30s; both couples have two preteen children; both have annual incomes of about $40,000 per year; in fact, the homes of the two couples are identical in structure and interior design. Although demographically similar these couples, as we will see, engage in very different energy-related behaviors. The Noblins exhibit many *energy intensive* behaviors, whereas the Gilmers have adopted many *energy efficient* behaviors. We will look at each couple in a typical day and examine some of the differences in their daily activities with respect to energy consumption.

ENERGY INTENSIVE BEHAVIORS

John and Barbara Noblin have awakened this winter morning at 7:00 a.m. John (as usual) complains that the heat has dried up his nasal passages so that he did not sleep very well, and Barbara (as usual) asks him why he doesn't talk to their doctor about his problem. After his ten-minute shower, John goes downstairs to the kitchen dressed in his T-shirt and trousers and makes breakfast for himself and their two children.

It is nice and warm in the Noblins' house. In fact, it is always 70° F. in their all-electric home because Barbara has made it a rule that the thermostat must always be set at 70°, day or night. Barbara feels that anything less than 70° F. is "dreadful," and John agrees. Also, Barbara had heard that turning the thermostat up and down wastes energy; hence, the rule. Their $325 electric bill for January, however, indicates that something may be wrong.

After Barbara arrives in the kitchen, has her breakfast, and helps get the children off to school, John puts the garbage out. He neatly puts all the garbage in one plastic bag and carries it to the front of the house.

Now Barbara and John are ready to go to work. John drives the family station wagon ten miles into the city to the high school where he works as a mathematics teacher. Barbara also works in the city, as the manager of a branch bank, and takes the Noblins' second car to work. Although the work trips of Barbara and John are relatively short, both their cars average only about 15 mpg, and last month alone their gasoline expenditures were over $120 for commuting and weekend driving.

Even though it is the middle of the winter, Barbara is wearing only a light coat, dress, and loafers. Barbara says that she can "always dress for spring" because their home is warm, the bank is always kept at 72°, and she only has to contend with the cold when she goes to and from her car.

In addition to his teaching at the high school, John serves as a liaison between students, faculty, parents, and community services. One problem that has led to many complaints from the community surrounding the school is that the school has become an "eyesore." The building seems to be in the middle of a garbage heap. Everywhere there are wrappers from fast food stores, bottles and cans, and other litter. John is not sure what to do about this problem. He has told different groups at meetings that the school does not have funds to hire additional sanitation services for the school. It has been a particularly hard day today, and as John trudges through the snow (and debris) to his car, he finishes his coffee and throws the styrofoam cup to the ground in disgust.

As usual, John and Barbara arrive home in a foul mood. The reason is that, although both have short commutes, both John and Barbara always leave work at 5:00 p.m. and experience the rush-hour "snarl." Tonight, their ten-mile trips each took about 40 minutes in bumper-to-bumper traffic.

Barbara says she is cold and irritable, and when she comes in she turns the heat up to 72° F. to get the house "toasty." After dinner, the Noblins and their children spend the evening in their den reading and watching television. The room faces the north and the wind seems to be creating a draft through the windows and through the room. John tells Barbara that he probably should have put storm windows in, as they had discussed last spring. As the family leaves the den to prepare for bed, everyone remarks on how nice and warm it is in the rest of the house—the part of the house no one has been in this evening.

ENERGY EFFICIENT BEHAVIORS

Susan and Robert Gilmer also rose at 7:00 a.m. this morning. Actually, it is rather cold in their house right now—in fact, it is 55° F. But Susan and

Robert and their two children have found that with two heavy blankets they can sleep quite comfortably when it is cool at night in their home. As he does every morning, Robert picks up his robe, puts on his slippers, goes downstairs, and turns the thermostat from 55° F. to 65° F. He then goes upstairs to take a shower. Although Robert and Susan have adopted many energy efficient practices, Robert insists on a leisurely, warm shower each morning. But to save on water and energy, he has installed shower-flow controllers in both of their showers.

Robert, Susan, and the children meet in the kitchen for breakfast, and each is wearing a brightly colored sweater, warm trousers, and boots or high-topped shoes. After breakfast, Robert clears the table and separates all the garbage into a special "recycl-it" can located in the kitchen. The can contains separate compartments for food scraps, paper, and metals. If separated, the paper and metal are picked up by the sanitation company as part of their new recycling program. The food scraps are put into a worm-laden compost pile that is later used for the family's garden in the spring.

About 8:00 a.m., while everyone is getting ready to leave for work or school, Susan turns down the thermostat to 55° F. In order to see if these thermostat set-backs worked, Robert kept records of electricity consumption in his all-electric home last January and compared consumption to the prior January when the weather had been quite comparable (and they had kept their thermostat at a constant 68° F.). Robert was surprised that they actually used 30 percent less electricity with the thermostat set-back procedures.

This experience also prompted Robert and Susan to have more insulation blown into their attic and walls. The insulation job cost $512, but last month their electric bill was only $130. Robert has continued to monitor regularly their electricity use and has estimated that the addition of the extra insulation saved about $40 last month alone. Robert is amazed when he hears stories from friends about utility bills of $300 to $400 per month.

Susan works in the city at an administrative position for an electronics firm. Last year her company decided to try a special commuting plan, because company officials felt that providing additional parking space for private cars was a poor capital investment. The company instead leased ten large vans that can comfortably seat about 12 people each and offered them to employees who were willing to pick up other employees (who pay a small fee for the service) and take them to work. On the weekends Susan and Robert have free use of the van, and thus they have sold their car.

Robert works at the university which is located on the outskirts of the city. Everyone thinks he's a hardy soul or a pioneer of sorts, because almost every day he takes his moped to work. He drives the moped on the sides of the roads, and for most of the trip he can use bicycle lanes. When the weather is particularly poor, he takes the bus. While some people still think Robert is a bit "weird," he points out that for the entire prior year he only paid $60 for gas and maintenance of his moped.

Until a couple of years ago, the heating system in the university buildings was the subject of much gallows humor. People in Robert's department used to talk about having "sauna meetings" in their seminar room. An overhaul of the heating system, including individual area thermostats and a program of incentives for the least consumption of energy by departments, has reduced energy use at the university by almost 40%. Robert admits that sometimes it is a bit chilly in his office, but for the most part he has gotten used to the cooler temperatures and simply dresses warmer.

Robert has also found a novel way for his students to earn some extra money. After complaining for years that he felt like he was living in a "paper mill," he decided to do something constructive with all the paper that circulates around the university. With his help his students have set up special, convenient areas in each department for people to leave their no-longer-needed papers. The recycling program has proven to be popular with the students, faculty, and administration. The students fund a party each semester with the money earned from selling the recyclable paper to a local paper mill.

By leaving work at off-peak times, Susan and Robert have been able to make their trips home from work quicker and easier. Susan's company has instituted a flexible-work-hour program, and she generally leaves work at 4:15 p.m. because she usually arrives at work promptly at 8:15 a.m. Robert likes to arrive at work a bit later, around 9:30 a.m., and thus leaves at about 6:00 p.m.

After dinner, the Gilmer family spends most of their evening in their den. Late last winter Susan came up with a good idea for saving energy, but remaining comfortable. Since most of their evenings are spent in one or two rooms, why should the entire house be heated in the evening? Thus, after dinner, the Gilmer's usually turn their thermostat down to about 55° F., but use a small electric space heater in the room(s) where they spend their evenings. With this strategy, the main heating furnace usually does not go on during the four or five hours in the evening that the Gilmer family is active, but they remain comfortable nonetheless.

HUMAN BEHAVIOR AND ENVIRONMENTAL
PROTECTION: THE CONTEXT OF CHANGE

The scenarios indicated that at least from an end-use perspective, many aspects of environmental protection including littering, recycling, energy and water consumption, and transportation can be described in behavioral terms. *People and their behaviors make a dramatic difference!* For example, people have or have not adopted physical practices of life-style changes to recycle goods, drive less, or use less energy for residential heating or cooling. The chapters in this book will detail and document the effectiveness of strategies designed to develop, promote, and maintain proenvironmental practices.

Before proceeding in greater detail, let us underscore the previous point at an individual and then societal level. Most laymen, and indeed most professionals, in the energy field are accustomed to examining the structure of a home and then predicting the "home's" energy consumption. Obviously, there is a great deal of validity to this type of assessment; certainly at the extremes, structural characteristics of a home make a big difference in energy consumption. However, what is less commonly known, and has been shown in our examples, is that what people do in a home also makes a great difference in energy consumption. For example, it has been consistently found that in identical homes, occupied by people with similar demographic characteristics, energy use can differ by two or three fold (Socolow, 1978; Winett, Neale, Williams, Yokley, & Kauder, 1979). Further, when people move from a particular home, and the home is reoccupied by a second family, energy consumption patterns from the occupancy of Family One and the occupancy of Family Two are often totally *dissimilar* from each other (Socolow, 1978).

On a societal level, it has become increasingly clear that other Western countries have obtained an equal, and in some instances better, standard of living than the United States, but with per capita consumption of energy *considerably less* than in the United States (Hirst, 1976). The old argument linking the GNP and economic prosperity with high per capita energy consumption has, for the most part, been proven false (Stobaugh & Yergin, 1979). It seems to us, and increasingly for others involved in energy policy and environmental protection (see Lovins, 1977; Stobaugh & Yergin, 1979), that there is nothing incompatible with conservation, efficiency, environment, economic prosperity, and the "good life." We will discuss this point again a bit later. It can also be (and clearly has been) argued that the opposite is *not* true. Energy waste, particularly the drain on our economy fostered by our tremendous dependence on foreign oil, is incompatible with economic prosperity and a stable standard of living.

In this text, we describe procedures and programs for promoting proenvironmental practices that are cost effective for large-scale application. However, behavioral strategies alone are not sufficient for environment preservation. To be really effective, behavioral strategies generally need a supportive context, such as federal and state policies and programs. Behavioral procedures have usually been applied and are most effective at promoting individual change, or change within a system, i.e., "first-order change." For example, many behavioral studies have focused on motivating individual consumers to save energy in their homes, but have not directed attention to such issues as how utility rate bases are determined (i.e., the "system" level), which in turn affect consumer behaviors. However, it is possible that a focus on the individual level and evidence of behavior changes occurring under less than positive conditions can help to influence system or policy changes, i.e., "second-order change." For example, demonstration projects showing that companies and their employees enthusiastically accept and use van pools or that home owners have dramatically reduced their energy consumption with low-cost strategies, indicate that policies to further promote such practices would probably be acceptable nationwide and prove remarkably effective in saving energy. Thus, second-order or system change may be of *primary* importance. However, we take an interactionist perspective in this text and suggest that, while policies influence behavior, *at times* behavior changes can influence policy. This contextual perspective is illustrated by the following examples.

Example 1. Figure 1.1 shows an aesthetically pleasing 2.5-mile bike path that leads from a residential area through farms and backroads to the campus of Virginia Tech. Although the weather in this part of the country is almost ideal ten months of the year, the bike path receives relatively minimal use as a commuting modality to campus (Mayer & Geller, 1981). The apparent reasons for this limited use include the still relatively low cost of gasoline. But perhaps even more significant are campus policies that include free and convenient parking; indeed, new lots have been constructed on the spacious campus whenever current parking facilities become crowded. This is also shown in Figure 1.1.

Not only is the bike path minimally used, but observational data of 17,589 cars entering the campus parking lots indicated that *83%* were occupied by only the driver (Mayer & Geller, 1981). Efforts to promote bike ridership or carpooling through behavioral strategies (i.e., a first-order change) will probably not work until parking policies are changed (i.e., a second-order change). In behavioral terms, the cost of behaviors competing with the proenvironmental behaviors must be increased. Parking must become either more inconvenient or expensive in order to motivate substantial numbers of car owners to change their commuting strategies (e.g., and car pool, bicycle, or walk to campus). However, it is possible that a point will be reached when one of the cost factors (e.g., the price of gasoline) will start to tip the contingencies in favor of biking or walking. Successful promotion of biking or walking at that point may accelerate the institution of policies to further discourage driving to campus.

Example 2. Major federal legislation has required utility companies to offer their residential customers on-site home audits (Federal Register, 1979). In some parts of the country this program is quite literally a well-kept secret; in other parts of the country utilities are actively promoting their home programs. The main reason for a utility's enthusiastic endorsement of this program seems to be closely related to an economic contingency. That is, in some parts of the country utilities cannot raise their rates high enough to offset the capital investments needed for constructing new generating facilities. Under these conditions, conservation makes good economic sense to the utility company and the customer.

The Empty Bike Path at Tech

A Jammed Parking Lot at Tech

Fig. 1.1. Behavioral procedures and energy efficient practices need a supportive social, economic, and political context. In this example, procedures to increase ridership on the bike path will probably be ineffective as long as gasoline prices are relatively low, and free and abundant parking is available. Increased incentives for energy efficient behavior do not compete well with convenient, low-cost energy intensive behavior. Photos by Philip C. Lederach.

Such utility companies are prime candidates for instruction in more effective marketing, communication, and behavior change strategies, all directed
toward conservation. Under these conditions, where mutual benefits are
available to the company and its customers, we would expect behavioral
procedures to be readily accepted and extremely cost effective.

Example 3. Soft drinks and beer sold in nonreturnable bottles and cans
create litter problems, make recycling more difficult, and require that more
energy be used to produce new bottles and cans than would be needed if
bottles were reused. As shown in Chapters 3 and 4, a number of behavioral
procedures can be used to decrease littering and increase recycling practices.
However, one ideal large-scale approach to litter control and recycling has
resulted from the enactment of laws requiring deposits on bottles and pro-
hibiting the sale of drinks in nonreturnable bottles or cans (Geller, 1980b,
1981c; Osborne & Powers, 1980). Such laws directly affect littering and
recycling behaviors and also set the context for the even more effective use of
behavioral principles. For example, under a deposit system, bottles become
valuable, their collection becomes a rewarding activity, and other behavior
change strategies can be incorporated into this system to further increase
bottle collection. And engaging in these behaviors may result in increased
awareness and positive attitudes about a recycling ethic. The public is then
apt to accept other community programs aimed at litter control, resource
recovery, or energy conservation. However, "bottle bills" have only been
enacted in a few states (eight at the time of this writing). In other states, the
lobbying of private interest groups (e.g., beverage and container companies)
has prevented bottle bill legislation which would benefit the environment
and its inhabitants substantially.

Thus, behavior change strategies are maximally effective under supportive
policy or programmatic conditions. Where the costs (economic and/or social) of engaging in energy wasteful or environmentally destructive behaviors
are minimal or virtually nonexistent, procedures to promote proenvironmental behaviors will be ineffective. However, a most intriguing possibility
was a primary rationale for writing this book: behavior change in the face of
limited support, but with policies moving in a proenvironmental direction,
may accelerate the environment preservation movement by demonstrating the
feasibility of a low-cost behavioral approach and implying the acceptability
of proenvironmental policies.

Theoretically, many environment-related behaviors can be conceptualized
as choice behaviors (e.g., engagement in energy intensive versus energy conserving practices). The amount of time or effort we spend at a given behavior
relative to another potentially substitutable behavior is a function of cost,
plus perhaps social/psychological factors that can make a behavior more
"appealing," "attractive," or "rewarding" (Rachlin, Kagel, & Battalio, 1980;

Winkler & Winett, 1982). Furthermore, the cost and attractiveness of a behavior are a function of its "context." The price of energy and media communications about energy conserving behaviors are two examples of contextual factors. In our first example above, the economic cost of driving a single-occupant car is still relatively low, and only limited efforts have been made to denigrate this mode of transportation; instead, most efforts are to make cars more efficient (see Winett & Geller, 1981). Therefore, other potentially substitutable practices (walking, biking, etc.) have too high a real and perceived cost. Rapidly rising energy prices coupled with persuasive communication strategies showing the benefits of substituting energy efficient practices in the home, have led, however, to the adoption of such practices in some instances (see Winkler & Winett, 1982). In addition, as we have noted above, the performance of some proenvironmental behaviors may help to change the context, and hence the value and substitutability, of alternative proenvironment behaviors.

Table 1.1 summarizes this interactionistic perspective by indicating the potential outcomes of the previous examples and others under "positive," "negative," and more "neutral" conditions. The authors of this book, like most behavioral scientists, are experts in first-order change, but not in second-order or system change (see Fawcett, Mathews, & Fletcher, 1980). However, one of our aims is clearly to help accelerate system change through the promotion of behavior change.

Focusing on Behavior and Blaming the Victim

The examples in this chapter emphasize that one of the missing factors in many approaches to environmental protection has been the focus on modifying environment-relevant behaviors. Indeed, it seems to us that most environmental protection programs have been instituted as if people were not actually engaging in driving, heating, cooling, littering, and so on. The comparison between the two families depicted at the beginning of this chapter underscores the role that behavioral patterns play in energy consumption. For example, we estimate that the Noblin family at home, commuting, and at work consumed *three times* the energy used by their neighbors, the Gilmer family (and such differences, as noted above, have been actually documented in field research).

Does this mean that the energy situation and the degradation of our environment is strictly the fault of careless, wasteful, and ill-informed people? Our answer is a resounding no. Attributing fault solely to individuals would be another example of what William Ryan (1971) has called "blaming the victim." As we have discussed in the prior section, behavior must be seen in context. People will "pollute and *not* give a hoot" if the prevailing policies (and social norms) encourage those practices. Most people will continue to

Table 1.1. The Probable Role of Behavior Change Strategies in Promoting Environmental Practices Under Positive, Negative, or Neutral Political and Economic Policies.

Example of Environment Preservation Practice	Political and Economic Policies (Implemented at National, State, or Local Level)	Role of Behavior Change Strategies: Probable Outcomes
Residential energy conservation—weatherization, consumer behaviors	*Positive* for promotion if utility cannot afford to build new generating capacity and rates are high	Behavioral technology should be an important component in program's promotion and implementation and increase its effectiveness
Recycling of bottles for soft drinks and beer	*Positive* for promotion if a deposit law exists and bottles have value	Behavioral technology can increase the amount recycled and *expedite* the process
Carpooling, bike riding for commuting	*Negative* effects if gasoline prices remain relatively low and ample, inexpensive (or no-cost) parking is provided to single-occupant cars	Behavioral technology will probably have minimal or no impact on carpooling and bike riding
Water conservation behaviors and retrofitting	*Negative* impact if prices remain low and policies emphasize increasing supply and not demand management	Behavioral technology will probably have minimal or no impact on water conservation
Bus ridership for commuting	*Neutral* impact if gasoline prices are rising and most institutions are becoming somewhat less supportive of commuting by car	Behavioral technology can somewhat increase bus ridership and *accelerate* second-order change by showing viability of bus service and consumer response, thus leading to policies supportive of mass transit
Residential energy conservation—weatherization, consumer behaviors	*Neutral* effect if energy prices are rising and utilities and other institutions are at least tacitly supportive	Behavioral technology can somewhat decrease energy demand and *accelerate* second-order change by demonstrating savings that can be made, and consumer acceptance, thus leading to policies that better promote energy conservation

drive excessively in this country until policies are enacted (and social norms accepted) which discourage unnecessary driving. Indeed, focusing on the individual and blaming the victim for our current environment and energy problems is often a convenient way to divert attention away from the policies and systems that are the real cause (Ryan, 1971).

Thus, while we focus on individual behavior change in this text, our approach should not be construed as blaming people for our country's energy/environment predicaments or detracting from the obvious need for system-level modification.

Solar Panels

Nuclear Reactor

Fig. 1.2. "Soft" and "hard" energy technologies represent different commitments, visions of the future, and values. Photos by Philip C. Lederach

OUR POSITION AND APPROACH

We also recognize the focus on human behavior as a value-based position. The belief and commitment to change human behavior as an approach to environment preservation represents particular values, just as the belief and commitment to further development of "high" or "hard" technology represents others (Lovins, 1977). We have written this book from a conservation, efficiency, and generally "low" or "soft" technology perspective; although it should be clear that behavioral principles can be applied to increase the effectiveness of other approaches to the energy problem. For example, feedback strategies can be used to increase productivity in coal mining (Rhotton, 1980), and undoubtedly a range of behavioral strategies could be applied to reduce human error in the nuclear industry. At this point, none of the authors has expertise in these types of endeavors, and each one of us has quite intentionally chosen to promote conservation, efficiency and low technology strategies for environment preservation—a general approach which is consistent with our values and vision of the future. We are clearly not alone in emphasizing conservation and soft technology over productivity and hard technology. Energy analysts have increasingly supported such an approach (Brown, Flavin, & Norman, 1979; Stobaugh & Yergin, 1979), noting the tremendous potential savings at minimal monetary or life-style costs from conservation and soft technology, and the incredibly large capital investments required for hard technology strategies with frequently uncertain outcomes:

If the United States were to make a serious commitment to conservation, it might well consume 30 to 40 percent less energy than it now does, and still enjoy the same or even higher standard of living. That would require only modest adjustments in the way people live. Moreover, the cost of conservation energy is very competitive with other energy sources. The possible energy savings would be the elimination of all imported oil—and then some. . . . Conservation may well be the cheapest, safest, most productive energy alternative readily available in large amounts. . . . It does not threaten to undermine the international monetary system, nor does it emit carbon dioxide into the atmosphere, nor does it generate problems comparable to nuclear waste. And contrary to the conventional wisdom, conservation can stimulate innovation, employment, and economic growth [Stobaugh & Yergin, 1979, pp. 136-137].

Thus, contrary to perhaps common belief, *conservation can save substantial amounts of energy without any "sacrifices" and without "endangering" our economy or standard of living*. For example, consider a well-planned community with nearby and diverse shopping, many walkways and bikeways, and virtually no automobile traffic—and hence, no unsightly strips, minimal use of gasoline, clean air, and safe, increased pedestrian mobility. Are there any sacrifices implied by this example? Does this sound like a poor standard of living? Returning to the issue of conservation, it can also be asked, for the next 10 to 20 years are there really any alternatives? Not only do synfuels and nuclear power require tremendous federal subsidies for their development, making them currently *noncompetitive* with other energy sources and conservation (Lovins & Lovins, 1980), but the effective use of these alternatives, even with large subsidies, is at best 10 to 20 years in the future (Stobaugh & Yergin, 1979). The increased mining of coal and domestic oil production are other energy options that are being pursued, although neither can be seen as the solution and each has its problems, not the least of which is environmental degradation. Whatever mix of new and old energy sources we take into the twenty-first century, a strong commitment to conservation, efficiency, and environmental protection will be necessary. Events of the last decade have led us and others to believe that the failure to take conservation seriously can result in a bankrupt and polluted country when new energy systems are finally operational (Stobaugh & Yergin, 1979). If conservation is taken seriously, then we believe that the strategies and programs described in this text can be a significant contribution.

GENERAL PLAN AND PERSPECTIVE

We have prepared this book for two groups of professionals. The first group is fellow psychologists and their students who want to review the latest work in environmental protection, and perhaps become involved in the field. The second group is professionals already working in the environmental protection field who are not psychologists but want to gain an understanding of behavioral principles and their application to various environmental problems.

In many instances, the research described in this book—whether in litter control, recycling, energy and water conservation, or transportation management—is still at an "experimental" or "demonstration" stage of development. A good deal of the work has involved relatively short-term studies designed to assess the effectiveness of specific procedures. Although such short-term studies certainly provide instructive data for the planning and development of environmental programs, there is an urgent need for more interdisciplinary, longer-term investigations. Indeed, a primary goal of this text is to promote the integration of behavioral science into comprehensive, interdisciplinary proenvironmental policy.

An ideal, comprehensive approach toward promoting energy conservation and saving environmental resources must consider several points of intervention, as well as a variety of intervention strategies. For example, consider a $2 \times 3 \times 5$ factorial array, with the following variables:

1. two basic intervention *approaches* (i.e., physical versus behavioral technology),
2. three community *sectors* requiring direct intervention (i.e., the residential/consumer, governmental/institutional, and commercial/industrial sectors), and
3. five *targets* or domains for intervention within each sector (i.e., heating/cooling, solid waste management, transportation, equipment efficiency, and water consumption).

Each cell of the three dimensional, 30-cell matrix resulting from this factorial represents an area of expertise required in a comprehensive, environmental protection program. The physical approach basically involves the application of physical technology (e.g., architecture, engineering, physics) to preserve the environment and is often manifested in altering or adding to the structure of a building, purchasing or modifying equipment, using certain energy-saving devices, and applying expensive equipment to separate solid waste for resource recycling and/or for energy fuel. It is quite obvious that the type of recommended physical intervention (and necessary technical expertise) is dependent upon both the general target area (i.e., heating/cooling, solid waste management, transportation, equipment efficiency, or water consumption) and the community sector in which the intervention is applied (i.e., residences, institutions or industrial complexes).

The application of physical interventions for environmental protection usually requires human intervention, and therefore behavioral approaches are necessary to teach and motivate appropriate human action. Such human action (in residential, commercial/industrial or governmental/institutional settings) may involve the purchase of particular devices or equipment or the application of certain devices or equipment in certain energy efficient ways. For example, action in the consumer-transportation cell of the factorial includes both the purchase of an energy efficient vehicle and the adoption of energy efficient driving habits. Physical technology is required in this case to prescribe the most energy efficient vehicle and its optional use, whereas behavioral science is needed to recommend strategies for disseminating information regarding energy efficient vehicles and driving behaviors and for motivating desired public reaction. The situation is certainly complex, requiring much challenging research and development just for the consumer/transportation aspect of environment preservation. This book describes only modest beginnings in delineating effective behavior change strategies across the 30 cells of the $2 \times 3 \times 5$ energy array presented above. Indeed, there has been minimal behavioral work done in certain sectors and with certain targets.

The comprehensive model does make it apparent that environmental research requires expertise in both physical and behavioral technology, a point which has been frequently made by psychologists reviewing environmental protection research (e.g., Geller, 1980b, 1982; Lloyd, 1980; Reichel & Geller, 1981; Stern & Gardner, 1980, 1981; Winett, 1980). For example, Stern and Gardner (1981) stressed that almost all of the energy issues for which psychology is relevant are interdisciplinary and thus "psychologists must learn to understand and work with economists, engineers, marketers, building contractors, and/or members of other disciplines or professions (p. 339)." Johnson and Geller (1980) discussed a conceptual model for research collaboration between engineering and behavior analysis, illustrating the positive gains which could result from behavioral science input to engineering technology under four situational categories: (1) when the appropriate engineering technology has been developed and is available for widespread dissemination, (2) while the engineering technology is being researched and developed, (3) when available engineering strategies are not working or being applied as planned, and (4) when no engineering technology is available.

Several psychologists researching environmental problems have recently attested to the extreme lack of respect of the behavioral and social sciences among professionals from other disciplines (e.g., Becker & Seligman, 1981; Geller, 1980b, 1981c; Shippee, 1980; Zerega, 1981). Most of the behavioral and social science research related to energy conservation and environmental protection has been accomplished without grant support from state or federal agencies, and interdisciplinary advisory panels for energy conservation and environmental protection do not regularly consider input from social and behavioral scientists (see Geller, 1980b). Perhaps after behavioral and social scientists in general demonstrate the patience to learn the jargon of other disciplines and their approaches to problem solving, the experts from these other disciplines may be more apt to develop an understanding and appreciation for the potential of behavioral information in the development, dissemination, and evaluation of strategies to preserve the environment. This text was written not only to demonstrate the value of applied behavior analysis for environment preservation, but to facilitate an appreciation for interdisciplinary problem solving among both the physical and behavioral sciences.

Chapter 2
The Applied Behavior Analysis Approach to Intervention and Evaluation

By now the slogan disseminated by Keep America Beautiful, Inc. (KAB), "People Start Pollution—People Can Stop It," is familiar to most Americans. Most people understand that much of the litter problem is a behavioral problem and appreciate the validity of the KAB motto. Indeed, the community-wide litter-control program of KAB (described in the next chapter) is publicized as "the nation's first local-level waste-control program to be based on behavioral change techniques (KAB, 1977b, p. 1)." Now consider some more general environment and energy slogans: "People Destroy the Environment—People Can Restore It!" and "People Consume Energy— People Can Conserve It!" As discussed in Chapter 1, these statements are as valid as the KAB litter-control motto, and behavioral change techniques are as appropriate for saving environmental resources as for controlling litter. Thus, behaviors which contribute to environmental degradation and energy waste can be decreased on a large scale, and behaviors which preserve environmental resources and conserve energy can be increased on community-wide levels. Further, it is often possible to influence environment-related behaviors through simple manipulations of environmental stimuli and response consequences.

It is noteworthy that several psychology-based studies have correlated individuals' actions, demographic characteristics, personality traits, or value systems with individuals' awareness or concern for environmental protection (e.g., see review by Van Liere & Dunlap, 1980). Although such attitude-behavior, correlational studies are probably more numerous than those aimed at finding strategies for directly influencing environment-related behaviors (e.g., see annotated bibliographies by Frankena, Buttel, & Morrison, 1977; and Weigel, Woolston, & Gendelman, 1977), we seriously doubt that this correlational research will have any practical significance for energy conservation or environmental protection. The attitude/value measurement scales are not consistent across studies and their reliability and validity may be questioned (see Hendee, 1971; Van Liere & Dunlap, 1981). Furthermore, it has been shown that what people indicate on a questionnaire (or in an interview) is often inconsistent with their actual behaviors (e.g., Bickman, 1972; Deutscher, 1966, 1973; Wicker, 1969, 1971). Finally, even if significant and valid relationships are found between individual characteristics and environment-related attitudes or behaviors, it is not clear how such results could be used to alleviate environment/energy problems. Thus, we are convinced that behavioral science (as introduced in Chapter 1) holds the answers for large-scale, cost-effective modification of environment-related behaviors.

The general approach is to define specifically and objectively the target behaviors which need to be changed (i.e., increased or decreased in frequency) and then manipulate environmental stimuli or events *preceding* and/or *following* the target behaviors in order to effect behavior change in desired directions. This chapter defines the basic behavioral principles which should be considered when implementing and evaluating behavior change programs for environment preservation. The remaining chapters of this book review the successes and failures of actual attempts to apply behavioral strategies for modifying responses in environment-improving directions.

TARGET BEHAVIORS

The variety of human responses related to environmental protection are numerous. Each cell of the 2 × 3 × 5 environment/energy array introduced in Chapter 1 suggests several behaviors that people make in particular situations (at home, work, school, business location, or in transition), that directly or indirectly consume environmental resources, and can be altered so as to be more protective of the environment. Of course, defining these environment-related responses and making specific recommendations regarding desirable change often requires interdisciplinary input. For example, with regard to energy conservation, engineering data is required to advise which appliance or vehicle is most energy efficient; architectural data is often helpful in defining optimal insulation techniques and landscape designs for conserving energy in home heating and cooling; biological data is necessary for prescribing optimal composting procedures; and information from physics and human factors engineering is relevant for defining energy efficient ways of using appliances, vehicles, industrial machinery, conservation devices, and heating or cooling systems.

Some strategies for conserving energy and preserving the environment require repetitive action while others do not. For example, one class of energy conservation behaviors require repeated occurrences in order to effect significant energy savings (such as setting back room thermostats each night, riding in a car pool and driving 55 mph or less, taking shorter showers, turning off lights when not needed, placing recyclable paper, metal, glass and biodegradable trash in separate containers, opening window shades during the day and closing them at night, and wearing more clothes in order to withstand lower room temperatures). On the other hand, a particular conservation strategy may require only one occurrence of the target behavior (such as installing a thermostat that automatically changes room temperature settings at preprogrammed levels, purchasing an energy efficient vehicle, wrapping insulation around the water heater and inserting a shower flow restrictor in the showerhead, changing light bulbs from incandescent to fluorescent, operating a high technology waste separation system, installing a solar heating system, and adding insulation to an attic). Notice that each of the examples given here for the "repeated-response" category has a concomitant behavior listed in the "one-shot" category (which is not always the case, of course).

For "one-shot" behaviors, the user usually pays an initial high cost in time and money for the subsequent convenience of not having to make continued response input. Selecting one target behavior over another for environmental protection may often be a complex decision process requiring a careful examination of the long-term costs and benefits of each alternative. Indeed, a complete cost-effectiveness analysis often requires interdisciplinary input, including physical and psychological data which may not be available. For example, just deciding whether to install a shower flow restrictor requires much field data which is currently not available. In fact, valid information regarding the amount of hot water and energy conserved with a shower flow restrictor cannot be estimated until human reaction to this low-cost device is field tested. Will people take longer or more showers (or switch to baths) if their shower flow is limited? To what extent does a flow restrictor lessen perceived (or real) shower comfort? Does the flow restrictor promote increased adjustments in water temperature (perhaps due to surges of hot or cold water), with concomitant increases in water usage, inconvenience, and discomfort? It is noteworthy that the U.S. Department of Energy (DOE) did not undertake an adequate field test and cost-effective analysis of shower flow restrictors before distributing them to 4.5 million New England households in a recent $2.6 million DOE program (U.S. DOE, 1980).

Regarding the distinction of repeated versus one-shot responses for energy conservation, Stern and Gardner (1981) indicated that "frequently repeated behaviors usually involve curtailment while one-shot actions usually involve efficiency (p. 334)." While most conservation behaviors requiring repeated occurrence involve a cut-back or curtailment on energy consumption, numerous "one-shot" behaviors also imply curtailment. For example, insulating walls, ceilings, and water heaters; inserting water conservation devices; installing thermostat controls; tuning up engines; and putting air in underinflated tires all involve changing existing facilities or equipment so that less energy is consumed (i.e., a curtailment). In addition, many conservation strategies involve *both* a one-shot investment and repeated actions. Thus, one can purchase a window fan to substitute for an air conditioner or a moped to substitute for an automobile, but energy conservation does not occur unless the individual makes repeated decisions to use the more energy efficient machine. Likewise, energy saving settings on new energy efficient appliances (dishwashers, air conditioners, clothes dryers and washing machines, and industrial equipment) are not worth much unless they are continuously used. And special receptacles for separating trash are not energy conserving unless they are used appropriately each day and the contents transported to a recycling center.

Stern and Gardner also concluded that "behaviors involving adoption of energy efficient technology generally offer more potential for conservation than behaviors involving curtailed use of existing energy systems (p. 334)." Given the lack of appropriate engineering and human factors data such an assertion is quite risky and could actually be detrimental to the energy situation if taken seriously. In other words, one could take this statement to mean that individuals should go out and purchase new energy efficient appliances, vehicles, machinery, and even heating and cooling systems, rather than modifying existing equipment or structures and/or changing usage habits with respect to their present situation. Not only is such a recommendation impractical with regard to large-scale environment preservation, but the purchase of new equipment rather than the repair of existing equipment implicates increased consumption of environmental resources to produce the new and dispose of the old. Selecting the most appropriate environment-related behavior(s) to modify in a particular situation requires a comprehensive analysis of environmental costs and savings throughout the production, use, and eventual disposal of the commodities involved; such long-term, interdisciplinary information is sorely needed.

Regarding the presumption by Stern and Gardner (1981) that repeated curtailment behaviors have relatively low conservation potential, it is noteworthy that Winett and his students recently showed that residents (n = 49 households) saved a mean of 15% of their overall winter electric bill and 27% of electricity for heating by setting back their thermostats from an average of 65° F. to 62° F. when at home and to about 59° F. when asleep or not at home. Likewise, in the summer, residents (n = 35) saved about 16% on overall electricity use and 35% of electricity for cooling by slightly raising the air conditioning thermostat and, when appropriate, using fans or natural ventilation for cooling. In both the winter and summer studies, people reported no loss of comfort when following these "curtailment" procedures (see Chapter 5 for more details). These savings from actual field observation were significantly higher than the 4% estimated winter savings reported by Stern and Gardner (1981) for setting back room thermostats from 72° to 68° F. daily and to 65° F. nightly.

Besides repeated and one-shot behaviors, there is an additional set of potential target behaviors to consider for environmental protection. These have been termed "peak shift behaviors," usually referring to changing the time when individuals emit energy consumption behaviors. For example, reducing peak demands for energy decreases the need for power companies to build or borrow supplementary generators or other energy sources (e.g., nuclear). Indeed, electricity suppliers have been willing to vary their rates according to peak demand (i.e., peak-load pricing), although residents have found it difficult to shift various energy consuming tasks (Kohlenberg, Phillips, & Proctor, 1976).

Peak shifting has usually been associated with residential energy consumption (e.g., changing cooking, showering, and sleeping times), but it may be even more feasible as an environment preservation strategy for other community sectors. Consider, for example, the peak shift advantages of altering the scheduling and/or length of work shifts at industrial complexes and government agencies through the adoption of flexible work schedules or a four-day work week. Certain large-scale changes in work schedules could result in peak shifts and energy savings at the work setting, at home, and during commuting. For example, the major function of urban transit systems is to serve people going to and from work, and since most of such commuting occurs during two short rush periods a day, numerous bus drivers make nonproductive runs or actually sit idle most of the day (Zerega, 1981). Before instituting large-scale shifts in work schedules it is necessary to do comprehensive, multifaceted pilot testing in order to define the most energy efficient plan without disrupting family life, leisure activity, and other functions of a "healthy" community (see Winett & Neale, 1981a).

From a discussion of general issues related to the selection of target behaviors for environment preservation programs, we now progress to a delineation of the behavioral principles on which interventions to change targeted behaviors can be based. Once again we remind the reader that this chapter is designed to introduce the behavioral approach for environment preservation. Examples of applications are given in this chapter to illustrate concepts and techniques, but the remaining chapters should be relied on for comprehensive reviews of the literature in specific research domains and for recommended behavioral strategies to conserve energy and protect the environment in particular situations.

ANTECEDENT (OR PROMPTING) STRATEGIES FOR MODIFYING BEHAVIORS

Behavior change strategies for energy conservation and environmental protection can be generally categorized as antecedent or consequence strategies (Tuso & Geller, 1976). Antecedent strategies (sometimes referred to as prompting or response priming procedures) are stimulus events occurring before the target behavior and are designed to increase the probability of the target if the response is desirable or to decrease the likelihood of the target response if it is undesirable. Prompts for environment preservation have been displayed through television commercials, verbal statements from parents, teachers, public officials, and peers, and through environmental manipulations such as beautified waste receptacles, containers with separate bins labeled for different types of recyclable trash, parked police cars along a highway, and thermostats and appliance controls with special settings for energy conservation.

The nature or format of the prompting strategy implies different types of control. Some prompts for environmental protection have been *general* exhortations or appeals with no specification of the target response (e.g., *Use energy wisely*; *Help keep our community clean*; *Please dispose of properly*; *Don't be a litterbug*), while others have taken the form of *specific* instructions which indicate the particular target behavior to emit or avoid (e.g., *Drive 55 mph to conserve energy*; *Deposit for recycling in green trash receptacle; Turn off lights when leaving room*; *Don't leave handbills in shopping carts*; *Don't trample the grass*). Note that some prompts (general and specific) exhort the occurrence of behaviors and are thus response-*approach* prompts; whereas other prompts attempt to get people to avoid certain behaviors and are response-*avoidance* prompts (Geller, Koltuniak, & Shilling, 1981). Educational information (disseminated through books, magazines, newspapers, pamphlets or workshops) represents general prompting if facts are given with no specification of desirable or undesirable behaviors, although much environmental information has occurred as *specific* prompts, including particular recommendations for approach or avoidance action accompanying the facts and figures.

Some prompts announce incentive or disincentive conditions by specifying pleasant or unpleasant consequences which will follow occurrences of the target response (e.g., 5¢ per returnable container; one raffle coupon per pound of recyclable paper; persons depositing litter in this container will sometimes be rewarded; $2 for a 10% decrease in electricity use; $1 per week for each 5% reduction in miles driven with automobile; $50 fine for littering). Some prompts announce incentive conditions and also signal when the pleasant or unpleasant event is available, thus serving as discriminative stimuli for the target response, such as a sign displayed intermittently to indicate that reinforcement is presently available for a particular response. Other prompts do not specify a contingency but do serve as a discriminative stimulus, because they signal that a pleasant or unpleasant consequence is available if the response is emitted. In this latter case, it is presumed that the public has already become aware of the contingency. Thus, a police car signals the availability of an unpleasant consequence if speeding occurs (without defining the particular contingency). In the transportation conservation experiments by Peter Everett and his students (discussed in Chapter 6), only the special campus bus with three large red stars signalled the availability of a positive reinforcer (a quarter or token) for boarding. The reinforcement contingencies for the studies by Everett et al. were announced in the campus newspaper, (an announcement prompt which did not serve as a discriminative stimulus for bus riding).

Table 2.1 summarizes our discussion so far concerning the definition of different antecedent or prompting strategies for modifying behaviors. Four main categories of prompts are defined according to whether or not the prompt announces response consequences and whether or not the prompt signals the availability of a response consequence. Specifically, some prompts announce a pleasant or unpleasant consequence that will follow a particular event, while others do not specify a consequence strategy. Approach prompts often announce a pleasant consequence for the desired behavior, whereas avoidance prompts are apt to threaten an unpleasant consequence if the undesired response occurs. Further, some prompts occur at the time and location of a particular response-consequence contingency and are therefore discriminative stimuli which set the occasion for the occurrence or avoidance of the target behavior. Prompts that neither announce nor set the occasion

Table 2.1. Matrix defining four categories of antecedent (or prompting) strategies for promoting environment preservation. Within each category, prompts exhort either response occurrence (approach) or response avoidance. When the antecedent neither announces nor signals a consequence strategy, it may be a *General* Prompt or a Response-*Specific* Prompt.

Announce Consequence Strategy

	YES	NO
Signal Availability of Consequence — YES	"5¢ per aluminum can when this sign is displayed" "10% increase in electricity cost during display of this sign"	Red Star Bus Police Car
Signal Availability of Consequence — NO	"Token for riding buses with Red Star" "$50 fine for littering"	"Please dispose of properly" (General) "Don't trample the grass" (Specific)

for a particular contingency are *general* appeals or exhortations which do not refer to particular responses, or are *specific* exhortations which instruct the individual(s) to emit or avoid certain target behaviors.

Prompting procedures without concomitant consequence strategies are relatively cheap and easy to administer, but as shown in earlier reviews of the literature, the efficacy of prompting strategies for energy conservation and environmental protection has been limited (e.g., Geller, 1980a, 1980b, 1981c; Shippee, 1980; Winett, 1980). In summary, prompts which did not announce or signal a consequence were only successful in promoting a substantial amount of compliance related to environmental protection when they: (1) specified what behavior was desired or undesired (i.e., a *specific* appeal); (2) were administered in close *proximity* with the opportunity to emit the requested response; (3) requested the occurrence of responses which were relatively *convenient* to emit (approach prompts) or the avoidance of responses that were not accompanied by powerful approach contingencies (avoidance prompts) given in *polite*, nondemanding language. For example, Delprata (1977) and Winett (1978) were successful in prompting occupants of public buildings to turn off room lights when they placed messages at light switches which specified that the lights should be turned out when leaving the room; Geller, Witmer, and Orebaugh (1976) and Geller, Witmer, and Tuso (1977) found 20% to 30% compliance with antilitter messages on handbills when the prompt politely requested that the handbill be deposited for recycling in a conveniently located (and obtrusive) trash receptacle.

On the other hand, educational programs and informational packages without special incentive provisions have been quite unsuccessful in motivating the occurrence of relatively inconvenient and/or time-consuming energy conservation strategies (e.g., Geller, 1982; Geller, Ferguson, & Brasted, 1978; Hayes & Cone, 1977; Heberlein, 1975; Kohlenberg et al., 1976; Palmer, Lloyd, & Lloyd, 1978; Winett, Kagel, Battalio, & Winkler, 1978), and handbills with a general plea and specific instructions regarding a campus paper recycling program were not sufficient to get residents of university dormitories to bring recyclable paper to a particular collection room (Geller, Chaffee, & Ingram, 1975; Witmer & Geller, 1976), even when the specific prompts were given personally to dorm residents via verbal exhortation and a flyer (Ingram & Geller, 1975).

One additional antecedent strategy for influencing behavior is labeled modeling (see Bandura, 1977b), which refers to the demonstration of specific behaviors and sometimes includes the explicit presentation of pleasant or unpleasant events following the behavior. Modeling can occur via live demonstrations or on a movie screen (e.g., television, film, or videotape), and actually implies the presentation of: (1) a specific prompt with the announcement of a reinforcement contingency (i.e., the model receives a pleasant or unpleasant consequence following a specific response), or (2) a specific prompt without the specification of a reinforcement contingency (i.e., no response consequences are shown).

These two different prompting strategies implied by modeling procedures are illustrated by the public service television advertising developed and funded by the Virginia Division of Litter Control. In particular, the first T.V. spot sponsored by the state litter control agency in 1978 showed a well-known actor picking up a crumpled piece of paper from the ground (modeling a desired response), and the verbal message was, "Isn't it time we cared?" (a general prompt). In contrast, two years later the T.V. spot sponsored by the Virginia Division of Litter Control showed a driver throwing a paper cup out of his car window while stopped at a city intersection (modeling a specific undesirable response); then a variety of individuals (including a police officer) ridiculed the driver for his destructive and wasteful littering response (an unpleasant response consequence).

Energy studies and environmental protection programs have essentially ignored modeling strategies, yet modeling (through television or video cassette) has the potential of reaching and influencing millions of residents. Indeed, in two recent studies by Winett and his students (detailed in Chapter 5), a 21-minute videotape program (showing specific conservation practices) was found to reduce the heating bills of 33 households an average of 27% and the cooling bills of 23 households an average of 33%.

Prompts perceived as demands, rather than polite requests, may elicit psychological reactance and actually motivate behaviors contrary to those desired (Brehm, 1966; 1972). Individuals may perceive verbal or written prompts as a threat to their personal freedom and may not only disregard the request, but in fact emit a response contrary to the instructions in order to assert their freedom. This notion was supported in a field study by Reich and Robertson (1979) who distributed antilitter flyers at a public swimming pool and found significantly more littering of flyers with the message "Don't litter" than fliers with the message "Help keep your pool clean" (Experiment 1). Fliers with the antilitter message "Don't you *dare* litter" were littered significantly more often than fliers with the message "Keeping the pool clean depends on you" or "Help keep your pool clean" (Experiment 2). Likewise, Geller and his students (detailed in Chapter 3) found that significantly more patrons of a shopping center complied with a specific, *polite* prompt at the bottom of distributed handbills (i.e., "Please dispose of in trash can in front of Woolco") than with a specific, *demand* prompt (i.e., "You must dispose of in trash can in front of Woolco").

In summary, we have defined four categories of approach and avoidance prompting. That is, stimuli presented to influence behavior may or may not announce the availability of a particular consequence following the target response; and some antecedents are only displayed at the time the response consequence is available and thus serve as discriminative stimuli. Many prompts for environment preservation neither announce the availability of a response consequence nor serve as a discriminative stimulus for a response-consequence contingency. These antecedents are written or verbal statements or demonstrations that appeal to certain actions or environmental outcomes. Specific prompts urge the occurrence or avoidance of certain behaviors, while general prompts do not. Specific prompts which appear too demanding or controlling may actually cause more harm than good. The advantages and disadvantages of particular prompting strategies will be reviewed in subsequent chapters, but at this point it is noteworthy that antecedent strategies alone have rarely been effective in influencing the occurrence of environment-relevant responses that require more effort (i.e., response cost) than adjusting a room thermostat (Winett, Hatcher, Leckliter, Fort, Fishback, & Riley, 1981), flicking a light switch (Delprata, 1977; Winett, 1978), purchasing drinks in one container over another (Geller, Farris, & Post, 1973; Geller, Wylie, & Farris, 1971), or dropping a handbill in a conveniently located trash receptacle (Geller, 1975; Geller et al., 1976; Geller, Mann, & Brasted, 1977). However, the frequency of inconvenient environment preservation behaviors has been increased with the addition of consequence strategies.

CONSEQUENCE STRATEGIES FOR
MODIFYING BEHAVIORS

Behavioral consequences can be pleasant (technically termed positive reinforcers if the frequency of the preceding behavior increases), or they can be unpleasant (technically termed negative reinforcers or punishers if the preceding behavior decreases in frequency). Furthermore, the variety of pleasant or unpleasant consequences which can facilitate environment preservation is limitless, especially if the *contingency manager* is creative. Consequences can be distinct stimuli (a monetary rebate, a self-photograph, a traffic fine, a verbal commendation or condemnation) or opportunities to engage in certain behaviors (the right to drive in a priority lane, write name on "Energy Conserver" poster, attend or host an environmental clean-up party). And stimulus events or response opportunities can be given or taken away from an individual as a result of specific *responses* or *outcomes*.

Punishment and negative reinforcement procedures to preserve the environment usually take the form of laws or ordinances (fines for speeding, littering, watering lawns, strip mining, and polluting air or water), and require extensive enforcement and legal personnel to make an impact. A beneficial behavioral impact occurs via *punishment* when individuals make the undesirable response, receive an unpleasant consequence, and are subsequently less likely to repeat the punished response. On the other hand, a behavioral impact occurs via *negative reinforcement* when individuals emit environment-protecting behaviors in order to avoid the aversive consequence for a particular environment-damaging response.

Applied behavior scientists have demonstrated empirically a variety of reasons for preferring positive reinforcement over punishment and negative reinforcement, including the fact that positive reinforcement is usually most acceptable, and can be easiest to administer and most cost effective in the long run. Therefore, behaviorists working for environment preservation have avoided the use of negative reinforcement and punishment procedures. However, governments and communities have applied positive reinforcement to protect our environment much less often than punishment and negative reinforcement, as manifested through bills, laws and ordinances. Indeed, the "bottle bill" of eight states (which specifies monetary remuneration for the return of certain drink containers for recycling) is the only large-scale, positive reinforcement procedure attempted by government and has probably caused more widespread controversy than any of the negative reinforcement and punishment procedures established by federal and/or state governments for environment preservation (see Chapter 4 for reviews of the issues and ramifications of bottle bills).

The positive consequences applied for environment preservation by behavior scientists have varied widely. Some consequences have been given contingent upon the performance of a particular *response*, whereas other consequence strategies have not specified a desired behavior but were contingent upon a given *outcome* (e.g., on the basis of specified reductions in energy consumption or increases in environmental cleanliness). The following *response*-contingent consequences were successful in increasing the frequency of the target behavior significantly above baseline levels: (1) raffle tickets per specified amounts of paper brought to a recycling center (Couch, Garber, & Karpus, 1978-79; Ingram & Geller, 1975; Witmer & Geller, 1976); (2) $5 payment if room thermostat is set at 74° F. in summer and all doors and windows are closed when air conditioner is running (Walker, 1979); (3) a merchandise token (redeemable for goods and services at local businesses) for riding a particular bus (Deslauriers & Everett, 1977; Everett, Hayward, & Meyers, 1974); (4) a coupon redeemable for a soft drink following litter deposits in a particular trash receptacle (Kohlenberg & Phillips, 1973); (5) $1 and a self-photograph for collecting a specially marked item of litter (Bacon-Prue, Blount, Pickering, & Drabman, 1980); and (6) points exchangeable for family outings and special favors for reduced use of certain home equipment, including the television, music system, oven, and furnace (Wodarski, 1976).

Examples of *outcome*-contingent consequences applied by behavior scientists include: (1) 10¢ for cleaning a littered yard to criterion (Chapman & Risley, 1974); (2) tour of mental health facility for 20% or greater reduction in vehicular miles of travel (Foxx & Hake, 1977); (3) $5 for averaging a 10%

reduction in miles of travel over 28 days, and $2.50 for each additional 10% reduction up to 30% (Hake & Foxx, 1978); (4) $2 per week for 5% to 10% reduction in home-heating energy, $3 for 11% to 20% reduction, and $5 per week for reductions greater than 20% (Winett & Nietzel, 1975); and (5) 75% of energy savings from expected costs returned to the residents of a master-metered apartment complex (Slavin & Wodarski, 1977; Slavin, Wodarski, & Blackburn, 1981).

The variety of energy conservation studies which showed beneficial effects of giving residents frequent and specific feedback regarding energy consumption may also be considered *outcome* consequences (see Chapter 5). The consequence was typically an indication of energy consumption in terms of kilowatt hours, cubic feet of gas, and/or monetary cost. Such a consequence can be pleasant if the feedback implies a savings in energy costs, or unpleasant if the feedback indicates an increase in consumption and costs. Most of the feedback studies for environmental protection have targeted residential energy consumption, and for most of these studies the feedback was given individually to target residences. Methods of giving such consumption feedback have included: (1) a special feedback card delivered to the home monthly (Seaver & Patterson, 1976), weekly (Kohlenberg et al., 1976; Winett et al., 1978), or daily (Becker, 1978; Hayes & Cone, 1977; Palmer et al., 1978; Seligman & Darley, 1977; Winett, Kaiser, & Haberkorn, 1977; Winett, Neale, & Grier, 1979; Winett, Neale, Williams, Yokley, & Kauder, 1979); (2) a mechanical apparatus that illuminated a light whenever current levels exceeded 90% of the peak use level for the household (Blakely, Lloyd, & Alferink, 1977; Kohlenberg et al., 1976); (3) an electronic feedback meter with digital display of electricity cost per hour (Becker & Seligman, 1978a; McClelland & Cook, 1979-80); and (4) training packages for teaching and motivating residents to read their own electric meters regularly and record energy consumption (Winett, Neale, & Grier, 1979).

A few feedback studies have targeted transportation conservation, showing that vehicular miles of travel (vmt) can be reduced with public display of vmt per individual (Reichel & Geller, 1980), and vehicular miles per gallon (mpg) can be increased with a fuel flow meter indicating continuous mpg or gallons-per-hour consumption (Lauridsen, 1977) or public display of mpg for short-run and long-haul truck drivers (Runnion, Watson, & McWhorter, 1978). In addition, one feedback intervention targeted litter control, demonstrating a 35% average reduction in ground litter following daily displays of litter counts on the front page of a community newspaper (Schnelle, Gendrich, Beegle, Thomas, & McNees, 1980). Television is also being investigated as a way to provide community feedback and influence environment-related behaviors (Rothstein, 1980). These and other feedback studies are discussed in more detail in subsequent chapters.

Whereas *response* consequences provide specific information regarding the appropriateness or inappropriateness of a particular behavior, most *outcome* consequences (including consumption feedback) do not prescribe changes in particular responses. In other words, a specific consequence of a response serves to prompt the occurrence of a similar response (if the consequence was pleasant) or an avoidance of that response (if the response consequence was unpleasant), while outcome consequences which are not associated with specific behaviors (such as consumption feedback) may not necessarily prompt specific behavior changes. Thus, outcome consequences should be less influential than response consequences, although we are not aware of a field study which makes this important comparison.

A good example of a consumption feedback intervention with a specific response prescription involved the application of a simple apparatus consisting of a blue light connected to a home's central air conditioning and a thermostat located on the outside of the house (Becker & Seligman, 1978b). Obtrusively located in the kitchen, the blue light flashed repeatedly when the air conditioning was on and the outside temperature was below 68° F. and stopped flashing when the air conditioning was turned off. In Chapter 5 we discuss the relative efficacy of these and other feedback techniques for motivating reductions in energy consumption.

Table 2.2 summarizes our discussion of consequence strategies up to this point. Four basic consequence strategies are defined, as determined by the *nature* of the consequence (pleasant or unpleasant) and the *action* with regard to the consequence (i.e., whether the consequence results in an *application* of a pleasant or unpleasant event or whether the consequence is the *removal* of a pleasant or unpleasant event). The examples given in the matrix of Table 2.2 illustrate the distinction between response-based and outcome-based contingencies. In other words, the application or removal of a pleasant or unpleasant event may occur after the contingency manager, the individual in charge of administering the consequence(s), observes a particular behavior or set of behaviors (i.e., response-based contingency) or after s/he observes a particular environmental outcome which is presumably the result of certain behaviors (i.e., outcome-based contingency).

The label reinforcement is used when the goal is to increase the probability that a response or outcome will reoccur, whereas punishment refers to consequence strategies for decreasing the likelihood of responses or outcomes. Desired behaviors or outcomes can be increased by making the application of a pleasant consequence contingent upon their occurrence (i.e., positive reinforcement) or by removing an unpleasant consequence following their occurrence (i.e., negative reinforcement). Under negative reinforcement contingencies, the desired response or outcome is motivated by the *avoidance* of an unpleasant event which may never have been experienced (e.g., a monetary fine) or by the *escape* of an ongoing aversive stimulus (e.g., high utility rates). Behaviors or outcomes are decreased in frequency by following the

Table 2.2. Matrix defining four types of consequence strategies for promoting environment preservation. The first example in each cell is a *response*-based contingency, whereas the second contingency is based on a specified *outcome*.

Nature of Consequence

	Pleasant	Unpleasant
Apply	POSITIVE REINFORCEMENT -one raffle coupon per delivery of paper to "Recycling Center" (response based) -$2 rebate per 10% decrease in monthly electricity consumption (outcome based)	POSITIVE PUNISHMENT -name of potential car pooler is listed on "Gas Waster" poster when observed driving to work alone (response based) -child calls adult a "litterbug" after leaving a picnic table with food packaging on it (outcome based)
Remove	NEGATIVE PUNISHMENT -three-month suspension of license for driving 80 mph (response based) -$5,000 fine for Kepone contamination of river (outcome based)	NEGATIVE REINFORCEMENT -five days in jail avoided for picking up litter along five-mile stretch of highway (response based) -increase in utility rates avoided for 5% decrease in water consumption (outcome based)

(Left margin label: Action with Consequence)

undesired behavior or outcome with an aversive consequence (positive punishment) or with the removal of a pleasant event (negative punishment). Note that the positive versus negative distinction in the definition of consequence strategies refers to whether the consequence is applied (positive) or removed (negative) in order to influence behaviors or outcomes and is *not* concomitant with the distinction between pleasant and unpleasant consequences.

The same consequence strategy can actually be differentially perceived as positive or negative, reinforcement or punishment. For example, reduced energy consumption following an exorbitant electricity bill may be perceived as resulting from a decrease in energy wasteful responding through *positive* punishment (e.g., the electricity bill was an embarrassing, aversive stimulus, indicating selfish consumption of environmental resources) or through *negative* punishment (e.g., the electricity bill represented the loss or removal of the resident's money), or through a combination of both positive and negative punishment. On the other hand, the same residents may reduce their consumption following a high electricity bill to avoid receiving another similar bill (negative reinforcement) or to receive a lower electricity bill (positive reinforcement). This rhetoric may seem like only word games or suggest that behavior scientists really don't know what they are doing, but the point is quite practical and important. The contingency manager may indeed define a contingency in one way (e.g., "I'll apply positive reinforcement by offering $5 rebates to residents with 10% reductions in monthly water use"), but the target population may perceive the contingency differently (e.g., "We'd better reduce our water consumption in order to avoid losing our $5 rebate"— negative reinforcement). And if a pleasant consequence is not earned (as specified in a positive reinforcement contingency), the target population may perceive a punishment contingency that was not intended by the behavior manager (e.g., "We lost our $5 rebate because we used too much water"— negative punishment). Given that reinforcement or punishment contingencies may not be perceived as they were intended, why is this important?

Recall that earlier in this chapter the point was made that antecedent strategies that are perceived as intrusive demands rather than polite requests may not only be ineffective but may in fact influence the occurrence of contrary behaviors. Such a result is consistent with psychological reactance theory (Brehm, 1966, 1972) in that individuals who feel controlled by external events (such as a demanding prompt) are expected to resist compliance when possible or emit contrary behaviors in order to assert their personal freedom. Obviously, consequence strategies can also influence perceptions of external control and elicit a perceived need to maintain personal freedom; therefore consequence strategies can encourage the occurrence of responses to counteract the control specified by the particualr contingency. Such "counteraction" may involve: (1) an ignoring of the contingency, (2) an active resistance to emit the target behavior, or (3) direct counter-control measures, i.e., attempts to reverse the situation and exert the external control over the administrator(s) of the original consequence strategy. The important point here is that certain consequence strategies (i.e., response or outcome contingencies) are more likely than others to reduce perceived freedom.

In his classic discussions of relationships between perceived freedom and response-consequence contingencies, Skinner (1971) explained that people are more apt to feel controlled by extrinsic events when they are responding to avoid or escape aversive consequences (i.e., negative reinforcement) than when they are responding to earn pleasant consequences (i.e., positive reinforcement). Furthermore, punishment procedures are the clearest demonstration of one person's external control over another. Thus, positive reinforcement is the consequence strategy which is most likely to preserve one's perceptions of personal freedom and least likely to promote resistance and counteraction. Positive reinforcement is the consequence strategy most apt to be accepted by the community at large, and is the predominant consequence strategy applied by behavior scientists for environment preservation.

However, we started this discussion of perceived freedom and consequence strategies with the notion that a particular contingency may be perceived differentially. A program manager may have intended to implement a positive reinforcement contingency, but a majority of the clients could actually perceive this consequence strategy as negative reinforcement and consider that not earning positive reinforcement is a punishment procedure. Therefore, resistance to an *intended* positive reinforcement program may actually occur because perceptions by a majority of clients imply that the program was interpreted as an attempt to exert control through negative reinforcement and punishment.

At this point, it is critical to emphasize that behavior scientists have *not* typically concerned themselves with perceptions and interpretations by the individuals targeted with particular consequence strategies. The definition of a consequence strategy (including the target behavior or outcome, the nature of the consequence, and whether the consequence is applied or removed) is specified by the program administrator; the contingency is positive or negative, reinforcement or punishment according to such intention. This is obviously the most objective and straightforward approach to the categorization of contingencies. However, the intention of this discussion was to introduce the notion that a particular consequence strategy may not necessarily be perceived as intended, and that such perceptions can determine relative acceptance or resistance to attempts at controlling behavior. Because such discrepancies between perceptions of program administrators and recipients can have critical ramifications for program evaluation and development, we suggest that attempts be made to assess the definition of consequence strategies from the clients' point of view. This is, however, an innovative concept in applied behavior analysis, and therefore optimal, objective techniques for assessing perceptions of consequence strategies in field settings must await appropriate research (see Wolf, 1978).

Animal/Laboratory versus Human/Field Research

The basic principles of applied behavior anlaysis which have been used to modify environment-related behaviors and to evaluate the behavioral impact of environment preservation programs were originally researched and developed in laboratory settings with pigeons and rats as subjects. In these animal/laboratory situations, influential parameters were readily manipulated by the behavior manager (the experimenter), and relationships between experimenter input (i.e., independent variables) and subject output (i.e., dependent variables) were usually obvious and unequivocal (e.g., Skinner, 1938). Thus, the definition of strategies for modifying behavior were simply as specified by the experimenter; there was no need to consider perceptions of the subject. The behavioral technology developed in the animal laboratory is certainly applicable to humans in their natural habitat (as will be demonstrated repeatedly in this text), but definitions of parameters and relationships between independent and dependent variables have been equivocal and some have required consideration of moderating factors which are not directly observable. For example, natural settings often do not allow for straightforward manipulation of laboratory-defined contingencies. And as discussed above, the cognitive activity of humans can result in perceptions of threatened freedom and unexpected, undesirable outcomes.

In a provocative address, Jack Michael (1980), one of the foremost authorities in experimental behavior analysis, indicated that numerous field applications of positive reinforcement are so unlike the standard laboratory specifications that it is actually inaccurate to label the field strategy positive reinforcement. The problem is not usually with the objective definition of target behaviors, nor with the acquisition of pleasant consequences which are successful in motivating an increase in the rate of target behaviors. Rather, the delay between the target response and the consequence is often so long in field applications of reinforcement techniques that principles of behavior from animal laboratory research cannot be used to predict or interpret findings. In the animal/laboratory situation the pleasant consequence must follow the target response within a few seconds in order to be effective. However, many field applications of positive reinforcement have included substantial delays between target behaviors and pleasant consequences. Furthermore as discussed above, some positive reinforcement programs have reinforced the environmental *outcome* of unspecified behaviors (which is a contingency without an animal-laboratory analogue).

Our point here is that many extensions of the experimental analysis of behavior to human situations have differed siginificantly from the laboratory analogue upon which they were supposedly based. Therefore, it is often inappropriate to refer to laboratory studies when predicting and interpreting findings and refining intervention strategies. When evaluating, interpreting, or designing behavioral approaches toward environment preservation, it is often most appropriate to go no further than the studies critically reviewed in this text for procedural verification, experimental support, and theoretical integration.

It is noteworthy that the standard categorization of consequence strategies is dependent upon response outcome. In other words, if a response increases in frequency following an immediate consequence, the strategy is termed reinforcement; and if the response consequence decreases subsequent occurrences of the preceding response, the contingency is termed punishment. Thus, stimulus events or response opportunities are pleasant if organisms respond to receive them (positive reinforcement) or stop making responses which result in the removal of them (negative punishment). Consequences are unpleasant if organisms respond to escape or avoid them (negative reinforcement) or stop making responses which result in their occurrence (positive punishment). Note that this direct relationship between the definition of a response-consequence contingency and its effect on behavior implies continual evaluation of behavioral impact, resulting in statements of response-consequence relationships which are always accurate (i.e., true by definition). For example, according to the technical definitions of the consequence contingencies, positive reinforcement always works. If a target behavior does not increase following a consequence that the experimenter believed was pleasant, then the consequence was not really pleasant (i.e., it was not a positive reinforcer).

This definitional system works well for laboratory studies, because in such situations experimenters can maintain control over factors that determine the value of consequences. They can apply or remove such consequences immediately following the occurrence of target behaviors, and can observe almost immediately the behavioral impact of such consequences. Because of this situational control, instances when contingencies do not influence responses in predicted directions (i.e., increases or decreases in rate of occurrence) are relatively rare. When such inconsistencies do occur, experimenters receive rapid feedback and make appropriate adjustments either in the nature of the actual contingency or in the definition of the contingency. However, substantial losses in control, predictability, and feedback result when behavior analysis is extended to field settings for environment preservation. An ineffective contingency can result from many uncontrollable factors other than the definition of an appropriate consequence, and evaluation procedures (when existent) are often imprecise with regard to the impact of a given consequence on a particular behavior. Indeed, many field applications have targeted the responses of several individuals simultaneously, and impact is evaluated with regard to a group rather than an individual. Thus, when the overall impact reported for a consequence strategy is in a desired and predicted direction, it is quite possible for individuals within the target group to be uninfluenced by the contingency or to be influenced in undesired (or nonpredicted) directions.

Our point here is that applications of behavioral interventions for large-scale environment preservation are not readily controlled nor evaluated, and therefore making definitions of consequence strategies contingent on response impact (as in animal/laboratory studies) is cumbersome and often impossible. Therefore it is often advantageous to derive field contingencies on past research in similar settings and to define a particular consequence strategy in terms of the intentions of the program administrators. If an appropriate evaluation shows unexpected and undesired effects, we recommend that program managers consider the large variety of contaminating factors that are possible in human/field settings rather than simply assuming that the consequence was inappropriate. Furthermore, cataloging field contingencies independently from response impact is consistent with the definitional scheme for antecedent strategies. The categorization of prompting techniques (see Table 2.1) has been based on characteristics of the particular procedure, regardless of behavioral effects. This is probably the case because variations in antecedent strategies have originated in the field extensions of behavior analysis; most antecedent approaches to environment preservation do not have animal/laboratory analogues.

Scheduling Response Consequences

Differential techniques for scheduling response consequences were defined, researched, and developed in the animal laboratory, and the resultant principles of behavior have critical ramifications for field contingencies. In simplest terms, response consequences can usually have more desirable behavioral effects if they occur intermittently rather than continuously. For example, the rate of behavior can reach higher levels under intermittent rather than continuous reinforcement; when a response consequence is removed entirely (technically termed extinction) the response rate will usually continue at desired levels for longer periods when the pre-extinction, reinforcement schedule had been intermittent rather than continuous. This behavioral principle is technically referred to as greater "resistance to extinction" following intermittent rather than continuous reinforcement. It is important to note two qualifications here: (1) It is usually most effective to *begin* a reinforcement program with a continuous reinforcement procedure and fade into intermittent scheduling; and (2) An intermittent reinforcement schedule that provides very few reinforcement opportunities can result in a low rate (or even extinction) of the target response.

A variety of reinforcement schedules have been studied in the animal laboratory, each determining characteristic and predictable response patterns while the reinforcement schedule is in effect *and* when the schedule is removed. We will discuss only the most basic and simple reinforcement schedules here, since only these are relevant for the current state of the art in behavior analysis for environment preservation.

The dichotomous categories, ratio versus interval and fixed versus variable, define the basic classification scheme for reinforcement or punishment schedules. The *ratio* versus *interval* distinction refers to whether the administration of reinforcers is determined by response frequency (i.e., ratio) or by a minimal time duration between consecutive consequences (i.e., interval). In other words, a behavior manager might determine systematically when to offer pleasant or unpleasant consequences by counting occurrences of the target response (a ratio schedule) or by timing the interval between opportunities for pleasant or unpleasant consequences (an interval schedule). The consequence schedule is *fixed* if the response frequency or minimum interval between consequences is constant throughout an intervention period and is termed *variable* if the response frequencies or consequence intervals that determine the schedule of consequences fluctuate throughout the intervention period.

For a *fixed ratio* five schedule (i.e., FR 5), a consequence is presented immediately after every fifth occurrence of the target response; for a *variable ratio* five schedule (i.e., VR 5) the number of responses required for a consequence varies, but averages to five responses per consequence. An FI 5 minute schedule is a *fixed interval* schedule, where the minimal interval between reinforced (or punished) responses is five minutes; for a VI 5 minute schedule the interval between opportunities for reinforcement or punishment fluctuates between consequence presentations but averages to five minutes.

Fixed ratio schedules are noted for their promotion of high response rates, while variable ratio and variable interval schedules typically influence steady and regular response rates. Resistance to extinction is often higher following variable than fixed schedules of reinforcement, although fixed ratio schedules have resulted in record-high response frequencies during lengthy extinction periods.

Since most human consequences in natural settings do not occur after every occurrence of given responses or outcomes, schedules of reinforcement and punishment are significant entities throughout our daily existence. However, occurrences of reinforcement and punishment do not always fit the basic laboratory definitions of ratio versus interval and fixed versus variable. In fact, most field applications of reinforcement schedules for environment preservation are only loosely related to the laboratory definitions, and many situations represent a combination of different consequence schedules. For example, the weekly raffle or lottery has been a popular incentive procedure for encouraging environment-preserving behaviors and represents a scheduling of pleasant consequences related loosely to continuous reinforcement, fixed interval, and variable ratio schedules. More specifically, in resource recovery projects by several investigators (e.g., Couch et al., 1979, Geller et al., 1975; Jacobs, 1978; Witmer & Geller, 1976), individuals received raffle coupons each time they made a specified newspaper recycling response. Coupon reinforcement occurred on a continuous schedule and was presented after each *delivery* of a recyclable item (a response consequence) or for each specified *amount* of recyclables (an outcome consequence). The weekly raffle offered an opportunity for participants to cash in their coupons (i.e., an FI one week schedule), but only those coupons drawn at the raffle could be traded for an actual prize. The raffle drawings were analogous to a variable ratio schedule, since only a small proportion of the individuals attending the raffle received a prize, and the number of prizes per individual varied from zero to a maximum defined by the total number of prizes raffled off. It is noteworthy that classifying the raffle drawing itself as a particular type of reinforcement contingency is cumbersome and probably inappropriate; the target responses are not immediately reinforced and it is difficult to identify a precise ratio between response and reinforcement frequency.

Hayes, Johnson, and Cone (1975) introduced the term "variable person ratio schedule" (VPR) for situations when reinforcers are delivered after a single response among a variable number of persons rather than after a variable number of responses by a single organism (as in the laboratory definition of variable ratio schedule). For example, Kohlenberg and Phillips (1973) gave a coupon redeemable for a soft drink to an average of every tenth person who used a particular trash receptacle, and Deslauriers and Everett (1977) gave a coupon exchangeable for discounts at local businesses to an average of every third person who boarded a special campus bus. Although the investigators referred to these schedules as VR10 and VR3, respectively, it is actually more appropriate to consider these consequence schedules as variable *person* ratio schedules, since the delivery of consequences was dependent upon frequencies of individuals making a particular target response rather than frequencies of responses emitted by one individual.

Note that fixed person ratio (FPR), variable person interval (VPI), and fixed person interval (FPI) are also possible in human/field settings. Under FPR scheduling, a consequence is delivered after every fixed number of individuals who make the target response. For VPI and FPI schedules, consequences are available after fixed or variable periods of time, and the consequence is presented to the first person who makes the target response after the consequence is available. The subsequent chapters of this text offer situations where these various scheduling techniques were implemented to encourage environment-preserving activities, but much research on the scheduling effects in field settings is still needed.

It is instructive to contemplate the variety of daily situations where human behavior in natural settings is controlled by *combinations* of consequence schedules which are analogous to those defined above. For example, consider that highway patrol officers are scheduled to sample vehicle speeds at particular locations along a highway throughout each day of a work week. This aspect of their assignment would represent a fixed interval schedule along the target highway, since the occasion for drivers to receive aversive consequences for traveling more than 55 mph would occur at fixed time periods per location. Now suppose the officers do not assess the speed of every vehicle, but average three radar measurements per minute in heavy traffic. This would represent a VPI 20 second schedule. Note that from the perspective of individual drivers who habitually exceed 55 mph on interstate highways, a schedule most analogous to variable ratio is in effect. In other words, the most consistent violators of speed limits receive a number of traffic fines in their life for speeding, but such punishment occurs only intermittently following varying occurrences of speed-limit violations. The density of this variable ratio schedule for a particular driver (i.e., the ratio of violations to fines) is dependent upon many factors, including the rate and route of travel, the use of techniques to detect radar traps, and alertness to situations when vehicle speed could be measured. So we return to a primary theme of this chapter: extending basic principles of behavior to the natural environment of humans requires creativity to expand and adjust laboratory-based technology, flexibility to appreciate and consider unobservable determinants of behavior, patience to cope with numerous uncontrollable variables, and courage to risk unpredictable and undesirable outcomes.

EVALUATION STRATEGIES

The continuous evaluation of the efficacy of an intervention or program is an integral component of applied behavior analysis. Cost-benefit and cost-effectiveness analyses are frequently used by environmental protection agencies, but it is our contention that some of this work has proceeded without much use of evaluation methodologies employed in behavior analysis research. However, in many instances the behavioral approach to evaluation is most appropriate, as illustrated by the following comparison between two approaches toward assessing the effectiveness of statewide litter control programs—the standard method versus applied behavior analysis.

Several states have recently added a division among their community service agencies to deal with statewide problems in solid waste management. The legislative action that has established such agencies has usually included a mandate for a periodic, comprehensive evaluation of the various types of litter found across the state. These surveys are conducted at the initiation of the agency and thereafter at least annually, in order to demonstrate the utility of the states' programs to control litter, reduce waste, and promote resource recovery. To satisfy mandates for periodic litter surveys, most states have hired consultants who have conducted elaborate large-scale counts and classifications of statewide litter.

It is certainly refreshing to find a substantial evaluation aspect to a government program, even if it is expensive (averaging about $35,000 per survey). However, in our opinion, periodic statewide litter surveys provide little information relative to the design and refinement of litter control programs. Such surveys do determine the relative contributions of specific items to the states' litter, but offer no data regarding the efficacy of specific litter control strategies. Most state litter control programs include at least improved enforcement of antilitter ordinances, public service advertisement on radio and television, community workshops on proper solid waste management, the establishment of community recycling centers, and the introduction of litter control and recycling information in school curricula. Thus, an observed reduction in comprehensive litter counts from baseline (i.e., when the litter control agency was established) to a post-treatment period (i.e., after several months of litter control strategies) can only indicate that *something* the state did to discourage littering and/or encourage litter pickup *may* have been effective. Actually, there are a number of extraneous variables unrelated to the litter control programs which could influence such surveys, such as variations in weather, population density, and land usage. But even if there were assurance that a state's litter control program was the primary determinant of a reduced litter count, such data could not be used to improve subsequent strategies for litter control, since there is no information regarding the efficacy of a single program component. An applied behavior analysis approach to evaluating litter control strategies (and other environment preservation programs) includes techniques to account for extraneous, contaminating variables and provides information relevant to the refinement of particular interventions.

The evaluation procedures followed by applied behavior analysts are based on research techniques in animal laboratories. Consider the following experimental situation. A white rat is pressing a lever and receiving a food pellet on the average after every fifth response (i.e., a VR 5 reinforcement schedule). After a 30-minute session in this situation, the animal is removed from the experimental chamber and returned to its home cage until the same time on the next day, when the rat will be again placed in the same setting for 30 minutes under a VR 5 reinforcement schedule. At the end of each session the experimenter reads a response counter which indicates the number of responses the animal emitted per 30 minutes. This response rate measure obtained each day is marked on a graph, with response frequency as the vertical axis of the graph (i.e., the ordinate) and consecutive days as the horizontal axis (i.e., the abscissa). After several days, an examination of the data points on this graph shows a stable rate of behavior (i.e., the response rate is similar each day). At this point the rat is injected with an appropriate dosage of amphetamine (e.g., 2 mg. per kilogram of body weight) before being placed in the operant chamber. The treatment phase of the experiment has begun.

Now our rat is injected daily with a specified amount of amphetamine before given a 30-minute reinforcement session on VR 5. This treatment phase continues until a stable rate of lever pressing occurs (i.e., until fluctuations of response rate within the 30-minute reinforcement session are minimal and the overall response rates per 30-minute session are approximately the same). A comparison between the stable response rates during baseline and treatment suggests the behavioral impact of the treatment intervention (in this case an increase in response rate will occur). However, it is possible that behavior was influenced by another factor which changed at the onset of treatment (e.g., maturity of the subject); therefore, to be sure that the experimental treatment was responsible for the observed behavior change, the treatment is withdrawn (i.e., no more amphetamine injections), and 30-minute reinforcement sessions are continued until a stable rate of responding is obtained. The conditions of this third phase are exactly like those during the initial baseline phase, and therefore, it is termed "baseline." This experimental paradigm is referred to as an ABA withdrawal design, with A referring to baseline and B to treatment.

Experimental behavior analysis in the animal laboratory is certainly more complex than the above example, especially with regard to experimental manipulations, but the basic evaluation procedure is usually followed. A stable rate of responding is obtained during a baseline (or pre-treatment) period, and one specified variable is then manipulated for a treatment phase and remains constant until response rate in this condition is stable. Subsequently, the treatment intervention is removed and response rate is measured until a stable response rate is reached. Therefore, the behavioral impact of a particular intervention is readily assessed without complex data transformations and statistical anlayses, and only a single subject is needed to show the behavioral impact of treatment strategies. To assess the generality of effect, the same procedures are implemented with other subjects or in other environmental settings.

Applying this experimental evaluation paradigm to field settings with human subjects has required various extensions and compromises (as was also the case with field applications of reinforcement scheduling). But the basic procedures from the laboratory model have usually been attempted, and we recommend these for evaluating the efficacy of environment preservation programs. For an evaluation procedure to provide information pertinent to program refinement, the following recommendations should be specifically considered (although field evaluations have rarely satisfied all of these suggestions):

1. Before implementing a treatment intervention, obtain measures of specific ongoing responses (or of response outcomes) which are directly relevant to the goals of treatment. More specifically, the target response or response outcome measured during baseline should be that which the intervention is designed to increase or decrease in frequency. Repeated measures of the responses of the *same* individuals would be ideal, but rarely possible in field experiments.

2. Observe the target response(s) or response outcome(s) at several times under the same baseline conditions and, if possible, obtain a frequency measure (i.e., number of occurrences per unit time) so that response rates can be calculated. It is usually better to obtain several repeated measures on relatively few individuals (or at relatively few locations) rather than a few measures on several individuals (or at several locations).

3. Continue baseline measures until a clear picture of response or outcome level is obtained, i.e., until stability is observed or variability is explainable. Decide when to implement treatment on the basis of the baseline observations, not according to some preset time schedule.

4. Implement a particular treatment procedure to influence the response (or response outcome) measured during baseline. Note that treatment can certainly consist of a variety of behavioral strategies, but in such cases the results can only indicate the impact of the *entire* treatment package. To obtain information relevant to the refinement of treatment programs, it is necessary to test the impact of separate components of a program. This is done by implementing individual intervention strategies independently.

5. Obtain repeated measures of the target response (or response outcome) during the treatment period until the measure(s) appear relatively stable, and then withdraw the treatment strategy for a second period of baseline.

6. To test different intervention strategies (or separate components of a particular treatment package) follow the five recommendations above for each strategy. This could be done with the same individual(s) at the same location(s) by following an ABACADA paradigm, where individual behavior change strategies (i.e., B, C, and D) are separated by periods of baseline. For each of the conditions in this paradigm, it is advisable (although not always possible) to continue repeated measures until the data is relatively stable so that changes due to specific treatment interventions are readily discernible. However, in this instance the *order* of different treatment interventions may have an effect. In such cases, experimental designs are available which balance for order, such as the Latin Square design applied by Geller et al. (1973) to study strategies for promoting the sale of returnable soft drink containers (see Chapter 4 for details).

Figure 2.1 illustrates the results of an ABA design at a field setting. As will be discussed in Chapter 4, this study was among the first attempts to influence environment-related behaviors and involved the daily observation of the number of returnable and nonreturnable bottles purchased by grocery store patrons. At this point it is instructive to note the similarities and differences between this field investigation and the model ABA design from the animal laboratory. The field study included a baseline, treatment, baseline order of conditions and added a follow-up phase after the second baseline to assess maintenance of impact (also common in laboratory analyses of behavior). Also, the treatment intervention essentially represented one component (i.e., the distribution of handbills at the door of the store which urged the purchase of drinks in returnable containers); therefore, the controlling influence of a treatment effect could be identified. Indeed, the immediate and prominent increase in the dependent variable during treatment and the immediate and sustained decrease in the data shown during the second baseline and follow-up observations suggest a significant behavioral impact of the handbill-prompting intervention, without the need of complex data transformation or statistical analysis.

However, the extension of experimental behavior analysis to naturalistic settings with human subjects has resulted in compromises of the model laboratory paradigm, and some of these are typified by the results shown in Figure 2.1. First, the dependent measure was not the rate of responding

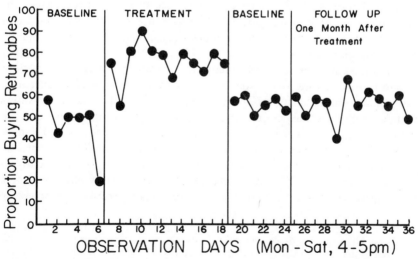

Fig. 2.1. An ABA withdrawal paradigm. The proportion of grocery store customers who purchased more than 50% of their drinks in returnable containers under baseline, treatment, and follow-up conditions (redrawn from Geller, Wylie, & Farris, 1971).

observed from a single subject. The dependent variable represented instead an aggregate measure of individuals who made the target response on consecutive days. Each observation day represented a different sampling of individuals, with no indication of the proportion of individuals on each day who had been recorded in an earlier sample. As noted by Nietzel, Winett, MacDonald, and Davidson (1977), it is perhaps most appropriate to consider that the environmental setting (in this case the grocery store) was the single organism subjected to applied behavior analysis. Indeed, this is a recurring situation in many naturalistic experiments which involve observations of large numbers of people, since individuals cannot usually be tagged and identified from one observation session to the next. One recent exception has been the field observation of behaviors associated with a person's automobile, since license plate numbers can be recorded and repeated observations of the same individual can be studied (see Geller, Johnson, & Pelton, 1981; Geller, Talbott, & Paterson, 1981; Johnson & Geller, 1981).

Figure 2.1 illustrates a serious weakness, unfortunately common among field extensions of behavioral analysis: the relatively small amount of observation time per experimental condition and lack of stability in the dependent variable prior to the initiation of a change in conditions (see Hersen & Barlow, 1976). In contrast to the laboratory setting, field observations require continuous on-site performance by research personnel and concomitant cooperation by the management staff of the particular milieu. At least two individuals are needed at some points to make independent observations of the same behaviors (in order to measure inter-observer reliability*), and additional staff is often needed to manage the treatment procedures. The result is often as shown in Figure 2.1; the duration of the observation sessions is shorter than desirable and the number of observation sessions per condition is less than optimal.

Given the vast number of extraneous factors which can bias observations in naturalistic settings, it is especially risky to change experimental conditions before the data are relatively stable. For example, Figure 2.1 shows that the initial baseline period was quite short (only seven days) and included substantial fluctuations in daily percentages. Several factors could have caused the daily fluctuations (e.g., changes in soft drink prices, weather, and store patronage) and contributed to the increase in returnable-bottle customers during treatment. The rapid return to baseline levels after treatment was withdrawn provides convincing evidence that the treatment intervention

---

* Reliability is assessed by determining the percentage of agreement between independent observers or different sources of data. Generally, at least 80% agreement is considered a minimal acceptable standard (Kazdin, 1975). For example, if two independent litter categorizations agree on 65% of possible items, the integrity of the dependent measure would be questionable. In such a case, conclusions from any experimental manipulations would be difficult to interpret.

(handbill prompting in this case) was a primary determinant of observed behavior change. However, one could be even more certain that the treatment manipulation was the most significant cause of the observed increase in target behaviors if bottle buying behavior had been observed under a continuous baseline condition at another grocery store *and* if the sale of returnables at this setting did not increase when the treatment intervention was introduced at the target milieu. Actually, such a comparison condition has been used quite often to overcome the additional extraneous variables encountered and the compromises in methodology and design needed when extending behavior analysis beyond the laboratory.

For example, when Everett et al. (1974) studied the effects of a positive reinforcement procedure to increase bus ridership (details presented in Chapter 6), they not only applied an ABA paradigm on one bus (the experimental bus) but also measured bus ridership on a control bus that never received the incentive intervention. The results of this field study are depicted in Figure 2.2, and illustrate the advantages of this ABA-control group design. Thus, comparing bus ridership during the baseline and treatment conditions

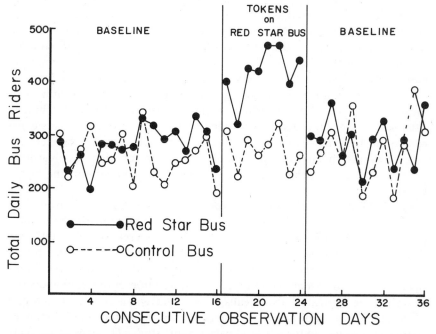

Fig. 2.2. An ABA withdrawal paradigm with a control group. The daily frequency of bus riders on a control bus and on the experimental bus (i.e., the Red Star bus) during baseline conditions and during treatment when tokens were distributed (redrawn from Everett, Hayward, & Meyers, 1974).

on the experimental bus suggests a marked impact of treatment. The additional observation that bus ridership on the control bus did not change when treatment occurred on the experimental bus, however, provides especially convincing evidence that the treatment manipulation was the critical determinant of increased bus ridership on the experimental bus.

As will be discussed in Chapter 5, there is a particular need to use a control group when evaluating the impact of strategies to decrease residential energy consumption. Since weather changes can actually have a greater influence on heating or cooling energy than almost any reasonable conservation strategy, it is advisable to measure the energy consumption of a non-treatment control group as well as obtaining both baseline and treatment data of the experimental group(s) so that effects of treatment can be assessed independently of effects due to seasonal variation. Figures 5.3 and 5.5 in Chapter 5 depict this ABA-control group design for two energy conservation studies conducted by Dick Winett and his associates.

If the control group in this ABA-control group design were given the treatment intervention sometime after the experimental group received treatment *and* if an immediate change in the control group were observed that was similar to the change observed in the experimental group when the same treatment was introduced, our assurance that we have observed a cause-and-effect relationship would increase even further. Such a paradigm would represent a combination of the ABA-withdrawal paradigm and the final evaluation procedure to be discussed—the multiple baseline design. A multiple baseline approach does not include a withdrawal of treatment, but involves the systematic application of staggered AB phases so that treatment is introduced in one situation while baseline measures continue in another situation. Indeed, the multiple baseline design was introduced as a compromise to the ABA-withdrawal paradigm for circumstances where ethical considerations obviate the withdrawal of treatment or when the treatment intervention may be expected to have a permanent impact on the target behavior.

Figure 2.3 depicts results from a recycling study by Luyben, Warren, and Tallman (1979-80) and illustrates the multiple baseline approach to evaluation. The number of aluminum cans collected each week from four different college dormitories was recorded under two different experimental conditions. The switch from a "single recycling container" per dorm to a "multiple recycling container" condition (i.e., the addition of five containers per dorm for the deposit of drink cans) was staggered successively from one dorm to the next, with one dorm remaining in the initial single container condition throughout the entire 11 weeks of the study. The beneficial effects of multiple containers is shown by comparing changes in the dependent measure across dormitories experiencing different experimental conditions. In other words, at points where the multiple container intervention was

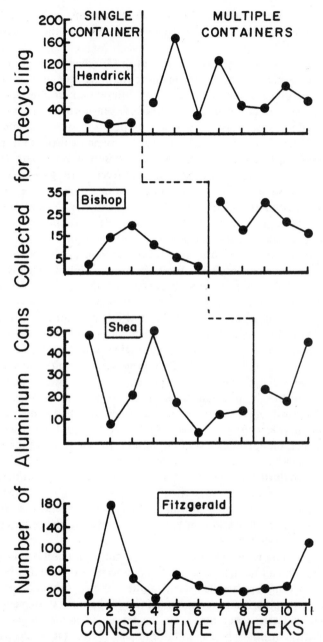

Fig. 2.3. A multiple baseline design across subjects and settings. The number of aluminum cans collected per consecutive week at four dormitories, with staggered introduction of a Multiple Recycling Container condition wherein five containers labeled for can recycling were added to the dorm (redrawn from Luyben, Warren, & Tallman, 1979-80).

introduced, the number of cans collected increased substantially at the treatment dorm while showing no consistent fluctuation at the non-treatment dorm(s).

It is noteworthy that the dormitories in the Luyben et al. study (across which the two experimental conditions were compared for the multiple baseline design) involved different subjects and different environmental settings. Hence, extraneous uncontrolled bias in the between-dorm comparisons could have occurred from two sets of variables—population and environment. The observed differences would have been more convincing if the multiple baseline comparisons had occurred across only different *environments* (i.e., if container recycling of the same subjects in different settings was compared) or only different *subjects* (i.e., if container recycling in the same environmental setting was compared across two groups of subjects). Such "pure" comparisons across only one set of variables is often difficult to achieve in naturalistic settings, but the definitions of the multiple baseline design do specify comparisons across only one set of variables, either environments, subjects, or behaviors (see Baer, Wolf, & Risley, 1968; Hersen & Barlow, 1976). In fact, definitions of the multiple baseline design include a specification of three types: (1) multiple baseline across environmental settings, (2) multiple baseline across subjects, and (3) multiple baseline across behaviors. An example of multiple baseline across behaviors would be an observation of baseline levels for two responses (e.g., number of newspapers and number of soft drink containers recycled) of the *same* subjects in the *same* environmental setting, an application of a motivational strategy to one of these behaviors, and finally an application of the treatment intervention to the second behavior. Note that for a valid assessment, the two behaviors should be independent (i.e., change in one does not necessarily influence a change in the other); such independence is often difficult to achieve, although such an independence assumption is testable by observing the amount of concomitant fluctuation during baseline recordings. Of course, when multiple baseline comparisons are made across settings or across subjects, it must also be presumed that the target behavior and its particular context (i.e, its subject or its milieu) are relatively autonomous with respect to the other context(s) in which the behavior is measured.

Table 2.3 summarizes the three types of multiple baseline designs discussed above and a fourth type which has not been defined earlier but one we believe can be quite applicable in field studies for environmental protection. We define this evaluation paradigm as a multiple baseline design across *time*, requiring systematic observations of the target behavior at two or more specified time periods while maintaining the environment, behavior and subject(s) constant. As summarized in Table 2.3, one example of such a paradigm would be the measurement of vehicular speeds on a particular highway at two different time periods (e.g., when the same drivers are travel-

Table 2.3. Four Types of Multiple Designs with Examples of Differential Points for Treatment Application.

Treatment Application Varied:	Dependent Measure	Initial Treatment Application	Second Treatment Application
1. Across Settings	Room Temperature	At Home	At Work
2. Across Subjects	Shower Duration	Brother	Sister
3. Across Behaviors	Number of Drink Containers	Aluminum Cans	Steel Cans
4. Across Time	Speed Limit	Morning	Evening

ing to work in the morning and driving home in the afternoon) with the initial implementation of a treatment strategy (e.g., by parking an empty police car along the side of the road) at only one of these times.

Summarizing this section on evaluation strategies, we have emphasized the frequent observation of target behaviors during periods when a particular treatment strategy has been applied and when the treatment was not in effect. We have defined three basic paradigms for varying the treatment and non-treatment periods: (1) ABA-withdrawal, (2) ABA-withdrawal with a non-treatment control group, and (3) a multiple baseline design with comparisons across settings, subjects, behaviors, or time. One of these evaluation paradigms was used in most of the studies described in subsequent chapters, although compromises from the ideal conditions of the laboratory experiment are common. Indeed, because such compromises occur and because the nature of these compromises varies from study to study, the impact of intervention strategies is not always straightforward and is open to subjective opinion and alternative interpretations. Thus, it is important to have a basic understanding of the *ideal* evaluation approach when interpreting the *real* evaluation procedures followed by particular experiments. From such an understanding of the methodology, findings, and interpretation of these experiments comes a realization of ways to decrease the discrepancy between real and ideal approaches toward treatment evaluation.

Chapter 3
Litter Control*

It is especially appropriate to start our discussions of specific behavioral applications for environment preservation with litter control—not because it is the most serious or pressing environmental problem, nor because behavioral analysis is most applicable in this problem area—but because more behavioral research has actually targeted litter control than any other single aspect of environmental preservation. Indeed, the first published account of behavioral analysis for environmental protection studied the cost effectiveness of particular response priming and positive reinforcement procedures for encouraging litter pickup in a movie theater (Burgess, Clark, & Hendee, 1971). Several publications already review the behavioral work in this area (e.g., Brasted, Mann, & Geller, 1979; Cone & Hayes, 1978; Geller, 1980a; Osborne & Powers, 1980; Robinson, 1976; Tuso & Geller, 1976) and the most comprehensive community approach to encouraging environmental-protection behaviors today has targeted litter control. The Clean Community System of Keep America Beautiful, Inc. (KAB) is currently the most influential large-scale plan for organizing, motivating, and evaluating community action toward the solution of environmental/ecological problems. This program is specifically concerned with litter control, but is relevant for many other aspects of environment preservation, and we will critically review the KAB program as an action model applicable to a wide variety of community, environmental problems in this chapter.

LITTER CONTROL AS A BEHAVIORAL PROBLEM

The behavior analysis of litter control, as with any problem area, should start with a definition of the problem and a specification of the behaviors relevant to that problem. Litter is misplaced solid waste, from the carelessly discarded cigarette butt to the rusting hulk of an abandoned automobile. To

* Portions of this chapter were adapted from Geller, E. S., Applications of behavior analysis to litter control. In D. Glenwick & L. Jason, *Behavioral community psychology*. New York: Praeger Publishers, 1980, 254–283.

define an item as "misplaced" requires that the environmental setting be considered. While a used paper cup in a waste basket or on the floor of a movie theater may not be considered litter, the same cup along a roadside or in someone's back yard usually would be. Likewise, the junked car is more likely to be considered litter in an open field than as one of many in the common and unsightly "automobile graveyard." Almost any unused item can be considered litter if found in a socially unacceptable location.

Since the definition of "socially unacceptable" may vary among individuals, discarded items may not be uniformly perceived as litter. While most people would percieve the empty bottle on the roadside as litter, paper cups and bottles scattered about the grounds of a football stadium may be seen by some as a natural and appropriate consequence of spectator activity. Furthermore, an automobile filled with soil and actually functioning to keep a river on course is not "misplaced" and is not litter according to local residents, but to the canoeist on the river the unsightly hulk may be considered useless and misplaced (Osborne & Powers, 1980).

The Problem with Litter

The most obvious and frequently discussed consequence of littering is environmental defacement. Indeed, this consequence results in a nationwide cost of over $1 billion each year; half of this expense is for collecting litter from public areas such as highways, forests, parks, and beaches, and the other half is for cleaning litter from private, business, and industrial property (KAB, 1970; Seed, 1970). Simply combatting the four billion tons of litter found along our highways each year (Ward, 1975) costs each state an average of $1 million per year, ranging from $35,000 in Alaska to $4 million in California (Johnson & Leonard, 1973; Seed, 1970). Other less published but more serious liabilities of littering were summarized as follows by Freeman Advertising Associates in a presentation to the Virginia Division of Litter Control in October, 1977.

A safety hazard. Insurance companies estimate that 500 to 1,000 people are killed or injured each year in the United States as a result of vehicles striking or swerving to avoid litter on highways.

A fire hazard. Every 12 minutes a home is destroyed or damaged by a fire starting in rubbish and litter. Litter feeds building fires, and the burning of trash and debris accounts for one-third of all forest fires.

A health hazard. Litter breeds rats, roaches, flies and mosquitoes; it spreads disease.

A hazard to animals. To foraging wildlife and domestic animals alike, litter holds the threat of injury and death [Freeman Associates, 1977, p. 1].

Figure 3.1 illustrates the perilous effects of littering to wildlife, natural consequences that are rarely included in antilitter campaigns. The young gull

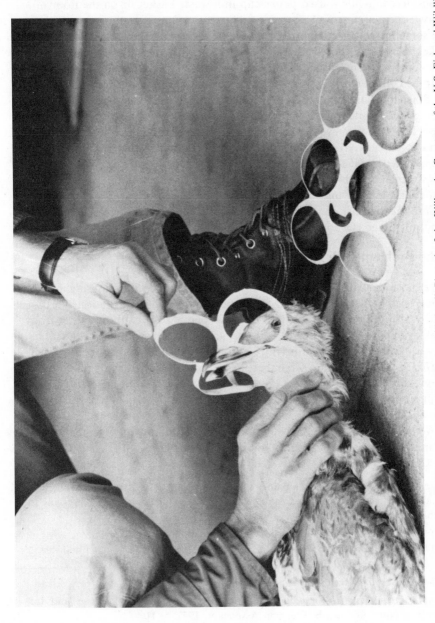

Fig. 3.1. Litter can be dangerous to wildlife; it was deadly for this ring-billed gull. Photo by John Wilbrecht. Courtesy of the U.S. Fish and Wildlife Service.

in Figure 3.1. died on a Michigan beach, strangled by a plastic six-pack can binder. The metal pull-tab rings from throwaway drink containers are also particularly hazardous to birds and fish. Some birds find the pull-tab rings attractive as nesting materials, and fish are instinctually attracted to the shiny metal rings. The result has been cases of a small bird "found dead with a pull-tab ring jammed over its face," and small fish have been found "girdled by pull-tab rings (Ward, 1975, pp. 2-3)." Larger fish have been discovered with a pull-tab ring lacerating its digestive tract, and hospitals across the country have reported the occurrence of pull-tabs "showing up in human stomachs, inadvertently swallowed by a person who'd dropped the tab into the can (Ward, 1975, p. 3)." In fact, it has been estimated that all domestic and wild animals eat bits of trash accidentally, and often such ingested litter can kill the animal or at least leave it in poor physical condition (Ward, 1975). Litter is certainly a physical liability for humans, too. One study showed "that in California alone, it cost $1.5 million a year to pay for medical attention for people involved in litter-related accidents (Purcell, 1981, p. 53)."

One final consequence of litter is related to the issues of waste reduction and resource recovery covered in Chapter 4. Litter actually represents a waste of energy if it could have been prevented by waste reduction techniques (e.g., using less packaging or returnable containers), or if the litter could be collected and reused (i.e., recycled) in the production of goods. For example, refilling returnable soft drink containers an average of 15 times requires 24,240 Btu, whereas the production of throwaway containers for the same number of soft drinks consumes 80,000 Btu (Mitchell, 1976). In fact, Oregon's litter-reducing bottle bill enabled a savings of 1.4 trillion Btu in 1974—enough energy saved to provide the annual home-heating needs for 45,000 Oregonians (Waggoner, 1976).

Characteristics of the "Litterbug"

One probable reason why the first behavioral research in environment preservation dealt with litter control is that litter is so clearly a behavioral problem: it obviously results from people littering. In fact, if "litterbugs" could be influenced to dispose of trash properly, many of our litter-control problems would be solved. Thus, it may be worthwhile to attempt to identify any special characteristics of the litterbug, so that behavioral-control strategies can be custom designed for particular types of individuals. Are there special characteristics of the litterbug?

Perhaps the most frequently cited document related to litter control is the summary of a litter survey conducted by Public Opinion Surveys, Inc. for KAB (Public Opinion Surveys, Inc., 1968). This document identifies specific demographic variables related to littering, concluding that: (1) twice as many males litter as females; (2) adults between the ages of 21 and 35 are three times more likely to litter than persons over 50, and are twice as likely to litter as persons between the ages of 35 and 49; (3) farmers and residents of smaller communities (with populations under 2,500) are more apt to litter than residents of large cities; and (4) individuals from small households (one or two persons) litter less often than persons living in households with five or more residents. However, before deciding that the primary target for antilitter campaigns should be the young male from a relatively large family in a rural environment, one should consider: (1) that the results of this "classic" litter study were derived from personal interviews, not behavioral observations; (2) that verbal statements regarding littering have often not corresponded with actual behaviors (Bickman, 1972; Heberlein, 1974); and (3) that some behavioral studies have not replicated the survey results. Actually, from interviews regarding littering it might only be safe to conclude that certain individuals (e.g., younger males) are more likely to admit to having littered.

Unfortunately, only a few behavioral experiments have examined individual characteristics of the litterer. For example, Heberlein (1971) handed flyers to 7,000 persons walking a street in Wisconsin Dells, Wisconsin, and of the 58 persons who were observed to litter, more were males than females, more were younger than older, and more were single than married. Also, Finnie (1973) observed 272 persons purchase hot dogs from street vendors in downtown Philadelphia and recorded characteristics of the 91 persons who littered the waxed paper used to wrap their hot dog. Litter rates were *not* higher for males than females, but people under 18 years of age were more likely to litter than the two older age groups (i.e., ages 19 to 26, and over age 26). There were slight tendencies for blacks and blue-collar workers to litter more often whan whites and white-collar workers. However, the behavioral results from both the Heberlein and Finnie studies must be considered with extreme caution, due to the small sample sizes and the difficulties shown by others in catching the "litterbug" (Heberlein, 1974; Shelby, 1973).

One behavioral procedure that reliably recorded the sex of the litterer for a relatively large sample size found equivalent littering rates from males and females. Over a series of studies Geller and his students distributed handbills to more than 18,000 patrons of supermarkets and later collected the littered handbills from the premises (Geller et al., 1976; Geller, Witmer, & Tuso, 1977). The 9,000 or more handbills given to males were inconspicuously marked with a small dot so that those deposited inside the store (appropriately or inappropriately) could be categorized according to the sex of the handbill recipient. Throughout these studies about 2,000 individuals littered their handbills, whereas approximately 3,500 individuals deposited their handbill in a trash receptacle. Neither inappropriate nor appropriate handbill disposals were influenced by the sex of the handbill recipient, and sex did not moderate the significant effects of particular disposal instructions included on the handbills. Although the sample size was large and the data was reliable, generalizations from the results of these studies may be critically limited by the use of only one milieu, i.e., a large grocery store in a semirural setting.

Thus, there is really insufficient evidence for making any conclusions regarding individual characteristics of the "litterbug." Verbal reports are very apt to be inconsistent with actual behaviors, and the behavioral data is likely to be unreliable or limited by environmental constraints. At this point it may be safest to say that everyone is a potential litterer in certain situations, and that it is presently most cost effective to alter situations so as to decrease littering by the most frequent user of the particular environment. Indeed, it may be that younger persons are most likely to litter in certain situations, but research has also suggested (as discussed later in this chapter) that younger persons are the most useful participants in antilitter programs.

METHODOLOGIES FOR EVALUATING LITTER CONTROL STRATEGIES

Researchers who have counted items of litter as a dependent variable have not always considered the same items in their measurements. For example, LaHart and Bailey (1975) and Powers, Osborne, and Anderson (1973) included items measuring 1 inch by 1 inch or larger in their litter contents; Chapman and Risley (1974) included only items 2 inches or more in diameter; Hayes, Johnson, and Cone (1975) and Finnie (1973) and the Denver Research Institute (1973) omitted items smaller than a cigarette pack in their surveys of highway litter. In those studies small misplaced items like cigarette butts and matches were not included in the litter measurements but have been included in the litter measurements of other investigations (e.g., Crump, Nunes, & Crossman, 1977; Geller, Brasted, & Mann, 1980). Thus, varying criteria for litter-count data make a comprehensive analysis of relationships between litter accumulation and environmental setting impossible. Even more incompatible with such an analysis are those reports which do not specify a size criterion for their litter counts (e.g., Baltes & Hayward, 1976; Dodge, 1972; O'Neill, Blanck, & Joyner, 1980).

Measures of litter volume (Dodge, 1972) and weight (e.g., Baltes & Hayward, 1976; Burgess et al., 1971; Chapman & Risley, 1974) are easier to obtain and are perhaps more reliable than item counts, but can only be sensitive to changes in independent variables when large amounts of litter are involved. As with the litter-count measurement, variations in size criteria for litter make between-study comparisons of weight and volume difficult or impossible.

A frequently used measure of litter control which provides reliable data, comparable between studies, is a count of experiment-produced litter that is removed from (or remaining in) the field setting after a given period of time. For example, Clark, Burgess, and Hendee (1972) planted particular categories of litter items (i.e., beverage cans, nondeposit bottles, deposit bottles, and crushed paper bags) in certain areas of a forest campground and later counted the number of pieces of planted litter found in the campground after certain experimental conditions. An analogous procedure was used by Heberlein (1974), Robinson and Frisch (1975), and by Geller and his students (Geller, 1973; 1975; Geller et al., 1976; Geller, Witmer, & Tuso, 1977). In these litter-control studies, individuals were given potential litter (i.e., paper cups or handbills) and measures of littering were obtained by counting the experiment-produced litter remaining in particular environmental areas after a certain duration of time.

The "planted" litter procedure by Clark et al. (1972) provided for a systematic analysis of the types of litter most likely to be collected from a particular environmental setting (i.e., clean-up behavior), whereas the handbill-distribution procedures enabled a study of the areas of a given environment most likely to be littered (i.e., littering behavior). For example, Clark et al. found that only the deposit bottles were picked up in the absence of other incentives. Geller et al. (1976) found that the less obtrusive (and perhaps more socially acceptable) areas of a grocery store attracted the most handbills (e.g., shelves, tables, and shopping carts rather than the floor). However, the environmental ethics of such procedures may be questioned since they may create litter that is irretrievable by the research staff. Some of the planted litter in the Clark et al. study could have blown to areas that the experimenters did not subsequently clean, and although Geller et al. cleared the movie theaters and grocery stores of the distributed handbill litter, often as many as 50% of the handbills were taken from the experimental setting and became potential litter in a milieu that researchers could not clean.

Some investigators have attempted to observe and count the occurrences of actual littering behavior. Finnie (1973) did not report difficulty in counting and categorizing by sex, age, and race those individuals who littered a waxed-paper, hot dog wrapper along streets in the Philadelphia central business district. However, since observer reliability checks were apparently not taken in Finnie's study, the difficulty of catching and categorizing a "litterbug" could not be assessed. On the other hand, Heberlein (1974) compared the number of distributed handbills that littered the hallways of a college classroom building with the number of individuals actually observed dropping a handbill and reported that the observer was able to spot only 58 of the 138 litterers (i.e., a 42% hit rate). Likewise, even with several observers Shelby (1973) was able to catch only 36% of the individuals who littered a handbill. Heberlein (1974) reported that those who dropped handbills appeared "circumspect," some walking closely behind other persons and dropping the handbill "in such a way that it was difficult to determine just who had littered (p. 7)." Consequently one should be suspect of data derived from observations of littering behavior unless appropriate reliability checks are offered.

Syrek (1977b) recommended an "aggregate area" measure of litter, whereby the collected litter is spread out on a flat sheet of plastic so that the items touch each other with minimum overlap and minimum gaps, and then this area is expressed in square feet. This method "avoids the problem of how to treat broken pieces when using the item count methods . . . provides a more realistic measure of the actual visual impact of litter than does the volume count method . . . is a better index to use as a standard for acceptable cleanliness than an item count . . . (and) is easy to compute and less subject to counting error (Syrek, 1977b, pp. 62–63)." However, this appears to be a very tedious and time consuming procedure.

The Evaluation Procedures Recommended by Keep America Beautiful, Inc.

The Photometric Index (PI), developed especially for KAB by the American Public Works Association (KAB, 1977j), has perhaps the most potential as a reliable, communitywide strategy for assessing litter accumulation. The PI procedure is a critical aspect of the litter control training course offered to communities that join the Clean Community System (CCS), and is detailed in a CCS program module which must be purchased by communities participating in the CCS (KAB, 1977j).

Since there are more than 166 CCS cities across 22 states (KAB, 1979a), the PI system is probably the most widely used procedure for evaluating the impact of litter-control programs. (The CCS program has been implemented in six countries besides the United States: Australia, Bermuda, Canada, Great Britain, New Zealand, and South Africa [KAB, 1979a]). The first procedural step in developing a PI requires the preparation of an acetate overlay to be used in systematically counting the litter accumulations on photographs of community areas. This overlay is produced by using masking tape to mark a 16 by 6 foot rectangle and 24 squares 2 by 2 foot within it on a dark, flat, clean, paved surface; photographing this rectangle/grid; developing the photo to the same size that will be used for the litter-accumulation photos (e.g., 3 by 4-1/2 inch or 8 by 10 inch); tracing the photographed matrix on a piece of clear plastic; and finally sub-dividing each of the 24 squares of the matrix into four equal sections. The result is an acetate overlay with a 6 × 16 matrix similar to that shown in Figure 3.2, but exactly compatible with the litter-accumulation photographs taken with the

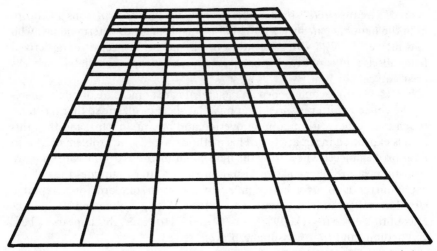

Fig. 3.2. The 96-cell overlay used for litter counting when determining a photometric index.

camera lens used to photograph the rectangle/grid. A 35- or 28-mm camera with a wide-angle lens and ASA 200 film are recommended.

Determining the PI for a community at a particular time requires the following procedures: (1) identifying locations to be photographed by following a systematic and random sampling methodology detailed in the CCS program module, (2) using precise setup techniques for photographing streets, front yards, vacant lots, parking lots, loading docks, and commerical refuse storage areas so that all photos (about ten per each of the six location categories) are taken at the same distance and height from the target area, (3) developing the film at the size used to make the plastic overlay, and (4) scoring the photos by placing the matrix over the photograph and counting the number of squares that contain at least one item of litter. A magnifying glass is recommended in order to see items as small as matches. "Anything that can be classified as man-made, or man-used (KAB, 1977j, p. 9)" should be considered litter if it is misplaced. If an item covers more than one square, it counts for as many squares as it touches. The litter score for any photograph will range from 0 to 96, and the overall PI is calculated by summing the litter accumulation scores of all photographs and dividing by the number of photographs taken. It is noteworthy that recent CCS workshops have demonstrated a slight refinement of the PI procedure. That is, 2 by 2 inch slides are developed of target areas rather than prints, and the litter count consists of using an overhead projector to project the acetate overlay shown in Figure 3.2. over a slide projection of individual scenes so the number of matrix cells containing litter can be readily counted. Indeed, a group of individuals can do this type of counting at the same time, thus increasing reliability.

Communities under the CCS plan first determine a baseline PI. It is then recommended that follow-up PIs be taken at least every three months subsequent to the initiation of a comprehensive litter-control program. When obtaining follow-up PIs, the CCS team is instructed to *avoid* taking photographs in areas that were photographed previously.

There is a very strong tendency to want to return to the precise sites included in the base line [sic] for the follow-up measurements. *It must be resisted at all costs.* The validity of PI—one of the factors that makes it the only objective technique for measuring litter accumulation—rests in the random selection of sites each time measurements are taken [KAB, 1977j, p. 5].

In our opinion the evaluation technique specified in the above quotation from the CCS manual represents the most serious flaw among the current CCS procedures. If certain areas are systematically omitted from the selection, the sampling procedure becomes a sampling procedure without replacement and is not completely random. More importantly, "experimenter expectancy" could certainly bias the area sampling and field photographing during follow-up measurements (Rosenthal, 1966; Rosenthal & Rosnow, 1969). The CCS team's desire to find a reduction in litter accumulation could affect "unintentional" selections of littered areas during baseline and clean areas during follow-up. Moreover, the expectancy or desire to demonstrate an effective litter control program could result in photography that targets the dirtier section of a particular community location during baseline and cleaner sections during follow-up. For example, it is not difficult to imagine a photographer varying the camera view a little (inadvertently or even deliberately) in order to catch litter during baseline sampling and to avoid litter during the follow-up PI.

Perhaps the most critical problem with the CCS procedure of comparing baseline and follow-up PIs is that a more objective and informative approach to evaluating treatment effects is available. As discussed in Chapter 2, follow-up photographs should be taken periodically at *each* of the baseline areas. In this case, each particular milieu would be viewed as the target subjected to a particular treatment program (see Nietzel et al., 1977). First, baseline data should be collected by taking systematic measurements before implementing a particular treatment intervention. Periodic recordings should then be obtained at the same target location(s) after initiation of the treatment procedure. Of course, an appropriate alternative evaluation strategy with the PI would be a multiple baseline design across locations, as discussed in Chapter 2. Baseline PIs would be taken at two locations. One location would then receive the treatment intervention and PIs would again be taken at both locations. The other location would subsequently receive the particular treatment and then treatment PIs would again be obtained at both locations.

The randomization techniques recommended by the KAB staff for determining a baseline PI are quite appropriate, except investigators should be careful not to omit important community areas from the specific location categories given in the CCS manual (e.g., picnic areas, parks, schools, entertainment facilities, highways). As discussed above, we recommend that all follow-up photos be taken in the baseline areas and that treatment evaluation include attention to the scores of individual photographs. The PI scores for each category location (i.e., streets, front yards, vacant lots, parking lots, loading docks, and commercial refuse-storage areas) should be analyzed separately before calculating a composite score. Thus, it would be instructive to study whether certain areas are more affected than others by a particular antilitter program.

However, even with these changes in the CCS analysis of PIs there exists another potential artifact that should be considered when evaluating changes in the PIs of a community. Intuition and empirical evidence suggest that environmental litter will be much more prevalent during warm rather than cold weather, when more people are out-of-doors (see Osborne & Powers, 1980). Thus, a significant decrease in a community's PI from baseline to a follow-up measurement three months later could occur primarily as a result of a seasonal change rather than the litter-control program. Therefore, the CCS manual should emphasize what it does not even mention: that follow-up PIs be taken during the same month as baseline PIs, and that comparisons between these PIs represent the more accurate estimate of treatment effects.

It is only fair to point out that the published reports of declines in PI scores for CCS communities have not demonstrated seasonal biasing in expected directions. Table 3.1 lists 21 CCS communities, the months that baseline and treatment PIs were taken, and the recorded percent reductions in litter accumulations calculated by subtracting each treatment score from its baseline PI, dividing the outcome by the baseline score, and multiplying this result by 100 to convert proportions to percentages. The data depicted in Table 3.1 taken from a *CCS Bulletin* (KAB, 1979b), demonstrate impressive results of the CCS program and do not vary systematically as one would expect if weather changes had biased the measurements. Thus, with an expected seasonal bias, the first seven communities in Table 3.1 should show the greatest percentage decrease in their PIs, since treatment PIs were taken in colder months than baseline PIs, and seasonal changes alone should influence reductions in litter. On the other hand, the last seven communities in Table 3.1 should have demonstrated the smallest percent changes in PI, since treatment PIs were taken during warmer months than baseline PIs, and therefore the seasonal differences should have increased environmental litter. Such trends are not indicated from comparisons of individual comparisons in Table 3.1. The mean percentage change in PI was −41.1% for the first

Table 3.1. Percent Change in Photometric Index (PI) as a Function of Months in which Baseline and Treatment PIs Were Taken.

Community	Baseline Taken	Treatment Taken	Percentage Change
Camp LeJeune, NC	June '78	Feb. '79	−55%
DeKalb County, GA	Oct. '78	Jan. '79	−23%
Denver, CO	July '77	Mar. '79	+19%
Farmington, NM	Nov. '77	Feb. '79	−53%
Grand Prairie, TX	July '76	Feb. '79	−70%
Sumter County, AL	July '78	Feb. '79	−57%
Portsmouth, VA	Aug. '77	Feb. '79	−49%
Athens, AL	April '77	April '79	−38%
Gastonia, NC	Jan. '78	Jan. '79	−49%
Huntsville, AL	June '78	June '79	−69%
Muncie, IN	April '78	April '79	−66%
Onslow County, NC	March '78	March '79	−9%
Riverside, CA	Feb. '77	Feb. '79	−64%
Roanoke, VA	May '78	May '79	−60%
Charlotte, NC	Feb. '74	May '79	−74%
Florence, SC	Jan. '79	June '79	−28%
Hampton, VA	Dec. '78	April '79	−11%
Memphis, TN	Feb. '79	May '79	−27%
N. Myrtle Beach, SC	Jan. '78	April '79	−70%
Port Arthur, TX	Feb. '77	April '79	+10%
Rome, GA	Oct. '76	June '79	−54%

Note. For the first seven communities treatment PIs were taken during *colder* months than baseline (mean PI change = −41.1%); for the next seven communities baseline and treatment PIs were taken during the same month (mean PI change = −50.7%); for the last seven communities treatment PIs were obtained during *warmer* months than baseline (mean PI change = −36.3%).

seven communities, −50.7% for the next seven communities, and −36.3% for the last seven communities.

Assuming the absence of contamination due to experimenter expectancy or weather factors, what do changes in PI indices like those shown in Table 3.1. tell us? Each of the 21 communities reported their PI reductions as demonstrated success for their litter abatement program. What can we learn about litter control from such data? By now the reader is well aware that such data, even if valid, can tell us nothing about the relative efficacy of a particular intervention strategy. The litter control program for each community included the implementation of a variety of strategies, from ordinance refinement and enforcement to public awareness campaigns, in settings from school classrooms to business organizations. Indeed, since most litter control programs include several litter clean-up campaigns, it is never clear whether a significant decline in a community's PI is due to a decrease in littering or an increase in litter pickup.

One slight modification of the standard PI procedure that could help distinguish between littering and litter pickup effects would be to take two sets of PIs at the same locations, with a litter pickup immediately after the first set of PIs. The first PIs would indicate litter *accumulation* over a particular period of time, influenced both by the amount of littering in the area and the litter collection (or cleanup) schedule for the area. The second set of PIs, occuring a fixed period after the first PIs and the litter pickup (e.g., one or two weeks), would represent the amount of litter *generation* for a particular time period and would reflect littering behavior independent of litter clean up in the area.

Daniel B. Syrek and associates (1975, 1977a, 1977b) of the California Institute for Applied Research have used the litter accumulation vs. litter generation distinction for their comprehensive litter surveys of California, Washington, and Kentucky. Prior to the initiation of a statewide litter-control program Syrek's survey teams counted, categorized and picked up the accumulated litter in randomly selected areas of the state from highways to parks. After a week or so the teams then returned to the same locations for a systematic count and categorization of the generated or "fresh" litter. After an extended period of time (and subsequent to several months of a state-wide litter control program), Syrek et al. returned to the same community locations where baseline counts were derived for a post-treatment survey of accumulated and generated litter. Although Syrek's methodology does not suffer from the expectancy bias inherent in the evaluation procedure recommended by KAB (i.e., Syrek's teams completed pre- and post-treatment surveys at the same locations), his methodology cannot provide feedback for refining a litter control program. Indeed, an observed reduction in generated litter from such an evaluation technique can only indicate that something the state did between pre- and post-treatment surveys to discourage littering and/or encourage litter pick up *may* have been effective, although seasonal variations were not accounted for in such litter surveys. In defense of Syrek et al., it is probable that Syrek's survey techniques were not designed to evaluate the relative efficacy of litter control strategies. Rather, the comprehensive litter counts and categorizations accomplished by Syrek et al. were used to determine the relative contributions of specific items to the litter stream and were considered during the definition of contingencies for statewide litter taxation (Samtur, 1979). Nevertheless, a Syrek-type litter survey is quite costly (e.g., $40,000 for Syrek's pre-treatment 1979 survey in Kentucky), especially considering the questionable applicability of the survey results.

Summarizing this discussion of approaches toward evaluating litter control strategies, we propose the following rules for consideration when designing an evaluation scheme or when assessing the validity of another evaluation methodology: (1) use a variety of dependent measures and attempt to assess verbal intentions, personal attitudes, and actual behaviors; (2) include at least a pre-treatment (or baseline) and a post-treatment assessment of each dependent variable; (3) if extraneous factors other than the treatment intervention could influence the dependent variables (e.g., such as weather affecting litter counts), then a control group should be employed which does not receive treatment but is assessed at the same time as the treatment group(s); (4) two individuals should observe and record the dependent measures independently whenever there is room for human error (e.g., when counting or categorizing litter on the ground or in a photograph, when observing litter-related behaviors, and even when weighing trash); and (5) examine the data of individual people and settings before calculating composite scores. With regard to this last point, a careful study of individual change scores from baseline to post-treatment can offer valuable information about the idiosyncracies of people and environments. It is sometimes necessary to make special refinements in intervention programs for special people and environments, and the nature of such refinements can be determined only from a detailed analysis of separate people and settings.

BEHAVIORAL STRATEGIES FOR LITTER CONTROL

In this section we discuss the variety of behavioral approaches to litter control which have been implemented and evaluated, paying particular attention to the advantages and disadvantages of each technique. The procedures used to test the effectiveness of these behavioral control strategies were all based on the general approach summarized above. Baseline data was gathered on the target behavior (e.g., frequency or volume of litter pickups or disposals), and the treatment intervention was then implemented and data usually gathered during this period. Subsequently, the treatment intervention was usually withdrawn and follow-up data was obtained.

Each behavioral strategy that was implemented to facilitate responses related to litter control can be categorized as an *antecedent* strategy or a *consequence* strategy. As discussed in Chapter 2, antecedent strategies refer to conditions implemented before the opportunity to make the target response, while consequence strategies include those interventions which manipulated the occurrence of specific events after the target response had occurred.

ANTECEDENT INSTRUCTIONS AS ANTILITTER PROMPTS

Among the earliest litter-control studies were those evaluating the behavior impact of response-priming instructions given to individuals in community settings in order to encourage responses related to litter control. For example, the treatment intervention used by Geller et al. (1971, 1973) to encourage the purchase of returnable rather than throwaway drink containers was merely the distribution of one-page flyers to incoming store customers which urged the purchase of drinks in returnable bottles by appealing to both environmental and financial advantages. Systematic comparisons between baseline and treatment conditions showed that an average of 20% more customers purchased their soft drinks in returnable bottles when the handbill was distributed than when this antecedent strategy was not in effect.

Larger-scale antecedent strategies than the customer prompting technique applied by Geller et al. (1971, 1973) were studied by Dodge (1972) and Schnelle et al. (1980). Dodge significantly decreased the volume of litter left at campsites in a small Alaskan community by instituting a communitywide antilitter campaign with promotion posters, propaganda handouts, car bumper stickers, information pamphlets, newspaper announcements, and window displays. Schnelle et al. observed a 35% average reduction in ground litter from baseline levels when an initial front-page newspaper article urged an antilitter campaign (including photographs of extremely littered areas and children picking up litter), and when subsequent daily newspaper articles published the litter counts in the form of histograms. The beneficial effects of this large-scale, prompting and feedback intervention only lasted while the newspaper articles were published; litter counts taken one month after the last newspaper article indicated a return to baseline levels of environmental litter.

Several studies by Geller and his students (Geller, 1973, 1975; Geller et al., 1976; Geller, Witmer, & Tuso, 1977) were designed to determine the effects of placing antilitter instructions on disposables. For many years the beverage companies have been putting antilitter prompts on the top of drink cans (e.g., "Please don't litter;" "Please dispose of properly"), and recycling prompts have been recently substituted for the antilitter instructions on aluminum cans (e.g., "Please don't litter;" "Please recycle"). Geller et al. wanted to find out if such instructions influence the disposal location of the item on which the instructions were printed.

The basic paradigm for this series of studies was as follows. Researchers stood at the entrance to a particular environmental setting, (college classrooms, movie theaters and grocery stores were used) and distributed a one-page flyer to incoming patrons. The flyer contained information relevant to the environmental setting (i.e., special sales of the week for the grocery store and a listing of the movie actors and actresses for the theater), and special antilitter instructions were sometimes boldly printed at the bottom of the handbill. During baseline conditions there was no antilitter prompt at the bottom of the flyers, while during treatment special antilitter instructions were added to the bottom of the distributed flyers. The nature of these instructions systematically varied between treatment conditions in order to study relationships between message content and disposal behaviors. One type of message was exactly as printed on many beverage cans (i.e., a general antilitter appeal), whereas other handbill messages instructed the handbill recipient to make a specific disposal response. The different types of handbill instructions evaluated in one study are presented in Table 3.2.

The handbills were distributed for a fixed amount of time (e.g., 20 minutes before the movie) or until a certain number of individuals had received the handbill (e.g., 100 males and 100 females for the grocery-store studies). After the handbill recipients had left the milieu, two teams of data recorders systematically searched the environment for handbills and categorized the handbill locations as appropriate disposals (in a trash receptacle) or inappropriate disposals (on floor, shelves, counters, seats, shopping carts).

In general, the nonspecific instructions ("Please don't litter;" "Please dispose of properly") only slightly decreased the number of handbills which littered the particular environment (i.e., 5 to 10% reductions from baseline) and did not increase the number of trash can disposals. On the other hand, specific instructions that identified a desirable disposal location resulted in a substantial amount of compliance: from 20 to 35% of the theater and grocery-store patrons consistently deposited their flyer in a waste receptacle. No more than 10% of the distributed handbills were found in waste receptacles when the handbill contained only general and antilitter instructions.

Table 3.2 depicts the location distributions of handbills given to grocery-store customers as a function of the message content at the bottom of the handbill. The data is summarized from one publication (Geller et al., 1976), but is quite representative of the results from other similar investigations by Geller and his students (Geller, 1973, 1975; Geller, Witmer, & Tuso, 1977). It is noteworthy that many grocery-store patrons complied with the specific instructions, especially when a rationale was given for the particular request (e.g., see the Recycle Appeal in Table 3.2). Requesting customers to avoid handbill deposits in a particular location was only effective when the message also specified an alternative deposit location (compare the impact of the Avoidance-General Alternative with that of the Avoidance-Specific Alternative in Table 3.2). Furthermore, from 10 to 20% of the customers on any given day even complied with an antisocial request to litter their handbill. As shown in Table 3.2, an average of 13.2% of the customers dropped their handbill on the floor of a grocery store when requested to do so. This is a very significant increase from the floor disposals observed in each of the other conditions (i.e., never more than 2%).

These findings indicate rather consistent antilitter effects of response-priming or prompting techniques, which are relatively economical to implement on a large scale. However, it should be realized that the absolute magnitude of the behavioral change was often quite low. Therefore, to have

Table 3.2. Behavioral Impact of Different Messages on Sales-of-the-Week Flyers Handed to Incoming Patrons of Two Grocery Stores.

Intervention Label	Message Content*	Total No. of Flyers	Location Percentages†				
			Green Can	Other Cans	Carts	Floor	Other Litter
Baseline	None	3141	2.7	2.3	22.5	1.2	14.5
General Appeal	*Please* don't litter. *Please* dispose of properly.	1582	4.7	3.2	21.8	.5	9.1
Specific Appeal	*Please* don't litter. *Please* dispose in *green* trash can located at rear of store.	1631	19.7	3.8	17.0	.4	9.1
Recycle Appeal	*Please* help us recycle. *Please* dispose for *recycling* in *green* trash can at rear of store.	1840	25.0	4.6	14.8	1.2	11.0
Demand Instructions	You *must* not litter. You *must* dispose in *green* trash can at rear of store.	1652	19.5	3.8	17.1	1.7	9.2
Avoidance-General Alternative	*Please don't* dispose of in carts. *Please* dispose of properly.	946	9.0	3.9	15.1	1.1	14.9
Avoidance-Specific Alternative	*Please don't* dispose of in carts. *Please* dispose in *green* trash can located in rear of store.	907	24.1	2.9	8.6	1.2	12.7
Litter Instructions	*Please* litter. Dispose of on *floor*.	1440	5.8	3.1	22.4	13.2	16.0

* The italicized words were actually underlined on the handbill.
† The percentage of total handbills unaccounted for were taken from the store.
Source: Adapted from Geller, Witmer & Orebaugh, 1976.

a substantial environmental impact prompts need to be applied to large numbers of people over long periods of time. Even more critical to the efficacy of behavioral prompting are the following characteristics of the prompts which have had the most behavioral influence: (1) the prompt was administered in close proximity with the opportunity to emit the requested response, analogous to point-of-purchase advertising (see Tillman & Kirkpatrick, 1972); (2) the prompt specifically stated what response was desired; (3) the prompt requested a response that was relatively convenient; and (4) the prompt was given in polite, nondemanding language. The following discussion of some failures to find reliable behavioral effects of prompting demonstrates the need to consider these four characteristics of successful prompting strategies when designing interventions for promoting environment preservation.

One of the first reported attempts to prompt antilitter behaviors was accomplished in 1969 by Heberlein (1974). University of Wisconsin students entering two introductory psychology classes and two introductory sociology classes were given a "conservation handbill" that included only a short three-sentence message urging students and faculty to keep the campus of the University of Wisconsin beautiful. As these students and the students from two other psychology and sociology classes were leaving the 50-minute class (n = 728), they were then handed a small flyer advertising a record store. Observers counted the number of flyers deposited in the hallway outside of the four classrooms and found that 11.4% of the students littered their flyer, but the littering rate was not significantly lower for those students who had previously recieved the conservation handbill.

One possible reason for the lack of an effect from prompting in the Heberlein study may be that the conservation prompt was only a general antilitter message and did not request the occurrence of specific behaviors; the prompt, in other words, did not prime a response. As discussed above (and summarized in Table 3.2), the evaluation research by Geller and his students demonstrated only minimal antilitter effects of the general antilitter prompt: "Please don't litter;" "Please dispose of properly." For example, for his first evaluation of antilitter prompting, Geller (1975) distributed approximately 4,200 "sales-of-the-week" handbills to grocery store patrons over 30 days, one-third with no antilitter message, one-third with the general appeal, and one-third with specific disposal instructions. The following overall percentages of handbills littering the store were found: 34.8% litter for handbills with no antilitter prompt, 30.0% litter for handbills with the general prompt, and 19.0% litter for handbills conveying the specific instructions.

It may also have been that the Heberlein prompt was too remote in time from the opportunity to litter. For example, in order to interpret their findings that a prompting strategy was only effective in increasing the purchase of returnable bottles when it was applied in a small, quick-stop grocery store (not when applied in two large supermarkets), Geller et al. (1973) presumed that the effectiveness of a handbill prompt varies inversely with the time interval between handbill receipt and and the opportunity for the requested behavior. At the small convenience store (where about 20% more customers bought their soft drinks in returnables when instructed to do so), customers typically purchased only a few items and therefore relatively little time elapsed between receiving the handbill prompt and purchasing soft drinks. However, at the large grocery stores (where the same prompting strategy was ineffective), several minutes usually intervened between handbill reception at the store entrance and the soft-drink selections at the beverage counter. Supporting the notion that prompting effects are immediate and short-lived were observations that behavioral differences resulting from differential handbill messages persisted at similar rates over long periods of time in the same milieu, after most subjects had recieved each of the different behavioral requests. For example, several individuals consistently purchased soft drinks in returnable bottles (Geller et al., 1973), or deposited their handbill in a particular trash receptacle (Geller, 1975; Geller et al., 1976) *only* when the handbill they received at the time had requested the particular response. Indeed, after reporting the transient nature of prompting effects, the relatively small behavioral effects of general prompts, and the substantial behavioral effects of specific prompts, Geller (1975) concluded that, for community-wide litter control, one should "display *specific* antipollution instructions *continuously* in each milieu that may set the occasion for polluting behaviors (p. 128)."

Attempts to Prompt Litter Pickup

It must also be pointed out that prompting strategies may not be influential when the requested response is relatively inconvenient, such as picking up litter that another person has left and depositing it in a trash receptacle. In fact, behavioral studies suggest that people will rarely collect litter from an environment unless the litter interferes with the individual's pleasures (as in the field experiment by Crump et al., 1977) or unless consequence strategies are used to reward individuals for collecting litter from the environment (as in the studies to be discussed later). For example, in one experiment Bickman (1972) planted two empty soda cans near a trash receptacle in front of the Smith College Library. In one condition passing pedestrians saw another college student (the model) kick one of the cans and walk on, and in another condition the model picked up one of the cans and deposited it in the trash can. When subjects in neither condition picked up the littered can (n = 20), observations were stopped and the litter was made more obvious in a second field study. In one situation of this second study, a small trash can was tipped over and crumpled pages from a newspaper protruded from the receptacle; in another situation a single, crumpled page of a newspaper was placed several feet from a small trash can. In both cases the litter was placed in the immediate path of individuals entering or leaving the school library or a store near the college. Of the 409 students and 97 nonstudents who passed the litter only five students and three nonstudents (1.4%) picked up any of the planted litter.

A series of ten experiments by Geller and his students, partially reported by Geller (1976), and Geller, Mann, and Brasted (1977), supported Bickman's observations that few people will pick up noticeable litter, and further that prompting techniques have only minimal effects in encouraging people to pick up environmental litter.* This is especially discouraging considering the vast amount of money being spent nationally by Keep America Beautiful, Inc. and locally by the state litter-control committees to prompt litter pickup behaviors via television advertising. Table 3.3 summarizes the environmental and prompting conditions of ten field experiments which essentially involved the placement of "clean" litter (i.e., crumpled paper, and soft drink cans) next to a trash receptacle and then observing the behavior of individuals who passed the area.

As listed in the first column of Table 3.3, the environmental settings were a university campus, an indoor shopping mall, and steps leading to a row of motel rooms. The litter was in the immediate path of passing pedestrians for the latter two situations. As summarized in the second column of Table 3.3, the trash receptacle was either a 50-gallon drum or a beautified trash receptacle shaped and painted like a cardinal (see Figure 3.3). One of the following antecedent conditions was occasionally added: (1) a fake dollar bill was next to the litter; (2) college students completed an environmental-concern questionnaire ten minutes before approaching the litter; (3) two individuals (confederates of the experimenter) walked down the motel steps in front of the subject and one picked up and deposited *one* litter item; (4) both of the confederates walked down the motel steps in front of the subject and both picked up and deposited *one* litter item; (5) one of the two confederates (who walked down the motel steps in front of the subject) continued to pick up and deposit the litter in the subject's presence while the other confederate walked on; (6) both confederates continued to pick up and deposit the litter in the subject's presence.

As depicted in the right-most column of Table 3.3, subjects rarely picked up and discarded the planted litter. A noteworthy observation was that 11 out of the 13 children (aged 9 to 12) who passed the planted litter on the university campus picked up and deposited the litter in the bird receptacle.

---

*Many students at Virginia Tech contributed to the accomplishment of these studies, especially David Barachie, William Brasted, Kathy Brehony, Kim Cuddihy, Cindy Gelmine, Ken Hearn, Kim High, Elizabeth Jenkins, Millard Mann, Ann McGovern and Laura Wipple.

Table 3.3. Litter Pickup as a Function of Particular Antecedent Conditions.

Environmental Setting	Experimental Condition	N		Pickup Frequency**		Total Pickup Percentages
		Males	Females	Males	Females	
University Campus (Summer)	Grey 50-Gallon Drum	172	151	0	1	.31
University Campus (Summer)	Attractive Bird Receptacle	167	153	8	11	5.94*
Indoor Shopping Mall	Attractive Bird Receptacle	1603	1612	3	8	.34
Indoor Shopping Mall	Attractive Bird Receptacle & Planted Bogus Money	1610	1609	6	11	.53
Motel Steps	Standard 50-Gallon Can	20	20	1	0	2.5
Motel Steps	Standard Can & Preliminary Environment-Concern Questionnaire†	14	6	0	0	0
Motel Steps	Standard Can & One Model Picks Up One Litter Item‡	21	20	2	2	9.8
Motel Steps	Standard Can & Two Models Pick up One Litter Item‡	22	20	3	4	16.7
Motel Steps	Standard Can & One Model Continues to Pick Up Litter‡	20	20	6	10	40.0
Motel Steps	Standard Can & Two Models Continue to Pick Up Litter‡	20	20	11	14	62.5
	TOTALS	3669	3631	40	61	MEAN 1.4

* Included 11 out of 13 children.

† The subject was leaving a 50-minute probability learning experiment.

‡ The subject was leaving a 50-minute social decision experiment in which s/he had performed with two other individuals (i.e., confederates of the experimenter who served as the litter pickup models).

**Number of individuals who picked up at least one piece of planted litter.

Only when one or two confederates continued to pick up the litter did a substantial number of college students stop to "pitch in." When one or two confederates picked up only one piece of litter and then walked on, the subject apparently didn't feel enough social pressure to make a similar anti-litter response. It is noteworthy that for most situations a few more females than males stopped to pick up and deposit the litter. Thus, females are not only less likely than males to *admit* to littering (Public Opinion Surveys, Inc., 1968), they may also be more apt to clean up someone else's litter, even though they are *not* less apt than males to litter items like hot dog wrappers and handbills (Finnie, 1973; Geller et al., 1976; Geller, Witmer, & Tuso, 1977).

Response Priming and Psychological Reactance

In addition to specifying desired responses which are relatively convenient and are required shortly after the antecedent prompt, the response-priming (or prompting) situations should be stated in polite rather than demanding terms. Demands rather than polite requests may elicit psychological reactance and actually encourage behaviors contrary to those desired (Brehm, 1966, 1972). Individuals may perceive verbal or written prompts as a threat to their personal freedom and not only disregard the request, but in fact may emit a response contrary to the instructions in order to assert their freedom. This hypothesis is illustrated by the few grocery-store customers who filled their shopping carts with throwaway bottles immediately after reading the handbill that requested returnable-bottle buying (Geller et al., 1971, 1973) or who threw their handbills on the floor after reading the antilitter message (Geller et al., 1976), and acccompanied such defiant acts with a statement like, "Nobody is going to tell me what to do!"

Psychological reactance may also have influenced more trash-can disposals of handbills with a general antilitter message ("Please dispose of properly") than handbills with a prompt that specified one particular trash receptacle for handbill disposal (Geller, 1973). For this latter illustration, the handbills were distributed in a movie theater where littering may be perceived as a given freedom. The request for disposals in one specific trash can may have been perceived by some as particularly unreasonable and a threat to their freedom to litter or to use any of a number of available trash receptacles, and have influenced some handbill littering. In this particular study, actually 36 out of the 64 distributed handbills with the *specific* antilitter request (56%) were appropriately discarded in one of the theater's trash cans, whereas 45 out of 66 handbills distributed with the *general* antilitter appeal (68%) were disposed of in one of the theater's trash cans.

Recent field experiments were designed precisely to study the potential role of psychological reactance during behavioral prompting and to provide

Fig. 3.3. The beautiful bird receptacle which influenced some litter pickup, especially from children. This cardinal trash receptacle was manufactured by the Jackson Company, Pomona, California. The capacity is 50 gallons, and the colors are bright and authentic, with red body, black face mask, and orange bill. Photo by John G. Cope.

more convincing evidence than the post hoc interpretations given above that one should attempt to minimize threats to perceived freedom when designing prompting procedures. In particular, Reich and Robertson (1979) delivered 90 flyers conveying only a brief statement to children over ten years of age at a public swimming pool. The dependent variable was the number of each type of handbill collected as litter from the pool and surrounding park areas. Significantly more flyers with the message "Don't Litter" were collected as litter (i.e., 15 out of 30) than were handbills with the message "Help Keep Your Pool Clean" (i.e., 6 out of 30, p $<$ .05). The third type of flyer ("Obey Pool Safety Rules") was littered on 9 out of 30 occasions.

In a follow-up experiment, Reich and Robertson added two more flyer-prompts to their procedure: "Don't You *Dare* Litter," and "Keeping the Pool Clean Depends on *You*." In this design, the most demanding message, "Don't You *Dare* Litter," resulted in the greatest number of littered handbills: 11 out of 30. The other two antilitter prompts, "Keeping the Pool Clean Depends on *You*" and "Help Keep Your Pool Clean," resulted in the least number of littered handbills (3 and 4 out of 30, respectively). Thus, the results of this research demonstrated important limiting effects of antilitter prompting which may be interpreted with a theory of psychological reactance, even though the number of handbills used for each condition was relatively small and the subjects were of a narrow age range.

Geller and his students (as partially reported by Geller, 1980a; and Brasted et al., 1979) also compared varieties of language forcefulness in requesting an antilittering response in a field setting but used a greater variety and number of subjects than Reich and Robertson.* In this study handbill advertisements were distributed to individuals using one of three entrances to a large, indoor shopping mall (see diagram of environment in Figure 3.4). Each handbill included a general antilitter prompt ("Please dispose of properly"), a specific prompt ("Please dispose of in trash can in front of Woolco"), or a demand prompt, ("You *must* dispose of in trash can in front of Woolco.") Another independent variable in this field study was the placement of an attractive bird receptacle (see Figure 3.3) as a substitute for one of two unobtrusive trash receptacles in the mall. The 50-gallon, unobtrusive cans were made of wooden slats that matched the mall decor (see Figure 3.5 later in chapter for a schematic of the design).

Two trash can conditions alternated between the 16 observation days. In other words, three types of antilitter prompts (general, specific, and demand) were distributed on each of eight days when the attractive trash can was positioned in front of Woolco (Location 1 in Figure 3.4) and was the speci-

* For this project the research supervision by Mark Augustine, William Brasted, Steve Grover, Millard Mann, and Elizabeth Watson, and the research activities of Virginia Tech students in Dr. Geller's Social Psychology classes (Fall, 1976 and Winter, 1977) are greatly appreciated.

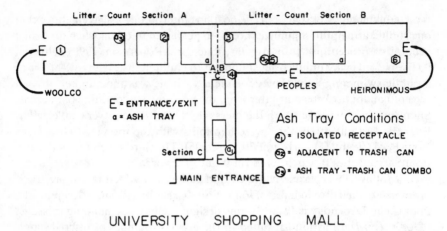

UNIVERSITY   SHOPPING   MALL

Fig. 3.4. A schematic of the university mall showing entrances to stores where Brasted, Mann, and Geller (1979) distributed handbills, and locations of trash can and ash tray receptacles for the studies of trash can designs (from Geller, Brasted, & Mann, 1980).

fied disposal point for the specific and demand instructions. On alternate days, the handbill distributions occurred when the attractive receptacle was located in a more central area of the shopping mall (Location 4 in Figure 3.4) and the standard, unobtrusive trash can was located in front of Woolco. To comply with the request of the specific and demand prompts, those individuals receiving the handbill at two of the three mall entrances needed to traverse a considerable distance in order to reach the specified disposal point (i.e., about 200 feet for one entrance and 350 feet for the other). Enroute to this disposal point they had to pass the central location (Location 4 in Figure 3.4). On half of the 16 observation days the attractive receptacle was in this central location and the unobtrusive can was at the specified disposal point; on alternate days the attractive and unobtrusive cans were reversed. At a third entrance (Woolco in Figure 3.4) the handbills with antilitter prompts were distributed in the immediate vicinity of the receptacle which was specified as the disposal point in the instructions.

At the end of each observation day (after the shopping mall closed), the handbills were collected from each of the mall's six trash receptacles and categorized according to the handbill's distribution point (i.e., mall entrance) and the type of prompt on the handbill (general, specific, or demanding request). For those handbills distributed at the two entrances located a considerable distance from the receptacle specified for disposal (N = 1440), significantly fewer demand-prompt than specific-prompt handbills were deposited in the specified trash can and more demand-prompt than specific-prompt handbills were found in the centralized trash can ($ps < .05$) *when* the attractive trash receptacle was located in the central mall area as an obtrusive alternative to obeying the demand. However, when the attractive receptacle was located at the disposal point and the unobtrusive can was at the central location, significantly more of the handbills conveying the demand than the specific prompt were disposed as requested in the Woolco can ($p < .05$). These findings suggest that the reactance elicited by the demand prompt was only sufficient to motivate noncompliance *if* a convenient and attractive alternate response was available.

When the attractive trash receptacle was at the specified disposal point, those 1,200 individuals who received the demand-prompt handbill directly in the vicinity of this can obeyed the behavioral request significantly *less* often than did the 1,200 people who received the specific-prompt handbill ($p < .01$). However, when the standard, unobtrusive receptacle was located at the specified disposal point, those 1,200 people who received the handbill conveying the demand prompt were more apt to dispose of it in the specified can than were those 1,200 individuals who received the specific-prompt handbills ($p < .05$). In this case, it was perhaps the simultaneous bombardment of antilitter stimuli (i.e., the antilitter prompt on the handbill and the colorful, antilitter trash can with its own antilitter prompt) that was sufficient to elicit reactance.

These field observations and those by Reich and Robertson suggest that certain aspects of antilitter prompting can actually influence a boomerang effect and cause some individuals to actively attempt to avoid compliance. Such findings have critical implications for the design and application of litter-control prompts. In fact, the overall behavioral effects of any change strategy may be the net outcome of two motivations aroused by that procedure: the motivation to comply with a reasonable request and the motivation to regain perceived freedom by not complying. In some litter-control situations, attempts to gain more compliance by applying additional behavior change strategies may actually be more influential in increasing the desire to regain threatened freedoms than to make the environmentally-conscious response. For example, it is possible that antilitter signs that threaten a large fine for littering may elicit more psychological reactance than environmental consciousness, especially when it is so easy to litter without being caught. Much additional field research is obviously required in order to clarify those aspects of litter-control programs that contribute to "behavioral reactance"— an overt defiance of requested behaviors. Given the research accomplished so far, it is at least advisable to be polite and nonthreatening when instructing specific antilitter behaviors and to limit the number of litter-control prompts in a given milieu.

Environmental Litter as an Antecedent

Among the earliest investigations of litter-control variables were field experiments designed to determine the validity of the common sense notion that "litter begets litter." Most of the field research tabulating the frequency of littering under littered and non-littered environments showed antecedent environmental litter to increase littering behavior, but it is also clear that both the absolute amount of littering and the extent that littering was influenced by antecedent litter was moderated by the nature of the environmental setting. The first published account of littering as a function of antecedent environmental cleanliness was based upon observations of individuals who purchased hot dogs from vendors in two "littered" and two "non-littered" sections of the Philadelphia central business district (Finnie, 1973). A total of 91 out of 272 individuals (33.5%) littered the waxed-paper hot dog wrapper. Of those 143 individuals who purchased hot dogs in relatively non-littered environments, approximately 24.5% littered the hot dog wrapper, but 42% of the 129 hot dog purchasers in the littered section of downtown Philadelphia littered their hot dog wrappers. Since Finnie did not report interobserver reliability checks, the validity of the observations may be suspect, especially given reports of difficulty in detecting litterers (Heberlein, 1974; Shelby, 1973) and the possibility of bias due to the observer's expectations (Rosenthal, 1966; Rosenthal & Rosnow, 1969).

Finnie's results have been replicated with an experimental procedure that enables reliable measurements of littering. With this paradigm, investigators distribute handbills to individuals in a defined setting that is either littered or clear of handbills and later collect and count the handbills deposited throughout the environment. When this paradigm was implemented in a post office located in the Student Center Building at Georgia Institute of Technology, 70.8% of the 1,743 students who received a handbill when the post office was prelittered with similar handbills deposited their handbills on the floor of the post office (Robinson & Frisch, 1975). When the post office was clear of littered handbills, 25.9% of the 1,358 students littered their handbills.

The rate of littering was much less in the hallway of a classroom building at the University of Wisconsin than on the streets of Philadelphia or in the Georgia Tech post office, but students were four times more likely to litter when the hallway was already littered with coffee cups, milk cartons, and handbills than when it was clean (Heberlein, 1974). More specifically, of the 728 total students who accepted a handbill advertising a local record store, 11.4% littered the handbill; 16.3% littered the handbill when the hallway was prelittered, and only 3.6% littered a clean hallway.

The frequency of handbill littering in a grocery store setting was even less than in the classroom building, but a consistent, five-fold increase in littering occurred after the grocery store had been littered with handbills (Geller, Witmer, & Tuso, 1977). Handbills listing specially-priced food items were given daily to incoming store patrons for two-hour periods. For eight days, a non-littered condition (during which the store was kept clear of littered handbills) was alternated with a littered condition (during which the store was littered with 140 handbills). On any non-littered day not more than 1 percent of the distributed handbills were deposited on the floor (a total of 6 out of 616 handbill recipients), whereas during each of the littered conditions approximately 5% of the patrons dropped their handbills on the floor (a total of 32 of 639 customers).

The critical role of the environmental setting on littering and litter pickups was shown by the observations of Crump et al. (1977) in a forest milieu. On the mornings of four consecutive Fridays, these investigators removed all litter from two picnic sections of Hanging Rock Picnic Complex in the Uinta National Forest in northern Utah. On the second and fourth Fridays they then implemented a Littered Condition by scattering 20 pieces of paper, 20 beverage cans, and 20 miscellaneous items throughout each of the two picnic areas. The litter counts on the four following Saturday mornings actually indicated that more litter was left on the ground for the nonlittered than littered conditions. In particular, for the first nonlittered conditions (Week 1) there were 47 and 46 pieces of litter left in the east and west picnic areas, respectively, compared to 23 and 32 pieces of litter in the east and west sections for the first littered condition (Week 2). Similarly, for Week 3 (nonlittered condition), 57 and 92 pieces of litter were found, compared to 26 and 27 pieces of litter collected during Week 4 (littered condition). Thus, not only did a littered picnic area *decrease* the probability of littering, but it also influenced some individuals to pick up litter. In fact, Crump et al. actually observed that when people entered a littered picnic area they frequently picked up and immediately disposed of the litter surrounding their picnic area.

Although Crump et al. offered no interpretation for their unusual findings, it is our opinion that the difference between the Crump et al. results and those of other researchers (e.g., Finnie, 1973; Geller, Witmer, & Tuso, 1977; Heberlein, 1974; Robinson & Frisch, 1975) may be explained by considering that only in forest areas did environmental cleanliness play a significant role in the ongoing behaviors of the subjects. People travel to scenic picnic grounds to appreciate the aesthetic outdoor setting, and environmental litter near a picnic area interferes with the pleasures of an outdoor picnic. Therefore, disposing of nearby litter before picnicking enables one to avoid perceiving unsightly litter (negative reinforcement) and to enjoy the aesthetic qualities of the outdoor setting (positive reinforcement). Indeed the occurrence of such antilitter behaviors before a picnic could prompt picnickers to dispose of their own trash after picnicking. In contrast, the ongoing behaviors of people walking along a busy street, shopping in a supermarket, and leaving a college classroom or post office are not inhibited by a littered environment. In fact, people in these situations are usually so involved in the task at hand that they rarely attend to the littered ground or floor, and certainly would not be expected to stop their reinforced behaviors and make the inconvenient response of picking up another person's litter.

Trash Receptacles as Antecedent Strategies

The observed relationships between environmental litter and littering are as intuitive as the findings of the field research on the litter control impact of the trash receptacle placement and design. For example, Finnie (1973) measured the antilitter effects of adding trash receptacles along highways and urban sidewalks, and of using obtrusively decorated trash receptacles. For one study he placed a large "Peli-can" on each side of one highway and positioned a road sign signaling its availability one-quarter of a mile in front of each can. Peli-cans without prior signs were placed on a second six-mile highway section, and a third highway had no litter receptacles. Conditions were rotated every month for three months so that each highway received each condition. Monthly litter counts were made in test areas 1000 feet long by 30 feet wide at distances of one mile and six miles from the litter cans. The results demonstrated an overall 28.6% reduction of highway litter due to the trash cans, and such reductions were apparent six miles from the receptacles. The litter counts were not significantly influenced by signs preceding the litter receptacle.

Finnie's research in downtown Richmond, Virginia, also showed antilitter effects of increasing the availability of trash receptacles. On two 16-block stretches of sidewalk he placed no trash cans, one Peli-can per four blocks, or one Peli-can per block. He rotated the first two conditions every 2 weeks for 12 weeks, and then rotated the first and third conditions for two, two-week periods. Daily litter counts of the 30-foot, middle section of each block indicated only a 6.8% reduction of litter for the one-can-per-four-block condition over the area with no receptacles. However, the eventual addition of a trash can for every block of sidewalk resulted in a 16.7% decline in sidewalk litter.

For a third study of increased trash-can availability as an antilitter strategy, Finnie observed a total of 272 individuals in four sections of downtown Philadelphia who purchased hot dogs wrapped in waxed paper. He added trash receptacles in two areas and removed all litter cans from the other two areas. About 33% of those who purchased hot dogs were observed to litter the waxed paper wrapping; the average percentage of litterers was 24% in the area where trash cans were available and 42% in the sections without trash receptacles.

Finnie also studied the litter-control effects of an obtrusive, beautified trash receptacle in downtown St. Louis by counting daily the litter along city blocks. Each week two blocks had no trash receptacles, two blocks had standard 55-gallon drums, and two blocks had a colorful "Clean City Squares" litter can that identified corporate sponsors. Each week these three conditions were rotated so that after six weeks each condition appeared twice per block. Compared with no trash receptacles, an overall litter reduction of 3.15% was observed with the regular cans, while a 14.7% reduction in litter was demonstrated with the specially decorated trash receptacles. Although these results appear to demonstrate remarkable antilitter effects of attractive receptacles, Finnie suggested that some of this difference may have been the result of litter blowing out of the 55-gallon drums that had no lids. A critical weakness in each of Finnie's experiments is the lack of independent reliability checks of the litter counts and the observations of littering behavior.

O'Neill et al. (1980) also showed antilitter effects of an obtrusive, unusual trash receptacle. Observations were made along the grassy slope of the general admissions area to the Clemson University football stadium after each of ten football games. Two trash can conditions and a baseline (No Receptacle) condition were implemented simultaneously in different areas of the setting. For one trash-can condition, a bright orange, 55-gallon drum was placed in one area of the grassy slope. The other trash-can condition involved the placement of a special trash receptacle in another area of the slope. This receptacle resembled a hat, modeled after the type commonly worn by students at the games. On the front of the hat was a hinged lid on which the word "push" was painted. When the lid was pushed, a mechanical device lifted the top of the hat and the word "THANKS!" appeared. This special trash can typifies both an antecedent and consequence strategy for litter control. Thus, the obtrusive appearance of the receptacle may prompt trash can disposals (i.e., an antecedent influence). After disposal occurs the novel consequence (i.e., a mechanical "Thank You") could reinforce the disposal response, thereby increasing the probability of subsequent disposals in the special trash receptacle. It is even conceivable that such reinforcement from a trash receptacle could influence some individuals to pick up litter in order to make an appropriate disposal response.

After each football game, O'Neill et al. found substantially more trash in the hat can than in the standard one: totals of 5.3 kg. vs. 2.6 kg. The litter counts in the 20 by 20 feet areas surrounding the trash cans and in the similar baseline area demonstrated that the area in the immediate vicinity of the regular can contained consistently less litter than the areas remote from any receptacle, and the area in front of the special hat can was consistently less littered than the area in front of the standard one. It is noteworthy that no litter-count differences were found in areas relatively remote from the receptacles (i.e., 90 feet away). These authors did not report any reliability checks for their dependent measures. Another weakness of this study and of Finnie's evaluation of a beautified trash receptacle summarized above is the short observation period. It is quite possible that the antilitter effects of obtrusive trash cans are only short-lived and only as long as the trash receptacle is a novelty.

A field study by Geller et al. (1980) compared the antilitter effects of beautified trash receptacles with unobtrusive trash cans over a relatively long period of time (41 weeks), and included procedures to assure reliable measurements. The setting was a large indoor shopping mall in Blacksburg, Virginia, which contained six unobtrusive trash receptacles enclosed in wooden frames that matched the decor of the mall. The location of these trash receptacles is indicated in Figure 3.4. Two beautified trash cans, one resembling the Virginia state bird (as shown in Fig. 3.3) and the other resembling the national bird (i.e., an eagle) were sometimes used in place of the regular receptacles at Locations 1 and 2; both locations were in "Litter-Count Section A" of the mall.

For 41 consecutive weeks the plastic trash bags within each of the six trash cans were collected three times per week. After a five-week baseline period (15 measurements of each trash can), the trash cans in Locations 1 and 2 (see Figure 3.4) were replaced with the attractive bird receptacles for seven consecutive weeks (the Eagle at Location 1 and the Cardinal at Location 2). The regular cans were then reinstated for six weeks. Subsequently, the bird cans replaced the regular can at Locations 1 and 2 for eight additional weeks; finally the weight measurements were obtained over a 15-week period with the regular trash cans in place of the special bird cans.

The weight data indicated that even over long periods of time the decorated bird cans consistently attracted more trash than the standard, unobtrusive receptacles. In fact, for all but one weight measurement the amount of litter in the two bird cans was higher than any other pair of trash cans. The overall weekly average was 15.05 lbs. per bird can vs. 9.34 lbs. per regular can. Table 3.4 depicts the distribution of trash among the three pairs of trash receptacles for each alternation of the two conditions (i.e., regular cans vs. bird cans at Locations 1 and 2). Although Locations 1 and 2 were usually the most

Table 3.4. Weekly Distribution of Trash Among Three Pairs of Trash Cans.
(Mean Pounds per Week and Percent of Weekly Totals)

Intervention Condition	Trash Can Locations			Totals of Weekly Means
	1 & 2	3 & 4	5 & 6	
Baseline (5 wks.) Jan. - Feb.	16.1 lbs. (41.9%)	14.4 lbs. (37.5%)	7.9 lbs. (20.6%)	38.4 lbs.
Birds 1 & 2 (7 wks.) Mar. - Apr.	25.6 lbs. (59.3%)	11.0 lbs. (25.5%)	6.6 lbs. (15.2%)	43.2 lbs.
Followup (6 wks.) Apr. - May	16.3 lbs. (43.2%)	13.3 lbs. (35.3%)	8.1 lbs. (21.5%)	37.7 lbs.
Birds 1 & 2 (8 wks.) May - July	34.6 lbs. (53.7%)	16.1 lbs. (25.0%)	13.7 lbs. (21.3%)	64.4 lbs.
Followup (15 wks.) Aug. - Dec.	23.7 lbs. (38.1%)	22.1 lbs. (35.5%)	16.4 lbs. (26.4%)	62.2 lbs.

popular trash-disposal areas, it is clear that these locations were prominently more popular when the bird receptacles were used. It is noteworthy that the average weekly totals across all six receptacles were consistently higher when the birds were in Locations 1 and 2, indicating that the beautified trash cans did not only influence a redistribution of the trash normally disposed of in one of the standard mall receptacles, but that the bird cans seemed to attract litter that would *not* have been deposited in another mall receptacle.

On every other weekday for ten days when the bird cans were used and for ten days when they were not, counts were made of all litter in the mall. The floor design of the mall enabled separate counts in three sections of the mall (labelled A, B, & C in Figure 3.4). The obtrusive bird cans were only used in Section A. The litter counts took place at 10:00 p.m. (after the mall closed) and were accomplished one section at a time by two data observers. Each observer started at opposite ends of a given section and systematically tabulated each observation of litter on the floor, benches, tables, and in shopping carts with separate categories for paper, cups, cigarettes, boxes, cans, bottles, matches, and miscellaneous. The checkered floor design of the mall made litter relatively easy to detect and categorize. These litter counts were repeated by each observer until the two, independently derived litter totals were not different by more than three items.

Table 3.5 depicts the distribution of litter throughout the three mall sections for ten days of each condition (i.e., bird cans vs. regular cans in Section A). This data indicates that the overall amount of litter in the mall did not change when the obtrusive bird receptacles were used, but the distribution of the litter throughout the mall was significantly influenced by the presence of the beautified trash receptacles, $\chi^2 (2) = 21.77$, $p < .001$. Specifically, less

Table 3.5. Distribution of Litter Among Three Sections of the Shopping Mall for Ten Days per Receptacle Condition.

Litter Count Section	Bird Can in Section A	Regular Can in Section A	Totals
Section A	388 items (38%)	451 items (48%)	839 items
Section B	429 items (42%)	313 items (34%)	742 items
Section C	198 items (20%)	169 items (18%)	367 items
Totals	1015 items	933 items	1948 items

Note. The item frequencies were derived by averaging the ten-day totals for each data observer and rounding to the nearest whole item.
Source: Adapted from Geller et al., 1980.

litter was found in the vicinity of the special bird receptacles than in the vicinity of the standard trash cans (as also shown by Finnie, 1973 and O'Neill et al., 1980), but the areas more remote from the bird cans (Sections B and C) actually attracted more litter when Section A contained the bird cans as opposed to the regular receptacles. It was as if the attractive receptacles with their antilitter prompts merely influenced "litterbugs" to avoid littering in the immediate area of the prompt. Thus, the extra trash which the bird cans consistently attracted were probably from individuals who would not have littered their trash in the mall area.

A subsequent litter experiment at the University Shopping Mall (Geller et al., 1980) was designed to study relationships between the design and usage of the mall ash trays. Intermittent observations of the four large ash trays in the shopping mall indicated that the ash trays were often used for inappropriate disposals of paper, cans, bottles, cups, etc., and trash cans rather than ash trays were used to put out cigarettes and cigars. Further, it was evident that the appropriate use of ash trays (i.e., for disposing of matches, cigarettes and cigar butts), decreased as a function of the amount of inappropriate litter in the ash tray. As a result of these observations, a field study was designed to measure systematically the appropriate and inappropriate usage of ash trays in three environmental conditions.

One ash-tray condition was a special ash tray-trash can design that combined an ash tray with a trash receptacle so that if an individual approached the receptacle it was equivalently convenient to use either the ash tray or the trash can. Figure 3.5 illustrates this ash tray-trash can receptacle as well as the regular ash tray; the vertical slats surrounding the receptacles were dark-

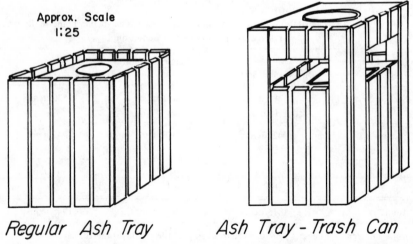

Approx. Scale
1:25

Regular Ash Tray   *Ash Tray - Trash Can*

Fig. 3.5. Scale drawings of the standard trash receptacle and the combination ash tray-trash can receptacle studied by Geller et al. (1980).

stained wood which blended with the decor of the mall. The other two ash trays were not combined with trash cans, but they represented different degrees of ash tray-trash can proximity, and therefore different degrees of consumer convenience regarding the receptacles' specialized functions. One regular ash tray (as illustrated in Figure 3.5) was positioned immediately adjacent to a 50-gallon trash can with a similar design and appearance, while the other ash tray was positioned in the shopping mall with 100 feet between it and the nearest trash can. The locations of these three receptacles in the mall are indicated in Figure 3.4.

On each of the 48 consecutive days, two researchers independently categorized the items discarded in each of the three ash trays as appropriate disposals (cigarette butts, cigar butts, and matches) or inappropriate disposals (candy, paper, peanut shells, toothpicks, gum, cans, bottles, straws, pull tops, cups and tops, etc.) and then counted their tallies. The independent item counts were repeated for each ash tray until full agreement was reached.

The results of this study of ash tray litter were striking and quite relevant for the design and placement of trash receptacles. A direct relationship between ash tray-trash can proximity and the number of appropriate ash tray deposits was consistently observed. In particular, the ash tray combined with a trash can collected the most appropriate ash tray litter and the least inappropriate litter for all but two of the 48 observation days, whereas the ash tray that was relatively isolated from other trash receptacles collected the least amount of appropriate litter and the most inappropriate litter on all but three of the 48 observation days. The average daily frequency and percentage of appropriate and inappropriate litter items per ash tray condition are depicted in Table 3.6 and show substantial effects of ash tray-trash can proximity on ash tray contents; i.e., $\chi^2(2) = 23.57, p < .001$. Thus, a simple

Table 3.6. Average Daily Frequency of Ash Tray Content over 48 Consecutive Days.

Ash Tray-Trash Can Proximity	Appropriate Disposals*	Inappropriate Disposals†	Totals
Ash Tray-Trash Can Combo	22.2 items (89.5%)	2.6 items (10.5%)	24.8 items
Ash Tray next to Trash Can	7.7 items (50.3%)	7.6 items (49.7%)	15.3 items
Ash Tray Alone	3.2 items (16.4%)	16.3 items (83.6%)	19.5 items
Totals	33.1 items	26.5 items	59.6 items

* Cigarette and cigar butts, matches.
† Paper, candy, peanut shells, toothpicks, gum, cans, bottles, straws, pull tops, cups and covers, other inorganic and organic matter.

change in the design of a trash receptacle influenced marked increases in appropriate ash tray use, which not only improved environmental aesthetics, but also reduced the likelihood of a fire caused by mixing paper disposals with cigarette butts. In fact, after the results of this experiment were shown to the manager and janitors of the University Shopping Mall, all of the standard ash trays were removed from the mall and each of the standard trash receptacles have been converted to the combination ash tray-trash can receptacle.

Modeling as an Antecedent Strategy

Children and adults are influenced daily by watching the behaviors of others. Indeed, much of our socialization process results from observation learning as we attend to the behaviors of other individuals in our environment and later attempt to copy the behaviors of model(s). Thus, a model demonstrating one or more behaviors can be considered an antecedent strategy for influencing the behavior(s) of observers. Behavioral research has shown clearly that modeling strategies are more effective when the model is liked and respected by the observer(s), and when the model is reinforced for the demonstrated behaviors (Bandura, 1969; Bandura & Walters, 1967).

Advertising agencies rely on modeling effects to sell products. Magazine advertisements and T.V. commercials typically show well-liked and respected individuals using the advertised product and often depict very pleasant consequences for persons using the promoted product. Modeling has even been used in public service announcements on T.V. to encourage litter control. For example, a litter control commercial in Indianapolis a few years ago showed William H. Hudnut, the mayor, tossing a piece of trash in a waste receptacle. This antilitter response was labeled "The Hudnut Hook," and a plea was made for people to become "Hudnut Hookers." Similarly, the Virginia Division of Litter Control sponsored a public service announcement during which movie actor Ed Nelson picked up a piece of litter from a wooded area and verbalized the state's litter-control slogan, "Isn't it time we cared?"

Very little behavioral research has attempted to determine the behavioral impact of modeling for litter control. Previously discussed research on litter pickup behavior by Geller and his students (see Table 3.3) indicated that relatively few college students stopped to pick up litter in their path, even after another student had picked up and disposed of one of the littered items. Even when subjects approached a situation where a student (i.e., a confederate of the experimenter) was collecting and depositing in a nearby trash can all of the littered paper and drink containers in the path of the subject, only 40% of 40 subjects stopped to pick up at least one item of litter.

The meager research on modeling strategies for litter control suggests that it may not be as influential as one might expect in getting people to make the relatively inconvenient response of picking up environmental litter. Indeed, if live models were relatively unsuccessful in promoting litter pickup, it is doubtful that T.V. modeling of litter pickup will facilitate a similar response in the real world. However, a provocative investigation by Jason, Zolik, and Matese (1979) offers some encouragement for the use of "on-the-spot" modeling. These investigators used a modeling strategy to attack the most offensive type of litter: dog feces along urban sidewalks and streets. Not only does dog litter detract from the overall aesthetic quality of life in a community, it also represents a potential health hazard, since many infections and parasites are transmitted from dogs to humans (Cruickshank, Standard, & Russell, 1976).

For seven consecutive days (five hours per day) baseline data taken along both sides of a street 405 feet long indicated that only 5% of the 42 dog owners whose dogs defecated in the target area picked up after their dogs, and this low pickup rate resulted in a one-week accumulation of 19 pounds of dog defecations in the target area. After baseline, three signs with the message, "Protect Children's Health. Pick Up Your Dog's Droppings" were posted on each side of the street for seven more days. During this period only 6% of the 49 dog owners whose dogs defecated in the target area picked up after their dogs, suggesting the ineffectiveness of the antecedent sign strategy.

The modeling strategy implemented by Jason et al. involved a person approaching every dog owner who entered the target area and showing the dog owner how to use a plastic bag to pick up dog feces. With his hand in the bag, the model placed the bag on the ground with the bag opening facing the ground. Then the model closed his hand on the ground, inserted the bag inside out, and picked up the bag. After this demonstration the plastic bag, called a "pooper scooper," was offered to the dog owner. This intervention continued for seven days (five hours per day) and resulted in 82% of 22 dog owners picking up after their dogs. When this modeling procedure was removed for seven days of follow-up recording, 63% of 24 dog defecations were picked up. Then the modeling procedure was reintroduced for seven additional days (35 total hours), and 84% of 19 dog owners picked up their dog's defecations.

On the surface, the modeling intervention used by Jason et al. appears remarkably successful in encouraging individuals to make a very inconvenient and unpleasant antilitter response. However, it is possible that dog owners avoided walking their dogs in the target area when the modelers were present or may have hurried into another area before their dogs could defecate. In fact, the frequency data indicated that both of these avoidance behaviors occurred, and suggests that part of the apparent efficacy of "pooper-scooper modeling" was due to a redistribution of dog defecations outside of the target area. Specifically, the number of individuals who walked their dogs in the target area when observations were made (i.e., 7:00 to 10:00 a.m. and 4:00 to 6:00 p.m.) was 165 for initial baseline, 149 during the signs,

116 during the first week of modeling, 104 during follow-up, and 97 during
the second week of modeling. The number of dogs observed defecating was
42, 49, 22, 24, 19, respectively, for the five consecutive one-week conditions:
baseline, signs, modeling, follow-up, and modeling. However, even considering that the modeling intervention influenced several dog owners to avoid
the necessity of a pickup response in the target area by having their dog
defecate in another area, it is important to realize that substantially more
owners picked up after their dogs during the modeling intervention than
during any of the other experimental conditions (i.e., 34 out of 41 defecations during modeling vs. 20 out of 115 defecations during the alternative
conditions). Jason and his associates demonstrated total elimination of dog
litter when the target areas were surrounded by foot-high stakes connected
with string, but this stimulus control strategy clearly resulted in only a
redistribution rather than a decrease in overall rates of community dog litter
(Jason & Figueroa, 1980).

An additional benefit of this behavioral analysis of urban dog litter was
large-scale publicity of the problem in the target city (Chicago) and eventual
support for a city ordinance that requires all dog owners to carry some type
of "pooper scooper" when walking their dogs. Indeed, during the week
following the Jason et al. study, the police in the district north of the study's
target area were instructed to dispense plastic bags to dog walkers. Thus,
the Jason et al. study is an excellent example of how the systematic behavioral analysis of a community problem can be instrumental in prompting
community support for action to abate an environmental problem, and how
the nature of the desirable community action for problem abatement can
develop from a systematic evaluation of potential behavioral strategies for
environmental protection. In a follow-up study, Jason, McCoy, Blanco, and
Zolik (1980) were successful in training the members of a community group
to apply pooper-scooper prompting.

CONSEQUENCE STRATEGIES FOR LITTER CONTROL

As discussed in the previous section, antecedent strategies for litter control
(also termed prompting or response priming) are often insufficient when the
desired antilitter response is relatively inconvenient, such as picking up environmental litter. This was also concluded from published reviews of behavioral community research (e.g., Geller, 1980a, 1980b, 1981b, 1981c; Osborne
& Powers, 1980; Tuso & Geller, 1976) and was empirically supported by
recycling studies (discussed in Chapter 4) which compared the behavioral
impact of prompting techniques with procedures combining both antecedent
(prompting) and consequence (positive reinforcement) strategies (Geller et
al., 1975; Ingram & Geller, 1975; Witmer & Geller, 1976). The *combination*
of response priming and response reinforcement has been quite effective in

influencing individuals to collect litter from both indoor and outdoor settings.

At a free-admission zoo, Kohlenberg and Phillips (1973) intermittently offered a coupon redeemable for a soft drink to individuals who deposited trash in a particular trash container. During this consequence strategy a sign near the trash receptacle indicated that litter depositing would sometimes be rewarded. For consecutive 20-minute intervals (12:00 p.m. to 8:00 p.m.), litter deposits in the trash can were independently recorded by two research assistants throughout four consecutive two-week conditions: *Baseline I*—No intervention was implemented. *Reinforcement I*—The contingency sign (or prompt) was displayed and a variable person ratio (VPR) reinforcement schedule was in effect so that on the average the target response of every Nth person was reinforced (N was 7, 10, or 20 on different occasions, representing VPR7, VPR10, and VPR20, respectively). *Baseline II*—The contingency sign was present, but no reinforcers were delivered; and *Reinforcement II*—The antecedent contingency sign and a VPR10 schedule was in effect. For these four conditions the number of litter deposits was 703, 4577, 2403, and 6032, respectively. The reinforcement contingency influenced children less than ten years of age to a greater extent than individuals in the other age categories (i.e., 10 to 20 years, and more than 20 years).

A practical disadvantage of the successful antilitter interventions used by Kohlenberg and Phillips is that someone must be available to administer the reinforcement schedule. A more cost effective application of this type of reinforcement strategy for litter control is represented by the "talking trash can": a trash receptacle with a spring-return lid over its trash-deposit opening that can be readily modified to deliver a tape-recorded message whenever the lid is pushed for a trash deposit. At least three behavioral psychologists have built a "talking trash can," but only short-term anecdotal evidence is available to attest to the beneficial behavioral impact of this consequence strategy (Corey, 1977; Geller, Mann, & Brasted, 1977; Silver, 1974). The special hat receptacle built by O'Neill et al. (1980), however, was analogous to a talking trash can, and as discussed earlier had beneficial antilitter impact for each of ten college football games. Instead of a verbal consequence, a Thank-You sign was displayed whenever the lid to the hat receptacle was pushed. Thus, special trash receptacles which offer interesting and/or novel stimuli when used may be very cost effective in encouraging antilitter behavior, but long-term behavioral tests of such a consequence strategy are needed. One critical weakness of *economical* trash cans offering a consequence following litter disposal is that such systems are "wired" to present the consequence when the lid to the receptacle is pushed, so that it is not necessary to drop litter into such a receptacle in order to receive the reward. However, more expensive trash receptacles have been designed and built which include a photoelectric relay system to detect trash (Corey, 1977), but again the cost effectiveness of such an intervention is yet to be systematically evaluated.

The first published evaluation of both prompting and reinforcement strategies for litter control was by Burgess et al. (1971) and was among the most instructive litter-control studies. The field setting was a movie theater on Saturday afternoons when most of the audience were children. The following antilitter strategies were implemented at different matinee showings and were compared with respect to percent of total theater litter found in theater trash receptacles after the movie:

1. *Extra Receptacles*—doubling the number of trash cans in the theater (the authors didn't indicate the number of trash cans in the theater).
2. *Antilitter Film*—showing an antilitter cartoon before the feature.
3. *Litter Bags*—distributing litter bags to theater patrons with the verbal instructions, "This is for you to use while you are in the theater."
4. *Litter Bags + Announcement*—same as Litter Bags condition with the addition of the following announcement at intermission, "Put your trash into the litterbags and put the bag into one of the trash cans in the lobby before leaving the theater (p. 78)."
5. *Litter Bags + 10¢ Reward*—same as Litter Bags condition with addition of instructions that a bag of litter could be exchanged for a dime in the lobby.
6. *Litter Bags + Ticket Reward*—same as Litter Bag condition with addition of instructions at beginning of film and at intermission that a bag of litter could be exchanged for "a free ticket to a special children's movie (p. 78)."

The results of the Burgess et al. study indicated superior effects of the reinforcement strategies, although distributing litter bags and presenting verbal instructions on their use was quite influential in removing litter from the theater. Specifically, the following overall percentages of total theater litter were found in trash receptacles:

1. *Baseline*—17.5%
2. *Extra Receptacles*—16%
3. *Antilitter Film*—21%
4. *Litter Bags*—31%
5. *Litter Bags + Announcement*—57%
6. *Litter Bags + 10¢*—94%
7. *Litter Bags + Ticket*—95%

Baltes and Hayward (1976) also applied prompting and reinforcement procedures to promote the use of distributed litter bags, except their environmental setting was a football stadium rather than a movie theater, and the subjects were largely university staff and students rather than children. More specifically, four types of messages were written on litter bags and dispensed to people entering the football stadium at Penn State University. One section of the stadium was used for baseline measures while other sections were used as treatment areas. At the entrance to one treatment section, every third person received a litter bag conveying the message that bags filled with trash could be exchanged for a prize if returned to a designated area. At another entrance, every third person received a litter bag bearing messages that "Litter can hurt" and "Others will disapprove of your littering." The third prompt condition, implemented at another entrance, asked people to be appropriate models for others and reduce cleanup costs by disposing of litter properly. The final group at yet another entrance received litter bags that conveyed no message. The dependent variable was the weight of the litter remaining in the designated sections after the game, and demonstrated that all four treatment conditions resulted in significantly less trash left in their respective stadium sections than in the control (or baseline) section. However, there were no significant differences among the various strategies to encourage litter bag usage. An overall 45% less stadium litter was found in the treatment areas than in the control (or baseline) section.

A recent study by Cope and Geller (1981) evaluated antecedent and consequence strategies for encouraging large-scale usage of vehicle litter bags. The environmental setting for this study was a fast-food restaurant in Blacksburg, Virginia, and the special trash receptacle shown in Figure 3.6 was used. This trash receptacle was designed by the Jackson Company of Pomona, California, in response to increasing attention given to vehicle litter bags as a litter-control device. Indeed, a receptacle that makes it convenient to dispose of litter bags and provides a clean replacement bag may certainly be a valuable contribution to community litter control, given apparent (not empirically tested) antilitter effects of vehicle litter bags, the Washington State law that requires litter bags in all vehicles (including boats), and the distinct possibility that additional states will mandate the usage of vehicle litter bags. The field experiment by Cope and Geller was designed to study the public's reaction to this special receptacle for disposal and distribution of vehicle litter bags and to evaluate the efficacy of specific antecedent and consequence interventions for encouraging the usage of this special receptacle.

Throughout the ten-week study, two observers were posted daily at the drive-in window of a fast-food restaurant (from 12:00 to 1:00 p.m. and from 4:30 to 6:30 p.m.), and independently and unobtrusively recorded whether drivers took a litter bag, deposited a litter bag, and had a litter bag in the front seat of their vehicle.* This data was gathered during each of the following conditions.

1. *Baseline* (one week)—The only intervention was the special litter-bag receptacle located in front of the drive-in window to a Wendy's fast-food restaurant.

2. *Antecedent Prompt* (two weeks)—One of the observers approached the driver *before* s/he reached the special trash receptacle and verbalized,

---

* The litter bags for this project were donated by Keep America Beautiful, Inc., Pennsylvania Roadside Council, Inc., and Wendy's Old Fashioned Hamburgers.

Fig. 3.6. The "Put and Take Litter Receptacle" manufactured by the Jackson Company, Pomona, California. The height is 48 inches, the size of the base is 22-1/2 inches by 25-1/2 inches, the trash capacity is 45 gallons, and the surface is finished in Du Pont's automotive enamels. The disposal chute is convenient for both walk-up and drive-up, and the litter bag dispenser holds approximately 25,000 pull-down-tear-off poly bags.

"Hi, just checking to see if you have a litter bag in use today."

3. *Follow Up* (three weeks)—The prompt condition was removed, and baseline was reinstated.

4. *Reinforcement* (two weeks)—A reinforcement contingency was defined by an obtrusive 2.5 by 3 foot sign, facing oncoming cars before reaching the special receptacle, which displayed the message,"FREE LARGE DRINK FOR AN AUTOMOBILE LITTER BAG IN USE DURING THESE HOURS, LUNCH - 12:00 TO 1:00 AND DINNER - 4:30 TO 6:30." Whenever an observer saw a litter bag in the car (with some trash in it), s/he gave the driver a coupon and explained that the coupon was awarded for litter-bag usage and that it could be exchanged for a large drink of his/her choice.

5. *Follow Up* (two weeks)—The reinforcement condition was withdrawn, and baseline was reinstated.

As shown in Figure 3.7, the percentage of Wendy patrons who took a litter bag from the special receptacle increased substantially from baseline when an observer merely indicated that litter-bag usage was being observed. The mean percentage of drive-in customers who took a litter bag from the special receptacle increased from 23.5% during baseline to 33.8% for the prompt intervention. After the verbal antecedent was removed, litter-bag taking decreased to a level below the initial baseline, but increased to 28.6% when the reinforcement contingency was implemented. The removal of reinforcement then resulted in a return to the pre-treatment level (i.e., 16.4% taking a litter bag).

More important than taking a litter bag is using one, and Figure 3.8 depicts the percentage of drive-in customers who had a litter bag in use in their vehicle for each of the experimental conditions. The initial baseline revealed very low litter-bag usage (mean of 5.1%), which consistently increased (to a mean of 19.6% usage) during the antecedent prompt. When this intervention was removed, litter bag usage dropped somewhat to a mean of 14.3%, and subsequently increased to record-high levels following the initiation of the consequence strategy to a usage mean of 30.6%. Withdrawal of reinforcement resulted in an immediate decrease in bag usage to a mean of 18.3% using litter bags. It is noteworthy that the drinks for the successful reinforcement condition were gladly donated by Wendy's in return for the goodwill resulting from their support of a community antilitter project. Thus, a reinforcement strategy similar to that evaluated by Cope and Geller may be quite cost effective for promoting communitywide usage of vehicle litter bags.

The fact that someone must be available to administer a reinforcement schedule can be a practical disadvantage of the antilitter strategies discussed so far to promote the use of litter bags (Baltes & Hayward, 1976; Burgess et al., 1971; Cope & Geller, 1981). The antilitter investigation by Powers et al. (1973) introduced a consequence strategy which did not require human in-

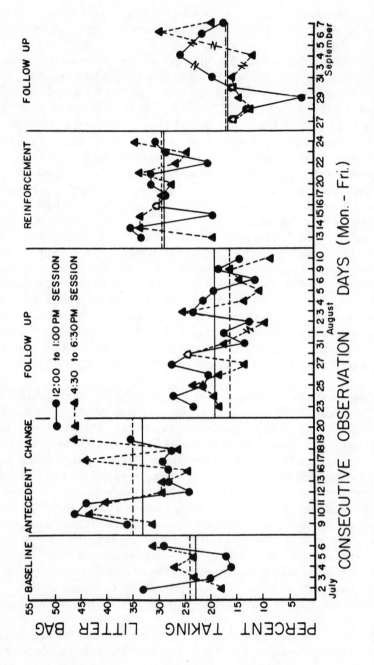

Fig. 3.7. Percent of drive-in patrons at Wendy's who took a litter bag from the "Put and Take" receptacle during baseline, prompting, and reinforcement conditions.

90

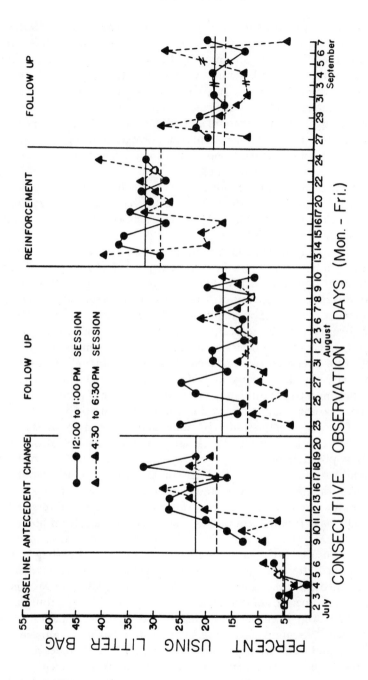

Fig. 3.8. Percent of drive-in patrons at Wendy's who had a litter bag in their car with some trash in it during baseline, prompting, and reinforcement conditions.

tervention and therefore may be more applicable for some situations. Specifically, these investigators constructed two "litter stations" in an unsupervised, heavily-used U.S. forest area north of Logan, Utah. Each litter station consisted of a compartment between two 55-gallon trash barrels that held plastic litter bags and information cards. During two-week periods with only an antecedent intervention, a sign was posted at the front of each litter station instructing park patrons to fill a litter bag with trash, tie it, deposit it in a trash can, and then to fill out an information card and deposit it in the card container. A reinforcement condition was alternated every three weeks with the antecedent strategy and involved the use of a sign that offered people a choice of one of two contingencies. Individuals could indicate on the information card whether they preferred to receive (by mail) 25¢ or a chance at a weekly, $20 lottery in exchange for each bag of litter, two-thirds filled and placed in the trash barrel.

Of the 187 bags of litter (1,658 lbs.) turned in during the 21 weeks of the Powers et al. study, 139 bags (or 74%) were deposited under the reinforcement condition. It is noteworthy that most participants (73%) chose the lottery contingency. The survey of three park areas before and after the reinforcement conditions showed substantially less metal and paper litter (44% and 19% reductions, respectively) as a result of the reinforcement procedure. Consequently, Powers et al. demonstrated significant antilitter effects of an unsupervised reinforcement procedure, although the authors could not determine how many individuals filled out information cards without collecting a bag of litter, and the relative number of participants per users of the area was disappointingly low (about .04% participation).

The use of litter bags in the studies by Baltes and Hayward (1976), Burgess et al. (1971), Cope and Geller (1981), and Powers et al. (1973) did not necessarily imply litter pickup. In other words, a filled litter bag in these studies could have resulted from the user simply putting his/her own litter into the bag, rather than picking up and disposing of another person's litter. In fact, rewarded deposits at the litter stations designed by Powers et al. could actually have resulted from individuals bringing trash from home.

Clark et al. (1972) also applied a prompting and reinforcement strategy to encourage the use of litter bags, except in this research litter-bag usage definitely implied litter pickup. The dependent variable was the number of pieces of planted litter remaining in sample areas of a large forest campground during two periods of four consecutive days. For the first four days, no contingencies were in effect, but during the second four-day period, children were given a 30-gallon plastic bag, instructed to look in certain general areas for litter, and were offered a choice of a Smokey Bear shoulder patch, a Junior Forest Ranger badge, a Smokey Bear comic book, a wooden ruler, a Keep Washington Green pin, or a small box of Chiclets gum in return for the used litter bag, not necessarily filled. During the reinforcement contingency the number of planted pieces of litter decreased from 160 to 24 in three days, as compared to a decrease from 160 to 64 pieces during the comparable baseline period. The efficacy of these reinforcement procedures is apparent when considering the fact that in exchange for reinforcers valued at three dollars, approximately 175 pounds of litter were collected, an amount that would have taken the forest service personnel up to 20 hours of work at a cost of approximately $55. It is noteworthy that the planted litter with a built-in value (i.e., the returnable soft drink bottles) were picked up almost as readily during the baseline period as during the subsequent reinforcement condition. The special environmental benefits of returnable, rather than throwaway, drink containers are discussed further in Chapter 4.

A series of other antilitter studies also applied inexpensive reinforcement procedures to encourage environmental cleanup. It is instructive to review these investigations briefly, not only to point out certain practical strategies and their impact, but also to examine particular weaknesses of each study which should be considered when designing programs for community litter control. The research by Chapman and Risley (1974) demonstrated a potential disadvantage of using the "payment-for-litter bag" technique for motivating litter pickup. In an urban, low-income housing project, local children were provided with litter bags and told to fill them with litter from yards in the area. The following three strategies for encouraging litter pickup were evaluated: (1) only a verbal appeal (i.e., prompt) to fill the bag; (2) a payment of 10 cents for each filled bag; and (3) a payment of 10 to 40 cents, contingent upon cleaning assigned yards to a specified "cleanliness criterion."

Chapman and Risley measured both the weight of the trash turned in and the amount of litter on 25 randomly selected yards. The greatest amount of trash was turned in under the "Payment-For-Bags" contingency, although the "Payment-For-Clean-Yards" contingency resulted in the greatest reductions of yard litter. The discrepancy between treatment outcomes—98 pounds of litter collected and an average of 27 litter pieces per yard for Payment-For-Bags versus 28 lbs. of litter collected and 12 litter items per yard of Payment-For-Clean-Yards—suggests that children brought litter from household and commercial trash containers under the Payment-For-Bags condition. Indeed, during this contingency the investigators received litter that could not have been picked up (e.g, coffee grounds, flour, cigarette butts and ashes). In fact, a disadvantage of a Payment-For-Bags contingency is that large rather than small pieces of litter will be turned in, since they are more convenient to pick up and will contribute more to bag volume and the subsequent reward for a filled litter bag.

It is possible that the reduced amount of litter collected during the Payment-For-Clean-Yards condition of the Chapman and Risley study (compared with pounds of litter collected during the Payment-For-Bags condition) was partially due to children disposing of yard litter in areas other than that defined by the investigators. Since rewards were contingent on only clean yards, the investigators had no control on where the collected litter was subsequently deposited. Perhaps some children even deposited litter from target yards on adjacent non-target yards. This would be among the most convenient litter-deposit behaviors, and there was no explicit contingency to prevent the littering of collected litter.

To promote environmental clean up, a cost-effective contingency is needed that will motivate the collection of small pieces of litter and prevent undesirable disposals of collected litter. Such a contingency was implemented and evaluated in three field studies (Bacon-Prue et al., 1980; Hayes et al., 1975; LaHart & Bailey, 1975). This contingency has been termed a "marked-item technique" and is somewhat analogous to an Easter-egg hunt. More specifically, certain pieces of litter are specially marked and the retrieval of any of these marked items qualifies for a prize. Since for this strategy all collected litter must be brought to a central location for examination, proper disposal is guaranteed. Small items of litter may be marked and should therefore be collected from the environment. Furthermore, it is possible that a marked-item strategy may actually reduce littering by those involved in the program, since extra environmental litter will make it more difficult to find marked items. In fact, participants in a marked-item, litter control contest (e.g., at an outdoor event) may actually encourage other people in the area not to litter in order to increase the chances of finding the specially marked litter.

LaHart and Bailey (1975) evaluated the impact of five different litter-control strategies, including a marked-item technique. The subjects were 43 classes of elementary students during their visit to the Junior Museum in Tallahassee, Florida. Each class of students received one of the following litter-control interventions before walking on the museum's nature trail: (1) a statement that littering is a problem; (2) prior experience with educational materials on litter; (3) a five-minute lecture which identified the economic, environmental, and health problems caused by litter; (4) specific verbal instructions to pick up litter; and (5) a marked-item strategy that included an antecedent statement of the litter problem, a request to pick up litter, and a verbalization of the contingency that a special plastic antilitter badge would be given to anyone who found one of five specially marked pieces of planted litter.

Consistent with our prior discussion of antecedent strategies for litter control, none of the antecedent interventions studied by LaHart and Bailey resulted in children picking up environmental litter. However, the marked-item strategy resulted in 38 out of 50 pieces of planted litter being picked up—a 76% litter reduction. However, three of the antecedent strategies did reduce significantly and equivalently the amounts of litter dropped by the children after a lunch break (i.e., the one-sentence statement of the problem, the five-minute lecture and the prior educational experiences). It is noteworthy that the two strategies that attempted to encourage the children to pick up environmental litter (i.e, specific instructions to pick up litter and the marked-item contingency) had no impact in discouraging the inappropriate disposal of lunch litter. This result indicates response-specific effects of behavioral interventions for litter control, suggesting the use of multi-component behavioral strategies for protecting the environment against litter (e.g., educational programs, antilitter prompts, and litter pickup contingencies). Apparently children in the marked-item condition did not realize that their own littering would decrease their chances of finding a marked item. The marked-item strategy may decrease littering if the relationship between littering and finding marked litter were made explicit to contest participants.

Hayes et al. (1975) implemented a marked-item strategy at the Robert F. Kennedy Youth Center, a federal prison in Morgantown, West Virginia, and demonstrated prominent reductions in ground litter as a result. The rate of littering by the participants (130 boys from 18 to 20 years of age) was not measured, and the investigators did not specify that littering would reduce the probability that any given piece of collected litter would be marked. The marked-item procedure was initiated by locating special receptacles and litter bags in a certain cottage, and distributing flyers that announced that marked litter had been placed in a particular outdoor area and that finding a marked item would result in 25¢ or a special privilege such as late bedtime or access to a coffeehouse. The flyer also informed the residents of another outdoor area that they were responsible for keeping clean but that contained no marked litter. This procedure was applied to three outdoor areas of the prison yard at successive time periods (i.e., after 17, 22, and 36 days of baseline, respectively), resulting in a multiple baseline design across locations. Systematic litter counts during baseline and treatment conditions showed successive reductions in ground litter of 55%, 88%, and 71% in the three areas respectively. A total of 32 persons participated (24% of those eligible), and 71 of the 97 marked items (73%) were returned. No changes in litter counts occurred in the control area specifically assigned as the "area of responsibility" for certain participants. Unfortunately, this latter result suggests a lack of stimulus generalization and supports a prior conclusion of this chapter that extrinsic rewards are necessary to motivate litter pickup behavior.

One serious disadvantage of the marked-item strategy implemented by Hayes et al. (1975) was the relatively large amount of work needed to accomplish the procedures. Most time consuming was the necessary search through each bag of litter for marked items, and because of this procedural component, Hayes et al. actually questioned the large-scale applicability of their marked item technique. However, a follow-up study by Bacon-Prue et al. (1980) introduced an ingenious procedure for detecting marked litter, which may make the item-marking technique very cost effective for many community and institutional settings. These investigators marked certain litter items by spraying them with "clue spray" (commercially available from Sirche Laboratories, P.O. Box 30576, Raleigh, North Carolina 27612 at $12.65 per 6 oz. can) which is not visible unless the object is placed under an ultra-violet light. When an individual touches an item marked with clue spray, fluorescent particles are transferred to his/her hands. By placing an individual's hands under a black light, it can be determined whether or not the items marked with clue spray had been touched. Thus, clue spray enables rapid marking of litter, and efficient and reliable detection of the pickup of marked litter.

Bacon-Prue et al. evaluated their refinement of the marked-item strategy at a residential retardation facility in Whitfield, Mississippi. After baseline litter counts, the marked-item intervention (termed a "littery lottery") was introduced to the residents by instructions read in school and recreation classes and posted in each cottage. These instructions indicated the time each day (3 to 4 p.m.) when litter could be collected from the grounds in plastic, 30-gallon litter bags available at the Recreation Hall. The instructions further stated that some pieces of litter were marked in a secret way, and that having a marked item in one's litter bag would entitle the person to $1.00 per marked item and a self-photograph to be publicly displayed for a week and then given to the resident to keep. Staff members were on hand at 4:00 p.m. to determine which residents had touched the marked litter.

The littery lottery studied by Bacon et al. was clearly cost effective. For example, when the littery lottery was in effect the amount of ground litter decreased consistently, the average reduction amounting to 46 percent across five areas and 50 days. A total of 130 residents participated in the littery lottery, averaging 25 participants per week, and these participants collected a total of 2,400 gallons of litter. The weekly cost of the lottery was $50.25 which included trash can maintenance. Bacon-Prue et al. estimated that the cost of their item-spraying strategy was less than the cost of paying two resident workers to pick up ground litter and resulted in six times as much trash being collected. Indeed, after the investigators left the retardation facility, "littery lotteries" became standard biweekly practice throughout the institution.

It is instructive to note that the littery lottery actually provided for a variety of pleasant consequences which could have maintained participation. Besides the $1.00 per marked item, pictures were taken of individual lottery winners and groups of participants, and publicly posted. Furthermore, the social rewards of the special group event and/or the opportunity to walk out of doors and benefit the institution may have been critical reinforcers for some lottery participants. In this regard, it is noteworthy that all of the other consequence strategies applied to encourage litter pickup by children included social support and approval from adults as a consequence for the desired behavior.

It is quite possible that the adult attention which accompanied the announcement of a litter-control project and the awarding of dimes, trinkets, and antilitter badges was the critical factor in motivating environmental cleanup. Further behavioral community research is needed in order to specify the role of adult attention and approval for promoting litter control. Research in other applied areas clearly suggests that social attention and approval are very powerful reinforcers, so it is certainly advisable to add this social factor to the antecedents and consequences of a litter-control program whenever possible.

SUMMARY OF BEHAVIORAL STRATEGIES FOR LITTER CONTROL

In general, litter control studies have targeted two behaviors: the appropriate use of trash receptacles (resulting in litter prevention), and the collection of environmental litter (resulting in litter cleanup). The behavioral strategies for controlling litter can be categorized as *antecedents* (events presented *before* a targeted response, in order to influence its probability of occurrence) or *consequences* (events presented *after* a targeted response, in order to influence its subsequent probability of occurrence). Some litter control researchers have applied and evaluated only antecedent strategies, while other investigators have studied the relative contribution of both antecedents and consequences. Actually the use of consequence strategies for litter control has usually required the application of some sort of antecedent in order to announce the availability of certain consequences for the occurrence of certain responses.

The litter-control studies discussed in this chapter are reviewed in Table 3.7. For both antecedent and consequence strategies, the target behaviors and essential outcomes with regard to the targets are given. As shown in Table 3.7, antecedent strategies without reinforcing consequences have only been successful in preventing littering, not in promoting litter pickup. These antecedent strategies for litter prevention have included: (1) increasing trash can availability; (2) using beautified receptacles; (3) decreasing the amount of environmental litter; and (4) displaying antilitter messages or instructions. In addition, there is evidence that the effectiveness of antilitter instructions is a direct function of the specificity of the request and the convenience of the requested behavior. However, the relationship between increased specificity of the behavioral request and degree of behavioral compliance is limited when the antilitter message becomes so specific that it threatens one's per-

Table 3.7. Summary of Litter Control Studies

Litter Control Research	Antecedents			Consequences		
	Target	Strategy	Outcome	Target	Strategy	Outcome
Geller et al. (1971, 1973) [grocery store]	returnable bottle buyers	handbills at store entrance	20% increase			
Dodge (1972) [camping community]	campsite litter	community hand-outs, bumper stickers, & newspaper ads	from 2.15 to .18 quarts per party (~92%)[1]			
Schnelle et al. (1980) [city, population 30,000]	ground litter	newspaper articles (litter feedback)	35% reduction			
Geller (1973, 1975); Geller et al. (1976); Geller et al. (1977) [movie theater and grocery store]	handbill disposals	specific disposal instructions	20-30% increase in trash can disposals[2]			
Finnie (1973) [Richmond, VA & Philadelphia, PA]	highway litter	increased number of trash cans	29% reduction[1]			
	sidewalk litter		17% reduction[1]			
	littered hot dog wrappers	clean vs. dirty milieu	25% vs. 42%[2]			
	trash can disposals	decorated receptacles	15% increase[1]			
Heberlein (1974) [classroom building]	handbills on floor	clean vs. littered hallway	26% vs. 70%[1]			

Table 3.7. (Continued)

Study	Target behavior	Intervention	Result	Target behavior	Intervention	Result
Robinson & Frisch (1975) [post office]	handbills on floor	clean vs. littered post office	3.6% vs. 16.3%[1]			
Geller et al. (1977) [grocery store]	handbills on floor	clean vs. littered grocery store	1% vs. 5%			
Crump et al. (1977) [forest picnic area]	picnic litter	clean vs. littered picnic area	55% decrease in *littered* area.[1]			
O'Neill et al. (1980) [university football]	trash can disposals; ground litter	decorated trash receptacles	combined with consequences (cwc)	trash can disposals; ground litter	"Thanks" sign on trash can	51% increase[1] 66% reduction[1]
Geller et al. (1980) [shopping mall]	trash can disposals	bird receptacles	61% increase[3]			
	ash tray litter	trash can design	84% reduction			
Jason et al. (1978) [Chicago street]	dog feces	litter bag "Pooper Scooper," instructions & modeling	75% increase in pick up after defecation[4]			
Kohlenberg & Phillips (1973) [free admission zoo]	trash can deposits	contingency sign	230% increase	trash can deposits	drink coupon on VPR 10[5,6]	730% increase
Burgess et al. (1971) [movie theater]	litter bag usage	litter bags and verbal instructions	57% of theater litter[1]	litter bag usage	movie ticket or 10¢/bag[5,7]	95% of theater litter[1]

Table 3.7. (Continued)

Litter Control Research	Antecedents			Consequences		
	Target	Strategy	Outcome	Target	Strategy	Outcome
Baltes & Hayward (1976) [football stadium]	litter bag usage	litter bags with instructions	45% litter reduction[1]	litter bag usage	$1 lottery prize (20 per game)[5,7]	45% litter reduction[1]
Cope & Geller (1981) [fast-food restaurant]	automobile litter bags	verbal prompt by observers	+43.8% taking bags +28.2% using bags			
		verbal prompt & contingency sign	combined with consequences (cwc)	use of automobile litter bag	large drink for litter bag in use	+22% taking bags +499% using bags
Powers et al. (1973) [forest campground]	park litter	litter stations & contingency signs	cwc	park litter	25¢ or chance in $20 lottery per litter bag[5,7]	32% reduction (48 vs. 139 litter bags)[1]
Clark et al. (1972) [forest campground]	campground litter (160 items planted)	parental contact, instructions, incentives, 30-gallon litter bag	cwc	campground litter (160 items planted)	badges, toys, trinkets, comic books per bag[5,7]	96% collected (150-200 pounds)[1]
Chapman & Risley (1974) [urban neighborhood]	yard litter	verbal appeal & litter bag (VA)	34 pounds of litter turned in, 10 kids/day	yard litter	10¢/bag[5,7]	−29% from VA, 94 pounds litter, 25 kids/day
					10¢/clean yard[8]	−68% from VA, 28 pounds litter, 15 kids/day

Table 3.7. (Continued)

LaHart & Bailey (1975) [nature trail]	ground litter	lecture or education materials	no pickups, 67% decrease in littering[1]	ground litter	badge per marked item[6]	76% pickup, no decrease in littering[1]
Hayes et al. (1975) [federal prison]	ground litter	contingency flyer, special bags & trash cans	combined with consequences (cwc)	ground litter	25¢ or special privilege per marked item[6]	71% mean reduction
Bacon-Prue et al. (1980) [retardation facility]	ground litter	verbal & written instructions, loud bell	cwc	ground litter	$1 & picture per marked item (clue spray)[6,9]	46% reduction

[1] No reported checks on data reliability.
[2] Increase in disposals did not result in substantially less litter; instead, fewer handbills were taken from the environmental setting.
[3] Pattern of disposal changed; influence on overall disposal minimal.
[4] The number of "dog walkers" in the target area decreased by 55% during intervention, suggesting a change in pattern of dog defecations.
[5] Small pieces not apt to be picked up.
[6] Labor intensive.
[7] Could promote litter generation rather than litter pickup.
[8] No control for litter disposal after pickup.
[9] Group picture taken and publicly posted of all participants, and individual picture taken and posted of winners. What was the critical reinforcer?

ception of individual freedom. Under these circumstances psychological reactance may be elicited and actually result in decreased compliance and/or an increase in behavior(s) contrary to the request.

Modeling strategies are frequently used in public service advertising to promote litter control, but systematic investigation of the behavioral impact of modeling is rare. It is likely that demonstrating the appropriate use of a trash receptacle will influence some people to use the trash can for their own litter (see Geller, 1975), since this type of modeling is analogous to specific instructions. However, the results of a series of field experiments by Geller and his students showed that modeling litter pickup and trash-can disposal was relatively ineffective in encouraging people to pickup another person's litter. Indeed, some behavioral studies have shown that a positive reinforcement contingency must be added to an antecedent strategy in order to encourage substantial environmental clean up.

Consequences in the form of cash payments, lottery tickets, and inexpensive toys, trinkets and antilitter badges have all been used successfully to encourage substantial clean up of environmental litter. Disadvantages of consequence strategies have been the number of people and amount of time necessary to administer the program and the transience of the effect (i.e., litter is picked up only while the reinforcers are available). Furthermore, there is evidence that under some consequence strategies individuals may actually produce litter in order to obtain rewards for disposing of it. This latter problem has been combatted by rewarding individuals for finding specially-marked items of litter (Hayes et al., 1975; LaHart & Bailey, 1975). With this marked-item, consequence strategy small items of litter are also apt to be picked up because they could be marked, and participants may be less likely to litter their own trash since such littering decreases the probability that collected litter includes a marked item. The extra time and effort required to administer a marked-item procedure was lessened significantly when marking was accomplished with a fluorescent spray that can only be seen when the marked item is placed under a fluorescent light (Bacon-Prue et al., 1980).

Perhaps the greatest deficiency of the litter control research conducted to date has been the failure to study long-term effects of antilitter strategies. Each study was essentially a demonstration project designed to evaluate litter-related behaviors under specific short-term conditions. Antecedents may certainly lose their influence as people accommodate to their presence, and individuals could certainly become satiated on certain reinforcing consequences. However, the application of litter-control strategies in community settings can impact on many different individuals every day, and thus can remain novel to some of the observers and participants for long periods of time.

THE APPROACH TO LITTER CONTROL
BY KEEP AMERICA BEAUTIFUL:
STRENGTHS TO MODEL AND WEAKNESSES TO AVOID

Keep America Beautiful, Inc., is probably the most influential litter-control agency in the world to date. Although KAB was founded in 1953, it was not until the development of the Clean Community System (CCS) in 1977 that the organization began to have prominent large-scale behavioral impact. Indeed, as of this writing the CCS has been responsible for initiating community litter-control programs in more than 207 U.S. communities, and has spread its concepts and strategies to six other countries: Australia, Bermuda, Canada, Great Britain, New Zealand, and South Africa (KAB, 1979a). In this final section we will review the philosophy and procedures of the CCS, not only because of its far-reaching influence in community litter control but also because the CCS exemplifies an elegant working model for coordinating and encouraging community action toward the solution of environmental problems. By pointing out advantages and disadvantages of CCS policies, we will imply a general plan for organizing the proenvironmental strategies discussed throughout this text into community-action programs for environment preservation. Indeed, in at least one state the CCS system has already been expanded to coordinate communitywide energy conservation efforts (KAB, 1980).

Development of the CCS

Since 1953, KAB has been promoted as "a national, nonprofit, nonpartisan public service organization working with citizen groups, governmental agencies, academic institutions and private industry to stimulate individual involvement in environmental improvement through education, communications, demonstrations and research (KAB, 1976, p. 1)." The programming of KAB is supported by over 100 companies, trade associations and labor unions, and is "guided by a National Advisory Council of 82 major professional, civic, conservation, and youth organizations, representing nearly 70 million Americans and 20 agencies of Federal Government (Johnson & Leonard, 1973, p. 2)." The antilitter intentions of KAB have been recently questioned since much of the financial backing of KAB has come from the beverage and packaging industries* who continually campaign against legislation to ban pull-tabs on cans and no-deposit drink containers (see Mitch-

---

* Of the 90 industries listed as KAB members and contributors in the *KAB Annual Report* of 1976, at least 28 are directly involved in the production, distribution, or use of throwaway drink containers.

ell, 1976). In fact, as reviewed in a special issue of the *Environment Action Bulletin* (Rodale Press, 1976), the *Washington Star* reported a charge by environmentalists and government officials "that KAB is a 'front group' for bottlers and the throwaway bottle and can industry with a major purpose of blocking legislation to require returnable bottles (p. 1)." Such notions apparently prompted the withdrawal of the Environmental Protection Agency from KAB's advisory board (Rodale Press, 1976).

Although KAB has definitely not promoted antilitter bottle bills, the recent activities of KAB's three departments (program development, communications, and field services) have indicated sincere, enthusiastic, and productive efforts to follow up the ramifications of KAB's motto, "People start pollution. People can stop it." Actually, for many years the extent of KAB's antilitter involvement seemed to be only the public service advertisement of their provocative motto and the production and distribution of antilitter information and materials (e.g., antilitter posters and litter bags). However, since January 1976 KAB has been developing, implementing, and evaluating a comprehensive community approach to litter control and improved solid-waste management that has been receiving the optimistic attention of community leaders across the country. This innovative program is publicized as a behavioral approach to handling waste problems and is called the Clean Community System (CCS).

Philosophy of the CCS

A review of CCS documents indicates many behavioral aspects, although the program represents by no means a pure nor optimal behavioral approach to solid-waste management. Basic concepts of applied behavior analysis are prevalent in such CCS intentions as: (1) evaluating the waste-management situation of a community carefully and objectively before and during community interventions; (2) pinpointing particular community activities that should be changed in order to reduce litter accumulations and/or improve solid-waste management; (3) clarifying punishment contingencies (e.g., antilitter ordinances) so that they can be objectively enforced; (4) providing "over-correction" punishers for littering such as a requirement to pick up litter along roadways for a specified number of hours; (5) designing situations to prompt trash-disposal behaviors and make them relatively convenient (e.g., by increasing the availability of beautified trash receptacles, displaying antilitter messages in appropriate locations, and providing motorists with litter bags); (6) developing and promoting education programs that involve modeling and role playing of appropriate antilitter behaviors; (7) employing specific contingency contracts to commit reciprocal behavioral contributions toward designated program objectives; (8) monitoring and documenting program procedures and progress in order to maintain accountability and provide data for program refinement; (9) implementing checklist procedures to compare existing environmental situations and behavioral patterns with those that are more desirable; (10) creating particularly attractive areas in the community to serve as prompts for further antilitter action (e.g., beautified industrial parks, neighborhoods or commercial districts); (11) establishing small community-action projects to demonstrate beneficial antilitter and recycling programs and stimulate increased community involvement; (12) using television, radio, and newspaper media to focus public attention on individuals and groups who emit desirable antilitter behaviors; and (13) implementing a variety of special incentive programs to reward appropriate solid-waste management and improve the public image of people who contribute to the maintenance of a cleaner community.

However, the CCS advocates particular concepts and practices that are rather inconsistent with a "pure" and parsimonious behavioral science. For example, the CCS is advertised as a "normative systems change process . . . [that] identifies the network of attitudes, knowledge and beliefs which condone negative habits, and works to modify them* (KAB, 1977s, p. 1)"; and a major component of the CCS is an assessment of community *attitudes* before and during antilitter interventions. Nowhere in the CCS program modules nor in any other CCS document could we find a clear statement of empirical or theoretical relationships between norms, attitudes, and behaviors. However, it is apparent that the CCS presumed that inappropriate norms and attitudes cause littering, and the community's "normative system" should be targeted for change with the use of behavioral principles. In other words, the CCS applies behavioral science to change norms and attitudes—the presumed causal antecedents of littering.

As discussed in Chapter 2, the CCS goal to change attitudes directly with behavioral principles is exactly contrary to a basic premise of the behavioral approach to therapeutic intervention. A primary distinction between the behavior model and the medical model as strategies for therapy is that under the behavior model behaviors rather than underlying constructs like attitudes, feelings, beliefs, or norms are treated directly whenever possible, although changes in attitudes/feelings/beliefs may often be expected to follow behavior change (see, Ayllon & Azrin, 1968; Ullmann & Krasner, 1965). Indeed, operant principles of behavioral change were designed to influence behaviors, not attitudes.

Not only is CCS terminology often inconsistent with goals of decreasing the frequency of behaviors that cause litter and increasing the frequency of behaviors that reduce waste, but the CCS policy of surveying attitudes as an indication of program efficacy is overly emphasized. More specifically, to

---

* It is clear from other CCS documentation that "them" refers to attitudes, knowledge and beliefs rather than to habits.

measure the impact of the antilitter and waste-handling programs of a given community, the CCS team obtains both a Photometric Index (as described earlier) and a Community Attitude Survey before and during program implementation. Through telephone surveys or personal interviews, the CCS team and recruited volunteers measure litter-related attitudes and opinions of samples of individuals from the commercial, industrial, and consumer sectors of the community. Different individuals are sampled for each condition (i.e., baseline vs. treatment assessments), and comparisons between baseline and treatment measurements are between rather than within subjects as for the Photometric Index. Numerical scores from the twelve-question attitude survey are presumed to reflect "public understanding and beliefs about the littering problem and the factors contributing to it . . . [and] can give the committee implementing the CLEAN COMMUNITY SYSTEM a descriptive base from which to measure the effect of its educational efforts as well as insights into those prevailing negative norms which may require special change strategies if the program is to succeed (KAB, 1977d, p. 1)." Differences between many survey scores obtained before and during a CCS antilitter program are calculated as "a continuing, unbiased measure of its [the program's] impact (KAB, 1977d, p. 1)" and are published to provide evidence of changes in attitudes and understanding toward the littering problem and its contributing factors (see KAB, 1977n; 1977o), and to "provide positive reinforcement for those who hold (or have developed) acceptable norms and help to define these norms for others (KAB, 1977o, p. 1)."

Conducting attitude surveys may be valuable for increasing awareness of waste-management issues and problems, suggesting areas of concern, and even in recruiting community involvement in the CCS program, but it is doubtful that the attitudinal measures can be useful in defining behavior-change strategies or in evaluating the litter-control efficacy of applying behavioral interventions. There is just too much evidence suggesting that valid and useful attitude measurements are too complex for community programs (see Hendee, 1971), and that verbal reports of attitudes are often not reliable predictors of behavior (see Deutscher, 1966, 1973; Wicker, 1969, 1971). In fact, recent comparisons of littering behaviors and attitudes toward litter are particularly detrimental to programs that rely on attitude surveys for behavioral information (Bickman, 1972; Heberlein, 1974; Robinson & Frisch, 1975). Bickman (1972) observed 409 college students and 97 nonstudents as they passed litter (i.e., crumpled newspaper) that had been "planted" directly in their path and interviewed every fifth person who passed the litter. Although only eight (1.4%) picked up the litter, 94% interviewed replied "yes" to the question, "Should it be everyone's responsibility to pick up litter when they see it? (p. 324)."

Heberlein (1971) and Robinson and Frisch (1975) distributed handbills to individuals and then sent attitude questionnaires to individuals who were observed littering the handbill and to those who did not. Neither study found a significant relationship between litter-related attitudes and actual behavior. For example, those individuals who suggested more severe fines for littering were *not* less likely to litter than those who suggested less severe fines; those who perceived littering as more serious were not less likely to litter than were those who ranked littering as less serious (Heberlein, 1974). In fact, when Heberlein asked those individuals who were observed littering whether they had engaged in any of five deviant acts (among which littering was included), only 50% (18 out of 36) admitted to having littered.

Organization of the CCS

In our opinion the most impressive aspect of the CCS is the organizational scheme that promotes practical relationships between local government, businesses, and civic organizations for cooperative community action toward solving waste-management problems. The structure and dynamics of the current CCS may actually represent the best working model developed so far for organizing reciprocal community efforts toward environment preservation (e.g., resource recovery, energy conservation, and transportation management). Figure 3.9 outlines the organizational components of the CCS and lists the major functions of each component. Most of the information in Figure 3.9 and the following discussion of the CCS organization was gleaned from the CCS program modules (KAB, 1977a through 1977n) which each CCS community must purchase from KAB.

A particular community initiates the KAB-sponsored program by completing an Application for CCS Certification, whereby local CCS sponsors agree to certain behavioral requirements that reflect community commitment to an antilitter program. The major requirements for becoming a Certified CCS Community include: (1) a letter from the mayor (or other chief executive officer) that endorses the CCS for his/her community; (2) an evaluation of the community's current litter and solid waste situations by the public works/sanitation director; (3) willingness to purchase the CCS program modules for $125, or organize a three-member CCS project team that includes at least one representative from the commercial, government, and consumer sectors of the community and to send the CCS project team to a CCS training workshop for $75 per person; and (4) commitment to provide the first year's operating expenses for the local CCS program (i.e., $3,000 to $5,000 for communities with populations greater than 15,000 and $1,000 to $1,500 for smaller communities).

In return for their commitment to the CCS, KAB agrees to provide the following: (1) a "CCS Project Team Training Workshop" for the three-member CCS team from the local community; (2) CCS program modules that include organizing guides, a training manual, slide presentations and

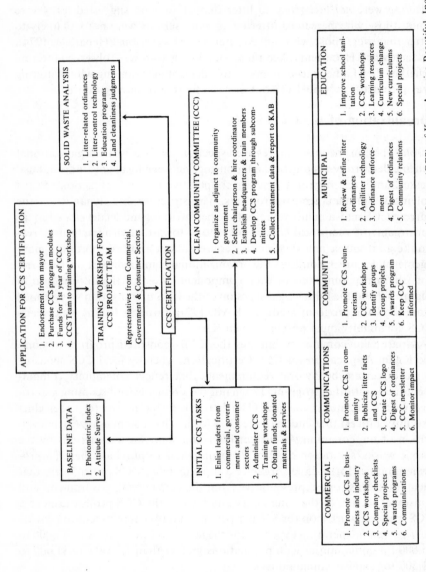

Fig. 3.9. A flow chart of the organization and policy of the Clean Community System (CCS) of Keep America Beautiful, Inc.

scripts, and research and evaluation materials; (3) participation in ongoing "brain-storming" communications between certified CCS communities; (4) publicity through KAB's national communications program (e.g., the *CCS Bulletin* and *KAB Reports*); (5) monitoring of local efforts and field counselling by KAB representatives; and (6) frequent KAB mailings that include program suggestions, case studies, and sources for additional program materials and information (KAB, 1977q).

After the CCS Training Workshop, the three-member project team returns home to initiate the CCS program. The team's home is now a Certified CCS community. Within 60 days the CCS project team must obtain the baseline Photometric Index (PI) and Attitude Survey (as discussed above) and begin a Litter/Solid Waste Analysis. The Litter/Solid Waste Analysis (KAB, 1977g) requires the cooperation of the community's sanitation/public works department and involves a detailed analysis of existing: (1) ordinances related to litter control (e.g., clarity of terms, fines, responsibility, enforcement); (2) physical resources for litter control (e.g., receptacles, litter bags, dumpsters, refuse collection equipment, and practices of the sanitation department); (3) enforcement practices concerning litter-control laws (e.g., authorized vs. actual implementation); (4) education programs related to waste-handling procedures (e.g., in public service and civic oranizations, commerical establishments, schools and the media); and (5) "cleanliness" of various land areas (e.g., commercial areas, parks, neighborhoods, roadsides, schools, shopping centers) as determined by subjective judgments (i.e., ratings of excellent, good, fair, or poor). Copies of the baseline PI, baseline Attitude Survey, and detailed Litter/Solid Waste Analysis must be fowarded to KAB after completion.

Another initial task for the CCS project team is to solicit the program involvement of key community leaders from the government, commercial, and consumer sectors of the community, such as city government officials, business and industry executives, and civic group leaders. More specifically, the project team presents the informational slide presentation of the CCS to these community leaders and seeks their advice for financial support and the organization of the local Clean Community Committee (CCC) that will essentially direct the local CCS programs. The CCC must have official sanction of the local governing body and actually be an adjunct to the community's government. If possible, the CCC members should include representatives from local government, business and industry, labor unions, the professional community (e.g., architecture, law, engineering), civic groups, public education, minority groups, and communications/media (e.g., T.V., radio, newspapers, advertising agencies.).

To formulate policy for the local CCS and be accountable for the implementation of such policy, the CCS must accomplish the following tasks: (1) establish a CCC headquarters; (2) hire an appropriate chairperson and executive coordinator; (3) participate in a CCS training workshop given by the CCS project team; (4) assign responsibilities for taking intermittent photometric indices and attitude surveys during implementation of CCS programs; (5) maintain channels of communication to keep community leaders (the mayor, city council, sanitation director, project supporters) aware of CCS progress; and (6) develop, evaluate, and refine the local CCS program that "will effect the changes in the normative system which will reduce littering in the community (KAB, 1977i, p. 4)."

The CCC must also establish a system of five subcommittees, each responsible for particular "normative system change strategies" of the total CCS program. Each subcommittee should participate in a CCS training workshop (given by the local CCS project team), and establish the necessary organizational support and policy to implement and evaluate assigned duties. The subcommittees of the CCC and their basic contributions to the CCS are as follows:

1. *Business and Industry.* (KAB, 1977b)—*to promote the involvement of local business and industry in CCS programs* by modeling antilitter behaviors, conducting CCS workshops for employees, demonstrating the use of checklists to evaluate the waste management practices of commercial establishments, developing special programs to reward antilitter behaviors in commercial settings, maintaining improved communications with employees and the CCC regarding current and potential antilitter activities, and by coordinating and promoting special antilitter projects, such as the company sponsorship of an antilitter television advertisement, a cleanup of an industrial park, a CCS training workshop, a special litter receptacle with the company's logo in the commercial district, or the distribution of litter bags to employees and customers;

2. *Communications.* (KAB, 1977c)—*to promote citizen participation in CCS programs* by developing systematic communication plans for each media outlet, creating a logo for the CCC, publicizing the litter problem and ways to solve it, documenting and distributing a digest of local sanitation ordinances, maintaining communications among the CCC members with a newsletter, focusing public attention on individuals who contribute to the CCS, and by monitoring the results of Community Attitude Surveys in order to assess the impact of public communications and refine future practices;

3. *Community Organizations* (KAB, 1977e)—*to promote group volunteerism toward CCS efforts* by identifying existing community organizations, organizing workshop sessions for community organizations, enlisting volunteer groups for special CCS projects, organizing award programs for recognizing special antilitter behaviors, encouraging neighborhood groups to organize for the purpose of solving local litter and waste-management problems, keeping the CCC informed of organized CCS action, and by translating CCS programs into action projects compatible with particular community groups

(such as conducting attitude surveys, receptacle-placement field tests, litter-accumulation counts, mini-park development campaigns, junked-car retrieval programs, resource-recovery centers, or cleanup projects at parades, fairs and sporting events);

4. *Municipal Operations* (KAB, 1977h)—*to assist the local government (especially the sanitation department) manage litter and solid waste* by reviewing and refining existing litter-related ordinances, working with the Communications Sub-Committee on a digest of waste-management ordinances, encouraging stricter enforcement of litter-related ordinances, by suggesting improvements in community relations programs and technological resources for waste management, and by defining and monitoring the litter-related roles of municipal agencies;

5. *Education* (KAB, 1977k)—*to sustain effective CCS programs through educational institutions* by improving sanitation practices on school property, giving informational workshops to school personnel and students, locating learning resources applicable to litter/solid waste education, modifying existing curriculums to include topics related to litter control and solid-waste management, developing and promoting new curriculums on municipal sanitation (with such topic areas as the history of refuse disposal, current and future innovations in trash disposal, definitions of litter and ways to stop it, the workings of the sanitation department, litter-law enforcement and the roles of public education in reducing litter), and by encouraging the involvement of students in antilitter activities (such as projects to design and decorate trash cans and litterbags, or plant gardens and build compost piles in appropriate sections of school grounds).

In summary, the CCS of KAB deserves serious attention as a comprehensive, working model for involving entire communities in collaborative action toward community goals. In fact, an interdisciplinary team of university professors and students at Virginia Polytechnic Institute and State University modeled their scheme for organizing community activities toward energy conservation after the CCS Plan (Geller, 1978; Geller, Bowen, & Chiang, 1978; Geller, Brasted, & Augustine, 1978). Further, the CCS policies of evaluating community programs in terms of overt behaviors or behavioral consequences, and of rewarding individuals and groups for emitting behaviors that support particular program goals are commendable and quite compatible with behavioral technology. However, some CCS procedures reviewed earlier do not reflect a true behavioral approach to community problem solving and could actually be markedly improved if made more congruent with applied behavior analysis. Most critical is the fact that the basic evaluation procedures for assessing the outcomes of CCS programs allow for unnecessary experimenter bias and risky interpretation. For example, procedures for deriving the Photometric Index do not account for sequential factors and are particularly susceptible to experimenter expectancy effects. Instead of gathering baseline and intervention data from different environments and comparing group averages, both baseline and treatment data should be obtained from the same environmental settings and studied according to ABA withdrawal or multiple baseline designs (as reviewed in Chapter 2). Furthermore, it is unlikely that the results of the CCS Community Attitude Survey offers enough practical information to make such data collection cost effective. Less time and expense should be devoted to interviewing citizens regarding their waste-management opinions and habits, and more time should be spent making reliable observations of environment-behavior relationships.

The CCS plan is a provocative, first approximation to an optimal application of behavioral science to community planning for environment preservation. The CCS plan represents a framework within which many of the behavioral strategies discussed in this text could be organized for large-scale application. Indeed, it would be instructive for the reader to refer to the CCS plan in the context of the subsequent chapters of this text. The next four chapters address problems caused by responses that damage the environment more critically and permanently than littering, and thus require immediate communitywide applications of behavior change strategies.

Chapter 4
Waste Reduction
and Resource Recovery*

The average person in the United States throws out three to five pounds of trash each day, amounting to three tons per year for the average family of four and over 150 million tons per year for the entire country—enough trash to fill the Superdome in New Orleans twice every day of the year. The annual cost for collecting and disposing of these wastes is $4 billion per year and is expected to increase to $6 billion a year by 1985 (Purcell, 1980, 1981). The result is unnecessary U.S. imports, energy waste, inflation, and environmental degradation!

Waste reduction and resource recovery are distinct waste management approaches for conserving environmental resources, reducing waste collection and disposal costs, and alleviating energy shortages. *Waste reduction* refers to decreasing the generation of waste by reducing the consumption of environmental resources, while *resource recovery* refers to the extraction of resources from discarded materials for use in manufacturing (see Humber, 1975). More detailed definitions of resource recovery programs (e.g., League of Women Voters of U.S., 1972) distinguish between using wastes to produce the original commodity (i.e., *recycling*) and changing wastes into other materials (i.e., *reclamation* or *conversion*). According to this distinction, the use of waste paper to produce paper, re-refined oil to produce lubricants, crushed glass to make glass, or scrap iron to produce steel is recycling, whereas burning garbage to generate energy (termed refuse derived fuel) or using crushed glass for road building is reclamation or conversion. A third term that is sometimes associated with recycling (e.g., League of Women Voters

* This is an expanded and updated version of two prior reviews: Geller, E. S., Saving environmental resources through waste reduction and recycling: How the behavioral community psychologist can help, in G. L. Martin & J. G. Osborne (Eds.), *Helping in the community: Behavioral applications*, New York: Plenum Press, 1980, 55-102; and Geller, E. S., Waste reduction and resource recovery: Strategies for energy conservation, in A. Baum & J. E. Singer (Eds.), *Advances in environmental psychology, Vol. III: Energy conservation: Psychological perspectives*, Hillsdale, N.J.: Erlbaum Associates, 1981, 115-154.

of U.S., 1972) but more often referred to as waste reduction (e.g., Wahl & Allison, 1975) is "reuse." Reuse occurs when a product is used over again, usually by another person and sometimes in refurbished form, such as a returnable bottle, a retreaded tire, a dress from Goodwill Industries, or a car radiator from the junk yard. Since reuse decreases manufacturing energies and waste generation directly, while requiring the recovery of used resources, it is understandable that the terms recycling and waste reduction have been used interchangeably when referring to this process. Since recycling requires manufacturing energies and produces wastes of its own and reuse does not, many environmentalists advocate reuse over recycling (Purcell, 1980, 1981).

Some waste management "experts" claim that waste reduction is the only direct method for saving resources and conserving energy and consider resource recovery to be a costly, post hoc alternative (e.g., Quarles, 1975; Wahl & Allison, 1975; Wendt, 1975). However, other "experts" (usually with an alliance to industry) view resource recovery as the only comprehensive, long-term approach to problems of solid waste management and resource conservation (e.g., King, 1975; Van Tine, 1975; Walker, 1975). Actually, an optimal approach to saving resources should include both waste reduction and resource recovery strategies (see, Humber, 1975). For example, packaging materials may not only be reduced (waste reduction), but much packaging can be produced from recycled paper (James, 1975). Indeed, the president of the Pillsbury Company reported that from 1965 to 1975 his company accomplished a 36% reduction in the amount of metal consumed in packaging—a savings of 11.1 million pounds of metal per year. Each year the company also uses about 50 million pounds of recycled paper (Peterson, 1975).

Strategies for resource recovery may be dichotomized as high-technology or low-technology. A *high*-technology recovery system is quite expensive but is most convenient for the consumer. Nonseparated garbage is collected as usual and transported to a "resource recovery" plant that mechanically separates out paper, glass, aluminum, and metal for reuse in product manufacturing and then burns the remaining refuse with coal and oil to produce steam for electricity generation or oil via a process called pyrolysis (see Seldman, 1975, 1976a, 1977). The types and amounts of materials separated from trash before it is processed varies among resource-recovery facilities, as does the particular energy conversion process.

In contrast, the *low*-technology approach to resource recovery refers to the more economical but less consumer-convenient system of separating garbage into reusable materials at the place where the waste was produced (the residence, institution, or factory) and then transporting separated waste to appropriate manufacturers (e.g., paper to a paper mill, glass to a glass factory, and aluminum to a can company). In other words, the product distribution chain is reversed, and the consumer becomes the first rather than the last link (see Margulies, 1970). It is noteworthy that high versus low technology approaches to resource recovery are quite incompatible and implicate a conflict between physical and psychological strategies for energy conservation. For example, an expensive resource recovery plant requires some minimum quota of trash each year to be profitable and thus serves as a disincentive for waste reduction and low-technology resource recovery (see Seldman, 1977).

The most obvious disadvantage of the high-technology approach to resource recovery is the very high and often underestimated expense of such a system. For example, the Baltimore Pyrolysis plant was scheduled to open in 1975 at a cost of $16 million, but its operation was delayed because of $10 million in additional costs, and a system in St. Louis to convert 6,000 tons of garbage per day into refuse-derived fuel (RDF) cost $70 million (La-Breque, 1977). In addition, the maintenance of a high-technology system is quite expensive, as illustrated by the fact that the "hammermills" needed to shred the trash in the St. Louis RDF plant cost nearly $4,000 for the 6,641 tons of garbage processed between November 1973 and April 1974 (Environmental Action Foundation, 1977b). Indeed the annual cost of simply operating a high-technology system is substantially higher than the standard landfill approach to solid waste management (Seldman, 1976b).

Other disadvantages or problems with the high-technology approach to resource recovery are: (1) operating the resource recovery plant consumes much energy and pollutes the air, sometimes with heavy metals (Environmental Action Foundation, 1977b; Seldman, 1975); (2) using RDF with coal and oil as an energy source causes more air pollution than does using coal or oil alone (Seldman, 1975; 1976a); (3) contracts between resource recovery plants and cities specify some minimum quota of trash each year (below which some cities must pay additional fees) and thereby establish a "disincentive" to reduce waste (Environmental Action Foundation, 1977b; Seldman, 1977); (4) a reliable technology is not available for separating aluminum (the most valuable recyclable) from the solid-waste stream, and glass separation is only slightly more advanced than aluminum recovery (Environmental Action Foundation, 1977b); (5) the storage of shredded waste can be a fire hazard (Environmental Action Foundation, 1977b); (6) locating reliable markets for the energy resources produced by resource recovery plants is sometimes difficult, and market prices vary widely (Environmental Action Foundation, 1977b); and (7) since paper and organics (comprising 55% to 75% of municipal solid waste) are more valuable when recycled than burned for Btu (see Seldman, 1977), increasing amounts of these materials will be removed from the solid-waste system via *low*-technology recycling, and therefore the garbage input to justify the operation of *high*-technology systems can be seriously threatened (Seldman, 1976b). With regard to this latter point, low-technology, source-separation programs were operating in more than 75 cities in 1976, but two years earlier no such programs existed (Seldman, 1976a).

Some experts have argued convincingly that the low-technology approach to resource recovery is more desirable than high-technology systems even in big cities where large amounts of concentrated trash are available for convenient transport to high-technology recovery plants (see report of the Committee for the Development of a National Recycling Policy prepared by the Institute for Local Self-Reliance, 1980). For example, "design shortcomings and technological bugs" in New York City's resource recovery plants have prompted serious consideration of "instituting low-technology recycling on a citywide basis." In fact, a large-scale, low-technology program was initiated in East Harlem in 1979, and its fantastic success has been attributed to a "coupon-incentive idea" that provides coupons per specified amounts of recyclables. "People save the coupons like green stamps and redeem them for movie, play, or sports event tickets that have been donated (McDermott, 1980)." This coupon intervention obviously relates directly to reinforcement principles, and in fact, raffle coupons were shown five years earlier to be a cost-effective method of promoting resource recovery (e.g., Geller et al., 1975). Experimental behavioral analysis can contribute substantially to the design, evaluation, and refinement of strategies for promoting community-wide recycling. This chapter critically reviews those behavioral studies that have provided information for the low-technology approach to waste reduction and resource recovery.

Before reviewing specific behavioral approaches toward waste reduction and resource recovery, it is instructive to consider the varieties of items that are discarded daily and to examine potential ways of saving the environmental resources used to produce and dispose of our trash. Municipal waste can be categorized into the following five categories: durable waste, nondurable waste, packaging waste, food waste, and yard waste (Wahl & Allison, 1975), and each of these trash categories are potential targets for particular waste reduction and/or recycling strategies. Figure 4.1 illustrates the variety of residential waste items that can be recycled and result in waste reduction and the conservation of environmental resources.

Durable Waste

Durable goods include large appliances such as televisions, refrigerators, lawn mowers, and furniture which the consumer decides to replace or discard. Often the discarded appliances are damaged beyond repair, but they usually contain valuable scrap materials. Too often the appliances were discarded because it was more convenient and rewarding to purchase a newer model. Because most durable wastes are large, they take up much valuable space in dumps, land fills, and open fields. Automobiles are perhaps the

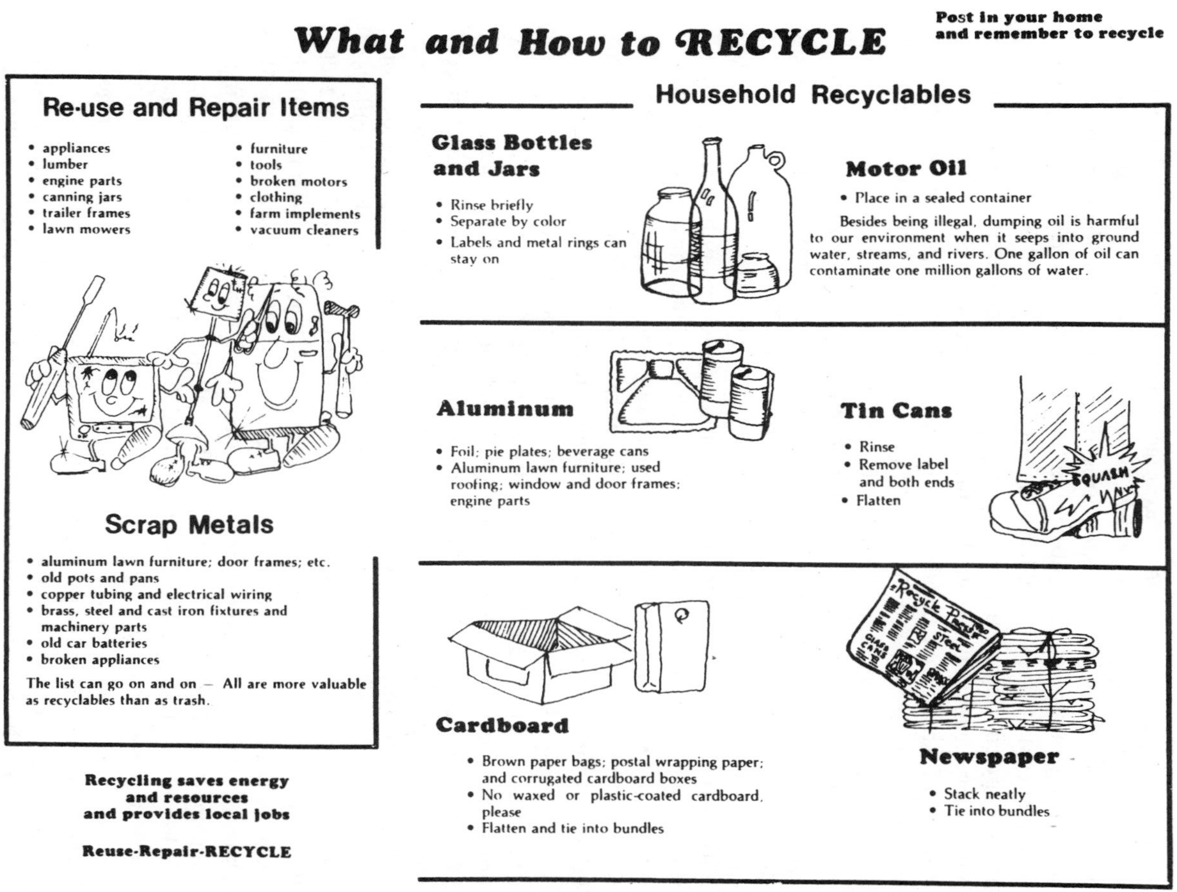
What and How to RECYCLE
Post in your home and remember to recycle
Re-use and Repair Items
• appliances
• lumber
• engine parts
• canning jars
• trailer frames
• lawn mowers
• furniture
• tools
• broken motors
• clothing
• farm implements
• vacuum cleaners
Scrap Metals
• aluminum lawn furniture; door frames; etc.
• old pots and pans
• copper tubing and electrical wiring
• brass, steel and cast iron fixtures and machinery parts
• old car batteries
• broken appliances
The list can go on and on — All are more valuable as recyclables than as trash.
Recycling saves energy and resources and provides local jobs
Reuse-Repair-RECYCLE
Household Recyclables
Glass Bottles and Jars
• Rinse briefly
• Separate by color
• Labels and metal rings can stay on
Motor Oil
• Place in a sealed container
Besides being illegal, dumping oil is harmful to our environment when it seeps into ground water, streams, and rivers. One gallon of oil can contaminate one million gallons of water.
Aluminum
• Foil; pie plates; beverage cans
• Aluminum lawn furniture; used roofing; window and door frames; engine parts
Tin Cans
• Rinse
• Remove label and both ends
• Flatten
SQUASH
Cardboard
• Brown paper bags; postal wrapping paper; and corrugated cardboard boxes
• No waxed or plastic-coated cardboard, please
• Flatten and tie into bundles
Newspaper
• Stack neatly
• Tie into bundles

Fig. 4.1. A flyer prepared and distributed by the Lane Economic Development Council in Eugene, Oregon, to promote residential recycling. Do you think such prompting is sufficient to encourage substantial participation in community recycling?

most obvious and unsightly of the durable wastes as demonstrated by the automobile graveyard.

The extreme difficulty for the average consumer to transport large durables to repair shops, recycle centers, or scrap yards means that such wastes will often be left in garages, backyards, or public spaces. With appropriate advertising and by offering substantial financial rewards, it may be possible to influence the relocation of large, durable wastes. It may be more practical and energy conserving if recycling centers would include their own "free" pickup service and offer a small remuneration for consumers who report the location of a recyclable durable and perhaps make an appointment to be on hand when the pickup is to be made. Indeed, Hayes et al. (1975) suggest that a "marked item technique" would be a financially practical procedure for getting bulky durables that litter the public environment to recycle centers. Thus, certain durables could be specifically marked unobtrusively by officials from redemption centers and the reporting and/or the appropriate relocation of these marked items would result in a large financial reward. It is noteworthy that large-scale social attention (such as public recognition through the news media) may be as powerful a reinforcer as large sums of money for maintaining the more inconvenient recycling behaviors and may have the further desirable consequence of modeling appropriate recycling behaviors for the newspaper reader, radio listener, and television viewer.

Tires are considered among the most intractable and indestructible municipal wastes (Kiefer, 1974; Wahl & Allison, 1975), "not suitable for conventional collection, processing, landfill, or incineration operations (Westerman, 1975, p. 84)." However, the number of discarded tires would be reduced markedly if more were recycled for producing roofing material, shoe soles, or playground equipment (Seldman, 1976b) and if significant numbers of consumers were persuaded to purchase longer lasting steel-belted radials. Radials are initially more expensive than standard bias-ply tires, but in fact the total life cost of the radials is less since they will generally last more than twice as long as standard tires (Wahl & Allison, 1975; Westerman, 1975). Thus, a campaign to promote the purchase of radials would need to convince consumers to delay economic gratification. Perhaps an increased emphasis on the safety advantages of steel-belted radials would promote an increase if consumers were provided with economical trade-in incentives. In fact, with at least one-sixteenth inch of tread remaining the radial tire can be retreaded to out-perform the standard bias-ply tire (see Kiefer, 1974).

Oil was not included among the municipal wastes categorized by Wahl and Allison (1975), but used oil is certainly a critical durable waste that can cause severe damage to environment and wildlife if discarded improperly and is an important target for resource recovery programs. For example, it has been estimated that Americans discard approximately 350 million gallons of motor oil per year that could be recovered and re-refined to save 1.3

million barrels of oil per day (Resource Technology, Inc., 1981). Resource Technology, Inc. is a Kansas-based corporation that has developed and put into operation a new technology for re-refining used oils. The outcome of this re-refining process is a base oil that is almost equivalent to virgin base oil and suitable for compounding into high quality lubricants. According to

Fig. 4.2. An advertisement poster to promote oil recycling. Will this prompt be sufficient to encourage large-scale oil recovery or will it be necessary to add incentive strategies?

Resource Technology, Inc. (1981), this process uses no chemicals or solvents and generates no hazardous wastes. However, this re-refining process requires large-scale cooperation of many individuals at the consumer, commercial, and government levels. Several behavioral strategies discussed in this chapter are relevant for the development of cost-effective programs for promoting oil recycling, and the potential targets for application are numerous (e.g., from individual car owners who could change their own oil for recycling, to gas station attendants and managers of vehicle fleets who discard large amounts of used oil daily). However, community programs for recycling oil are rare, and it is clear that research and development of promotional strategies are sorely needed in this area.

A recently introduced strategy for recovering durables that is particularly cost effective and in need of strategies for motivating behavioral input has been termed *highgrading* by the few agencies that have practiced the technique (Appelhof, 1980a; Gravino, 1981; Knapp, 1981). For example, in Lane County, Oregon, highgrade recyclers locate at the local landfill to recover and clean recyclable metals, including aluminum, cooper, brass, cast iron, and heavy steel. Cards distributed to landfill users which explained the metal recovery program were effective in prompting most individuals to keep metals separate from the rest of their trash and to drop them off in the "metals recovery area" adjacent to the landfill dump. During one ten-week period, two highgraders (each working an average of 24 hours per week) processed 15 tons of metals that met market requirements (Knapp, 1979). Another highgrading program at the landfill in Berkeley, California employs three to six full-time workers doing metal salvage, metal processing, and direct sales and as of July 1980 was producing from 100 to 150 tons of recyclable metal per month at values ranging from $5,000 to $7,000 (Appelhof, 1980a). Behavioral research is required for the development of this promising resource recovery technique; strategies for promoting communitywide highgrading need to be tested and the costs and benefits of highgrading evaluated.

Nondurable Wastes

A majority of the nondurables are paper-based materials (e.g., newspapers, magazines, tissues, towels, paper cups and plates) that can be used as a raw material for paper manufacturing (i.e., recycling) or burned as a fuel for energy production. Nondurable goods are also prime candidates for waste-reduction programs since many on the market could be replaced with reusables. Indeed, since reusable alternatives for nondurable throwaway commodities are still available (although in decreasing amounts), behavior motivation approaches to waste reduction could attempt to influence the purchase decisions of consumers. Here again the convenience of the throwaway is difficult to overcome, even when economics may favor the reusable. To avoid the inconvenience of washing cloth handkerchiefs, diapers and napkins, dishes and glasses, consumers make the more costly, negatively reinforced response of using paper tissues, disposable diapers, and paper napkins, cups and plates. And who wants to carry durable, reusable plates and cups to a picnic when a more effortless response is available? (The water and energy needed to wash certain reusables may be more costly than producing compatible disposables; this possibility demands rigorous field testing and extensive cost-effective analyses.)

It is noteworthy that attempts to promote the sale of paper dishware will often refer to safety and sanitation advantages over glass alternatives. For example, a mother in a 1979 television advertisement of Dixie Cups refers to the cuts that her child had received from broken glass, and how such accidents will be avoided by using paper drink containers. Of course, the viewer is not informed of the availability of safe, reusable plastic cups, nor of the energy waste and waste management problems caused by large-scale substitution of paper cups for plastic drink containers. Perhaps, advertisers should be required to indicate the environmental cost associated with their product. Alternatively (or in addition) it may be warranted to charge the manufacturer and the consumer for the waste-management costs of producing and purchasing nondurables that have durable substitutes. In certain cases it might then be possible to offer refunds for the return of durables to recycling centers.

Packaging Wastes

The major portion of municipal waste includes the cans, bottles, cartons, boxes, and wrappings in which consumer goods are transported and sold. "About 50% of the nation's paper, 8% of the steel, 75% of the glass, 40% of the aluminum, and 30% of the total plastics output are used solely to wrap and decorate consumer products . . . one dollar out of every $11 spent on groceries goes to packaging, which works out to $400 per year for the average family of four (Purcell, 1981, p. 54)." The unnecessary excess in packaging material is further demonstrated by the estimate that if the amount of packaging in the U. S. *per capita* would have been controlled at the 1958 level (the year that marked the beginning of the "packaging explosion"), the U.S. "would have saved more than 566 trillion BTUs, the equivalent of 267,000 barrels of oil each day . . . (Wahl & Allison, 1975, p. 24)."

Governmental controls certainly provide the greatest large-scale impact toward decreasing waste due to unnecessary packaging, but such regulatory litigation usually requires the vote or social pressure of the public. For example, to date public support has enabled governmental restriction of nonreturnable drink containers in eight states (i.e., Oregon, Vermont, South Dakota, Maine, Michigan, Iowa, Connecticut and Delaware) and local bottle regulations in more than 15 communities (e.g., Oberlin, Ohio and Bowie and Howard Counties, Maryland). One state (Minnesota) has enacted a law to regulate new package designs so that they maximize energy conservation and minimize detrimental impact on the environment (Wahl & Allison, 1975). Public support for packaging regulations may actually depend upon the development of community resource-conservation projects, and vice versa. Cooperating in one community waste-reduction or resource-recovery program may not only result in positive attitudes regarding that particular program, but may in fact increase the probability of behavioral and attitudinal support for additional efforts toward resource conservation and waste reduction. It is perhaps no coincidence that Oregon was the first state to ban the throwaway drink container in 1971, and since 1973 several large-scale, cost-effective, and energy efficient resource-recovery systems have been developed and tested in Portland, Oregon (Duncan, 1975, 1976a, 1976b, Seldman, 1975) and a city-wide plan has been adopted (Buel, 1977).

Simple life-style changes on a large scale could truly make a substantial difference. For example, "if 70 million American households bought one-half gallon of milk a week instead of two quarts, they would reduce paper discards by 41.6 million pounds and plastic discards by 5.7 million pounds per year. They would save $145.6 million in packaging, along with over 1 trillion Btu of energy, enough to heat and cool 7,500 households for an entire year (Purcell, 1981, p. 54)."

Food and Yard Waste

Food and yard waste comprise the largest proportion of municipal waste—about 36% in 1973 (Wahl & Allison, 1975). However, a low-technology approach is available for disposing of these wastes which "has the highest 'net energy' yield of all recycling processes (Duncan, 1976b, p. 32)." This strategy is composting, which consists essentially of stock-piling food and yard wastes and intermittently turning the compost pile to allow oxygenation. The resulting compost (available after three weeks under appropriate environmental conditions and at least biweekly turning) can be used to up-grade soil characteristics by: (1) improving workability for plowing and planting; (2) increasing water-holding capacity and thereby increasing resistance to erosion; (3) providing trace minerals and some nutrients; and (4) decreasing soil compactibility so that the soil is better aerated and gas exchange around plant roots is improved (Institute for Local Self-Reliance, 1975). Further, by improving general soil structure and returning organic material to the soil, composting in vegetable gardens has been shown to increase the quantity and nutritional quality of yields. For example, a nine-year study compared the nutrients in potatoes, rye, and oats harvested from composted plots with that from noncomposted (but fertilized) plots and demonstrated 9% more potassium, 6% more nitrogen, and 4% more phosphorous per harvested pound of vegetables in the composted garden (Tietzen & Hart, 1969).

Soil can be further improved for gardening with the addition of another low-technology procedure that has just recently been receiving serious attention. This procedure is termed vermicomposting and involves the maintenance of a worm bin (e.g., a 2 foot by 2 foot by 8 inch plywood box containing from one to two pounds of worms) in which residents dispose of their food wastes and from which they obtain humus-rich, nutrient-laden vermicompost. Combining vermicompost with soil or adding it to a compost pile of yard waste (grass, leaves, twigs, etc.) results in an almost optimal medium for plant growth. Details for building and maintaining bins for vermicomposting are presented elsewhere, and research is currently underway to make these procedures more convenient, efficient, and acceptable to the consumer (e.g., Applehof, 1974, 1979, 1980b). For example, Mary Appelhof and Cheryl Poche of Kalamazoo, Michigan, and Scott Geller have been studying the feasibility of maintaining a worm bin in the home kitchen where usage would be most convenient and cost effective. The results of their comprehensive survey of attitudes related to the concept of residential vermicomposting indicated that 39.1% of 744 respondents (including home owners, apartment renters, high school students, college students and faculty) would be willing to try operating a worm bin in their home. An additional 36.6% of this sample had some concerns about using worms to compost food waste, but would be willing to learn more about vermicomposting. A minority of the respondents (24.3%) indicated that they could not stand the thought of composting with worms. These investigators are currently studying the efficacy of several techniques for encouraging vermicomposting, from informative pamphlets to television prompting and modeling. So far the only effective strategy for motivating residents to build and maintain a residential worm bin has been a workshop that includes actual demonstrations of vermicomposting.

Appelhof, Poche, and Geller are currently deriving optimal procedures for building and maintaining a residential worm bin and are preparing an operations manual. At this point it is safe to say that the procedures recommended for successful vermicomposting are extremely cost effective and require: (1) a small initial financial investment for bin materials, worms and worm bedding; (2) half a day to prepare the household compost bin (e.g., a 2 foot by 2 foot by 8 inch plywood box containing from one to two pounds of worms); (3) ten minutes each week to bury food waste in the bin; and (4) two hours every four months to collect the vermicompost from the bin and apply fresh bedding (Appelhof, 1980b). As the worms multiply they can be added to the

WORMS EAT MY GARBAGE

M.F. FENTON

Fig. 4.3. A residential worm bin for food waste conserves energy, saves landfill space, and provides vermicompost and worms for upgrading gardening soil. Given these obvious benefits, what will it take to encourage large numbers of residents to try vermicomposting?

household garden or compost pile, but in some settings there is a high probability that a local fisherman will claim to have even a better use for these "extra" worms.

Composting and vermicomposting require relatively minimal response cost—not much more effort than bagging food and yard wastes weekly for

Fig. 4.4. Worms and vermicompost material from a worm bin maintained by one of the authors (SG). The bin was started in November, 1980, according to the guidelines presented herein; and so far (for more than eight months) it has handled *all* of the food waste from three adults and two children. In cold weather the bin was kept indoors (with absolutely no aversive odors). The bin was moved outside in warmer weather, and it is only slightly inconvenient to transport food waste daily to the outdoor location. The response-maintenance reinforcers have included the convenient availability of plant fertilizer and fishing worms, and special social attention (everyone wants to see the "innovative" worm bin!). Photo by Bob Veltri.

the garbage collector or piling and burning leaves. However, before composting will occur to any great extent, education programs are necessary to teach and promote the appropriate procedures for meeting health standards (e.g., relatively free of odors, seepage, rodents, and insects) and for minimizing financial costs, energy consumption, and individual effort. Household vermicomposting will require the application of special tactics to overcome initial negative reactions to bringing earthworms into one's home. One approach might be to introduce vermicomposting in school science classes and include the building and maintenance of vermicomposting bins as individual or group activity projects. Such a project would be educational and contribute to the development of a waste reduction and resource recovery ethic.

The city of Brookhaven encouraged neighborhood composting by: (1) distributing free booklets that described procedures for composting and listed advantages; (2) establishing local demonstration centers to model appropriate composting techniques; (3) initiating highway beautification projects that require compost for growing trees and shrubs; (4) soliciting the cooperative behaviors of boy and girl scouts; and (5) running "compost-pile-building" contests between scout troops (Franz, 1971). One feasible contingency that may be very effective in motivating composting in communities with garbage pickup service would be for sanitation departments to charge households for *each* garbage bag or can that is collected from the residence rather than for just the garbage pickup. Indeed, in Grand Rapids, Michigan, residents must purchase tags for their garbage bags from the Sanitation Department, and one householder reported that vermicomposting resulted in fantastic financial savings. Most beneficial was the outcome that garbage bags without food waste did not elicit aversive odors and could therefore remain in the home until completely filled (Appelhof, 1981).

BEHAVIORAL STUDIES OF WASTE REDUCTION AND RECYCLING

Most of the socio-behavioral research related to waste reduction and resource recovery has focused on correlating recycling-related behaviors to attitudes rather than determining community interventions for increasing waste reduction or recycling behaviors (see Hendee, 1971; Weigel, Woolston, & Gendelman, 1977). However, it is likely that focusing on attitude-behavioral relationships has less immediate applied value than focusing on environment-behavioral relationships. As discussed in Chapter 2, opinions regarding environmental litter have not been related to actual littering behaviors (e.g., Bickman, 1972; Heberlein, 1974; Robinson & Frisch, 1975); even when significant relationships are found between individual characteristics and environment-related behaviors, the applied relevance for the development of community recycling programs is often obscure. For example, a review of several recent attitude-behavioral studies* suggested that the participant in a community antilitter or recycling program is likely to be well educated (Arbuthnot, 1977; Weigel, 1978), concerned about environmental quality (Levenson, 1974; Steininger & Voegtlin, 1976; Weigel & Newman, 1976), liberal in social, economic and religious philosophies (Arbuthnot, 1977; Weigel, 1978), relatively high in occupational status (Weigel, 1978), and relatively pessimistic about the improvability of environmental quality (Levenson, 1973).

Such correlational data suggests that educating the public regarding environmental concerns may facilitate community involvement in recycling projects and that the cooperation of liberal, well-educated individuals at high

---

* All of these studies related attitudinal measurements to environmental cleanup or recycling. Many other investigators have attempted to correlate personality and demographic factors with environmental attitudes.

socioeconomic levels will be relatively easy to gain. However, considering environment-behavior rather than attitude-behavior correlations is probably more beneficial for determining ways to motivate public cooperation in community reclamation programs. The need to examine such behavioral research is especially critical because simple education and advertising procedures have been relatively unsuccessful in encouraging participation in paper-recycling programs (Couch et al., 1979; Geller et al., 1975; Hamad, Cooper, & Semb, 1977; Ingram & Geller, 1975; Witmer & Geller, 1976). For example, Geller and his students have shown that a successful paper recycling program requires the application of individual or group reinforcement contingencies, even when the potential participants are large numbers of college students who should be quite aware of environmental/ecological concerns (e.g., Geller et al., 1975; Ingram & Geller, 1975; Witmer & Geller, 1976).

Waste Reduction Interventions

Specific procedures for reducing waste at its source are numerous, including: the use of reusable rather than throwaway products (e.g., returnable rather than throwaway drink containers, plastic rather than paper cups and plates, cloth napkins and handkerchiefs rather than paper tissues), the restriction of packaging materials used in shipping and selling products, the purchase of used rather than new commodities (such as clothing from Goodwill Industries, a car part from the junk yard, or a retreaded tire), the purchase of longer lasting, safer steel-belted radial tires, the production of packages that can be used for additional purposes (e.g., glass containers that can serve as a drinking glass, drink-storage container, or a canning jar), the repair rather than replacement of inoperative appliances, and the remodeling rather than destruction of old homes.

However, waste *production* decisions usually have more immediate payoffs than waste *reduction* decisions in terms of response convenience or economics, and therefore the promotion of waste reduction will often require the application of contingencies that offer special rewards for waste reduction-strategies. For example, the large-scale waste reduction program implemented by the Red Owl food stores in six midwestern states provided monetary refunds when shoppers returned certain packaging materials for reuse, i.e., 2 cents per shopping bag, 3 cents per egg carton, and 4 cents per refillable milk container (see Green, 1975 for a more complete discussion of this "bring 'em back, repack and save" program).

Mandatory bottle-deposit legislation is the one waste reduction strategy that has received the most attention. Amidst much controversy, the first statewide "bottle bill" became effective in Oregon on October 1, 1972. The bill required every beer and soft-drink container sold or offered for sale in

Oregon to have a refund value of not less than 5 cents, and it forbade the sale of pull-tab drink containers (Savage & Richmond, 1974). The initial Vermont bottle bill (effective in September, 1973) also provided a minimum 5-cent deposit on all beer and soft drink containers. A subsequent revision in Vermont's beverage container law banned nonrefillable glass containers as of January 1, 1977 (Loube, 1975). Moreover, the Fall of 1976 marked the initiation of a regulation by the Environmental Protection Agency that all federal facilities (including national parks and forests) handle only beverage containers with a 5 cent deposit (Fowler, 1976), and in December 1978 a bottle bill similar to that of Oregon and Vermont was implemented in Michigan and Maine, except in Michigan the mandatory deposit is 10 rather than 5 cents (Dernbach, 1977; Environmental Action Foundation, 1976b).

Some people report "a riproaring success' for the mandatory deposit litigation (e.g., Ruvin, 1975; Savage & Richmond, 1974; Skinner, 1975; Waggoner, 1976), while others insist that the bottle bills have done more harm than good (e.g., King, 1975; Van Tine, 1975). Included among the reported benefits of the Oregon and Vermont bottle bills are: (1) a 65% reduction in beverage-container litter for both states (Loube, 1975; Skinner, 1975), and a 35% decrease in all litter categories in Oregon (Savage & Richmond, 1974); (2) a bottle-return rate above 90% and an average of 8 to 12 refills per bottle in Vermont (Loube, 1975), and as high as 18 refills per bottle in Oregon (Savage & Richmond, 1974); (3) an 81% reduction of container purchases by bottlers and brewers in Oregon, thereby reducing solid waste by 350 million containers (Waggoner, 1976); (4) increased public awareness of waste reduction and recycling issues and consumer acceptance for other resource recovery projects in Oregon (Bree, 1977); (5) a decrease in litter-related warnings and citations in Oregon (Bree, 1977; Waggoner, 1976); and (6) a more than 100% increase in human energy and a 50% decrease in environmental energy in the production of drink containers (Savage & Richmond, 1974).

Most of the reported negative ramifications of the bottle bills seem to reflect social and economical adjustments, and therefore may be only temporary. For example, in Vermont price increases during the first year of mandatory deposits ranged from 20 to 40 cents per case of soft drinks, and from 40 to 60 cents per case of beer (not counting the 5 cent-per-bottle deposit), and sales of soft drinks and beer declined significantly (Loube, 1975). Similar effects occurred in Oregon during 1972, but in 1973 (two years after the initiation of mandatory deposits) sales of soft drinks and beer regained the increasing trend shown throughout the ten years preceding the Oregon bottle bill (Savage & Richmond, 1974). While some skilled jobs were lost, there were other less skilled jobs added (e.g., warehouse sorters, truck loaders and drivers), and in fact a net increase in employment was reported for Oregon (Ruvin, 1975; Savage & Richmond, 1974). In addition, beverage-related, transportation costs increased substantially in Vermont, but they are apparently declining with the use of fewer container types and sizes (Loube, 1975).

The hassles of handling and storing returnables (and the associated potential health hazards) prevail as a negative outcome of the bottle legislation (Loube, 1975; Serrin, 1979). This disadvantage would be eliminated entirely at retail outlets with the adoption of a community resource recovery network (like the ORE Plan outlined by Duncan, 1976b), whereby residents leave empty returnable bottles with their garbage for pickup by recyclers who then deliver the returnables directly to bottlers for reuse. The consumers' bottle-deposit refunds could be subtracted from the cost of the garbage pick up.

The cost effectiveness of mandatory deposit legislation requires a careful, long-term examination of many variables that change with a large-scale shift from throwaways to returnables. However, the environmental/ecological advantages of the bottle bills have been overestimated by environmentalists and underestimated by industrialists. Environmentalists claim a net energy savings and substantial litter reductions from the reuse of drink containers, while industrialists argue that the litter counts are biased and nonrepresentative, and estimate that the extra costs to transport and sterilize reusable containers actually make throwaways more energy efficient than returnables. Thus, there is an urgent need for objective, unbiased data regarding the energy, litter, economic, and social consequences of banning the throwaway drink container. As of this writing, eight states had enacted laws to ban throwaways, indicating that opportunities are certainly available for evaluating objectively the short- and long-term costs and benefits of such litigation.

Field studies to influence grocery-store customers to purchase their soft drinks in returnable rather than throwaway containers represented the first systematic attempt to apply principles of behavioral analysis for waste reduction (Geller et al., 1971, 1973). For both of these investigations the dependent variable was the proportion of customers who selected returnable bottles for more than 50% of their soft-drink purchases. Frequency data for calculating daily proportions were recorded by behavioral observers posted at the stores' checkout counters. The basic intervention for both projects was a simple antecedent strategy where all customers entering the grocery store during the observation period were handed a one-page flyer that stated the desired response and listed reasons for the request.

Geller et al. (1971) used an ABA design to study the effectiveness of waste-reduction prompting in three supermarkets. At three grocery stores, baseline measurements were obtained during daily one-hour sessions for six consecutive weekdays (including Saturday), and then the prompting intervention was implemented during the same one-hour time period each weekday for two weeks. Follow-up data (with the intervention removed) was obtained immediately following treatment for six consecutive weekdays and then for one month after treatment for two consecutive weeks. A problem with this experiment (and with the follow-up study by Geller et al., 1973) was that the same individual's behavior could not be observed under different conditions, and therefore the actual frequency of individuals influenced by the environmental interventions could not be measured. As discussed in Chapter 2, one could consider that the milieu (in this case the grocery store) was the "organism" subjected to applied behavior analysis.

The results of this study showed prompting to have no consistent influence over the returnable bottle purchases at two large supermarkets (Krogers and Mick-or-Mack). However, in a small, quick-stop store (Seven Eleven) where customers often purchased only one drink, the proportion of drink customers who purchased more than 50% of their drinks in returnables was higher on each treatment day than the highest baseline or follow-up day (see Figure 2.1). The mean percentage increase in returnable-bottle customers at the Seven Eleven store was 32%. The authors' interpretation of the between-store differences was based on economic influence. That is, certain drinks were on sale each week in the larger supermarket (while sales never occurred in Seven Eleven), and drink customers were more apt to be influenced by money savings than by waste-reduction prompting. This interpretation was in fact supported by a finer data analysis that correlated the particular drink flavors selected with price fluctuations, and by unpublished research that was accomplished in preparation for the Geller et al. (1973) experiment. Regardless of their container, drinks that were reduced in cost for a particular week were consistently favored.

The follow-up study (Geller et al., 1973) took place at the quick-stop, Seven Eleven store where the prices of soft drinks were stable from week to week. Over a four-week period, six, two-hour experimental conditions were varied within weekdays (including Saturdays) according to a Latin Square design. More specifically, the customers' bottle purchases were recorded for a baseline condition and for the following independent prompting conditions (two hours each per day): (1) a college student gave incoming customers a handbill that urged the purchase of returnable bottles by appealing to specific antipollution advantages of returnable containers; (2) a student distributed the handbill and on a large obtrusive "Pollution Chart" adjacent to the entrance/exit door, another student publicly recorded each bottle customer as a returnable-bottle customer (i.e., purchasing more than 50% returnables) or a throwaway-bottle customer; (3) a student distributed the handbill while a five member, mixed-sex group charted the bottle customers as they exited the store; (4) a male student distributed the handbill and three male students did the charting; (5) a coed distributed the handbill while three coeds charted the bottle customers.

Each of the five antecedent strategies influenced approximately equivalent increases in the proportion of returnable-bottle customers. The weekly percentage of returnable-bottle customers during baseline ranged from about 50% to 75% with a mean of 60%, whereas under the prompting treatments the weekly percentages were never below 60% and reached highs of 90%.

The overall mean percentage increase in returnable-bottle customers during treatment was 22.2%. The variations of two-hour experimental conditions within 24 consecutive weekdays provided much more representative samples than those of the prior study and made it likely that the same drink customer would contribute data for more than one condition. Indeed, the results of 76 interviews conducted during the last week of the project showed that 26% of the customers shopped at the Seven Eleven store at least six times a week, and that 63% of the patrons shopped at the store one to five times per week. Given the likelihood that many persons were observed under different conditions throughout the 24 consecutive weekdays, it is probable that some individual behavior change was reflected by the treatment effects. Actually, the possibility of between-session generalization could have certainly masked differential treatment effects, but the crudeness of the dependent measure also limited the extent that differential effects of antecedent strategies could be detected. Perhaps a ratio of the number of returnables to the number of throwaways purchased per customer (rather than the simple "returnable" versus "nonreturnable" categorization) would have been sensitive to the variations in antecedent strategies.

Figure 4.5 illustrates a prompting strategy proposed by environmentalists for reducing excessive packaging and the sale of nonreturnable drink containers. Thus, if containers were marked according to ease of recycling and if customers responded appropriately to influence increased demands for refillable or recyclable containers, it is likely that the packaging practices of manufacturers would be modified in environment-protective directions. To our knowledge this labelling technique has not yet been applied on a large scale and evaluated with regard to impact on consumers, manufacturers, and waste management. However, the studies reviewed above by Geller et al. (1971, 1973) suggest that the prompting strategy would influence a substantial number of purchase decisions *if* certain other powerful determinants of product selection were controlled (e.g., price, utility, and convenience). If implemented on a large scale, such a strategy would at least increase awareness of waste reduction issues and perhaps set the occasion for environment preserving decisions when other conditions, such as response consequences, are appropriate to motivate behavior change.

Waste Recovery Interventions

Although the market for wastepaper has traditionally been unstable and incentives are not yet available for encouraging major paper mills to use secondary paper on a regular basis (Smith, 1975), wastepaper has been the most frequent target for waste recovery programs. This may be the case for a number of reasons, including the facts that: (1) paper is the most convenient recyclable to separate from trash; (2) the abundance of recyclable paper in

Why Buy Trash When You Have A Choice?

Many product containers are costly to recycle.
Watch for these symbols on the shelves.
They will help you choose your containers wisely.

Refillable   **Recyclable**   **Costly to recycle**

Fig. 4.5. A prompting strategy that could have waste reduction benefits if implemented on a large scale.

households and institutions can make even relatively small-scale projects profitable; and (3) the environmental benefits from recycling paper are obvious. Recycling paper conserves energy (since secondary paper requires 60% less energy than virgin material to produce paper), reduces air pollution (since secondary paper emits 60% less air pollutants than virgin materials), saves landfill space by diverting significant portions of solid wastes from municipal garbage, and helps to preserve our forests (Environmental Action Foundation, 1977a).

Most of the behavioral research related to resource recovery has targeted paper recycling. To our knowledge, Geller et al. (1975) published the first account of a systematic attempt to analyze the behavioral effects of particular interventions designed to facilitate a paper recycling program. Three experimental conditions, lasting two weeks each, were alternated within three pairs of university dormitories according to a Latin Square design. The following conditions were varied so that each two-week condition occurred once for each dorm pair and at each of the three possible sequential positions (i.e., first, second, and third): (1) *baseline*—large, colorful posters tacked to bulletin boards announced the location of a Paper Collection Area (PCA) in the dormitory; (2) *contest*—$15 was awarded the dormitory of the pair (males vs. females) that delivered the most recyclable paper per capita in one week. A sign on the door to the PCA displayed the specifics of this contingency, including the two-hour period each day when deliveries would be tallied for the contest; (3) *raffle*—a numbered ticket for one chance in a weekly raffle of prizes donated by local town merchants was given for each delivery of at least one 8½ by 11 inch sheet of paper or cardboard. The rules for this contingency were posted on the door to the PCA, as was a list of the four prizes that were to be raffled off in the evening of the upcoming Friday.

The results of this study demonstrated a consistent advantage of extrinsic reinforcement contingencies: the contest and raffle contingencies were almost equivalently effective in markedly increasing program participation over baseline levels. The total pounds of paper delivered per experimental condition were 845 for baseline, 1,420 for the contest, and 1,515 for the raffle. The percentage of resident participation was consistently greater during the contest and raffle interventions than during baseline, but was lower than expected and desired during all conditions. The mean percent of dormitory residents who delivered at least one 8½ by 11 inch sheet of paper to the collection room over a one-week period was 2.2% for baseline, 3.9% for the contest, and 7.3% for the raffle. Geller et al. suggested that the low participation rates were due to ineffective antecedent strategies (i.e., response priming) rather than weak reinforcement contingencies. In other words, relatively few residents may have attended to bulletin-board announcements, and therefore a majority of the residents may have been unaware of the recycling program.

A follow-up to the Geller et al. study was accomplished one year later in different dormitories and attempted to refine the antecedent intervention of the earlier study with the personal distribution of flyers to each dormitory room (Ingram & Geller, 1975). More specifically, as a verbal prompt condition, a "prompt distributor" knocked on the resident's door, handed the resident a flyer that urged paper recycling and specified the location of the

PCA, and then said: "I would just like to remind you of the paper drive being held Monday through Friday from 5:30 to 7:30 in the basement." During a subsequent raffle condition the verbal prompt and flyer included a description of the raffle contingency (see Figure 4.6).

A noteworthy change in this follow-up experiment was the definition of the raffle contingency. Geller et al. (1975) rewarded each delivery of at least one 8½ by 11 inch sheet of paper to the collection room with a raffle coupon. This contingency resulted in some residents undermining the system by stacking their paper outside of the door to the collection room and then repeatedly delivering individual sheets of paper to the data recorder, receiving a raffle ticket for each delivery. The raffle contingency in the Ingram and Geller study did not encourage such repeated deliveries to the collection room since participants received one raffle ticket for each pound of recyclable paper delivered.

The results of the Ingram and Geller study were quite similar to those of Geller et al., suggesting that reinforcement contingencies are necessary for even minimal participation in a recycling program. The raffle contingency increased the percentage of resident participation as well as the pounds of paper collected, but as in the Geller et al. study, the frequency of dorm residents who delivered at least one sheet of recyclable paper to the collection center per week was discouragingly low. Similar results were shown in a third study (i.e., Witmer & Geller, 1976) which compared personal prompting with a raffle condition as implemented by Ingram & Geller (1975) and with a contest similar to that used by Geller et al. (1975).

Likewise, on another university campus in Virginia (James Madison University) Couch et al. (1979) observed prominent increases in paper deliveries at two dormitories as a result of a raffle contingency. The total weight of paper delivered to the two collection rooms was only 134 pounds during the first baseline week, averaged 763.7 pounds each week throughout the six weeks of the raffle intervention, and decreased to 240 pounds for the last week of the project when the raffle contingency had been removed. Throughout the entire eight-week experiment only 27% of the residents delivered some recyclable paper to the dorm collection room.

For each of the paper-recycling projects by Geller and his students, the raffle contingency was slightly more effective than the contest in encouraging program participation, suggesting an advantage to rewarding individuals rather than groups, at least when the group is large. Also notable is the cost effectiveness of the raffle and contest contingencies. The contest cost only $15 a week per dorm pair, and the raffle prizes were donated by community merchants for the publicity accompanying their support of a community ecology project. In fact, as a result of the three projects store managers were approached on 71 occasions for donations of raffle prizes and 60 of those requests (84.5%) resulted in a contribution of at least one raffle prize,

SAVE TREES

RECYCLE YOUR PAPER

WHERE : In Basement (Student Storage)
WHEN : 5:30 – 7:30 (Mon. thru Fri.)
Receive 1 Raffle Coupon Per 1 lb. Paper
Prizes This Week : $10.⁰⁰ Gift Certificate
from The Flower Box, Necklace from
Dickerson's, Assorted Bath Goods from
Frog Hollow, 2 Subs from Mr. Fooz.

Fig. 4.6. The flyer used by Ingram and Geller (1975) to announce a raffle contingency for rewarding the delivery of newspapers to a certain paper collection area.

amounting to a grand total of 74 prizes ranging widely in value from $1 to $30 and in kind (e.g., among the donated prizes were a pitcher of beer, a styled haircut, a bicycle rack, a wall poster, a submarine sandwich, a bottle of cologne, a record album, a steak dinner, and a sleeping bag). Furthermore, six different newspaper stories reported aspects of the paper drives throughout the two-year period. All contributing merchants were mentioned at least once, and on several occasions a picture of a store manager handing a prize to a raffle winner appeared in the newspaper. These examples demonstrate the potential community cooperation available if appropriate contingencies are implemented. The only real cost is the time and effort of people to organize, implement, and evaluate such large-scale, contingency management procedures.

The number of students who participated in the four university recycling programs described above was disappointingly low under all conditions. These results certainly suggest that university dormitories are inappropriate environments from which to run a paper recycling program, perhaps because the average dorm resident does not attend to poster or handbill announcements, because meagerly reinforced recycling behaviors are too inconvenient to fit into the busy daily routine of the average college student, or because the supply of recyclable paper per dorm resident is perceived as too minimal to make paper deliveries worthwhile.

These disadvantages of a university paper recycling program were less critical when a paper recycling contest was implemented and evaluated at an apartment complex (Reid, Luyben, Rawers, & Bailey, 1976). A "recycling box" was located in the laundry rooms of three apartment complexes during baseline and a handwritten sign on each laundry room wall identified the recycling box. The proximity and prompt condition had two components and was initiated at three apartment complexes at different times from the start of the 110-day study (i.e., after 20, 32, and 61 days). The proximity component of this intervention involved the distribution of two additional recycling containers (with identifying signs) adjacent to garbage dumpsters located in the parking lot for each complex. Prompting involved a verbal explanation of the newspaper recycling boxes during door-to-door interviews with the residents. The results indicated prominent and consistent increases in pounds of newspaper collected as a result of the proximity and prompt procedure. For example, at one apartment complex (72 residences) the mean pounds of paper collected daily increased from 7.91 during baseline to 16.48 pounds during the proximity and prompt intervention. These daily means were 9.16 versus 14.14 pounds at another apartment complex (48 residences) and 5.59 versus 8.99 pounds at the third complex (64 residences). An obvious advantage of this study, compared to other paper-recycling programs, was the small amount of maintenance labor.

A paper-recycling project implemented by Luyben and Bailey (1979) applied a positive reinforcement procedure unlike those reviewed earlier. For a baseline condition, these researchers placed a large plywood box at the entrance to each of four trailer parks in Tallahassee, Florida, that conveyed the message "Please recycle newspapers here." After four weeks of baseline at one trailer court and seven weeks of baseline at another, a prize and prompt intervention was initiated. This intervention involved the following procedures: (1) mounting a poster in the park's laundromat and distributing a flyer to each mobile home that announced the beginning of a "Newspaper Recycling Reward Program" for children in the trailer park; (2) distributing a registration card with each flyer that parents were requested to sign in order to give permission for their child to participate in the reward program; (3) driving a "recycling vehicle" to the park at 7:00 p.m. on designated collection days, weighing child-delivered newspapers, and then offering participants their choice of a toy within a particular price range. The price range was dependent upon how much paper the child had delivered: a toy selection from a 10- to 20-cent category for two pounds of paper, and a selection from a 30- to 50-cent category for eight pounds of paper. As a result of the prize and prompt intervention, the average pounds of newspapers collected per week increased from 242 during baseline to 616 pounds at one trailer park and from 132 to 212 pounds at the second trailer park. Removal of the prize and prompt condition after eight weeks resulted in returns to the lower baseline levels at each trailer court.

The prize and prompt procedure administered by Luyben and Bailey was analogous to the intervention previously used by other researchers for motivating children to gather litter from environments (e.g., Burgess et al., 1971; Chapman & Risley, 1974; Clark et al., 1972), and suffered from a weakness that also plagued these antilitter studies. The antilitter contingencies that gave children inexpensive rewards for bags of litter set the occasion for the undesirable behaviors of filling litter bags from sources of already collected litter (as discussed in Chapter 3). Rewarding children for used newspapers could have similarly resulted in the collection of unused newspapers from front yards or porches before they were retrieved by residents. It is also conceivable that such a contingency could work against waste reduction by influencing some children to nag their parents and friends to buy "extra" newspapers that would not normally be purchased. An additional undesirable side effect could have occurred as a result of the Luyben and Bailey price-scaling procedure that offered a more expensive toy for more paper. Specifically, this contingency could have promoted the accumulation of recyclable newspapers in children's trailers (perhaps with parental annoyance) until the pile was high enough to permit selection from among the most expensive toys. Hence, a simple positive reinforcement procedure can encourage a variety of undesirable behaviors; such behaviors may not be anticipated prior to program implementation and must therefore receive attention during continual program evaluation.

Hamad et al. (1977) organized a paper recycling contest in a public school (Grades 1 to 6), where a coupon redeemable for a hamburger was given to each participating student in the classroom that collected the most paper in 3½ weeks. The contest contingency was then dropped for two weeks, but the paper drive was still in effect as announced in class and on written memos given to the pupils to take home with them. During the initial contest, 11,254 pounds of paper were delivered to the collection site (a garage adjacent to the school grounds), but only 292 pounds of recyclable paper were delivered after the contest was dropped. When the contest contingency was reinstated for two weeks, 3,044 pounds of paper were collected. During the next two weeks when verbal appeals were given in class, but no extrinsic rewards were offered, the total collected paper was only 500 pounds. During the two contests *only*, daily feedback of the paper collected by each classroom was displayed on a thermometer-type scale in a hallway of the school. Thus, the contest included *two* major changes from the baseline or verbal prompt condition: a group competition and public feedback. Either one or both of these components was necessary in affecting the behavioral differences. The authors reported that 136 of the 271 potential participants (about 50%) delivered paper at least once, but they did not give participation rates per experimental condition.

The rate of participation and the quantity of paper collected were markedly greater in the Hamad et al. program than in any of the documented paper-recycling studies that had been established in college dormitories (see Couch et al., 1979; Geller et al., 1975; Ingram & Geller, 1975; Witmer & Geller, 1976). At least two factors contributed to this difference, and each should certainly be considered when developing recycling programs. First, it is probable that more elementary pupils than college students became aware of the recycling program implemented by Hamad et al., because in the elementary school prompting occurred in classrooms where the children were more or less a "captive audience." Further, the parents of the grade school pupils were prompted to join the recycling effort when the written memos reached their intended destination. Perhaps the factor contributing most to the superiority of paper recycling in an elementary school versus a college dormitory was that a much greater source of recyclable paper was tapped with the elementary school program. The supply of paper materials is usually substantially higher in a child's home than in a dormitory room. The university programs would have collected more paper if they had targeted more plentiful sources for recyclable paper, such as faculty and administrative offices, publication services, and computer centers. This was indeed the case in the program developed by Humphrey, Bord, Hammond, & Mann (1977), which is summarized later in this chapter.

The relatively high rate of participation in the Hamad et al. study compared with other recycling programs that attempted to motivate participation with a contest may be partially attributed to a critical distinction between the contest contingency defined by Hamad et al. and that by Geller et al. and Witmer and Geller. For both contingencies the reward was dependent upon the performance of the whole group, but the Hamad et al. contest involved an individual component not usually included in group contingencies. Only those pupils who delivered at least one sheet of paper to the collection site received the reward *if* their class won the contest. The dormitory contests administered by Geller and his students awarded the whole dormitory $15, and the dormitory to collect the most recyclable paper was the one whose residents specified a method for spending the contest winnings. Every resident in the winning dorm was permitted to enjoy the group reward (i.e., beer) which was purchased with the winnings. More contest participation might indeed have occurred in the dormitories if the contest contingency had been more like that defined by Hamad et al., so that only those residents who made a paper delivery could indulge in the beer drinking.

An important aspect of the Hamad et al. study was a cost-benefit analysis of their program that collected 7.5 tons of recyclable paper. Cost-benefit analyses should become standard procedure in the evaluation of waste-management programs. The authors considered four components in their analysis: (1) revenue from the sale of reclaimed materials = $148.42 earned, at approximately $20 per ton; (2) reduced solid waste = $166.00 saved, considering a national cost of $22 per ton for collecting, transporting, and disposing of solid waste (Environmental Protection Agency, 1974); (3) energy from the reuse of materials = $101.15 saved if the paper were burned as fuel, or $147.00 saved if the recycled fibers replaced virgin wood pulp in manufacturing paper; and (4) natural resource savings = the utility of not depleting natural resources for energy and/or product manufacturing. Weighing the first three benefits against the costs of the hamburgers ($47.24) and the 153 miles of truck transportation ($30.60), results in a net monthly gain of $337.72 for the short-term paper drive. However, the costs of managing the paper-collection center (53.5 hours) and transporting the paper to school (which the authors did not specify) must be considered in a complete cost-benefit analysis. Furthermore, it is noteworthy that the benefits were received by different parties and that the program participants actually contributed more costs than they reaped for themselves.

The cost of transporting the paper to the school by a "special" trip with a motor vehicle was a noteworthy energy cost for the Hamad et al. project. In fact, one of the two days the collection garage was open each week was Saturday, and therefore it is possible that a high percentage of the total 240 car or truck deliveries involved a transportation cost that served no other purpose but to deliver paper. Such energy costs for special transportation could be eliminated if the collection center were only open when parents normally drive their children to school, or better yet if contingencies were contrived to encourage children to carry small amounts of recyclable paper with them when walking to school each morning. Indeed, an advantage of developing recycling programs in public schools is that recyclable materials, readily available in the home, can ride "piggyback" with students without contributing extra transportation costs.

One year following the initial Hamad et al. study, these authors conducted a second study at the same elementary school which did not promote special automobile trips for paper deliveries (Hamad, Bettinger, Cooper, & Semb, 1979). Specifically, two large plywood boxes labeled "Newspaper Recycling" were placed at the school entrance and locked shut except during the collection period from 8:00 to 8:30 a.m. each school day. Since school began at 8:30 a.m., this collection procedure set the occasion for paper deliveries without extra transportation costs. Hamad et al. (1979) measured pounds of paper and frequency of participation during seven conditions, sequenced below:

1. *Baseline 1* (approximately nine weeks)—Students took home a memo from the school principal which detailed the paper collection times, indicated that proceeds would be donated to the school PTA, and encouraged participation.
2. *Public Feedback* (approximately six weeks)—A poster publicly displayed the cumulative pounds of paper contributed by each of the eleven classrooms. A small emblem of a tree was stamped next to each thermometer-type scale whenever 120 pounds of paper was collected. It has been estimated that 120 pounds of recyclable paper saves one tree from being cut down (NARI, 1973).
3. *Baseline 2* (approximately three weeks)—The feedback sign was removed.
4. *Goal Setting* (three weeks)—Students took home a second memo from the principal which introduced a school-wide collection goal of 20,000 pounds within the next three weeks, urged that each student bring some recyclable paper to school every day and aim for individual goals of 120 pounds for the next three-week period, and explained that the money collected during this period would be used to ,purchase small trees for those students who requested them. [The individual goal amounted to an average of eight pounds of paper per student per day, and therefore was probably unrealistic.]
5. *Baseline 3* (approximately three weeks)—Same as Baseline 2, except that small trees were given to students upon request on the first day.
6. *Self-recording* (approximately two weeks)—A chart for recording individual participation was distributed to each of the eleven classrooms, and every class roster included an announcement of the group contingency that an extra ten minutes of recess would be awarded the class if at least 75% of the students delivered at least one newspaper on seven of the next nine days.
7. *Baseline 4* (approximately one week)—Same as Baseline 2, except that on the first day the principal announced which classes had met the criterion for extra recess.

The large amount of paper collected by this recycling program by Hamad et al. (19,749 pounds in eight months) demonstrates the cost efficiency of using public schools and "piggy-back" deliveries for the recycling of resources used in the home (e.g., newspapers, aluminum and glass containers). However, the comparisons between experimental conditions resulted in some unexpected and·equivocal findings. Specifically, the feedback condition resulted in a mean of 157 pounds of paper per collection day, which was a decrease of approximately 50% from the mean across all baseline periods of 235 pounds. Increases above baseline were shown for the goal-setting and self-recording conditions (i.e., mean pounds per collection day of 366 and 296, respectively). Participation was markedly greatest during self-recording (i.e., 30% of the students participated compared to a mean of 2% participation for all other conditions), although only one class met the criterion for extra recess. Several factors could have contributed to the relatively low effects of the author's interventions. For example, the decline in paper deliveries from Baseline 1 to Feedback may have been due to a decline in student, parent, and/or teacher interest following the initial prompt (i.e., memo) from the principal. A dissipation of the novelty of having a school paper drive may have also attributed to a decline in participation. Of course, it is also possible and even probable that the students did not attend to the feedback thermometers, since there was no reinforcement contingency in effect. Further, the goal-setting intervention specified a somewhat unrealistic individual goal (eight pounds of delivered paper per student per day) and added a reward component (a small tree upon request) which was not contingent upon paper deliveries. Finally, a critical weakness of the self-recording intervention was an absence of a system for monitoring the students' daily recording of their participation in the recycling program.

The cost-benefit analysis by Hamad et al. (1979) indicated a net gain of $237.65, when the benefits to both the program participants and society as a whole were included in the calculations. The total cost of the program was estimated at $187.50, which included $41.20 for transporting the paper for resale, $25.00 for the trees distributed during the goal-setting condition, and $111.30 for labor. The benefit of $425.18 was the sum of $205.18 which was received from the sale of the newspapers and the estimate of $220.00 saved by preventing the newspapers from entering the solid waste stream. Another potential benefit not included in the author's monetary calculations is the reduced energy use when recycled paper rather than wood pulp is used to manufacture paper. Indeed, such a savings has been estimated at 13 million Btu of energy per ton of recycled paper (Hunt & Franklin, 1972). Furthermore, an extremely valuable (yet intangible) asset of school recycling programs is the impact on subsequent attitudes and behaviors of the participants. Indeed, personal involvement in a recycling program should not only increase awareness of conservation measures, but should also increase the probability of future conservation action.

The paper recycling program by Humphrey et al. (1977) demonstrated an approach to paper recycling that may be the most cost-effective, wastepaper-collection system that an average community could implement. The basic approach is cost effective on two counts. It is workable at large institutions such as schools, hospitals, industrial plants, and government buildings where large numbers of individuals may be readily organized for program partici-pation, the sources for recyclable waste paper are plentiful, and the target is to recover high-grade rather than mixed paper. Compared to mixed paper, the monetary return for high-grade paper is much higher (from $50-100 per ton in 1976), and the market is more stable (Environmental Action Founda-tion, 1977a).

The ten-week wastepaper recovery program studied by Humphrey et al. essentially involved workers in administrative offices separating high-grade wastepaper as it was generated. The efficacy of three relatively effortless methods of separating office wastepaper were compared: (1) using two per-sonal wastebaskets, one for resalvageable paper and the second for other waste; (2) using a divided wastebasket with one section for recyclable paper and the other for non-recyclable disposables; and (3) using one personal wastebasket for recyclable paper and a centrally located, public receptacle for non-recyclable paper and other disposables.

The program was initiated in 16 experimental areas of a large state univer-sity with a letter to all potential participants requesting cooperation in a waste-separation project. For half of the experimental areas, the department head or office supervisor contacted each program participant on two occa-sions to inquire about problems with the system and to encourage continued participation. The dependent variable was the quality of the contents in the recyclable containers as determined by weighing the recyclable and non-recyclable material and then calculating the percent of recyclable paper per container.

Overall, 90% of the material discarded in the recycle container was sal-vageable wastepaper. The less convenient, central-can procedure resulted in 83.6% recyclable wastepaper in the office trash cans, a significantly poorer quality return than either the two-wastebasket or divided-wastebasket pro-cedure which gave 92.3% and 92.7% recyclable paper, respectively. For each separation procedure the weekly percentages indicated a rather consistent deterioration in the quality of wastepaper separation over time, with a marked increase in quality during Weeks 3 and 7 when the personal prompts were given in 50% of the experimental areas. However, the extent of the prompting effects cannot be realized since the authors did not separate the weekly quality-percentages for the prompt and no prompt conditions. How-ever, the authors did report a slightly higher overall separation quality for the group that received the personal prompts (i.e., 92.5% versus 88.0%).

Unfortunately Humphrey et al. did not indicate the pounds of salvageable paper collected nor the amount of money received from selling the paper, so that the cost effectiveness and environmental impact of their program cannot be determined. However, the program represents a practical model for a straightforward and economical procedure of tapping a copious source of high-quality wastepaper. The participants in this study did suggest that the program would be improved if a more detailed list of recyclable and non-recyclable materials were distributed, and if the trash can for recyclable materials were obtrusively marked. Given the steady decline in separation quality, other program refinements should include at least a more systematic procedure of prompting program participation, and should perhaps also incorporate an individual or group contingency to reinforce the quality and/or quantity of wastepaper-separation responses.

An additional improvement in the office, paper-separation program implemented by Humphrey et al. would be to make the separation process more convenient and contamination less convenient. The "desk-top container" system recommended by EPA represents such an improvement (Environmental Action Foundation, 1977a). Each participant (e.g., office worker) is given a small 14 cubic inch, desk top container which holds a one- to three-week accumulation of high-grade, recyclable paper. When the container is full, the participant deposits the contents in a large, centrally located container. Such a system has been operating at EPA's headquarters in Washington, D.C. since November 1975, and currently involves about 2,700 individuals recycling 12.5 tons of high-grade paper per month. During the first year of operation EPA recovered 150 tons of high-grade paper and earned $11,000.

The incredibly low contamination rate for the desk-top container system (only 3%) is at least partially due to convenience. Not only is the special desk-top receptacle convenient for depositing used, high-grade office paper, but it is also inconvenient (or sometimes impossible) to use for non-recyclable paper and other disposables. Shade Information Systems, Inc., the company that has manufactured and promoted the desk-top container system since the summer of 1972 currently handles more than 400 accounts with a variety of private businesses, universities and government agencies that return over 750 tons of paper each month. Included among these accounts is the National Bureau of Standards which boasts a participation rate of 95% (out of 1,400 employees) and a recovery rate of 32%—a savings of $2,400 in disposable costs each year (Environmental Action Foundation, 1977a).

It is unfortunate that at the time of this writing only three behavioral studies had systematically studied the impact of behavior change strategies on the recycling of beverage containers. Defining the components of a cost-effective program for promoting the reuse or recycling of drink containers is particularly worthwhile for environment preservation. Containers for beer and soft drinks account for about half of all beverage and food containers sold in the United States, including packaging for meats, milks, cheese, vegetables, and candy (Hannon, 1973), and there are many environmental settings where procedures for recycling beverage containers are applicable. Consider further that the recycling of aluminum drink containers uses a twentieth of the energy required to produce aluminum cans from virgin ore and results in substantially less pollution of air and water (Purcell, 1981).

Luyben et al. (1980) evaluated can-recycling behaviors in university dormitories under two different experimental conditions. Throughout the entire 11-week study, a 23-gallon container bearing the message "Please Recycle Cans Here" was located adjacent to the soda vending machines in the main lounge of four undergraduate dormitories. In addition, a large sign which read "Please Recycle Cans" was posted on the soda vending machine of each dorm. Once per week a flyer urging the recycling of beverage cans and specifying the location of the dorm's recycling container was placed in each of the residents' mailboxes. These were the components of a "single container" condition. After varying periods of exposure to the single container condition, a "multiple container" condition was initiated at three of the four dorms according to a multiple baseline paradigm. For this intervention, five additional recycling containers and several additional posters were distributed throughout the dormitory.

Each day the number of steel (soda) and aluminum (beer) cans were collected from each recycling container and counted. The weekly record of recyclable cans collected showed prominent effects of the multiple container intervention. The weekly frequencies of aluminum cans are depicted in Figure 2.3 of Chapter 2 as an example of a multiple baseline design. Analogous results were found for steel cans. During the single container condition, the average number of cans collected per week at the three dorms where the multiple container condition was eventually implemented was 130 for steel and 49 for aluminum. the multiple container condition augmented these weekly averages to 165 for steel cans (an average increase of 11.7%) and to 128 for aluminum cans (a 25.7% average increase). The successive introduction of the multiple container condition (i.e., the multiple baseline design) showed that the increases in recyclable beverage containers was due to the intervention and not to seasonal changes in beverage consumption.

Thus, the outcome of the Luyben et al. study was consistent with newspaper recycling studies reviewed earlier, showing that substantial numbers of people will use a group recycling container (Hamad et al., 1979; Humphrey et al., 1977) and that such recycling behaviors will increase prominently if recycling containers are added to the milieu in order to reduce response cost (Luyben & Bailey, 1979; Reid et al., 1979). It is noteworthy that the single container condition resulted in substantial collections of recyclable cans (e.g., as much as 23% of all steel cans sold in the vending machine) and in some situations could be more cost effective than a multiple container procedure. For example, Luyben et al. reported that to be cost effective, the can-collection procedures should be incorporated into the regular assignment of the maintenance staff. This might actually be more feasible with a system more analogous to the single rather than multiple container condition of the Luyben et al. study.

Arbuthnot, Tedeschi, Wayner, Turner, Kressel, and Rush (1977) observed that prompting might be effective in encouraging relatively inconvenient participation in a community recycling program *if* the intervention procedure also included effective prompting of more convenient, recycling-related behaviors. Specifically, these investigators administered the following three antecedent conditions to individuals in Athens, Ohio, who were not participating in the community recycling program: (1) a door-to-door *survey* wherein graduate students interviewed residents regarding their knowledge of recycling issues; (2) an *appeal* condition immediately following the survey, wherein the residents were given a handout of helpful recycling hints and a plastic bag with which to save recyclable cans for one week; and (3) a *letter* condition, wherein individuals were sent a letter two weeks after the appeal condition which described the benefits of a communitywide recycling program, and included a request that the recipients mail an enclosed postcard to their city council representative in order to indicate their positive or negative attitudes toward expanding recycling programs in their community. Residents in a "Three-Step" group received each of these antecedent conditions; residents in three "Two-Step" groups received one of the three possible pairs of conditions (i.e., survey and appeal, survey and letter, or appeal and letter), residents in three "One-Step" groups were given only one of the antecedent conditions; a control group received none of the antecedent interventions.

The dependent variable in the Arbuthnot et al. study was the percentage of compliant subjects in each experimental condition who reported participating in the community recycling program one to two months and 18 months after the prompting intervention(s). Unfortunately, program participation was assessed via a "disguised telephone survey" and not with observations of actual recycling-related behaviors. The results showed that the probability of an individual reporting participation in the Athens recycling program was directly related to the number of prior prompts received *and* followed. For example, 87.5 percent of the 28 individuals who complied with the survey, appeal, and letter prompts reported participation in the recycling program one to two months after treatments. The reported participation rates were as follows for the compliant subjects in the other conditions: 80.0% of 23 individuals for the appeal and letter condition, 32.0% of 25 for survey and appeal, 20.0% of 28 for survey and letter, 8.3% of 24 for appeal alone, 0.0%

of 24 for letter alone, 5.9% of 34 for survey alone, and 0.0% of 22 for the control group. Practically the same participation percentages were reported 18 months after treatment.

The authors reported that 19 individuals refused to respond to the survey (14%), but did not report any other participation rates. It would have been valuable to know what percentage of the individuals contacted and prompted in each condition saved cans in the distributed bags and/or wrote a town council member about recycling. Apparently the authors overlooked such fine analyses of the participation rates because their study was really not designed as a behavioral analysis of participation in a community recycling project, but as an attempt to demonstrate a field application of the Freedman and Fraser (1966) "foot-in-the-door" principle (i.e., that compliance with an initial small request will increase the probability of compliance with a subsequent, more effortful request). However, the authors' conclusion that compliance with three recycling-related requests produced participation in the community recycling program is not necessarily valid. Instead, it is reasonable to assume that those individuals who were most likely to comply with a prompt to participate in a recycling program were also those who were most apt to comply with the prior request for recycling-related activity. In this regard, the multiple prompting technique was successful in selecting those individuals who would most likely emit relatively inconvenient behaviors in support of a community recycling project.

The thesis and dissertation of Harvey E. Jacobs at Florida State University (under the supervision of Jon S. Bailey) represents the most comprehensive behavioral analysis of residential resource recycling conducted to date. For his masters thesis (Jacobs, 1978), Jacobs studied strategies for increasing newspaper recycling among 700 residences in Tallahassee, Florida. The observation "sessions" were the first and third Saturday each month and consisted of driving by each of the households and collecting any newspapers or cans placed outside for recycling pickup. The dependent variable was the percentage of homes participating per session for each of five experimental groups defined below. Each group consisted of from 86 to 147 households.

1. *Information Only.* A flyer was delivered to the household every other week for eight weeks notifying the residents of the scheduled pickup of newspapers and aluminum cans and specified participation procedures.
2. *Penny-a-Pound.* The information flyer included a specification of the contingency that on the day following the collection, the participant would be paid a penny for each pound of newspaper.
3. *Lottery.* The information flyer included the definition of a variable person ratio contingency of reinforcement whereby each participant became eligible for a $5.00 prize which was drawn randomly from each session's participating households and distributed on the day following the collection.

4. *Weekly Pickup*. The information flyer specified a weekly collection of recyclable newspapers and cans, rather than the less frequent, biweekly collection for the other groups.

5. *Control*. Data was recorded from one group of residences who received no special information pamphlet nor any other experimental manipulation.

Each experimental group consisted of from 86 to 147 residences, and each experimental intervention was preceded by four baseline sessions (i.e., eight weeks). Furthermore, ten months prior to the start of the study all of the households had been notified of a biweekly collection service for recyclable paper and cans. It is noteworthy that the penny-a-pound condition rewarded only newspaper recycling, whereas the lottery condition apparently included an incentive for collecting both newspapers and aluminum cans.

The percentage of households leaving recyclable materials for collection was quite low for each observation session and experimental group, but relative to the controls, each treatment intervention influenced a significant increase in participation. More specifically, the average percent participation during baseline was 2.8% for information only, 4.1% for penny-a-pound, 2.9% for lottery, 3.4% for weekly pickup, and 1.1% for the control, while mean participation during treatment increased to 8.3% for information only, 9.0% for penny-a-pound, 14.2% for lottery, 8.8% for weekly pickup, and 2.0% for control. Although these changes indicate percentages increases of 193%, 120%, 390% and 193% for the information only, penny-a-pound, lottery, and weekly pickup, respectively, the mean amount of recyclable newspapers collected per group did not change reliably across any observation session. Indeed, a comprehensive cost-benefit analysis indicated that no group generated enough revenue to cover the expense of operating the intervention strategy. Actually, the interventions provided for only about 25% to 33% of the revenues necessary to maintain the program. However, it is noteworthy that treatment lasted only ten weeks (five observation sessions) and more favorable cost-benefit ratios may have resulted from a longer-term program.

For his dissertation research (as reported by Jacobs & Bailey, 1979a, 1979b), Jacobs accomplished a systematic behavioral analysis of a variety of potential determinants of residential recycling. The first experiment examined socioeconomic level as a correlate of participation in a community recycling program. Four neighborhoods were selected on the basis of their socioeconomic representation of lower, lower-middle, and upper-middle income levels within Tallahassee in Leon County, Florida. The residents were informed of weekly curbside pickup of recyclable newspapers and cans by a brochure delivered to their doors. After four to six weeks, a "reminder flyer" was distributed to the homes. Participation for the eleven-week study was a direct function of socioeconomic level, with approximate mean participation percentage of 3%, 8%, 16% and 25% for 417 lower, 555 lower-middle, and 250 upper-middle level households, respectively. The follow-up reminder flyer had no effect on the lower, and lower-middle income residents, but temporarily increased participation in the upper-middle and middle income neighborhoods—an initial rise of 10 to 12 percentage points.

In a second experiment, Jacobs and Bailey studied the advantage of having the collection service for recyclables scheduled on the same day as the garbage collection. For eleven weeks the collection of recyclable cans and newspapers occurred on Tuesdays for a large neighborhood in which half of the homes had their garbage collected on Tuesdays and Fridays, and half received garbage collection service on Mondays and Thursdays. Each week more residents with both garbage and recycling service on the same day rather than different days participated in the recycling program. The mean participation rate was 13.3% of 275 households for the same-day collection group and 8.3% of 369 households for the different-day collection group.

Jacobs and Bailey compared the effects of "door-to-door pamphleting" and "phoning campaigns" for a third field study of strategies to encourage residential recycling. A reminder flyer was delivered to the doors of one group of residents in a large middle income area after five weeks from the initial announcement of a neighborhood recycling program, while another group received the reminder handbill after eleven weeks from program initiation. Phone reminders were given to two other groups in this neighborhood five or eleven weeks from the start of the recycling program. Neither prompting procedure seemed to have consistent effects on program participation. Participation increased somewhat after the door prompt, but this change was temporary. The phone prompt appeared to have no effect on participation in the recycling program.

A fourth recycling study by Jacobs and Bailey compared two methods of notifying residents of a recycling program: door-to-door distribution of brochures versus a newspaper ad. Four days prior to the first scheduled pickup of recyclable cans and newspaper, a large, one-eighth page ad announcing the recycling program for a particular subdivision of approximately 140 homes was run in the only local paper. Half of the homes in the subdivision received an information brochure on the day that the newspaper ad appeared; the remaining homes received this brochure prior to the ninth observation session (i.e., 18 weeks after the newspaper ad).

The results of this study demonstrated marked advantages of the door-to-door brochure strategy over the newspaper ad. More specifically, the households which received only the newspaper ad at the start of the study showed consistently less participation during the first eight collection periods than the households which received the newspaper ad and the brochure (mean participation during this period was 2.9% versus 7.6% for these groups). Furthermore, when the group which started with only a newspaper ad was given a brochure, participation immediately more than doubled. Mean participation for the seven sessions following the brochure was about 7.9%, compared to a mean percent participation of 2.9% prior to the brochure intervention.

Three additional field experiments by Jacobs and Bailey investigated the beneficial effects of a special three-compartment, source separation container called a "recycl-it" which was sold by Sears, Roebuck and Co. For the first of these studies residences in an upper income area were divided into two groups of 63 houses each: a container group and a control group. An information brochure and the recycl-it were delivered to the container group along with instructions and a number to call in case of questions, whereas the controls received only the information brochure. Prior to the tenth collection week a reminder brochure was delivered to all 126 residences. The results suggested marked advantages for the recycl-it container. More specifically, on all but one week of this 20-week study the residents with a recycl-it showed prominently greater participation. The mean participation percentages were 19.3% and 7.8% for the container and control groups, respectively. The reminder brochure did not influence participation for either group.

The second experiment with the recycl-it containers was conducted in a lower middle-income neighborhood. Four groups of 18 to 20 residences each were defined as follows. Twelve weeks after the initiation of the recycling program each home in one group (Group C-1) received a recycl-it and instructions for its use. Each household in Group P-1 received a reminder prompt with recycling instructions on the same day that recycl-its were delivered to C-1. Five weeks later an additional group received the recycl-it (C-2), and another group received the door-delivered brochure (P-2). Seven weeks after these interventions C-1 and P-2 became the targets for an intensive prompting campaign, receiving a different recycle-prompting handbill twice a week for five weeks.

The distribution of the recycl-its (Group C-1 and C-2) resulted in an immediate, participation increase of about ten percentage points which declined after four weeks to near baseline levels of approximately 10-12% participation. The door-to-door distribution of reminder flyers had no apparent influence on recycling by Groups P-1 and P-2. The approximate baseline levels of 9% and 13% for Group P-1 and P-2, respectively, remained intact after prompting. The twice-a-week prompting program increased participation by an average of about ten percentage points for both container groups (C-1 and C-2), but had no influence on participation for the prompt groups (P-1 and P-2).

For a final experiment in this series, Jacobs and Bailey implemented an intervention package that included a variety of factors found previously to promote participation in a community recycling program. In particular, one of two experimental groups from a middle to upper-middle income area

THE RECYCL-IT

KEEP UP THE GOOD WORK

IF YOU'VE RECYCLED IN PAST WEEKS YOUR SUPPORT HAS BEEN APPRECIATED.
IF NOT, NOW IS THE TIME TO GET INVOLVED.

recycling helps--
all of us

WE RECYCLE
LEON COUNTY RECYCLING PROGRAM

Fig. 4.7. A successful residential resource recovery program may have to include the availability of special trash receptacles (such as the "recycl-it"), the distribution of reminder and encouragement flyers, and inexpensive rewards for recycling (such as a "We Recycle" sticker), as were included in the intervention package developed and evaluated by Jacobs and Bailey (1979a, 1979b).

received the following treatment package after seven weeks of baseline: (1) a recycl-it container with usage instructions; (2) a flyer reminding the resident of the weekly collection day and how to recycle; (3) a letter stating the contingency that a "We Recycle" sticker for mail box application would be awarded a household that participated in the program at least once; and (4) twice-a-week delivery of different reminder prompts for a consecutive five-week period. The second group received no treatment strategy.

During baseline the treatment (n = 20) and control (n = 14) groups displayed equivalent recycling participation, averaging from 20% to 25% weekly participation. However, upon implementation of the intervention package, the treatment group demonstrated a participation increase of 25 percentage points. Indeed, participation for this group averaged approximately 50% per pickup and did not drop for thirteen weeks, even after the termination of twice-a-week prompting.

SUMMARY AND CONCLUSIONS

This chapter identified issues regarding waste reduction and resource recovery for energy conservation and critically described the research contributions of behavior scientists which could be applied for the benefit of community resource conservation programs. Studies of correlations between attitudes and recycling-related behavior have identified some factors which may help to identify those people who are apt to participate in a resource recovery program (e.g., individuals who are relatively liberal, well educated, and of high socioeconomic status). Research that applied behavior analysis to problems of waste reduction and recycling have identified environmental factors which can increase the cost effectiveness of a community recycling program (e.g., reinforcement contingencies, specially designed recycling containers, response-feedback techniques). Indeed, most of the behavioral studies have demonstrated that a cost-effective recycling program requires some sort of incentive to encourage participation. However, it is our opinion that none of these studies were long term nor large scale enough to prescribe optimal conditions and contingencies for a communitywide, resource conservation program.

Table 4.1 summarizes the field studies that applied behavioral strategies to promote waste reduction or resource recovery. As with the summary table in Chapter 3, each behavioral strategy is categorized as an antecedent strategy (i.e., a stimulus preceding the opportunity to make the desired response) or a consequence strategy (i.e., a pleasant event following the desired response). As depicted in Table 4.1, most studies compared the impact between two or more behavior change strategies, although several interventions included a manipulation of both antecedents and consequences of the target behavior. Indeed, the implementation of a program to reward desirable behaviors in field or community settings requires a particular antecedent strategy for announcing the contingency, although some investigators did not specify the nature of the antecedent strategy used to promote their consequence strategy. The footnotes in Table 4.1 summarize critical drawbacks of certain studies, which are discussed in more detail in the text.

Table 4.1. Summary of Waste Reduction and Resource Recovery Studies.

Resource Recovery Research	Antecedents			Consequences		
	Target	Strategy	Outcome	Target	Strategy	Outcome
Geller et al. (1971, 1973) [grocery store]	purchase of re-turnable bottles	flyers distributed at entrance to grocery store	20% increase			
Geller et al. (1975) [college dorms][1]	recyclable paper	signs and posters in dormitory	141 lbs. per week, 2.2% partic.			
			combined with consequences (cwc)	recyclable paper	$15 for most lbs. per capita	237 lbs. per week, 3.9% partic.
				recyclable paper	raffle coupon per visit[2]	253 lbs. per week, 7.3% partic.
Ingram & Geller (1975) [college dorms][1]	recyclable paper	flyer per residence	58 lbs. per week, 2.9% partic.			
		personal delivery of flyer	47 lbs. per week, 4.3% partic.			
			cwc	recyclable paper	raffle coupon per pound	113 lbs. per week, 4.9% partic.

Table 4.1. (Continued)

Study	Material	Intervention	Result		Material	Consequence	Result
Witmer & Geller (1976) [college dorms][1]	recyclable paper	weekly flyer per residence	49 lb. per week, 2.6% partic.	cwc	recyclable paper	$15 for most lbs. per capita	544 lb. per week, 5.9% partic.
					recyclable paper	raffle coupon per lb.	820 lb. per week, 12.2% partic.
Couch et al. (1977) [college dorms][1]	recyclable newspapers	flyer per residence	cwc		recyclable newspapers	raffle coupon 1/2 lb.	764 lb. per week, +470%
Reid et al. (1979) [apartment complexes]	recyclable newspapers	recycling box in laundry room; signs	7.6 avg. lbs. per day				
		recycling box near dumpsters; signs; door to door appeals	13.2 avg. lbs. per day 74% increase				
Luyben & Bailey (1979) [trailer parks]	recyclable newspapers	recycle boxes, flyer per residence	175 lbs. per week, 52% increase				
		posters, flyers, recycling vehicle[3]	cwc		recyclable newspapers	2 lb. = 10-20¢ toy; 4 lb. = 20-30¢ toy; 8 lb. = 30-50¢ toy	414 lbs. per week, 108% increase
Hamad et al. (1977) [elementary school][3]	recyclable newspapers	in-class, verbal prompt	198 lbs. per week	cwc	recyclable newspapers	between class contest, public feedback	2,600 lbs. per week

Table 4.1. (Continued)

Resource Recovery Research	Antecedents			Consequences		
	Target	Strategy	Outcome	Target	Strategy	Outcome
Hamad et al. (1979) [elementary school][3]	recyclable newspapers	two newspaper recycling boxes, general memo		recyclable newspapers	public feedback, tree emblem per 120 lbs. of paper	−33% from baseline (157 lbs. per day), 2% partic.
		goal setting memo	cwc		small trees for all pupils	+56% (366 lbs per day), 2% partic.
		written and verbal instructions			10 minute extra recess for 75% partic.	+26% (296 lbs per day), 30% partic.
Humphrey et al. (1977) [administrative offices]	high-grade paper	two wastebaskets	%recyclable paper:[4] 92.3%			
		divided wastebasket	92.7%			
		public wastebasket & personal wastebasket	83.6%			
Luyben et al. (1979-80) [college dorms]	recyclable beverage cans	additional posters and collection containers	+11.7% for steel cans +25.7% for aluminum cans			

Table 4.1. (Continued)

Study	Dependent measure	Treatment	Results / Control			
Arbuthnot et al. (1977) [Athens, Ohio]	participation in community recycling program	1) door-to-door survey 2) appeal flyer & bag to save cans 3) letter & request	% compliance:[5] 1,2,3 = 87.5% / 2 & 3 = 80% / 1 & 2 = 32% / 1 & 3 = 20% / 2 = 8.2% / 1 = 5.9% / 3 = 0% / controls = 0%			
Jacobs (1978) [700 home neighborhood]	newspaper recycling (% partic. and inches of paper)	flyer per residence every other week (for 8 weeks)	+23% partic., no change in inches[6]	newspaper recycling	1¢ per lb.	+120% partic., no change in inches[6]
			cwc		coupon for weekly raffle for $5 prize	+39% partic., no change in inches[6]
			cwc			
Jacobs & Bailey (1979) [Tallahassee-Leon County community]	participation in neighborhood program for recycling newspapers and aluminum cans	brochure and follow-up flyer	partic. was direct function of SES. No effect of flyer for LM & lower income area			
			cwc	partic. in recycling program	pickup on same or different day as garbage	+33% for same-day schedule

Table 4.1. (Continued)

Resource Recovery Research	Antecedents			Consequences		
	Target	Strategy	Outcome	Target	Strategy	Outcome
		reminder flyer at residence vs. reminder phone call	slight, transient increase for only door prompt			
		newspaper vs. newsp. and door-to-door broch.	+200 to 400% due to residential brochure			
		three-compartment container = Recycl-it	100% increase			
		Recycl-it & 2 flyers/week for 5 weeks	+10% with RECYCLIT +10% with prompts			
		Recycl-it, incentive letter, two reminder flyers per week for 5 weeks	cwc	partic. in recycling program	mailbox sticker: "WE RE-CYCLE"	25% increase 50% partic.

[1] Poor source for recyclable paper.
[2] Undermining by repeated deliveries with one sheet of paper.
[3] Transportation costs could be excessive.
[4] No data on amount of paper collected.
[5] Participation judged by telephone interview, not behavioral observation.
[6] Cost-benefit analysis indicated that no intervention provided for a self-supporting program.

It would certainly be beneficial if behavior scientists would study the environmental determinants of recycling-related behaviors for longer periods of time and on a wider scale than prior research. Indeed, this is a valid criticism of most environment preservation research. However, an equally pressing problem is the large-scale dissemination of the information gathered from the behavior analyses of environment preservation programs. For example, strategies for encouraging recycling and for evaluating the behavioral impact and cost effectiveness of recycling programs have been shared at psychology conventions and published in psychology journals, but are rarely disseminated to individuals developing policy for actual waste reduction and recycling. In fact, outside of our discipline the utility of behavior analysis for resource conservation is hardly realized. For example, the fact that comprehensive, resource recovery plans applied citywide in Seattle, Washington, and Portland, Oregon, were based on a premise that people will participate in a recycling program if they are given specific instructions and a reasonable rationale (Duncan, 1975) suggests a lack of appreciation for (or knowledge of) the behavioral evidence.

Comprehensive evaluations of community resource recovery programs have been rare, and when attempted, an adequate assessment of critical human input has been notably absent (e.g., Lane Economic Development Council, 1981). Also, the noted absence of social scientists from the variety of interdisciplinary meetings on waste reduction and resource recovery that have occurred nationwide in recent years (e.g., Institute for Local Self-Reliance, 1980; Office of Solid Waste Management Programs, 1975; Seldman, 1977; Wahl & Bancroft, 1975) illustrates a lack of appreciation for the potential of behavioral science as a contributor to solving waste-management problems. Indeed, an important solid waste bill has established teams of specialists in technical, marketing, financial, and institutional areas to provide nationwide assistance for state and local governments regarding resource conservation and recovery, but a representative from the behavioral or social sciences has not been included on these teams, referred to as "Resource Conservation and Recovery Panels" (Environmental Action Foundation, 1976a). This deficiency is due to at least two factors: (1) minimal awareness of the critical role of behavioral and social factors in the outcome of recycling and resource recovery programs, and (2) insufficient contingencies to motivate the involvement of more than a few behavioral and social scientists in this problem area. The need to develop, evaluate, and refine strategies for disseminating the technology of applied behavior analysis for environmental problem solving is demonstrated further in each of the subsequent chapters.

Chapter 5
Residential Energy Conservation

It is possible to reduce the energy consumed in the typical American home by about 50% (Socolow, 1978). By "typical American home," we mean a detached home, townhouse, or apartment in the existing housing stock. The methods to accomplish these great savings are relatively simple and involve a comprehensive program of behavior changes and home retrofitting. The key is developing strategies that motivate consumers to make changes which in the long run will be highly beneficial to them and collectively to the entire country.

Table 5.1 presents a list of behaviors and retrofits that should be the focus of a residential energy conservation program. These practices primarily involve space heating and cooling and water heating, since these functions account for about 79% of energy consumption in the home (Stobaugh & Yergin, 1979). This chapter reviews the research that has applied and evaluated behavioral strategies for encouraging residential energy conservation. Unfortunately, these procedures have generally been applied in a relatively short-run, nonspecific way. For example, researchers generally have attempted to motivate consumers to make changes in the thermal environment of their homes but have not offered them a systematic plan for maintaining such changes. This strategy, of course, is unlike successful behavior change approaches in other areas which tended to focus on specific behaviors and processes. In addition as noted in Chapter 2, many energy conservation studies have only focused on outcomes (energy savings) without a careful analysis of the particular system involved (e.g., home heating or cooling) or an explication of the specific and optimal procedures to be followed.

There are also very few behavioral studies that have focused on retrofitting. This is probably the case for at least two reasons. Many disciplines tend to work alone, and the "hardware" aspects of retrofitting place it in the engineering field, a field that is unfamiliar to most behavior scientists. One of the objectives of this chapter is to show how physical technologies and

Table 5.1. Targets for Residential Energy Conservation: Heating, Cooling, Hot Water.

Retrofit

- Appropriate attic, ceiling, wall insulation (check 'R' value)
- Storm doors and storm windows
- Appropriate-sized heating and cooling units
- Use of renewable resources for heating and hot water (e.g., solar, wood)
- Insulate water heater
- Procure fans for the summer
- See Appendix at the end of this chapter for an extensive list of low-cost/no-cost retrofit strategies

Behavioral

- Thermostat control: 65° F. winter, 78° F. summer*
- Day set-back by 10° F. when house is empty (winter)
- Night set-back by 10° F. (winter)
- Turn off air conditioning when house is empty
- Turn air conditioning off or to 82° F. at night
- Do not heat or cool infrequently used rooms
- Set hot water thermostat at 120° F.
- Passive solar for winter (open blinds or shades to let in sun; close at night)
- Block out sun for summer
- Leave air conditioning off when windows are open
- Turn off air conditioning when outside temperature is less than or equal to 75° F.**
- For most nights, switch to fans for cooling
- Place fans in appropriate positions
- Dress very warmly in the winter
- Dress in light cotton in the summer

* Lower temperatures in the winter and higher temperatures in the summer can be adapted comfortably; see text.
** For most areas of the country, this means no air conditioning at night, but natural ventilation or fans.

behavioral technologies can be integrated for a comprehensive energy conservation program.

Another reason for limited research on retrofitting probably involves a "risk factor." It is one thing for consumers in a project to decide that they no longer want to change the thermostat as suggested by the program protocol; it is another to risk potential dissatisfaction with the home retrofitting program in which consumers have just invested a considerable sum of money. However, given the urgency of the energy situation in the 1980s, we will probably see different experiments on ways to promote home retrofitting. In the last section of this chapter, we describe such potential efforts.

Before starting the review, one note of caution is relevant when considering the effectiveness of particular strategies. Most of the behavioral studies were conducted in a different "price era." Indeed, it may be the case that marginally effective procedures in the 1970s will be highly effective now. On the other hand, many "easy" changes have already been made by consumers so that the former potential of some low-cost or convenient strategies may be reduced. Indeed, some procedures should probably be reevaluated in order to assess the interaction of procedural effectiveness with the spiraling costs of energy (Winkler & Winett, 1982).

ANTECEDENT STRATEGIES

Antecedent strategies, as discussed in Chapter 2, generally include any type of procedure instituted *prior* to the target behaviors or practices in order to promote initial occurrence or increased frequency of occurrence. For example, specific prompts might be applied to remind consumers to make day and night thermostat set-backs every day. In this section, we discuss informational and expectancy manipulations, modeling, and prompting as antecedent strategies for prompting energy conservation in the home.

Information

The first behavioral studies generally evaluated government informational approaches as they existed in the 1970s. For the most part, this meant that participants in these studies were given the booklets, brochures and pamphlets developed by the Federal Energy Administration and the Energy Research and Development Administration. They typically showed consumers different ways to save energy in their homes. Figure 5.1 provides an example from one such booklet.

Note that when evaluating the effectiveness of this approach, we are evaluating *both* content and medium of communication. Many studies (Heberlein, 1973; Hayes & Cone, 1977; Kohlenberg & Anschell, 1980; Palmer, Lloyd, & Lloyd, 1978; Winett, Kagel, Battalio, & Winkler, 1978; Winett & Nietzel, 1975) found that this type of information promoted no energy savings. However, it is not clear whether the information itself or the method of presenting the information was ineffective, or whether the failures should be attributed to both content and method. Since the specific information, if followed, would have resulted in energy savings and since alternative means of delivering the same information have been effective (Winett, Hatcher, Fort, Leckliter, Riley, Fishback, & Love, 1981), it follows that the method of presentation was probably ineffective. Nevertheless, the informational approach remains appealing because of its simplicity, low cost, public acceptability, and easy accountability. For example, a common reply in the 1970s from state DOE personnel when asked about residential energy conservation programs was: "We have a great program. We've sent out a million informational brochures." It is quite clear now that a million brochures sent to consumers does not equal a million kWh saved each day!

Modeling

One of the most effective methods to influence behavior involves the modeling of desirable practices, either in vivo or through video techniques (Bandura, 1977). This approach is particularly intriguing since television is a large-scale dissemination modality that is readily available. One of the important first steps here is to develop public service ads and programs for subsequent field testing of behavioral impact. To the best of our knowledge, there have been few television programs or spots that actually demonstrate step-by-step conservation strategies to consumers. This does not mean just telling consumers, "Insulate your home," but actually showing them all the processes involved in accomplishing a particular conservation strategy (e.g., from material purchase to specific application).

In a series of studies at Virginia Tech, Richard Winett and his students have started work in this area. The overall goal of these studies is to apply behavior analysis to the development and evaluation of guidelines for comfort standards in residential buildings. Basically, during the winter people were shown by a videotaped program how to successfully adapt to cooler temperatures in their homes by gradually changing thermostat settings, wearing warmer clothing, using extra blankets on their beds, being sensitive to the first sign of becoming cold, and so on. The 21-minute program was composed of a series of short vignettes in which viewers were first shown the negative outcomes of inappropriately approaching a situation. For example, in one scene a couple who failed to modify their dress and instead changed their thermostat settings abruptly, ended their vignette angry with each other and, of course, cold. This was immediately followed by a positive version of the same situation, i.e., appropriately modified dress, gradual change of the thermostat, and a happy ending. The couple was depicted as being friendly with each other, comfortable in their home, and also finding their electric bill lower than expected.

The models for the video program had social and age characteristics similar to the audience and the program was taped in a residence similar to the viewers' homes. These aspects possibly promoted viewer identification with the models and scenes. The programs also received high ratings by viewers across a number of dimensions. The show was judged as credible, informative, and appropriate for other energy conservation programs (Winett, Hatcher, Leckliter, Fort, Fishback, & Riley, 1981).

Most important, consumers significantly reduced their electricity consumption after viewing the program by about 14%. During the study, electricity was primarily used for heating homes, and about 26% of electricity used for heating was saved. A similar program was developed for a summer project, and the results of that study indicated savings comparable to the winter (Winett, Hatcher, Leckliter, Fort, Fishback, & Riley, 1981).

When the heat is on . . .

- Lower your thermostat to 65 degrees during the day and 55 degrees at night. You can save about 3 percent on your fuel costs for every degree you reduce the *average temperature* in your home. In addition, you can save about 1 percent on your heating bills for every degree you dial down *only at night*.

- Keep windows near your thermostat tightly closed, otherwise it will keep your furnace working after the rest of the room has reached a comfortable temperature.

- Have your oil furnace serviced at least once a year, preferably each summer to take advantage of off-season rates. This simple precaution could save you 10 percent in fuel consumption.

- Clean or replace the filter in your forced-air heating system each month.

- Check the duct work for air leaks about once a year if you have a forced-air heating system. To do this, feel around the duct joints for escaping air when the fan is on.

Relatively small leaks can be repaired simply by covering holes or cracks with duct tape. More stubborn problems may require caulking as well as taping. You could save almost 9 percent in heating fuel costs this way.

- If you have oil heat, check to see if the firing rate is correct. Chances are it isn't. A recent survey found that 97 percent of the furnaces checked were overfired.

If your oil furnace doesn't run almost constantly on a very cold day, call a service man.

- Don't let cold air seep into your home through the attic access door. Check the door to make sure it is well insulated and weatherstripped, otherwise you'll be wasting fuel to heat that cool air.

- Dust or vacuum radiator surfaces frequently. Dust and grime impede the flow of heat. And if the radiators need painting, use flat paint, preferably black. It radiates heat better than glossy.

- Keep draperies and shades open in sunny windows; close them at night.

- For comfort in cooler indoor temperatures, use the best insulation of all—warm clothing.

The human body gives off heat, about 390 Btu per hour for a man, 330 for a woman. Dressing wisely can help you retain natural heat.

Wear closely woven fabrics. They add at least a half a degree in warmth.

For women. Slacks are at least a degree warmer than skirts.

For men and women. A light long-sleeved sweater equals almost 2 degrees in added warmth; a heavy long-sleeved sweater adds about 3.7 degrees; and two light-weight sweaters add about 5 degrees in warmth because the air between them serves to keep in more body heat.

If every household in the United States lowered its average heating temperatures 6 degrees over a 24-hour period, we would save more than 570,000 barrels of oil per day or more than 3.5 percent of our current oil imports.

Cooling Energy Savers

Overcooling is expensive and wastes energy. Don't use or buy more cooling equipment capacity than you actually need.

Regarding air-conditioning equipment . . .

- If you need central air-conditioning, select the smallest and least powerful system that will cool your home adequately. A larger unit than you need not only costs more to run but probably won't remove enough moisture from the air.

Ask your dealer to help you determine how much cooling power you need for the space you have to cool and for the climate in which you live. (For further information, see page 19, Energy Efficiency Ratios.)

- Make sure the ducts in your air-conditioning system are properly insulated, especially those that pass through the attic or other uncooled spaces. This could save you almost 9 percent in cooling costs.

- If you don't need central air-conditioning, consider using individual window or through-the-wall units in rooms that need cooling from time to time. Select the smallest and least powerful units for the rooms you need to cool. As a rule, these will cost less to buy and less to operate.

- Install a whole-house ventilating fan in your attic or in an upstairs window to cool the house when it's cool outside, even if you have central air-conditioning.

It will pay to use the fan rather than air-conditioning when the outside temperature is below 82 degrees. When windows in the house are open, the fan pulls cool air through the house and exhausts warm air through the attic.

When you use air-conditioning . . .
- Set your thermostat at 78 degrees, a reasonably comfortable and energy-efficient indoor temperature.

The higher the setting and the less difference between indoor and outdoor temperature, the less outdoor hot air will flow into the building.

If the 78° F. setting raises your home temperature 6 degrees (from 72° F. to 78° F., for example), you should save between 12 and 47 percent in cooling costs, depending on where you live.

Fig. 5.1. A typical page from an information brochure. From "Tips for Energy Savers," Federal Energy Administration, Washington, D.C., 1977.

The participants viewed the video programs only once in a group situation. Future research is needed to determine the effectivensss of such programs when routinely delivered as repetitive television spots and when used in combination with other conservation strategies. For example, the Winett et al. study focused primarily on thermostat control, and people viewed the films in small groups. Whether or not viewing actual television presentations and spots will influence people to buy insulation, storm doors and windows, etc., is unclear from behavioral energy research. Certainly, the billion dollar advertising industry indicates that selling conservation on television may be extremely cost effective.

Expectancy

Included under the term "expectancy" are a number of procedures that involve changing the way people perceive a particular problem or situation. In some cases this can mean primarily disabusing people of incorrect beliefs and supplying them with correct information. The major rationale for this type of intervention is that correct information will yield predictable changes in behaviors. As the prior section on information strategies indicated, this probably will not be the case. However, correct information should be a component of large-scale behavior change programs to preserve the environment.

One example of misbelief apparently mediating residential energy consumption was identified by Becker, Seligman, Fazio, and Darley (1981). Their analysis of written responses to a questionnaire indicated that high usage of residential energy was correlated with the belief that high winter temperatures and low summer temperatures in the home are important for comfort and health. In fact, it is likely that there are some people who keep their residences at virtually the same temperature year round! Recent data suggests that a range of reasonable temperature settings probably does not affect health (Bell, Fisher, & Loomis, 1978). For example, sleep disturbances were not found even in effective temperatures (i.e., a combined measure of temperature and humidity) as high as 90° F. or as low as 50° F. (Rohles, 1978). Thus, the identification of what may be a common belief governing residential energy use has suggested different intervention strategies, including simply disabusing people of the health-temperature correlation, thermal adaptation training (discussed below), and tailoring conservation strategies to an individual's beliefs.

In a recent study, Winett, Hatcher, Leckliter, Fort, Fishback, Riley, & Love (1981) also found that people still have inaccurate information about thermostat set-backs. For example, many people thought that setting back the thermostat with conventional heating systems on a winter's evening resulted in more energy being used to "reheat" the house the next morning, compared to keeping the thermostat always set at 68° F. Not surprisingly, prior to this project's behavior change strategies, none of the residents set back the thermostat.

There also appears to be considerable misinformation about the payback period for retrofit investments in this era of escalating prices and double-digit inflation. For example, using some modest projections of home appreciation, fuel costs, and energy savings, it can be shown that even a substantial investment in home retrofitting (e.g., $5,000) is far superior in terms of potential payback than putting the same funds in bank certificates. This is true even when payback periods are as short as three to four years. These calculations are shown in Table 5.2.

Thus, in the energy field there are still some common misbeliefs. Focusing on supplying correct information should be a major priority, though it is unlikely that simply presenting correct information to the public will change energy-related practices. That is, correct information is probably a necessary, but not a sufficient, component of conservation programs.

Three other expectancy strategies are *goal setting*, *commitment*, and *cohesiveness* procedures. By goal setting, we simply mean having people select energy reduction goals as part of a conservation program or procedure. Goal setting seems to be an important component for feedback strategies discussed later in this chapter. Indeed, without difficult but achievable goals, feedback can be ineffective (Becker, 1978).

Commitment tactics involve having people make some type of meaningful public or private commitment to adhere to a specific program and its goals. Commitment procedures can include signing a statement, publicly voicing agreement to follow a program, giving testimonials, having one's picture in the newspaper—all, of course, directed toward following a particular conservation program (see Goldstein, Heller, & Sechrest, 1966).

By cohesiveness, we mean developing conditions so that people feel they are a part of a cooperative, concerted effort extending beyond the sum of the individual participants. For example, neighborhood energy conservation programs should not be "neighborhood" in name only, but rather designed as truly collaborative endeavors. Cohesiveness may be increased through face-to-face contact, participation in project planning, and the development of common group goals.

Prompts

Almost all energy conservation programs and procedures have used general prompts which may be loosely defined as verbal or written "messages" to promote conservation. Examples include signs that say "Use Energy Wisely" or television announcers who say, "Please conserve during the winter's energy shortage." The appeal of prompts is that they are simple, inexpensive, and

Table 5.2. An Exemplary Comparison of Projected Savings and Gains from Purchase of an Energy Conservation Retrofit Package versus Investment in a Certificate of Deposit*

Year	Projected Cost per kWh ($)	Projected Utility Bill†	Home Retrofit (Insulation, Storm Door/Windows, Attic Fan) Investment = $5,000 Tax Credit = $ 300 25% Savings	Home Appreciation (10% of $5,000)	Total Gain/Savings	Bank Certificate of Deposit Investment = $5,000 (9.5% interest) Gain	Total
1	.06	$ 2,048	$ 512	$ 5,500	$ 500 + $ 512 = $ 1,012	$ 475	$ 5,475
2	.07	2,389	597	6,050	$ 550 + $ 597 = 1,147	520	5,995
3	.08	2,730	682	6,655	$ 605 + $ 682 = 1,287	570	6,565
4	.09	3,071	786	7,321	$ 666 + $ 786 = 1,452	624	7,189
5	.10	3,412	853	8,053	$ 732 + $ 853 = 1,585	683	7,872
6	.11	3,754	938	8,858	$ 805 + $ 938 = 1,743	748	8,620
7	.12	4,095	1,023	9,745	$ 886 + $1,023 = 1,909	819	9,439
8	.13	4,436	1,109	10,720	$ 975 + $1,109 = 2,084	897	10,336
9	.14	4,778	1,194	11,791	$1,071 + $1,194 = 2,265	982	11,318
10	.15	5,119	1,280	12,970	$1,180 + $1,280 = 2,460	1,075	12,393
		$35,832	$8,974	– 5,000 (Investment) $ 7,970	$16,944	$7,393	$12,393

Gain/Savings $16,944
Plus Tax Credit + 300
Less Investment – 5,000
NET GAIN $12,244

* Consumption data based on results from Winett, Neale, & Grier, 1979, and Winett, Neale, Williams, Yokley, & Kauder, 1979.
† Note that the major savings come through the projected increase in energy costs and appreciation of the energy conservation package.

166

easy to deliver. However, investigations on the impact of prompts on environment preservation have shown definite limitations of this behavior change strategy (as discussed generally in Chapter 2 and specifically in Chapters 3 and 4). As shown in Chapters 3 and 4, variables that can make prompts more effective include their specificity, timing, and placement. For example, if the object is to modify how people use heat in their homes, television and radio prompts should not say "Conserve Energy," but, instead at 10 and 11 p.m. (after the news) should say, "Tonight, turn your thermostat down ten degrees before going to bed." This response should then be actually demonstrated in the television studio.

An example of a study evaluating the appropriateness and effectiveness of different kinds of prompts to conserve energy was conducted by Winett (1978). In this study, university-produced signs urging persons to conserve energy were placed in rooms where lights were frequently left on, even though the rooms were unoccupied. The sign was placed above a light switch, and a small sticker that also urged the savings of energy was then placed on the light switch. These conventional prompts had no effect; the lights were almost always left on (i.e., 100% of the 20 observation days) when the rooms were unoccupied.

In the next phase of the study, larger signs with specific information (when and who should turn out the lights) were placed near the exit point of the room. The lights were then left on for only 40% of the observation days. A similar reduction in lighting of unoccupied public places through use of signs with specific information has been found by other energy researchers (Delprata, 1977; Luyben, 1980).

Prompts can also be built into the environment and may be critical facets of other procedures or devices. For example, Becker and Seligman (1979) investigated the effectiveness of a light that went on in a highly visible part of the home when the air conditioning was on, but the temperature was below 68° F. outside. An average of 15% savings in energy consumption was found in homes equipped with this signalling device. As discussed later in this chapter, automated feedback devices will probably require some type of built-in prompt in order to assure that the consumer attends to the device and acts on the information provided.

A range of other strategies exists if prompts are made more public. For example, suppose a large sign illuminated in stores during the summer when the temperature was above 78° F., and informed customers that they were purchasing goods from "energy savers." Indeed, the sign could also indicate that conservation was contributing to monetary savings passed on to the consumer. Such "energy saver" signs could have mutual benefits for both businesses and consumers. Thus, this information and feedback strategy could save both parties money, while benefiting public relations and consumer awareness.

Thus, there are a variety of antecedent strategies that are effective in promoting changes in energy-related behaviors. However, an examination of many energy policies and programs suggests that antecedent strategies have rarely been appropriately used. Attention to the specificity, timing and placement of prompts, the medium of delivering correct information, methods for securing commitments to goals and creating cohesiveness are aspects of antecedent strategies that can be important components of conservation programs.

THERMAL ADAPTATION, ADJUSTMENT, AND COMFORT IN THE HOME

Considerable and highly sophisticated work on human comfort has been conducted in order to find the exact thermal parameters (i.e., temperature, humidity, wind) that most people find comfortable (Rohles, 1978). These studies follow a psychophysiological threshold-testing paradigm. Subjects are placed in small groups in a special environmental chamber and exposed to different thermal conditions. At each thermal condition, subjects are asked to anonymously vote on how comfortable, warm, or cold they feel using the nine-point scales shown in Table 5.3. Ideal thermal conditions are, thus, based on the votes of the subjects in these experiments. Once conditions have been determined, they have been used as input for comfort standards in buildings (ASHRAE, 1972). For example, according to these studies ideal comfort with only moderate clothing is achieved at about 75° F. (Rohles, 1981).

Several behavioral principles and data sources were used in the development of field-based comfort studies conducted at Virginia Tech which conceptualized comfort within a more dynamic framework than the prior laboratory research. First, it seemed likely that people could adapt and adjust to

Table 5.3. Standard Thermal Sensation and Comfort Scales.

Thermal Sensation	Thermal Comfort
9 = very hot	9 = uncomfortably hot
8 = hot	8 = hotter than comfortable
7 = warm	7 = much warmer than comfortable
6 = slightly warm	6 = slightly warmer than comfortable
5 = neutral	5 = comfortable
4 = slightly cool	4 = slightly cooler than comfortable
3 = cool	3 = much cooler than comfortable
2 = cold	2 = colder than comfortable
1 = very cold	1 = uncomfortably cold

different thermal environments, within reason. Historical and contemporary cross-cultural data indicate that people can live comfortably in a range of temperatures, particularly if clothing is appropriate. Second, adaptation may be successful if a gradual schedule of thermostat changes could be defined so that people hardly notice any differences in the thermal environment and, hence, remain comfortable. Third, a number of antecedent strategies (modeling, prompting) and consequence procedures (such as feedback) could be used to motivate people to change the thermal environment of their homes. Finally, data from prior studies have suggested that all of the above points are probably true (see Winett & Neale, 1979). For example, it has been found that energy savings were highly correlated with self-reported changes in thermostat settings. People reported that the changes they made were relatively easy, and more importantly seemed to maintain these changes, suggesting that they were "comfortable" (e.g., Winett, Neale, & Grier, 1979; Winett, Neale, Williams, Yokley, & Kauder, 1979).

The comfort studies at Virginia Tech have incorporated all these points in the following way:

1. Each all-electric household was provided with a gradual thermostat reduction schedule, as shown in Table 5.4. The specific reduction schedule received by a household was determined by the mean household temperature reported on a form by residents during a baseline period. For about two-thirds of the households, temperature and humidity were continuously recorded on a special instrument called a hygrothermograph, which was at table-top height and within several feet of the residence's only thermostat.

Table 5.4. Thermostat Change Schedule Used in a Conservation Project.

PROJECT CREATE
Thermostat Setting Reduction Schedule

Baseline = 69°F *When Home*		*Goal = 4° Reduction* *and Daily Set-Backs*	
Start Date *and Week*	*When Home*	*When House Unoccupied* *Day Set-Back*	*Sleeping* *Night Set-Back*
Feb. 3 1	68°F	58°F	58°F
Feb. 10 2	67°F	57°F	57°F
Feb. 17 3	66°F	56°F	56°F
Feb. 24 4	65°F	55°F	55°F
March 2			
	Maintain Settings of Last Week		

Thus, the thermostat change schedule was tailored to each household and continuous data were available on adherence to the schedule. Note that the schedule emphasized day and night set-backs, a procedure that should assure maximal energy savings with minimal discomfort (Beckey & Nelson, 1981).

2. Residents' efforts at following the thermostat reduction schedule were supported by a combination of videotape modeling and feedback on electricity consumption.

3. To aid adjustment and adaptation during the winter period, residents were provided with detailed lists of the "clo" or insulation value of clothing (Rohles, 1981). Table 5.5 provides a sample list of common articles of clothing with their clo value. Of course, residents were advised (and in some cases shown via modeling) to wear warmer clothing.

The results from the first winter study were quite striking. Participant groups that either received daily feedback on energy consumption and/or saw the modeling film described previously, now performed both day and night

Table 5.5. Sample of Women's Clothing and Associated Clo Values.

Description	Fabric Construction	Typical Fiber Content	CLO
Underwear			
Bra		Cotton	0.02
Panties		Acetate	0.02
Long Underwear			
Tops	Knit		0.25
Bottoms	Knit		0.25
Socks and Hosiery			
Panty hose		Nylon	0.01
Tights	Knit		0.25
Shoes			
Low Shoes			0.03
Knee High Boots, Leather			
Lined			0.30
Blouses			
Short Sleeve Blouse	Plain Weave	Rayon	0.17
Heavy Long Sleeve Shirt	Plain Weave	Wool	0.37
Pants			
Light Pants	Knit	Polyester	0.26
Jeans	Twill Weave	Cotton	0.26
Dresses and Skirts			
Heavy Skirt	Twill Weave	Wool	0.22
Sweaters			
Long Sleeve Sweater	Knit	Wool	0.37
Blazers and Vests			
Light Vest	Weave		0.20
Heavy Blazer	Weave	Wool	0.43

Table 5.5. (Continued). Sample of Men's Clothing and Associated Clo Values.

Description	Fabric Construction	Typical Fiber Content	CLO
Underwear			
Briefs	Knit	Cotton	0.05
Sleeveless Undershirt	Knit	Cotton	0.08
Long Underwear			
Tops	Knit		0.25
Bottoms	Knit		0.25
Socks			
Light Socks	Knit		0.03
Heavy Knee High Socks	Knit		0.08
Shoes			
High Shoes			0.15
Shirts			
Short Sleeve Light Knit	Knit	Cotton	0.22
Long Sleeve Woven	Plain Weave	Polyester and Cotton Blend	0.29
Pants			
Heavy Trousers	Twill Weave	Wool	0.32
Sweaters			
Sleeveless Sweater	Knit	Orlon	0.17
Sport Coats and Vests			
Heavy Vest	Weave		0.30
Heavy Sport Coat	Twill Weave	Wool	0.49

set-backs and were living at home in temperatures at a mean of 62° F. Most importantly, households (n = 50) making substantial changes in their thermostat settings reported no change in their perception of comfort. This was possibly true because these residents increased the clo value of the clothing they wore by about 10%. As expected, changes in the thermal environment led to very meaningful savings of overall electricity consumption of 15%, with 26% mean reduction in electricity used for heating. It was also found that temperature settings and energy savings were generally maintained throughout the heating season.

The control group (n = 20 residences) showed no changes in thermostat settings and energy consumption. For almost every hour of continuous readings from the hygrothermographs, control homes tended to show a virtually constant temperature of between 65° F. and 66° F. Thus, despite a great deal of information given about energy conservation during the study (e.g., through the media), control participants showed no change. These findings suggest the need for more systematic and focused approaches, as exemplified by the intervention groups in the study.

Several other issues were highlighted by the winter study's results, including:

1. The methodology used in the study demonstrated a field-based approach to studying comfort that may have greater external validity than laboratory studies.

2. Indeed, the results of the study were quite discrepant with prior laboratory studies that have been used to set comfort standards. Participants in the winter study reported comfort with temperatures and clothing (i.e., clo level) considerably below those reported in laboratory studies. For example, given the clothing worn by participants, the laboratory studies would have predicted comfort at 75° F., not 62° F. One set of possible explanations for these differences is that the field studies may be more representative of what conditions people are actually willing to live in, what trade-offs they may be willing to make (e.g., cost of energy versus feeling "toasty"), and how new information and behaviors may modify perceptions and self-reports of comfort. Then too, at home there is personal control over comfort, while this is not the case in the laboratory. The laboratory studies have essentially investigated comfort out of context. In this way, the laboratory studies may have defined *ideal* thermal parameters which may have more or less correspondence to life in the "real world," depending on the changing context. For example, when energy was very inexpensive, laboratory comfort and real-world comfort may have corresponded more closely.

3. The temperature changes achieved with no loss of comfort have energy policy implications. The thermal results seriously question those who depict changes in thermostat settings and other comparable changes as an unacceptable curtailment and "sacrificial" approach to conservation (e.g., Stern & Gardner, 1981). Note that people in the study reported they were comfortable at their new thermostat settings and maintained their settings through the heating season. Based on these results, we would like to relabel the thermostat change strategy from "sacrifice" and "curtailment" to an "efficiency strategy" (Winett & Geller, 1981).

The winter comfort study showed that simple strategies (set-backs) could save considerable energy and that comfort could be maintained at unexpectedly low temperatures. In a summer study, it seemed possible to markedly reduce electricity used for air conditioning with minimal change in interior home temperature and, hence, comfort. In this study, participants were given a range of strategies to achieve this objective, including: turning off the air conditioning when leaving the home for more than two hours; turning air conditioning to 80° F. or off when sleeping; substituting fans for air conditioning at night or using natural ventilation;* closing all windows, drapes, and blinds in the morning; and rearranging strenuous activities for cooler parts of the day. Thus, the major goal of this program was to have people

---

* On most summer nights, in most every part of this country it is sufficiently cool outside (65°-75° F.) that using air conditioning set at 76° F. is keeping a home *warmer* than the outside!

reduce one set of energy intensive practices (i.e., high air conditioning use) and substitute and increase other less energy intensive practices (e.g., use of fans). Following these procedures, it may be possible to maintain comfort. This approach also more generally illustrates an axiom in behavior change strategies: when focusing on decreasing one behavior, try also to increase an alternative behavior.

These procedures were supported by combinations of videotape modeling and feedback on electricity consumption. The most successful group (n = 11) reduced overall electricity usage by 20%; electricity used for air conditioning was reduced by about 45%. Hygrothermograph data indicated that in homes achieving these savings (16% overall reduction and 35% reduction for cooling across the study sample) temperatures during the intervention period were about the *same* as during baseline. Therefore, it is not surprising that there was no change in perceived comfort. Again, these simple strategies were highly effective, efficient, and hardly "sacrificial!"

Additional studies are needed to: (a) ascertain how this same substitution strategy can be used in the winter (e.g., using small portable heaters in occupied rooms and turning down the thermostat for the entire home; Rohles, 1981); (2) find through field-based research actual thermal conditions that most people can adapt and adjust to; and (3) develop large-scale methods for persuading consumers to follow steps that are found effective. The data from the studies discussed here indicate that substantial energy savings are possible via these simple strategies.

SUMMARY OF ANTECEDENT, ADJUSTMENT, AND ADAPTATION PROCEDURES

There are few investigations to report in this section because few energy conservation projects have evaluated such procedures as prompting, modeling, and goal setting. It appears that some of these procedures (e.g., videotaped modeling) may have a highly promising future as a fundamental component of large-scale conservation programs. At the very least, it is apparent that more work is needed on the effective qualities of these procedures, since they can be an integral part of most comprehensive conservation programs.

Perhaps, one of the problems with the use of antecedent strategies such as informational approaches is inappropriate expectations. There is, for example, extensive behavioral science literature showing that procedures that can effectively change information and attitudes may not necessarily change behaviors (Wicker, 1969). An example of the discrepancy in outcomes between information, attitudes, and behavior was found in a project by Geller (1981a). In this project an informational approach (workshops) was found to be highly effective in changing attitudes and intentions related to energy conservation. However, follow-up audits of some participants' homes indicated that changes suggested by the program had rarely been implemented. In light of the behavioral science literature, the result is not surprising and points toward combining antecedent procedures with consequence procedures that have been more effective in promoting behavior change. Correct information is probably a necessary component of any intervention, and may indeed influence knowledge and awareness, but by itself is usually not sufficient to promote behavior change.

CONSEQUENCE PROCEDURES

Consequences are events that contingently follow specific behaviors or practices. Knowledge of a reliable contingency between behavior and consequent events will often motivate behavior. For example, in states that have substantial tax credits for the purchase of solar hot water or heating systems, sales are reported to be quite substantial (Stobaugh & Yergin, 1979). Consequent events are also used to increase the frequency or maintain specific behaviors or practices. Indeed, the primary rationale of an inverted rate structure is to reward low-use consumers with low rates and punish high-use consumers with high rates.

However, consequence procedures need not be as tangible as the examples with tax credits and rate structures suggest. Feedback on performance, for example, is one of the most reliable ways to reduce residential consumption. In this section, we will review both rebate and feedback techniques.

Contingent Money

Large monetary rebates involving payments contingent on energy reductions were initially used to demonstrate that consumers could be motivated to reduce use. The results from studies using large rebates (price changes of over 200%) have shown reductions of from 12% to over 30% for periods approximating a heating or cooling season (Hayes & Cone, 1977; Kohlenberg et al., 1976; Winett, et al., 1978; Winett, Kaiser, & Haberkorn, 1977; Winett & Nietzel, 1975). Probably because many psychologists do not have backgrounds in economics (see Chapter 7), it was not realized at the time of these studies (during cheap energy) that rebate payments such as $2 per week for a 10% reduction or $3 for 20% were not cost effective.

However, rebates are one way to experimentally investigate the elasticity of consumer demand (i.e., change in demand/change in price; Battalio, Kagel, Winkler, & Winett, 1979) without altering the basic rate structure (although the impact of rate structure has also been investigated; Kohlenberg, Barach, Martin, & Anschell, 1977). Estimates of elasticity obtained by economists and used by power companies, the government, and politicians are often not derived from experimental data but aggregate data (Kagel & Winkler, 1972). For example, data sources might include total demand for one or two utilities under varying prices. Such data are often not appropriate for making predictions, yet they are usually the data base for computer models of demand. There is apparently a growing disillusionment with econometric models used by economists and others (Stobaugh & Yergin, 1979). The main problems are that the models developed by one econometrician tend to disagree with models of other economists, and the general method has lacked predictive ability (Stobaugh & Yergin, 1979; Waverman, 1977). The rebate studies conducted by researchers in different locales during the 1970s yielded consistent results and indicated (not surprisingly) that elasticity of demand was low. (Chapter 7 on water conservation presents more detail on the integration of behavioral and economic principles termed "behavioral economics.")

Interestingly, when rebate research was first conducted and presented to power company and university administrators, rebates were labeled "bribery" and considered "infeasible" (Winett, 1976). The social and economic context has much to do with how procedures are perceived. The Chrysler Corporation, for example, has been trying to survive in the 1980s by offering rebates for test driving or buying one of their cars. To the best of our knowledge, no one has called Chrysler's approach "bribery."

A reasonable rebate procedure could be enacted by utilities, and perhaps events in the 1980s will make rebates politically feasible. Table 5.6 is based on the actual average kWh use of upper-middle-class consumers in studies by Winett, Neale, and Grier (1979) and Winett, Neale, Williams, Yokley, and Kauder (1979) during normal (late spring) and peak (hot summer and winter) periods, and by high users during the winter. The table shows the

Table 5.6. The Possibility of Developing Rebate Systems During Peak-Use Periods as the Utility Rates Increase.

	Summer Peak Use and Old Rates	Regular Use and High Rate	Summer Peak Use and "Summer Rate"	Winter Peak Use and "Winter Rate"
Average Daily Use	80 kWh*	30 kWh*	80 kWh*	150 kWh**
Monthly Use	2400 kWh	900 kWh	2400 kWh	4500 kWh
Rate per kWh	2.5¢	7¢	9¢	9¢
Month's Bill	$60.00	$63.00	$216	$405
20% Reduction	480 kWh	180 kWh	480 kWh	900 kWh
Actual Cost	$12.00	$12.60	$43.20	$81.00

* Actual figures from Winett, Neale, Williams, Yokley, and Kauder, 1979.
** Actual figures from Winett, Neale, and Grier, 1979.

expected monthly bill during these three time periods if the marginal cost of electricity was 7 cents during the normal period and 9 cents during a peak period, rates that are actually much below those in some parts of the country when taxes and fuel adjustment costs are included (Craig & McCann, 1980).

In projects from 1974 to 1976, $5 per week or $20 per month was rebated for up to a 20% reduction. As shown in Table 5.6, the savings to the consumer under the summer rates and use pattern are almost double that amount and quadruple for the winter period. Thus, it would appear that a meaningful rebate system could be enacted, for example, where part of a consumer's reduction from expected use is matched by a rebate payment generated through special rates during peak-use time. By contrast, the first column of the table shows that when rates were low, even during a peak-use period, electricity bills were very low. Under those conditions a meaningful rebate system was relatively infeasible.

There are many varieties to the rebate scheme that can be developed and evaluated. These include "conservation lotteries," discounts on conservation equipment, and cash refunds. All of these could be tried, and perhaps the typical consumer may welcome such efforts. Some utilities may also find these procedures appealing. Obviously they have public relations value, but hopefully such procedures could actually reduce demand and, hence, also reduce the need for additional costs of generating capacity.

We also recommend that newly proposed tax credits, "conservation taxes" on gasoline, and the like receive some experimental field tests to ascertain effectiveness. For example, in the spring of 1980, a 10 cent tax on gasoline was proposed to promote reduced driving by the administration. One presidential hopeful proposed a much larger tax. Yet there were minimal data available to suggest that such taxes would have the intended effects. Likewise, it is unclear how much of a tax credit is needed to promote home retrofitting. These questions could, to some extent, be answered by behavioral-economic field studies.

Rebate and Other Strategies in Master-Metered Settings

Because energy was once inexpensive, particularly when bought in bulk, and presumably for convenience and savings in construction, many residential and commercial settings were developed using master meters. When this is the case, not only are individual occupants unaware of their own energy use, but there is little incentive for individual units to conserve. There is apparently a considerable amount of energy wasted in such settings (Slavin & Wodarski, 1977).

Slavin and his colleagues (Slavin et al., 1981; Slavin & Wodarski, 1977) have developed a group contingency, rebate procedure that involves paybacks to individual residents of master-metered apartment buildings consisting of an equal part of money saved through collective efforts. Management may also keep part of the savings. In other words, if an apartment complex of 150 units saved throughout a summer $4,000 from expected costs, each unit may receive $20 (75% of the total) with management keeping the remaining $1,000. This procedure has yielded some minimal, though meaningful, large-scale reductions (i.e., about 3% to 9%), but the individual payment is quite small. Effects of the basic procedure were enhanced by increasing the payment and by social processes that primarily involved having the residents meet each other to develop cohesiveness and make a commitment to conserve (Slavin et al., 1981).

Lou McClelland and her group at the Institute of Behavioral Science have also developed two practical conservation programs for master-metered settings (see also Newsom & Makranczy, 1978). The first program included persuasive communications, conservation information specific to a setting, feedback via newsletters, group meetings, and monetary incentives (McClelland & Belsten, 1979). This work is particularly promising, not only in showing short-run reductions of about 10% to 15%, but in demonstrating that: (a) such savings may be maintained because life-style changes were initiated by their program, (e.g., light bulb removal, closure of unused rooms) and (b) brief, intensive programs may be implemented at periodic intervals in the same institution and still be effective.

The other program of McClelland and her associates is called the Resident Utility Billing System (RUBS). The system involves the immediate passthrough of all energy costs to residents by billing each resident (on his or her rent bill) for a prorated share of the property's utility bill for the prior month. The share for each resident is based on the number of square feet in his or her dwelling. The resident is separately shown the amount on the bill for rent and energy, providing the basis for some monthly feedback. Preliminary results indicate reductions of 5% to 15% in the consumption of electricity and natural gas. Thus, RUBS may be an effective procedure because it involves both "group" and "individual" components and allows for positive and negative consequences.

Another strategy for promoting energy conservation in master-metered apartments was developed by Walker (1979). His technique entailed an immediate $5 payment to residents whose apartments had thermostats set at or above 74° in the summer and had windows and doors closed when air conditioning was on. Residents had agreed that an "inspector" could enter their apartments when they were home and see if their apartments met the simple criteria. Apartments to be inspected were drawn randomly at varying times. The inspector carried a thermometer which registered the temperature of the apartment within seconds so that the validity of the observed thermostat setting could be verified. Despite only checking a limited number of apartments each week, savings of from about 3% to 8.5% were found in a

175-unit complex. A cost-effectiveness analysis suggested that the cost of the electricity saved was more than the cost of the program, even at a low rate of 2.6 cents per kWh. It may be that this program and the program noted previously on comfort and adaptation were particularly effective because they targeted specific responses that if enacted would result in reductions of residential energy consumption. This strategy can be compared to those focusing on outcomes (i.e., reduction on overall energy consumption without specifying the process). As shown here and as discussed in more detail in Chapter 2, this distinction is hardly trivial and is an important consideration in the development of environment preservation programs.

More generally, it seems that many owners of master-metered apartment complexes are motivated to reduce energy use in their buildings. Higher energy costs mean higher rents with possibly lower occupancy rates in their settings. The higher rents also can take certain apartments out of a particular market (e.g., lower-middle class, or even middle class).

Despite the apparent cost effectiveness of master-metered procedures, we first recommend ascertaining the cost of single-metering or sub-metering any master-meter setting. Unfortunately, the cost is usually quite high. We next recommend studies to explore the feasibility of installing simple timing devices (e.g., on heating and cooling systems) and charging residents for electricity based on the time a system for their apartment is in operation. At present, the most viable procedure seems to be the "billing-pass-through" system (RUBS). In the long run, procedures that bring energy costs directly to the consumer should be more cost effective than other incentive procedures described in this section.

Peak-Load Management

Peak-load use, or peaking, can refer to either high seasonal or high time-of-day use. Reducing the peak demand is important since supplementary generators, other power sources (e.g., nuclear), or energy from other utility systems must be operationalized during peak demand periods. During nonpeak periods, these expensive supplementary systems are idle. From the producer's point of view, it would be beneficial if the peak could be flattened by curtailing consumption or switching some use to a nonpeak time. From a pro-environment perspective, less damage to the environment would occur if peak loads were lowered. In addition, the consumer may eventually realize lower rates if the peaks were flattened because of reduced operating costs for power companies. Thus, peak-load management is one area in which all parties seem to have a common interest.

As an incentive for consumers to modify their pattern of use, utility companies have been experimenting with reduced rates during nonpeak periods and higher rates during peak periods. This practice is called time-of-day pricing and reflects the true cost of energy at any given moment. To operate this system effectively, homes, buildings, and other installations must be re-metered, a considerable, but primarily a one-time cost. This cost can be justified if time-of-day pricing reduces peak-load use, or it can also be justified as a means of having consumers pay the real cost of energy when it is used.

Behavioral research of peak-load management has been limited, but apparently monetary incentives or frequent feedback that continuously signals consumption beyond a designated level, can reduce peak electricity use at least over a short-term period (Blakely et al., 1977; Kohlenberg et al., 1976). However, consumers seem to find it difficult to shift various energy-consuming tasks (Kohlenberg et al., 1976). This is not surprising since work schedules, which are similar for most people (Robinson, 1977), determine when we use various energy-consuming facilities and resources, including gasoline for transportation, hot water for showers, and electricity for air conditioning. For example, one study of federal employees in the Washington, D.C. area found that the time people engaged in certain practices (commuting, dining, watching television, preparing for work or bed) did not vary very much as a function of demographic characteristics, but the time of typical everyday activities was highly dependent on individuals' work schedules (Winett & Neale, 1980).

These data on work schedules suggest that a purely economic approach (i.e., time-of-day pricing) may not be very effective. The peak-load problem in different resources may be better approached through staggered and flexible work schedules (Winett & Neale, 1980). However, while time-of-day pricing may not flatten the peak-load demand, it seems reasonable for people to pay for the true cost of energy. But if it is correct that without large-scale implementation of alternative work patterns, consumers cannot easily change the pattern of their energy-related practices, then the introduction of time-of-day pricing could create a "windfall" for utilities. Clearly, some equitable policy must be developed for this problem. As suggested later in this chapter and throughout this book, most environmental problems need to be approached from a comprehensive perspective. For peak-load consumption, this would include careful study of time-of-day pricing (Craig & McCann, 1980) in conjunction with alternative work patterns.

Feedback

Feedback has been the most extensively studied and most successful consequence strategy for reducing residential energy consumption. In fact, we recommend that any other procedure or program noted in this chapter include a feedback component if possible. Indeed, if they are to be effective, previously noted price change or rebate systems need a feedback component to frequently inform consumers about their consumption and eligibility for differential rates or rebates (Kohlenberg & Anschell, 1980).

Exact and frequent information about consumption (i.e., feedback) seems important and effective for several reasons. Energy consumption in the home is still not a widely known unit of measure. For example, of about 700 persons in studies by Winett and associates, only a small fraction (1% to 2%) of participants knew how many kWh they used per month or day; in fact, most did not know where their electricity meter was located. Very few participants in these studies had ever experimented to see, for example, the effects on kWh consumption of varying use of appliances such as air conditioners or heaters. Also, current billing systems only indicate energy use for a long period of time (one or two months), with no attempt to tell the consumer (with a weather correction factor) how much energy they have used in relation to a comparison period. Thus, consumers have no way to assess quickly and accurately the success of their conservation efforts. Without information on the outcomes of conservation efforts, it is likely that many consumers will not maintain their new practices. This point is supported by recent data from Kohlenberg and Anschell (1980) who have shown immediate, but transient reductions in energy use with the introduction of price changes. The price change may have first prompted engagement in certain practices, but billing procedures with delayed feedback that is difficult to discern cannot support continual engagement in conservation practices.

Further, there is no expected use level for a given type of residence occupied by persons with particular life patterns. Indeed, even when households are matched on demographic characteristics of occupants, physical structure, and location (e.g., shade and sun), it has been found that electricity use can differ by two- or three-fold during the summer or winter (Seligman & Darley, 1977; Winett, Neale, & Grier, 1979; Winett, Neale, Williams, Yokley, & Kauder, 1979; Winett, Hatcher, Leckliter, Fort, Fishback, Riley, & Love, 1981). It has also been found that retrofitting two identical homes with prior differences in consumption levels will not change the proportional differences in energy use between the two homes, and completely different consumption patterns can emerge when occupants change (Socolow, 1978). Indeed, the large disparity in consumption patterns between identical residences is probably the most striking finding of the fine-grained analyses of household energy consumption performed in behavior analytic studies. It is a factor largely overlooked in current energy policy (Winett & Geller, 1981).

In contrast to the lack of knowledge of kWh use is the consumer's knowledge of "mpg" in cars. Automobile conservation programs and advertising are based on superior mpg performance, and a similar approach is probably needed in residential and commercial energy use. That is, a reasonable energy consumption goal could be applied to different residential and commercial buildings. Thus, feedback can fill a critical knowledge "gap." The exact information provided by consumption feedback may in part explain the behavioral impact of feedback (see Shippee, 1980).

In studies that assessed how, when, and with whom feedback worked, feedback was primarily given in written form or recorded on charts affixed directly to a residence (Becker, 1978; Hayes & Cone, 1977; Palmer et al., 1978; Seligman & Darley, 1977; Winett et al., 1977; Winett, Neale, & Grier, 1979; Winett, Neale, Williams, Yokley, & Kauder, 1979). Consumers were shown their energy use for a designated period (day, week, month) and then usually given a weather-corrected increase or decrease in percent based on their prior use levels. Sometimes energy use, savings, or loss was converted to money and termed "price feedback."

Figure 5.2 shows a feedback form used in a few studies. A series of smiles and frowns on feedback slips was used to indicate to consumers levels of reductions or increases. This was a ploy to maintain consumer attention and also to show that conservation can be made interesting and even fun. These seminal studies have helped to identify some basic parameters in feedback and other procedures. As energy prices continue to escalate, such seemingly

PROJECT CREATE

Dear Mr. Gilmer:

Our meter readings for yesterday (Mon, 2/16/81) showed that you used 150 kWh.
Taking into account your own prior use, weather conditions, and a control group's use, this represents a 25% reduction. This is at or above below your reduction goal of 20%.

Fig. 5.2. A feedback form used in early behavioral research. The daily form provided the consumer with information on kWh use, a weather-corrected percent increase or decrease from a baseline period, and if the percent decrease was under or over a reduction goal.

primitive techniques may become feasible for larger-scale implementation (Winett & Neale, 1979).

With regard to feedback parameters, it appears that feedback must be given at least several times per week to promote conservation (Seligman & Darley, 1977), but there are studies showing effectiveness of less frequent feedback (Hayes & Cone, 1981; Seaver & Patterson, 1976). It is unclear from these studies why feedback worked even when given very infrequently. This is a critical question, since it suggests that appropriate feedback on energy bills will curtail consumption.

Behavioral energy research also indicates that people may be "weaned" from frequent feedback. There is now consistent evidence for maintenance of reduced consumption for periods of 6 to 12 weeks after feedback had been terminated (Winett, Hatcher, Leckliter, Fort, Fishback, Riley, & Love, 1981; Winett, Neale, & Grier, 1979; Winett, Neale, Williams, Yokley, & Kauder, 1979). Maintenance of effect is particularly important when calculating the cost effectiveness of a procedure, as will be shown later in this chapter.

A meta-analysis of behavioral energy research has also found a relationship between the *cost* of energy, consumer *income*, and feedback *effectiveness* (Winkler & Winett, 1981). Not surprisingly, feedback did not appear to be effective when the cost of energy relative to income was low. The proportion of income expended for a commodity is called "budget share." Thus, if rates are low in your part of the country, feedback approaches will probably not work well, particularly with middle and upper income households. Where budget share was high, frequent (almost daily) feedback has yielded reductions in overall residential electricity use of from about 10% to 20% for periods up to an entire peak-use (seasonal) period (Winett, Neale, Williams, Yokley, & Kauder, 1979). Such simple feedback may be particularly effective if it is given to high-use consumers during peak-use periods (heating, cooling). For example, it was found that written feedback resulted in reductions of about 13% in electricity use even among low (11 kWh per day) to middle (21 kWh per day) level consumers during off-peak (spring) periods. However, as shown in Figure 5.3, reductions of up to 30% (representing savings of 15-20 kWh per day per household) were found when the same procedure was used in a higher use area during very hot (over 90° F.) and humid weather (Bittle, Valesano, & Thaler, 1980; Winett, Neale, Williams, Yokley, & Kauder, 1979). It is noteworthy that feedback to either individual households or individual households including additional information on the consumption of a group of households, as shown in Figure 5.3, was not effective until it became extremely hot and humid. At the time of this study (1977), the power companies in the Washington, D.C. area where the study was conducted were reporting record demand. Thus, feedback strategies may be helpful in avoiding brownouts and blackouts due to peak-load demand on peak-use days and in eventually reducing costs during these periods.

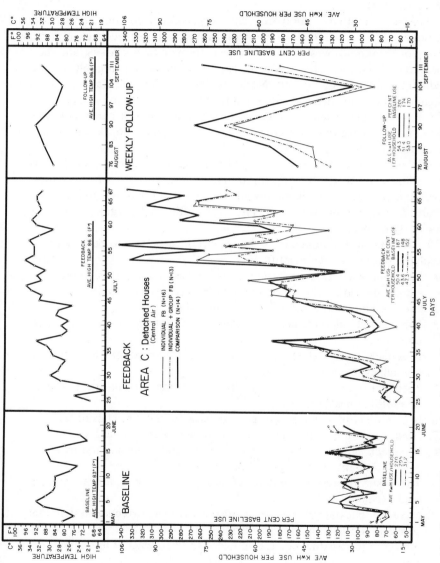

Fig. 5.3. Percent baseline and kWh consumption of two feedback groups and a no-treatment (or comparison) group during a mild spring baseline period, a mild then very warm summer intervention period, and a later summer follow-up period. Note that feedback was particularly effective during the warmest and highest electricity use period and that effects were maintained at follow-up.

Giving consumers goals, particularly difficult but achievable ones, apparently increases the effectiveness of feedback in decreasing energy use (Becker, 1978). It has been found that with easy goals, feedback can be ineffective (Becker, 1978).

It also appears that not only frequent and general prompting, but specific, personal information, is one of the important elements of feedback. When a group of households was given daily information on their kWh use and their increase or decrease as a group instead of as individual households, no reductions were found (Winett, Neale, Williams, Yokley, & Kauder, 1979). An additional study demonstrated that the information given must be credible. For example, when consumers did not understand or agree with how their energy use was corrected for changes in weather, feedback was ineffective (Becker & Seligman, 1979).

While goal setting and specific, credible information systems should be part of feedback tactics, the best type of information (e.g., kWh, percent change, cost) remains unclear. Perhaps, any information that is sensitive to consumer efforts and is credible will work. However, additional parametric work is obviously needed.

The following list summarizes the important aspects and parameters of feedback that have been identified:

1. Frequent or continuous feedback may be necessary, although there are studies indicating the effectiveness of less frequent feedback.
2. Specific and credible information is necessary.
3. Feedback should not simply prompt; specific information seems important.
4. Feedback is more effective when enacted in a situation where difficult but achievable goals are used.
5. Feedback may be particularly effective during seasonal peak and/or time-of-day peak periods.
6. It is more cost effective to direct feedback to high-use consumers.
7. Feedback is more effective when the budget share for energy is high.
8. Feedback can be effective in decreasing overall consumption by about 15% for an entire heating or cooling season.
9. There is evidence for maintenance of reduced consumption when feedback terminates.
10. Most feedback systems have included a weather correction system that converts consumption to a percentage increase or decrease. The contribution of the weather correction factor to the impact of feedback is not clear.

Direct Applications of Feedback

Written feedback.   Written feedback studies are often referred to as preliminary demonstrations and judged interesting and informative but impractical.

Table 5.7 presents data relevant to the practicality question. The scenario is a residential energy conservation program staffed by students or hard to employ persons. The site is a high-use area during a peak-use time. The rate structure reflects prices already in effect in at least one part of the country and probably "around the corner" in other areas. The expected costs to read meters, compute figures, and distribute information are based on actual costs for the written feedback procedure (Winett, Neale, Williams, Yokley, & Kauder, 1979). Not included in the costs are professional supervisory expenses and overhead (building and equipment), both minimal in this type of operation. Table 5.7 shows that the savings (based on a 15% reduction) in kWh and dollars actually exceed the costs of obtaining those savings. Further, if savings are maintained once feedback terminates, the cost effectiveness of this approach would then be outstanding.

Such procedures could also be implemented in commercial buildings using existing maintenance personnel to provide the feedback. The possible cost-effectiveness ratio here may be even better than in the residential area. Energy consumption in some commercial buildings is very high, and feedback may only involve one staff person reading the same energy meter and delivering the same feedback each day to everyone. While this procedure needs to be tried, caution is suggested since, as noted previously, group feedback systems have been relatively ineffective. To be effective, a group feedback system may require some individual components and/or attention to enhancement of group identity (cohesiveness).

Table 5.7. Potential Costs and Savings Using a Written Feedback Procedure in a High-Use Area During Two Peak-Use Periods with a Program Staffed by Minimally Trained Persons.

	Summer	*Winter*
1. Use Per Day[a]	80 kWh	150 kWh
2. Cost Per kWh[b]	$ .12	$ .12
3. Total	$9.80	$18.00
4. 15% Reduction	12 kWh	22.5 kWh
5. Savings	$1.44	$ 2.70
6. Cost to Read Meter[c]	$ .07	$ .07
7. Cost to Record, Figure Percentage Change, Place on Form[d]	$ .50	$ .50
8. Cost to Distribute Form[e]	$ .07	$ .07
9. Paper	$ .02	$ .02
10. Cost of 6-9	$ .66	$ .66
11. Savings (5) − Cost (10) Per Day	$ .78	$ 2.04

[a] Based on actual use from Winett, Neale, & Grier (1979) and Winett, Neale, Williams, Yokley, & Kauder (1979).
[b] Approximate Con Ed rate in 1981 (not including taxes and fuel adjustment).
[c] Based on 60 meters per hour at $4/hour.
[d] Based on five minutes for the data transformation for a worker paid $4/hour.
[e] Based on 60 households per hour for a worker paid $4/hour.

Feedback devices.　Given the costs of supplying written feedback, efforts have been directed toward the development and evaluation of devices which can provide different types of information or simply present a cue for a specific behavior. The effectiveness of devices that signal overuse during peak-use periods has been shown by Kohlenberg et al. (1976) and replicated by Blakely et al. (1977). In each of these studies, lights illuminated when consumption exceeded a specific predesignated level. The feedback lights were located in the kitchen of participant families or in other locations frequently used by the families, and reduction in consumption during peak-load periods was demonstrated.

Even simpler than these devices was a light-signal arrangement developed and researched by Becker and Seligman (1979). The feedback device was developed because many persons who follow the appropriate rule of only running their air conditioning with the windows closed are not aware of when it has cooled sufficiently outside for them to stop the air conditioner and open the windows. Here the light was connected to the central air conditioner and a thermostat located on the outside of the house. When the air conditioning was on and the outside temperature was below 68° F., the blue light, visible from the kitchen and the family room, blinked repeatedly. The resident could only stop the light by turning off the air conditioner. During a one-month test, 20 residences with the device reduced their electricity use by over 15% when compared to 20 very similar residences without the device.

Currently, there are a number of different devices with a range of digital displays (accumulated use, current use, cost, special signals) being developed and evaluated by the U.S. Department of Energy, the Honeywell Corporation, and independent investigators. There is at least one feedback meter available on the market that digitally displays the projected cost of electricity for one hour (i.e., the Fitch meter). An evaluation using a quasi-experimental design has shown average energy reductions of about 15% with this meter (McClelland & Cook, 1980). However, a better controlled study has reported no responsiveness with this same device (Becker, 1978). Further, it is unclear if the feedback from such devices promotes the same changes as feedback given in other forms, such as writing. For example, McClelland and Cook (1980) found that the Fitch device did not reduce energy used for heating or cooling but resulted in energy savings from other practices. As of this writing the contribution that such devices can make to energy conservation efforts is still unclear.

Available microprocessor technology assures that devices can be quite sophisticated and, perhaps, also have weather-correction and goal-setting functions. Tax credits are also given for the purchase of a feedback device. Therefore, if such devices are further developed and marketed, it is not difficult to imagine an energy or resource console located in a highly visible area of many residences that will monitor all the home's electricity, gas, water, and perhaps even air quality. Such devices may also be applicable to commercial settings. If the goal of these systems is to have people respond to the information presented, it is clear that methods are also needed to sustain people's attention to their system once the novelty of an energy console has decreased. Americans' apparently unhappy experiences with seat-belt warning devices and seat belts connected to ignition systems (Geller, Casali, & Johnson, 1980) also suggest that an energy console must maintain vigilance through nonaversive means.

Self-monitoring. While efforts are underway to develop cost-effective feedback monitors, it appears that it is possible to have a significant conservation effect with conventional equipment—namely, the regular energy meters that exist at every home. One question is whether people can be persuaded to read their (dial) meters at least several times per week and keep a record of their use. The self-monitoring research suggests that a good deal of prompting will be needed to accomplish this task (Richards, 1977). However, if a simple self-monitoring package were developed, it may then be possible to prompt self-monitoring efforts through newspapers, radio, and television. These same media could also give expected use statistics for each day and instruct consumers on how to calculate a percentage increase or decrease from a designated prior period.

While these large-scale interventions may seem fanciful, two points are noteworthy. First, many people are starting to record mpg and route mileage in their cars, and second, successful self-monitoring of energy consumption has been demonstrated.

Since self-monitoring seems to be a practical feedback approach, specific procedures for this strategy are detailed herein. The study for which these procedures were developed was conducted during the winter in an upper-middle-class, all-electric townhouse complex (Winett, Neale, & Grier, 1979). An initial question was whether people with a mean gross household income (in 1978 dollars) of $40,000 would even be willing to trudge out in the cold every day and read their outdoor electricity meter and then return to record their consumption for the day. Yet, even in the mild Washington, D.C. winter (the site for the study), the mean monthly bill for these well-insulated residences was about $200 at the low rate of 4¢ per kWh, meaning that the budget share for electricity was relatively high. In other parts of the country with harsher and longer winters, the cost for heating and subsequent budget shares was clearly much higher.

After an initial three-week baseline period, the following simple procedures were put into effect. At a group meeting, or in a few cases in individual homes, consumers received brief (10-minute) "programmed instruction" on how to read their meters and record and calculate kWh consumption each day. For purposes of recording the data, people were given weekly recording sheets as shown in Figure 5.4. These recording forms were set up with carbon copies, and every week a staff person picked up the forms to check on the accuracy of the recordings.

The project's own meter reader independently recorded meters about the same time participants were self-monitoring their meters. It was found that participants not only read their meters in over 90% of possible instances despite rain, sleet, and snow, but their meter readings were over 96% accurate.

As a further aid to self-monitoring, participants received a note every day indicating the "expected use" for the prior day (e.g., 112% of baseline, 87% of baseline, etc.). The expected use was actually the daily weather-correction factor. A participant could then compare his/her consumption on a given day to the prior baseline daily mean and then compare this figure to the expected use. For example, if a household's use on a given day was 40 kWh, compared to a mean baseline use of 50 kWh, the actual usage percentage (for comparison with expected usage) would be 80% (i.e., 40/50). As noted above, similar information is available from utilities and could be publicized.

Figure 5.5 shows the results of this study. There was a large no-treatment, comparison group and also another group that received daily, written feedback (as in prior studies) which indicated kWh use, percent increase or decrease in use, and whether or not a household was under or over a reduction goal. Since the effects of written feedback have been so reliable, this procedure provides a sort of "benchmark" from which to compare new techniques. In the project, self-monitoring participants reduced their electricity use by 7% to 8%, whereas the standard feedback group showed a 13% to 14% reduction. Reductions in electricity use were highly correlated with reported reductions in thermostat settings. Because the procedures were implemented with relatively high users during a peak-use period (i.e., winter heating), substantial monetary savings were evident. When the procedures were in operation, feedback participants saved an average of 19 kWh a day per household, or $23 a month per household; self-monitoring participants saved 9 kWh a day and $11 a month, despite the relative low cost of electricity.

In order to perform a cost-effectiveness analysis, all the costs involved in implementing these procedures across households were first itemized and totaled. These costs are shown in Table 5.8 and amounted to about $23 per household for self-monitoring and about $26 for feedback. These calculations were conservative since they included certain research expenses such as follow-up readings. Next, as shown in Table 5.9, the dollar savings across households for different phases of the study were calculated and totaled. For both self-monitoring and feedback, dollars saved exceeded dollars spent principally because of the maintenance of effect. However, when potential

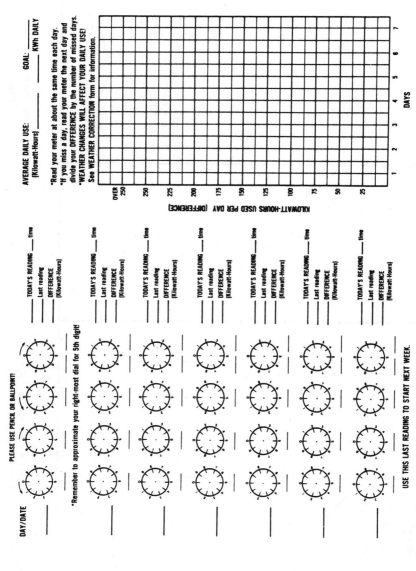

Fig. 5.4. A self-monitoring form for consumers to record daily readings on their electricity meter dials, calculate daily kWh consumption, and graph their daily kWh use.

189

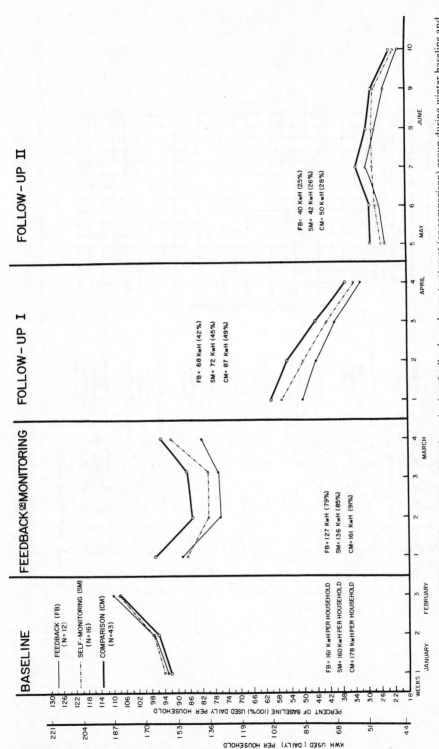

Fig. 5.5. Percent baseline use and kWh consumption of a self-monitoring, feedback, and a no-treatment (or comparison) group during winter baseline and intervention periods and a spring follow-up period. Note that the effects were maintained proportionally in the spring, although usage decreased with the warmer weather.

Table 5.8. Costs Involved in Self-Monitoring and Feedback.

	Self-Monitoring (N = 16)	Feedback (N = 12)
Recruitment (Handouts, Personal Contact, Travel)	$ 26.50	$ 18.50
Initial Meeting (Notes, Meeting, Travel, Extra Training)	$ 57.00	$ 46.00 (No Real Training)
Manual for Each Household (Forms, Clipboard, Instructions)	$ 22.00	$ 7.80 (No Clipboard)
Reliability and Feedback on Readings (Pick Up/Check Forms for Four Weeks/ "Troubleshooting")	$ 65.00	—
Daily Expected Use Note (Calculate from Comparison Group/Put on Form/Deliver for Four Weeks/Travel)	$143.00	—
Daily Feedback (Calculate Correction Factor/ Put on Form/Deliver for Four Weeks, Travel/Special Envelopes)	—	$196.00
Read Meters (16) (Daily for Four Weeks, Once a Week for Follow-Up)	$ 34.20	$ 30.00
Secretarial	$ 15.00	$ 15.00
TOTAL EXPENDED	$362.70	$313.30
TOTAL PER HOUSE	$ 22.67	$ 26.11

* All procedures are described in Winett, Neale, & Grier, 1979.

savings as shown in Table 5.9 were extrapolated to electricity rates higher than those in the study, potential savings far exceeded costs of the procedures.

The self-monitoring approach may be improved by encouraging consumers to make more sensitive calculations than in the project discussed here. For example, participants in the self-monitoring project were not asked to also record their daily percentage increase or decrease from baseline using the daily expected use figure. However, self-monitoring approaches may have potential as an individual component of communitywide feedback programs discussed in the next section.

Table 5.9. Savings from Self-Monitoring and Feedback at Different Rates for Electricity.*

	Self-Monitoring (N = 16)			Feedback (N = 12)		
	4¢	6¢	9¢	4¢	6¢	9¢
During 4-Week Intervention	$176	$264	$396	$276	$414	$ 621
During 1st 4-Week Follow-Up	$112	$168	$252	$156	$234	$ 351
During 2nd 6-Week Follow-Up	$129	$193	$290	$ 97	$146	$ 218
TOTAL	$417	$625	$938	$529	$794	$1,190
PER HOUSEHOLD	$ 26	$ 39	$ 59	$ 44	$ 66	$ 99

* Actual kWh savings found by Winett, Neale, & Grier, 1979.

Community-level feedback and monitoring. Because different communities and subcommunities have main utility lines, it may be possible to feed back use to an entire community and, thus, create an energy "self-controlling" community. In this situation, the use for an entire community could be monitored and displayed (e.g., use and percentage change) every day through cable television and charts located at frequented locations. To be most effective, the community feedback system would have to be coupled with individual monitoring and guidelines for specific conservation strategies. We say this because of the non-success of a group feedback procedure described above that did not use individual information and because of the limited success of master-metered interventions.

However, the practicality of community feedback is suggested by summer water shortages in 1977 in the Washington, D.C. area. Reacting to public concern, the media presented overall use and savings figures on a daily basis for different communities. A conservation effect was noted, and the shortage period included voluntary cutbacks in certain levels of water use. Indeed, at this point there are already experimental studies showing that media-based, community feedback can work. In one study, television feedback reduced a community's gasoline consumption (Rothstein, 1980), while another study demonstrated that feedback in newspapers was effective in reducing a community's litter (Schnelle et al., 1980).

Although we still have to describe much of the feedback work as preliminary, it appears that feedback should be an important component in individually based or larger-scale energy conservation efforts. As discussed later in this chapter, feedback may also be a significant variable in the diffusion of conservation ideas, practices, and hardware.

SUMMARY

Table 5.10 summarizes the targets, procedures, and results of residential behavioral energy studies in the order presented in this chapter. It is clear that research is still in the preliminary stages. In fact, there is only one study that actually focused on retrofitting (insulation, caulking, weather stripping, etc.) and used energy savings and retrofitting as dependent variables (Geller, Ferguson, & Brasted, 1978). Some of the possible reasons that behavioral studies have apparently avoided becoming involved in retrofitting have been noted in the introduction to this chapter.

Despite these limitations, the current work shows a number of strengths. For example, researchers have been careful to replicate procedures, expand on existing techniques, and attempt to investigate strategies that can potentially be implemented on a larger scale. Such an approach needs to be continued as behavioral researchers enter into more diverse areas of investigation. The purposes of these last sections are to indicate areas currently in need of research, to describe methods for disseminating of energy conservation strategies, and to outline plans for a more comprehensive residential energy conservation program.

AREAS IN NEED OF MORE RESEARCH

Hardware and Behavior Analysis

There is a need for behavioral input in the design and marketing of at least some kinds of energy hardware (see Johnson & Geller, 1980). The automatic thermostat set-back device provides one such example of the need to mesh behavior analysis with hardware. When used properly (e.g., appropriate night set-back and generally lower settings), the set-back device can provide excellent energy savings (Darley, 1978). As a study we previously described showed, most people never change their thermostat setting, thereby suggesting the need for the set-back device.

Table 5.11 presents energy and cost data to further illustrate this point. The energy consumption data is based on a study by Winett, Neale, and Grier (1979) in all-electric homes. Energy rates are placed at 6¢ per kWh, the mean rate for the country at the time of this writing. However, the consumption data was recorded from typical middle-class, reasonably well-insulated townhouses (described in detail in Winett, Neale, & Grier, 1979) which were

Table 5.10. Summary of Residential Energy Conservation Studies.

Residential Energy Research	Antecedents			Consequences		
	Target	Strategy	Outcome	Target	Strategy	Outcome
Hayes & Cone (1977) [apartments in West Virginia]	Electricity use, but not for space heating	Poster describing ways to conserve	No change	Electricity use, but not for space heating	Monetary rebates and daily feedback	20% to 30% reduction
Heberlein (1973) [apartments in Wisconsin]	Electricity use for space heating	Letters encouraging conservation and energy saving tips	No change			
Kohlenberg & Anschell (1980) [various types of residential units in the state of Washington]	Electricity use, but not generally for space heating	Information literature and booklets	No change	Electricity use, but not generally for space heating	Monetary rebates, rate changes, daily feedback, feedback over longer periods	Rebates and price changes marginally effective, but more effective with feedback; rate change had immediate, transient effects[1]

194

Table 5.10. (Continued)

Study						
Palmer et al. (1978) [houses in Iowa]	Electricity use	Appeal letter asking for reduction	No change	Electricity use	Daily written monetary and consumption feedback	10% reduction
Winett et al. (1978) [various types of residential units (n = 129) in Texas]	Electricity for space cooling	Pamphlet with conservation information	No change	Electricity for space cooling	High and low monetary rebates and weekly feedback	Weekly feedback ineffective; 10% reduction for low rebate; 16% reduction for high rebate[2]
Winett & Nietzel (1975) [30 houses in Kentucky]	Electricity and gas for heating	Pamphlet with conservation information	No change	Electricity and gas for heating	Monetary rebates and weekly feedback	15% reduction for electricity; no gas reductions[3]
Winett et al. (1981) [113 townhouses or apartments in Virginia]	Electricity for space heating and cooling	Information, demonstrations, videotape programs modeling conservation strategies	When used alone, modeling programs reduce use 9% to 15%; also combined with consequences (cwc)	Electricity for space heating and cooling	Daily feedback used alone or with modeling videotape programs	Feedback reduces overall use by 15% to 20%; more reduction with modeling[4]

Table 5.10. (Continued).

Residential Energy Research	Antecedents			Consequences		
	Target	Strategy	Outcome	Target	Strategy	Outcome
Becker (1978) [100 townhouses in New Jersey]	Electricity for space cooling	Goal setting: Hard goal (20%) and easy goal (2%), combined with consequence strategy	cwc	Electricity for space cooling	Written feedback (3 per week)	Feedback only effective when combined with hard goal; reduction of 15%
Becker & Seligman (1978) [townhouses in New Jersey]	Electricity for space cooling	Obtrusive blue light when A.C. on and outside temperature is below 68° F.	cwc	Electricity for space cooling	Written feedback (3 per week)	15% reduction[5]
Winett (1978) [university classrooms in Kentucky]	Electricity used for lighting in classrooms	Large signs requesting turning out lights after class	60% reduction in unnecessary lighting			

Table 5.10. (Continued).

Study						
Kohlenberg et al. (1976) [houses in the state of Washington]	Peak-load electricity use	Energy conservation booklets	No change	Peak-load electricity use	Light indicated when electricity use greater than 90% of peak for previous weeks; daily written feedback; payment of electricity bill	6% reduction; enhanced by payment[9]
Winett, Kaiser, & Haberkorn (1978) [12 apartments in Kentucky]				Electricity use	Monetary rebates and daily feedback	30% reduction for rebates; 15% reduction for feedback
Slavin et al. (1981) [master-metered apartments in Maryland]	Electricity use	Group meetings, commitment procedure	cwc	Electricity use	Rebates to individual apartments contingent on savings	6% reduction
Slavin & Wodarski (1977) [master-metered apartments in Maryland]				Gas use for heating	Rebates to individual apartments contingent on savings	5% reduction[6]
McClelland & Belsten (1978) [master-metered dorms in Colorado]	Gas use	Group meetings, conservation goals	cwc	Gas use	Feedback on energy use	10% to 15% reduction; some retrofits[7]

Table 5.10. (Continued).

Residential Energy Research	Antecedents			Consequences		
	Target	Strategy	Outcome	Target	Strategy	Outcome
McClelland & Cook (1977) [master-metered dorms in Colorado]	Gas use	Appeal flyer; booklet with conservation tips	cwc	Gas use	Feedback posted weekly; cash bonus to winning dorms	10% reduction
McClelland & Cook (1980) [houses in North Carolina]				Electricity use, but not for space heating/cooling	Energy monitor giving continuous cost feedback	12% reduction[8]
Newsom & Makranczy (1980) [master-metered dorms in Pennsylvania]	Electricity use	Flyers announcing contest	cwc	Electricity use	Feedback poster; small payment to winning dorm and payment on a raffle basis to person in winning dorm	6% reduction
Walker (1979) [master-metered apartments in Texas]	Electricity for space cooling	Rules for air conditioning use	cwc	Electricity used for space cooling	Home observations and $5 rebate for following rules	9% reduction[10]
Blakely et al. (1977) [houses in Iowa]				Peak-load use of electricity	Continuous mechanical feedback	10% decrease

Table 5.10. (Continued).

Study						
Seligman & Darley (1977) [29 townhouses in New Jersey]				Electricity used for space cooling	Daily feedback on electricity use	15% reduction
Winett, Neale & Grier (1979) [71 townhouses in Washington, D.C.]	Electricity for space heating	Participants taught self-monitoring; conservation pamphlets; phone prompts to continue self-monitoring	cwc	Electricity for space heating	Self-monitoring group receives weather correction information; another group receives daily feedback	7% reduction for self-monitoring; 14% reduction for feedback
Winett, Neale, Williams, Yokley, & Kauder (1979) [123 various residential units in Washington, D.C.]	Electricity for space cooling	Information booklets	cwc	Electricity for space cooling	Daily written feedback	15% reduction; greatest reductions for high users on peak use days[11]
Hayes & Cone (1981) [40 various residential units in Rhode Island]				Electricity use, but generally not for space heating	Monthly feedback on utility bill	10% reduction
Seaver & Patterson (1976) [119 various residential units in Pennsylvania]				Fuel oil for heating	Social commendation decal for saved oil; feedback on delivery bill indicating savings	20% reduction
Bittle et al. (1980) [353 various residential units in Illinois]				Electricity for space cooling	Different kinds of daily written feedback	11% reduction for high users, some differential effects due to type of feedback

Table 5.10. (Continued).

Residential Energy Research	Antecedents			Consequences		
	Target	Strategy	Outcome	Target	Strategy	Outcome
Geller (1981a); Geller, Ferguson, & Brasted (1978) [80 houses in rural Virginia]	Insulation of hot water heater; installation of water flow limiter	Pamphlets, workshops, face-to-face prompting	Attitudes favorable to conservation increased, but minimal change for targets			

[1] Study done in state of Washington under extremely low electricity rate.
[2] Study used to experimentally generate elasticity functions.
[3] Gas was extremely inexpensive at the time of the study; a small subsample that had more expensive electric heat reduced by 15%.
[4] Estimate of electricity saved for heating was 26%; estimate of electricity saved for cooling was 35%.
[5] Considerably more could have been saved if a higher criterion were used, e.g., 75° F.
[6] Minimal awareness of program by the residents.
[7] Retrofits were permanent, energy saving changes.
[8] Quasi-experiment; selection factors may have influenced outcome.
[9] Difficulty in modifying family schedule; may be better approached by alternative work.patterns.
[10] Used low temperature (74° F.) criterion unnecessary for comfort; more could be saved with higher temperature criterion; procedure appears cost effective.
[11] Upper-middle class users consume three to four times more electricity than lower-middle class users and are the better target for intervention.

Table 5.11. Potential for Electricity Savings With a Thermostat
Set-Back Device in the Winter.*

kWh per Day 171	Cost per kWh $.06	Total kWh per Month 5,130	Total Cost per Month $308

Prior Thermostat Setting	Change Settings			Percent Saved	Total Cost per Month Saved
	When Home (8 hours)	When Gone (8 hours)	When Asleep (8 hours)		
	Minimum Change				
69° F.	67°	67°	67°	7.4%	$ 22.80
	Moderate Change				
69° F.	65°	60°	60°	27%	$ 83.00
	Maximum Change				
69° F.	61°	55°	55°	44%	$137.00

* Consumption data based on Winett, Neale, & Grier (1979); maximum thermostat change based on Winett, Hatcher, Leckliter, Fort, Fishback, & Riley (1981). Figures based on each degree change over a 24-hour period equal to a savings of 3.7% of overall electricity consumption. Cost of device equals $65.

located in a suburb of Washington, D.C., an area with mild winters. For each degree Fahrenheit that the thermostat was lowered a 3.7% savings in electricity consumption was found, a result consistent with other research (Socolow, 1975). Using this finding and the results of the study on human comfort to determine reasonable temperatures in the home (Winett, Hatcher, Leckliter, Fort, Fishback, & Riley, 1981), estimates are provided for minimal to maximum day and night set-backs. Note that even with moderate changes, savings during one winter month are substantial; in fact, savings are more than the cost of the device. With major thermostat set-backs almost one-half of expected electricity costs could be saved!

Thus, if properly used, set-back devices could play a significant role in residential energy conservation. There may be some ways to further expedite the purchase of these devices, even though tax credits are available for their purchase. For example, advertisements could emphasize the need for changes in the thermal environment. Ads could also show respected individuals examining lower utility bills while comfortably dressed in sweaters. In addition, the device itself and accompanying instructions could emphasize a gradual change in temperature toward a target goal. Also, a second-generation device could be designed to give feedback, so that the consumer is aware of actual energy and monetary savings. If consumers find the device beneficial (i.e., temperature change gradual and comfort maintained) and can observe energy savings, the diffusion of this device throughout the country may be expedited. This point is discussed further below.

Tax-Credit Rebate Studies

There seems to be a consensus that current federal tax credits for home retrofitting are minimal and not very effective in encouraging retrofit conservation strategies (Stobaugh & Yergin, 1979). However, in some states where substantial tax credits are given for the purpose of solar equipment, business is apparently booming (Stobaugh & Yergin, 1979). While uncertain energy prices and policies cloud the future, it still seems worthwhile to conduct studies on the actual demand for retrofitting created by different tax-credit percentages. Such studies would be similar to early microeconomic studies that were conducted and discussed earlier where the effects of different levels of monetary rebates on energy demand were investigated (Winett et al., 1978; Winett & Nietzel, 1975). There are precedents for payments to citizens in experimental policy programs. For example, studies on the effects of various kinds of income maintenance and subsidy plans (Lynn, 1978), suggest that studies of tax credits and retrofitting are feasible. The tax-credit issue also provides another area for the experimental analysis described in this book to make a contribution to policy.

Institutional Arrangements

Various institutional arrangements should be investigated to determine their potential for change and their influence on residential energy consumption. For example, work hours greatly determine the time period when energy is used and, to some extent, the quantity of energy consumed. In other words, most peak-load problems may be directly attributable to time-of-day use, which in turn is dependent on work hours (Robinson, 1977). Therefore, it remains unclear whether politically feasible time-of-day pricing will significantly flatten peak-load patterns (Winett & Neale, 1979). Flexible work schedules tend to shift the time of day when specific energy consuming activities occur. Moreover, two studies found that flexible work schedules were rated as desirable by management and employees, and detailed time activity log and questionnaire data indicated that flexitime helped to alleviate some problems experienced by young families in coordinating work and home life and reducing commute time (Winett & Neale, 1980). Flexible work scheduling is only one example of an institutional change that could affect patterns of residential energy consumption. A range of other alternative work plans such as the four-day work week are also being investigated with regard to their energy saving potential (Winett & Neale, 1980).

Changing institutional arrangements is likely to result in a complex array of costs and benefits across different systems. For example, the four-day work week may decrease energy used for commuting and increase energy used for leisure activities, but reduce parental time available for children during the four work days. This is a problem because analyses of typical dual-earner families indicated that with the current five-day work week, employees spent about 11 hours per day working and commuting, leaving little time available for children or spouses. These analyses showed that increasing work hours on certain days would severely curtail what little time there was for family interaction (Winett & Neale, 1980). These important issues need to be assessed before programs are put into effect that may help with the energy situation, but be costly for other facets of our society.

Energy Efficient Communities

The different studies and programs discussed in this paper have been described in an individual manner and limited to the residential sector. Certainly, one pressing need is to determine the costs and benefits to a community which adopts a comprehensive plan for energy conservation. For example, such a community might have an extensive retrofit program, an elaborate system of walkways and bike paths, a water conservation program, and specific conservation goals.

While all indications from Davis, California are that such a community is quite viable and "civilized" (Lovins, 1977), the processes and outcomes need to be studied in other communities where social and economic circumstances have led to the initiation of comprehensive conservation programs. A careful evaluation across the different sectors (residential, commercial, governmental) and across different energy consuming practices could reveal directions for economic and physical adjustments, amounts of actual energy saved, losses and gains for employers and employees, changes in air quality, and specific modifications of life styles. More specific plans for becoming an energy efficient community are described in Chapter 8.

Social Diffusion

The application of social diffusion theory to energy programs has been discussed by Darley (1978). Basically, programs need to be implemented with components that will lead consumers to evaluate their conservation efforts as successful and subsequently to tell others of the beneficial outcomes and methods for obtaining such outcomes. These conditions help in diffusing innovations throughout the society.

Figure 5.6 presents some dimensions of diffusion theory as discussed by Rogers and Shoemaker (1971). Briefly, innovations are marketed through one or more media channels. Innovators are presumably affected by media messages (perhaps a case of information changing behavior) and are crucial in influencing later adopters ("early adopters" and "early majority") to adopt the new behaviors or products. It is essential that innovators are

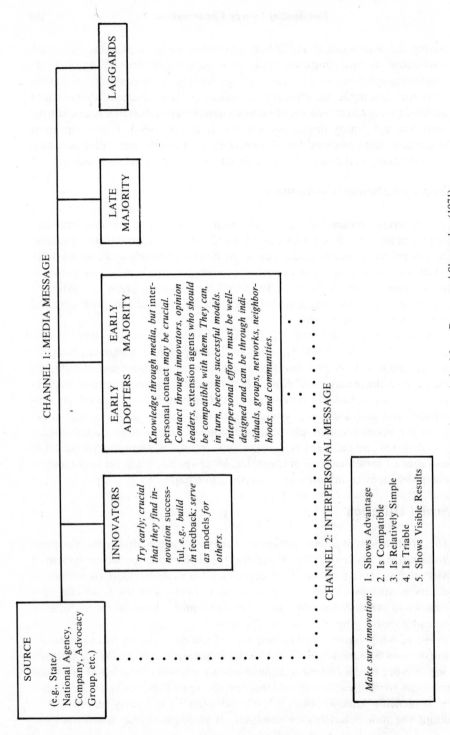

Fig. 5.6. A multistage model for the social diffusion of innovations as derived from Rogers and Shoemaker (1971).

successful and believe that the innovation has helped them. Thus, whenever possible it is of particular significance to incorporate feedback mechanisms into innovations.

Innovators can serve as successful models and influence the later adoption of the innovation by others. Feedback, modeling, and interpersonal contact may be crucial components in social diffusion (Darley , 1978). In addition, innovations should be: (1) advantageous in comparison to current practices or technology; (2) compatible with the prevailing culture; (3) simple to employ; (4) obtainable to some extent on a trial or "guaranteed or your money back" basis; and (5) show visible results (Rogers & Shoemaker, 1971).

The crucial role of behavioral analysis in the development and implementation of cost-effective programs should be apparent. This is true not only for the dissemination models described below, but for every energy program or procedure noted. All intervention strategies, from the small set-back device to communitywide interventions, have positive or negative diffusion potential.

DISSEMINATION MODELS

By dissemination models, we mean large-scale methods to promote effective residential conservation behaviors and life styles. Presently, efforts by utilities and state and federal agencies have been primarily directed to audit procedures. A "Class B" audit generally involves a customer-requested, computer-based, mailed audit system. Audit forms also have been distributed through organizations, fairs, and shopping mall exhibits. An example of questions from one such form is shown in Table 5.12. After consumers delineate the various physical aspects of their home and current practices (e.g., thermostat settings), the data are computer analyzed with the consumer receiving a list of conservation options (e.g., raise the insulation in your attic to R-30), each with associated potential savings (e.g., 15% per year), cost (e.g., $400), and pay-back period (e.g., two years). While the information seems useful, it is not surprising that the Class B audit system has not appeared effective in promoting change in the home (Kehoe & Geller, 1980). It is essentially a "one-shot" informational intervention. Yet, it is possible that as the energy situation worsens, the Class B audit could yield some energy savings. Its appeal is its simplicity and relatively low cost for large-scale implementation.

As of January 1, 1980, utilities were mandated to offer their customers Class A audits (U.S. Department of Energy, 1979). The major difference between Class A and Class B audits is that with the Class A system the original audit is supposed to be accomplished at the home site by a trained individual. Further, the auditor is to return to the home, explain the audit

Table 5.12. Sample of Typical Home Audit Questions.

Does your house have a cathedral or other type of raised ceiling which would be difficult to insulate? _____ Yes _____ No

How much insulation do you now have in your home?

Attic or Ceiling	_____ inches or	_____ R-value
Floor	_____ inches or	_____ R-value
Walls	_____ inches or	_____ R-value

What is the condition of the caulking, weather-stripping, and storm sashes? (See Information Sheet)

_____ Good, tight
_____ Average, loose in places, some repairs needed
_____ Bad, little, or none

What is the average *winter*-time heat thermostat setting? _____ ° F.

---

results in detail to the resident, and demonstrate some low-cost, no-cost conservation techniques (see Appendix).

The person-to-person aspect of this system suggests real potential for promoting energy savings. Yet, there are many unanswered questions about the Class A audit program; the first three in the following list were previously raised by Hirst (1979):

1. When it is not in the best interests of the utilities to offer such a service (e.g., rate increases are possible; generating capacity can be increased), will utilities promote the service in any meaningful way?
2. If the service were advertised, is it the kind of system that consumers really want?
3. How much will the service cost, and will consumers pay the full cost for it?
4. What kinds of auditor behaviors are important? The interactions of this person with the resident appear to be a key to the success of the program. Yet, it is unclear how these people are to be trained. Will their training be only technical or include interpersonal training? Will they do follow-up (prompting and feedback) visits?
5. How can feedback be built into the program? It appears crucial for people to receive positive feedback on the changes they have made in their homes. For example, people should know how much energy and money they are saving. Without this information the spread and success of this program (social diffusion) will probably be limited (Darley, 1978).
6. How can the program be financed? It is not clear if most consumers want or need retrofitting loans. It also has been recently proposed that utilities should gain a stake in conservation by allowing them to become involved in the retrofit business (U.S. Department of Energy, 1981).

Even if these questions and issues are resolved, we believe the Class A audit has two major problems as the primary dissemination model. It is simply too passive and may be limited in application. By passive we mean that it is an intervention in the "waiting mode" (Rappaport, 1977). In other words, the energy experts must wait until the resident has decided that the time is right to pursue conservation, rather than actively promoting conservation. It is analogous in some ways to high-powered psychotherapy. The therapy may be somewhat effective, but it is costly and depends a great deal on the individual person seeking out help. We are by no means dismissing this model, but rather suggesting that other models may have more impact.

The Class A audit may also be improved by a better conceptualization of dissemination stages. As discussed by Fairweather, Sanders, and Tornatzky (1974), dissemination strategies generally include approach, persuasion, and implementation stages. A more active, person-to-person approach stage seems needed; face-to-face (or telephone) prompting and feedback should also be included in the persuasion and implementation stages. Without more investment of personal contact (and dollars), we do not believe the Class A audit will be any more successful than the Class B audit.

Two other community models have been proposed and tested: a workshop model and a school-based model. Through local civic, social, and religious organizations, people can meet in relatively small groups and be shown the costs and benefits of different conservation strategies. This approach may be effective if the workshop meets at least several times, if techniques and materials are demonstrated to attendants, and if some procedures are used to reinforce people for their conservation efforts during the weeks the workshops meet and afterwards. We have much less confidence in the one-time, lecture-discussion workshop (Geller, 1981a; Geller, Ferguson, & Brasted, 1978).

Scott Geller and an interdisciplinary team from Virginia Tech field tested the one-time workshop approach in a number of communities in Virginia (Geller, 1981a; Geller, Ferguson, & Brasted, 1978). The goal of the program was to reduce energy used in the residential, transportation, and governmental sectors by providing local workshops to identified community leaders or otherwise concerned individuals. The workshops discussed and demonstrated energy-saving techniques. While participants rated the workshops highly and showed energy-related attitudinal change, home audits indicated that there apparently was not a transfer of attitude changes to residential energy-related practices. As discussed earlier in this chapter, this result should not be surprising. Workshops may produce changes in knowledge and attitudes, but other strategies must be added to the one-time workshop approach if actual behavior change is the goal.

There is some evidence that a task-specific curriculum for high school students (including audits and self-monitoring procedures) not only affected student behaviors, but also influenced parental practices in the home (Stevens, Kushler, Jeppesen, & Leedom, 1979). Schools can form a natural dissemination network for this type of program, and there seems to be promise of reaching a large group of people. It is also not a passive, but a much more active approach since information, strategies, and technologies are brought to the consumer with the program constructed around specific conservation tasks.

Another promising approach toward large-scale dissemination could involve extensive use of the media to demonstrate specific conservation behaviors. For example, a series of television spots and programs on conservation and efficiency in the home may not only impart information but change behaviors. These same programs can also be used to prompt conservation practices depicted in prior programs. The media approach is an active, population-based strategy with high potential cost effectiveness. As indicated earlier, there is a need to evaluate carefully the behavior impact of such programs, as this next example of a media-based program indicates.

An example of a large-scale, media-based effort to promote residential energy conservation was the "low-cost, no-cost" (LC/NC) program conducted in November 1979 by the Department of Energy in the New England states. The objectives of this program were to use a "fully integrated marketing effort designed to stimulate awareness of the LC/NC program and its components, and to motivate households to implement LC/NC energy savings actions (U.S. Department of Energy, 1980, p. 1)." To accomplish these objectives several strategies were used, including television, radio, newspaper advertising, and the postal delivery to 4.5 million households of a LC/NC booklet and a special shower flow limiter. The booklet and television ads advocated the adoption of 11 actions that were free or low-cost (less than $100 total) and could potentially save a household up to 25% of their energy consumption.

The actions included: (1) installing the shower flow device; (2) reducing the water heater temperature setting; (3) wrapping water heater tanks with insulation; (4) using cold water for the rinse cycle in electric dishwashers; (5) insulating around fireplace dampers; (6) insulating around the attic door; (7) caulking and insulating around electric outlets, exhausts, and ductwork; (8) turning off "anti-sweat" devices in refrigerators; (9) turning off pilot lights on heaters during the summer; (10) adjusting the bonnet or plenum thermostat on oil and gas-fired space heaters and tuning furnaces for maximum efficiency; and (11) adjusting draperies to let radiant heat from the sun in during the winter months and to keep out heat during the summer months.

Though the goals of this program were laudable and the methods used seem potentially effective, the actual impact of the program on householders' energy-related practices was not assessed. The evaluation of this program consisted primarily of telephone interviews to assess householders' awareness of ads and to indicate adoption of the LC/NC methods. There were no on-site observations of LC/NC practices, nor were comparative energy consumption data considered. The collection of such data would probably have been no more expensive than the collection of the abundant survey data.

The results of telephone surveys indicated a high level of awareness of the program and a high level of self-reported adoption and intention to adopt the LC/NC practices. However, recall the results reported by Geller, Ferguson, and Brasted (1978) from individuals presumably motivated enough to actually attend conservation workshops. There were large changes recorded on attitudinal instruments in that project, but virtually no observable changes in their households with respect to specific practices discussed at the workshops and endorsed by the participants on the attitudinal measures. The discrepancy between attitudinal and behavioral measures is a widely documented phenomena (Wicker, 1969). We readily acknowledge the political considerations in obtaining quick feedback on the public's awareness of the program, a case in point for this program (Seligman & Hutton, 1981), but clearly more could have been done in the evaluation.

There have been other large-scale media-based programs (such as health and safety campaigns) that have employed behavioral measures for at least a subsample (see Maccoby, Farquhar, Wood, & Alexander, 1977), and we urge that energy conservation programs which apply state-of-the-art marketing and intervention strategies also use state-of-the-art approaches to evaluation (as discussed in Chapter 2). Even if only a relatively small percentage of the 2.6 million spent on the LC/NC had been used for the collection of behavioral data, we would know much more about the feasibility of a media-based approach.

While each of the areas described needs more attention and research, even more critical is a comprehensive large-scale approach to residential energy conservation. In the following section we outline the elements of a comprehensive program that are based on current work and proposed research.

COMPONENTS OF A COMPREHENSIVE PROGRAM

Financial Incentives/Institutional Change

1. Substantial tax credits are needed for purchasing insulation material, heat pumps, solar systems, etc., and perhaps also for wood stoves and furnaces. However, before such tax credits are put into place, we recommend studies to assess the behavioral impact resulting from specific amounts or percentages of tax credits.
2. An inverted rate structure needs to be implemented which would involve very low rates for low users and very high rates for high users, particular-

ly applied during seasonal peak-use period. (It is conceivable that oil for heating could be allocated following a similar system.)

3. Utilities should have a stake in conservation by being able to do retrofit work and give loans for retrofitting. Indeed, such a program will probably be implemented soon (Federal Register, 1981).

4. Utilities should advertise through the media the availability of Class A audits. Customers should be charged a reasonable rate for the audit, but part of the audit fee should be reimbursable through a tax credit or used as a credit toward the retrofit.

5. "Energy stamps" should be used to help lower and lower-middle income families finance retrofitting.

Hardware

While much retrofitting technology is not esoteric, the development and marketing of various retrofit technologies and hardware need to proceed with input from the behavioral sciences (see Johnson & Geller, 1980). It is quite likely that some hardware will be inappropriately used because of lack of attention to behavioral variables. An example provided in this chapter was the thermostat set-back device that could yield savings up to 40% to 50% if behavioral factors are incorporated into its marketing and application.

Institutions

The potential for energy savings through organizational and institutional change should be thoroughly investigated. Flexitime and the four-day week are two alternative work patterns that could save energy, but they are likely to have marked effects on other systems. Before these practices are widespread, the multifacted impact of such institutional changes should be evaluated.

Communities

At least several model communities should be developed with the consent of their citizens in order to ascertain the different outcomes of various energy alternatives. For example, establishing an energy efficient community following "soft technology" (Lovins, 1977) could tell us the various tradeoffs involved in following that energy path. If judged successful, such a community could serve as a model for other communities.

Media

1. The media should be used extensively as previously discussed to demonstrate conservation practices and behaviors.
2. The media should be used to disseminate correct information concerning paybacks, thermal comfort and health, set-backs, and other low-cost, no-cost approaches.
3. The media should be used to *prompt* behaviors such as thermostat set-backs, passive solar techniques, and low-cost, no-cost methods.
4. The media should be used to deliver appropriate feedback. For example, energy use and cost data should be frequently shown for households that made retrofit and life style changes. Communitywide feedback should also be tried.

Local Support and Information

1. A conservation educational curriculum, particularly as it includes specific tasks for students, and perhaps a "conservation ethic" can be a program component. The aim of this preventive strategy is to train a future generation to live in a more energy efficient way. The possible spillover to parental practices can, perhaps, also yield significant energy savings.
2. Local groups and organizations should start home energy savings cooperatives. Rising prices, inflation, and a strong media effort should create the demand for such collaboration which would serve as a forum for information on services and advantages of particular strategies for the local climate. Most importantly, the group interactions could provide the mechanism for person-to-person contact which seems critical for social diffusion and behavior change (Rogers & Shoemaker, 1971). Successful "retrofitters" would then serve as guides and models for others.
3. Neighborhoods may be ideal for feedback programs. A neighborhood with some identity and cohesiveness could provide the conditions for group feedback to be effective. In addition, such programs could be conducted as part of a school's conservation curriculum. Students could help residents conduct home audits and even perform simple low-cost, no-cost retrofitting.

Evaluation

An excellent summary of the issues involved in evaluating energy conservation programs is provided in a recent paper by Seligman and Hutton (1981). They point out some of the obstacles involved in evaluating energy programs, including: (1) a lack of evaluation tradition in that field; (2) beliefs by government officials that controlled experimentation is impossible; (3) the low priority given social science conservation research by government; and (4) the political expediencies involved in developing, selling, and continuing conservation projects. While recognizing these constraints, Seligman and Hutton recommended active and high-level involvement of an evaluator in conservation programs as a way to demonstrate how feedback on program processes and outcomes can substantially improve conservation efforts. They further recommend that program evaluations follow an experimental or quasi-experimental model wherever possible, but with the evaluator also involved in helping to base program refinements on empirical data both in the early development stages (i.e., formative research on operations and implementations) and later outcome stages (i.e., summative evaluation).

Seligman and Hutton proposed that program evaluation follow the state-of-the-art methods from the social sciences and that information obtained from such evaluations also make theoretical contributions by being integrated into the social science knowledge base. For example, evaluations of conservation programs can tell us much about consumer behavior in response to marketing techniques and pricing strategies, particularly if measures are developed which are sensitive to the program's obejctives (e.g., the purchase and/or use of specific types of appliances). Thus, conservation programs and the social sciences can be equally well served if programs are carefully planned and field tested. This position of Seligman and Hutton is obviously in agreement with our perspective.

CONCLUSION

At the beginning of this chapter, it was indicated that 50% of the energy currently used in the typical home could be saved. For the most part these savings can be achieved through available, low-cost engineering technology and nonaversive life style changes. The conservation programs described in this chapter represent combinations of behavioral procedures, economic principles, and community and organizational strategies, in conjunction with simple retrofit and life style recommendations. If we are to reach the twenty-first century comfortably, broad and comprehensive conservation efforts must be continually instituted, evaluated, and refined.

Appendix to Chapter 5
Low-Cost/No-Cost Retrofit Strategies

LOW COST/NO COST—1980

Included in this appendix are 50 actions and retrofits that make up the low cost/no cost package. These are known and commonly available, inexpensive devices and retrofits that are likely to pay back in energy savings in less than two years. Some are energy or efficiency measuring devices that encourage and allow the homeowner to monitor the home's energy use. Some, such as the in-out thermometers for air conditioning ducts, allow the homeowner to know when the air conditioner is in need of service. Such information could easily save the homeowner 20% to 40% of the air conditioning costs.

These items and retrofits should not be evaluated for individual cost and savings, other than to confirm that they are:
1) Inexpensive
2) Likely to pay off in less than two years.
3) Generally applicable to the U.S. home.
This package should save one-third to one-half of the homeowner's energy and water consumption. The material cost will vary from house to house and should cost no more than $200. To put this material cost in perspective with other energy savings improvements, for $300-$400 the average house could be outfitted with storm windows, yet the savings may only be 2-6%. To bring an attic up to the R.C.S. recommended level of insulation from an existing 3½ inches would cost between $300–$700, but would save only 5% of the homeowner's energy bills.

The Heating System:

- Check firing rate and advise homeowner of reduction capabilities.
- Reduce blower cut-off limit switch to lowest setting or reduce aquastat

setting to minimum temperature setting that will still heat the house, or install modulating aquastat.

- Check burner efficiency and advise homeowner of alternatives.
- Perform economic analysis for vent damper or replacement burner.
- Remove insulation from duct joints and seal duct joints with flexible caulk. Then insulate ducts to 3½ inches.
- Insulate hot water pipes.
- In the basement, seal all cracks and voids between floor and all protrusions through the floor.
- Install flue stack thermometer.
- Install filter change alarm in forced air system.
- Balance distribution system with baffles, booster blowers, valves, etc.
- Install running time meter.
- Install thermostat fooler for night setback control.
- Install individual thermostats on electric baseboard heaters.
- Install radiator covers in rooms that are too hot.

The Cooling System:

- Install filter change alarm in window as well as central systems.
- Install In/Out thermometers across cooling coil.
- Install booster blower or other techniques to balance forced air system.
- Install two 20-inch window fans and outdoor thermometer.
- Install running time meter.

The Water System:

- Insulate hot water tank. Set thermostat to 140° F. or lower if a dishwasher is not used. Install heat trap.
- Install separate hot water line to the dishwasher.
- Install Temperature Regulation Valve (TRV) near hot water heater. If separate line cannot be run to dishwasher, install TRV in each hot water line as close to the water tank as possible but beyond the take-off point for the dishwasher.
- Install shower flow controllers in all shower heads and faucets.
- Install aerator cut-off switch in kitchen and bathroom sink faucets.
- Install shower head cutoff valve (optional).
- Install dual flush toilet mechanisms in all toilets.
- Insulate hot water lines.

In the Attic:

- Seal all cracks and voids around ducts, vent pipes, wiring chimneys.
- Strip insulation from around air duct joints and caulk those joints with flexible caulk. Then retape the joint.

- Check for heat bypasses in walls, around walls, above interior walls and dropped ceilings.
- Weatherstrip around the attic access door and insulate the back of it.
- If the attic has less than 3½ inches of insulation or safety hazards, make individual recommendations and calculations of cost and savings of bringing the attic up to various thicknesses of insulation.
- Install flapper dampers on *all* exhaust vent duct work from bathrooms, laundry rooms, kitchens, etc.

Sealing Up the House:

- Seal all cracks, voids, and openings around foundation, joist headers, toe moulding, windows, and doors from the *inside*.
- Remove any caulking and weatherstripping placed between outside siding and foundation.
- Install draft sealers behind outside wall electrical switches and receptacles.
- Seal heat bypass in hollow or cinderblock walls and in hollow walls.
- Stuff insulation in joist header cavity after caulking joints.
- Install thermally activated crawl space opening covers.
- Install door sweeps on leaky doors.
- Refit storm windows that don't close properly.
- Repair door sweep and weatherstripping of storm doors.
- Seal up fireplace with removable fireproof cover.
- Install dryer vent diverter, filter, and dirty filter alarm.
- Double glaze basement windows with clear plastic.
- Install fire retardant, sticky backed, expanded polyethylene foam to basement windows and infrequently used windows.

General Miscellaneous:

Install fluorescent fixtures or bulbs in high-use fixtures.

Chapter 6
Transportation Energy Conservation*

There are many environmental problems caused by or directly related to contemporary transportation systems. The impact of transportation on two main categories of environmental problems, resource depletion and environmental pollution, is dominant and overwhelming. With regard to resource depletion, passenger cars alone consume 27% of the nations's annual consumption of petroleum and natural gas (Sokolosky, 1979). In such cities as New York, Los Angeles, Washington, and San Francisco, 25% to 30% of precious land is devoted to roads and parking spaces for cars (Bruce-Briggs, 1977). In addition to the tremendous energy and land costs necessary to operate contemporary transportation systems, vast amounts of energy and other natural resources are needed for the production of these systems. The Motor Vehicle Manufacturers Association noted that in 1975 the United States automotive industry consumed 19% of the steel, 47% of the natural rubber, and 33% of the zinc produced in this country.

Environmental pollution is also highly correlated with contemporary transportation systems. Since the 1940s a major proportion of air pollution has been caused by the ever increasing population of private automobiles. The internal combustion engine is particularly responsible for carbon monoxide, hydrocarbons, nitrogen oxides, ozone, and lead (Purdom & Anderson, 1980). Other sources estimate that as much as 60% of all air pollution in the United States is produced by the automobile (Dorf, 1974).

Noise pollution is also pervasive in major urban areas and the major culprit is again transportation. In the Urban Noise Survey (U.S. Environmental Protection Agency, 1977) it was found that automotive sources con-

---

* This chapter was adapted from two previous works: Everett, P. B., Reinforcement theory strategies for modifying transit ridership, in I. Altman, J. Wohlwill, and P. Everett (Eds.), *Human behavior and the environment: Transportation*, New York: Plenum Press, 1982, in press; and Reichel, D. A., and Geller, E. S., Applications of behavioral analysis for conserving transportation energy, in A. Baum and J. E. Singer (Eds.), *Advances in environmental psychology, Vol. 3, Energy conservation: Psychological perspectives*, Hillsdale, New Jersey: Lawrence Erlbaum Associates, 1981, 52–91.

stitute the most pervasive noise disturbances in the urban enviroment. The study reported widespread annoyance with noise, problems of disturbed sleep, and speech interference. Purdom and Anderson (1980) reported that 51% to 68% of urban noise sources comes from motor vehicles.

Another source of pollution credited to motor vehicles is aesthetic pollution. Although this is more difficult to document than air and noise pollution because of its subjectivity, its existence cannot be denied. There is much agreement that sprawling auto junkyards, urban congestion, highway billboards, endless strip development and so on are aesthetically unpleasant. These attributes of contemporary urban life are direct products of motor vehicles.

Transportation is a dominant contributor to the environmental problems of resource depletion and environmental pollution in the United States. Because of their overwhelming number, passenger cars are the major culprits. For example, passenger cars used 59% of the petroleum products used by the entire United States transportation system in 1977. By comparison, aircraft used 8% and trains only 3% (National Cooperative Highway Research Program, 1977).

SCOPE OF THE CHAPTER

This chapter focuses on the dominant relationship between one mode of transportation (passenger cars) and environmental problems. The impact of passenger cars on the environment could certainly be decreased should more fuel efficient cars be developed and/or less polluting exhaust systems implemented. It is *not*, however, the intent of this chapter to discuss physical/technical solutions to the automobile-environment problem. Instead, the prime intent is to review strategies designed to change travel behaviors so that consumers: (1) reduce their vehicle miles traveled (vmt), (2) drive in a manner so that their miles per gallon (mpg) are increased, and (3) elect more energy efficient modes of travel such as mass transit, bicycles, walking and ride sharing (e.g., car and van pools). This chapter further focuses on consumer behaviors which are related to one environmental problem associated with passenger cars—energy consumption. Although many environmental problems are related to passenger cars, it would be a larger task than possible within the confines of this chapter to address them all. Indeed, some of the other problems of passenger cars (e.g., air and noise pollution) would be partially resolved should the energy issues be properly addressed.

Finally and most importantly, this chapter limits itself to a discussion of behavioral strategies that have evolved from experimental behavioral analysis (as reviewed in Chapter 2). The development of strategies to reduce energy consumption travel has evolved from perspectives other than the behavioral approach. For example, marketing theory and practice have suggested promotion and advertising strategies for increasing transit use (Weiglin, 1975). Economic principles have suggested: (1) gasoline pricing techniques to reduce fuel purchase for passenger cars, (2) parking price strategies to discourage intensive car travel in congested urban areas, and (3) pricing procedures to increase car pooling and transit use.

Strategies for changing travel behavior have also emanated from areas of psychology other than experimental behavioral analysis. For example, much research has focused on assessing people's attitudes toward certain attributes of various transportation modes that may be discouraging their use (Recker & Stevens, 1976). However, as is the case for addressing the many environmental problems associated with the passenger car, it would be beyond the scope of this chapter to discuss the multitude of travel-change strategies emanating from the numerous and diverse disciplines that have addressed the problems of transportation management. However, it is impossible to delete strictly economic applications and discuss only behavioral implementations. For example, economists have suggested pricing strategies (such as an income tax rebate) for buying a fuel efficient car. This can be considered a reinforcer as suggested by behavioral analysis and reinforcement principles (see Chapter 2) as well as a manipulation of a demand elasticity curve (see Chapter 5). The chapter deals with this issue by discussing strategies for changing travel behaviors that have evolved directly from behavior analysis and/or adhere to the tenets of the behavioral paradigm (whether intentionally or not).

A REINFORCEMENT MODEL OF ENERGY RELATED TRAVEL BEHAVIORS

A reinforcement model of energy related travel behaviors is presented in Table 6.1. It is appropriate to present this model before discussing specific examples of reinforcement applications for transportion. Two broad classes of travel behavior are identified in the model (single occupancy car driving and energy efficient travel), as are two contingent consequences of these responses (positive reinforcers and punishers). Additional categories have been developed under the heading "Energy Efficient Travel." They are increasing mpg, reducing vmt, and selecting another mode than the car. In each of the matrix cells (numbered one through four), there are speculations as to the kinds of events or consequences that might *normally* follow these behaviors.

The model has several shortcomings. First, it is static in time and space and does not account for the continual changes in the nature of behavior and consequences, nor for changes in environmental contexts and settings (as

Table 6.1. A Reinforcement Model of Energy Related Travel Behaviors.

			Consequences Contingent on Behavior	
			Reinforcers	Punishers
SINGLE OCCUPANCY CAR DRIVING			1 —Short travel time —Prestige —Arrival/departure flexibility —Privacy —Route selection —Predictable —Cargo capacity —Credit —Protection from weather —Quiet —Exhilaration (fun of driving)	2 —Traffic congestion —Gas and maintenance costs
ENERGY EFFICIENT TRAVEL	Single Occupant Car	Reduce vmt	3a —Cost savings	4a —Cancel trip —Constrained trip flexibility
		Increase mpg	3b —Cost savings	4b —Slow —Uncomfortable car (small) —Dangerous car (small)
	Select Mode other than Car (e.g. transit, car pool, vanpool, walk, bicycle)		3c —Make social contact —Cost savings —Healthy	4c —Long travel time —Exposed to weather —Dangerous —Crime —Immediate Costs (transit) —Noise —Unpredictable —Crowded —Limited cargo capacity —Limited arr./depart. flexibility —Limited choice of travel route

discussed in Chapter 1). Second, it does not incorporate schedule of reinforcement and reinforcement delay concepts (as discussed in Chapter 2). Third, it does not illustrate the different magnitudes of relative impacts of the various kinds of consequences following given behaviors. The model assumes that all the consequences have roughly the same impact. Yet in spite of these shortcomings, the model provides a systematic framework to illustrate how the existing environmental consequences overwhelmingly favor driving single occupancy vehicles. It should be emphasized that these existing environmental consequences were not designed by psychologists but rather by highway engineers, car manufacturers, economists, politicians, and so forth. Nevertheless, they are, however, reinforcers and punishers that do influence behaviors. From a behavioral analysis perspective, Table 6.1 suggests strategies one might institute in order to decrease single occupancy car driving and increase energy efficient travel. To accomplish this task, for example, the consequences of cells 1 and 4 could be reduced, and/or the consequences in cells 2 and 3 could be increased.

Additionally, the model demonstrates from a practical and theoretical perspective that there are appropriate and inappropriate consequences that a decision maker can choose from. For instance, the reduction of cell 1 consequences may be politically difficult, since it would entail a reduction of reinforcing events for citizens. Cell 2 manipulations, although favored by public policy makers, are theoretically inappropriate to manipulate. If one chooses to decrease car driving by punishing it and in turn increase energy efficient travel, something very different may happen. Any behavior which avoids a punishing event is reinforced. Therefore, under these circumstances the energy efficient alternative would not be specified, so it is not known what response (e.g., transit use) would be increased. For example, a government policy may strive to suppress car driving by requiring higher taxes on gas, yet car driving may remain high because of the purchase of black-market petroleum. Punishment procedures seem to be favored by policy makers, since they often seem easier to manage and sometimes lead to readily observed behavior change. Yet the unwanted behavioral side effects are not predictable and may lead to problems which outweigh management efficiency.

Manipulations in cells 3 and 4 are the most favored. Decreasing the amount of punishment which follows energy efficient travel (cell 4) would be a fruitful strategy. However, the precise identification of the behaviors which would be reinforced by such changes is difficult. Therefore, the consequences in cell 3 are both politically and practically the best to deal with. For example, increasing the number of reinforcing events that follow energy efficient travel requires an exact specification of the desired target behavior (e.g., bus riding, car pooling, biking) and may not evoke the politically sensitive reactions that often follow punishment procedures.

As mentioned above, the model presented in Table 6.1 needs additions that cannot be graphically represented in order to make it more complete. First, one must not only attend to the reinforcers and punishers that are consequent on various travel behaviors but also consider the schedule of these reinforcers and punishers. For example, the reinforcing consequence of privacy has a very high probability of occurrence consequent upon car driving, while privacy on mass transit is a much less predictable event (a very thin schedule of reinforcement), thus increasing the odds against transit ridership.

Second, one must consider delay of reinforcement parameters in a reinforcement model of energy efficient travel behaviors. The dollar consequences of using a private car are often deferred through a credit system, whereas an individual using a bus must pay immediately. As basic research has shown, immediate consequences have a greater impact on behavior than deferred ones. A more thorough examination of many environmental problems, such as the overuse of the passenger car, demonstrates even more strongly that the delay of reinforcement concept is a major factor in society's inability to change environmentally relevant behaviors. The immediate consequences (which indeed control behavior) for car driving commonly tend to favor the increase of car driving (e.g., speed of trip, prestige, privacy), whereas consequences that would have the best probability of suppressing car driving (e.g., depletion of resources, severe levels of pollution) are quite delayed several years in the future and/or are not easily identifiable. Deslauriers (1975) has presented a more detailed account of the effect of delay of reinforcement parameters on travel behavior. He noted that certain modes (e.g., the private automotible and dial-a-bus) will be clearly favored over a fixed route bus as a result of the reinforcement delay inherent in the different modes.

One final comment with regard to the model in Table 6.1 is appropriate. The model as presented is qualitative. It would be quite interesting and worthwhile to attempt to quantify the relative influences of behavioral consequences. In other words, does the reinforcing consequence of "privacy" for car driving have an equal, less than, or greater influence on behavior than does "crowded" as a punisher for transit use? Indeed, such quantification is the work of demand modeling. Demand modeling is a branch of applied economics that attempts to develop quantitative models of consumer behavior based on data such as income, housing, employment, life style, and so forth. A convergence of reinforcement perspectives with the demand modeling work would be most beneficial. Reinforcement theory could specify a general framework within which quantitative demand modeling could develop.

This brief overview of a reinforcement model of energy related travel behaviors provides the background for reviewing studies that attempted to modify travel behaviors through the application of reinforcement principles.

REINFORCEMENT PRINCIPLES
AND ENERGY EFFICIENT TRAVEL

The purpose of this section is to review several applications of reinforcement techniques to the task of increasing energy efficient travel behavior. As mentioned earlier, the chapter focuses on three specific behaviors. Studies that attempted to reduce vehicle miles traveled (vmt) by car drivers are first presented, then those that attempted to modify driving behaviors that lead to greater miles per gallon (mpg). Finally, the chapter reviews the larger group of studies that attempted to increase the use of more energy efficient modes of travel than the single occupancy passenger car. These latter studies address car and van pooling and transit use.

Reducing Vehicle-Miles-of-Travel

Reducing vmt is perhaps the most direct approach to reducing the energy consumed by passenger cars. Indeed, if each of the 100 million automobiles in the United States were driven 10 miles less per week, 3.5 billion gallons of gasoline, or 5 percent of the annual automobile demand for gasoline, would be saved annually (Federal Energy Administration, 1977). The Federal Government has realized this fact and it is reflected in the many "contingency plans" promulgated for energy emergencies. In addition to ration plans, strategies for allowing driving only on certain days, driving on a limited number of roads, closing gas stations, and reducing the amount of downtown parking are all aimed at reducing vmt.

Foxx and Hake (1977) published the first successful application of behavioral technology applied to the task of reducing vmt. Two groups were used: a Reward group received the opportunity to earn various prizes (e.g., cash, car servicing, tours) for reducing automobile mileage, whereas a Control group received no such incentives for reducing mileage. The twelve subjects in the Reward group were enrolled in one psychology course and the nine subjects in the Control group were enrolled in a different psychology course. Subject selection was instituted to insure that subjects did most of their driving with a single car, that little driving of the car was done by another person, that the odometer was functional, and that the subjects drove their own automobile to classes.

An ABA-withdrawal design was followed. No planned contingencies were in effect during the initial baseline, which varied from 23 to 30 days among individuals for the Control group and from 21 to 35 days for the Reward group. Subjects were required to bring their cars to an odometer check point at designated times. On the final day of baseline, subjects in the Reward group were given a guide which listed mileage-reduction goals from 10% to 50%, the prizes associated with each reduction, and the miles-per-day reduction needed to achieve the 10% to 50% reductions.

A mean reduction of 20% from initial baseline was obtained by subjects in the Reward condition. Subjects in the Control group actually showed a mean increase in mileage of 4.5% from initial baseline. During the post-treatment baseline, subjects in the Reward condition increased their mileage to a level equivalent to that of the initial baseline. Thus the efficiency of reinforcement in reducing vmt was clearly demonstrated.

A number of procedural weaknesses in this study were corrected in a replication and extension by Hake and Foxx (1978). In the second study, a short-term reinforcement schedule was incorporated by providing small weekly reinforcers in addition to the larger, end-of-treatment reinforcers of the earlier study. All subjects were commuting students, eliminating one problem of the earlier study which included dormitory residents with minimal essential driving.

Since subjects in the Reward group of the earlier study (Foxx & Hake, 1977) were students in one of the experimenter's classes, a design artifact could have been responsible for the obtained mileage reductions. Hake and Foxx (1978) examined the behavioral effects of this potential artifact (which they termed a "leader" variable). One-half of the subjects in the Reward condition were from a university class taught by the second author (n = 4) and one-half were from a class whose instructor was not involved in the study (n = 5). During treatment, subjects in the Reward condition could earn from \$1 to \$2 per week for 10% to 30% weekly mileage reductions relative to initial baseline. All of the subjects in a Self-Recording condition (n = 8) were from the same class taught by the second author. This group was the Control group, and these students were required to record their mileage. They were paid for this task but not for decreasing their vmt.

The Reward group obtained a 22.5% reduction in miles driven relative to initial baseline. The leader variable, manipulated only under the Reward condition, did indeed have a strong effect. The four students from the second author's class averaged a 40.3% reduction, whereas the five students from another class averaged only an 8.2% reduction. The Self-Recording group obtained a 12.6% reduction in miles driven relative to initial baseline. All subjects in this condition were students of the second author's class, thus the reduction may have been biased by the leader variable.

These results clearly demonstrated that contingency management may be applied effectively to reduce automobile mileage. Furthermore, the leader variable is an interesting phenomenon that demands further study because it may be applied very cost-effectively to reduce automobile mileage. The effect of a leader in the Hake and Foxx (1978) study suggests that supervisors, managers, and foremen in organizational settings could be incorporated in mileage reduction programs to motivate individual participation and to facilitate the efficacy of a self-recording intervention. The observed effect of a leader in the Hake and Foxx study could have been due to several factors, including a special respect for the author and his intentions, the prompt that students received by seeing the author in class, and possibly special statements made by the author.

A cost-benefit analysis by Hake and Foxx was based on absolute reduction in mileage relative to the average of both baselines and revealed a total of \$79.97 savings in terms of gasoline not purchased by the Reward group, whereas an overall savings of $20.40 was obtained for the Self-Recording group. Total prize money was $126.00 and $109.50 for the Reward and Self-Recording groups, respectively. Such an analysis reflects more costs than savings and can be criticized for not realistically reflecting the cost-benefit exchange. The total $100.37 saved in terms of gasoline not purchased by subjects is an "elusive" benefit that does not represent a tangible benefit to subjects nor to experimenters. Hake and Foxx (1978) recommended that the procedures would be more economical under any of the following conditions: (1) if the size of the monetary prizes were reduced; (2) if only drivers who used their car frequently were participants; and (3) if prizes were awarded for absolute miles reduced per day instead of for percentage reduction from baseline. This latter suggestion would eliminate the problem that a large percentage reduction may not necessarily result in an economical reduction if the subject drives very little.

A procedure that may be more economical and just as motivating is the use of a lottery or raffle. Geller and his students (Geller et al., 1975; Ingram & Geller, 1975; Witmer & Geller, 1976) have demonstrated the effectiveness of a raffle in encouraging participation in paper-recycling programs (see Chapter 4). One "chance" in a lottery or raffle could be made available for each 10% reduction in mileage per week, with additional bonus "chances" made available for each 10% reduction achieved over a month.

Reichel and Geller (1980) extended the work of Hake and Foxx (1978). In an attempt to determine a more cost-effective means of providing incentives for reductions in vmt, these authors compared a contest to a lottery procedure. In the contest, one group of five individuals competed against another group of six individuals for having the greatest percentage decrease in vmt for a three-week period. The prizes consisted of items contributed by local merchants, such as a kite, a T-shirt, and a dinner for two. The prizes could be distributed among the team members in any way desired. The teams became nonexistent following this treatment and the individuals from these teams were then subjected to a lottery condition for three weeks. In this procedure, a lottery ticket was given to each subject for each 5% reduction in vmt from the previous week. At the end of the lottery treatment, the holder of the winning lottery ticket received a free keg of beer. Additionally, the holder of the most lottery tickets received a $25 cash price.

Under the contest contingency (or group reinforcement), the nine subjects obtained a 23.8% reduction in vmt, while in the lottery condition (or individual contingency), a 27.8% increase in the average weekly driving was observed. The authors cite this as evidence of the potency of group over individual contingencies in certain situations. It should be noted, however, that there could be contaminating effects caused by using the same subjects sequentially in first the contest and then the lottery condition. Furthermore, since the lottery condition was implemented later in the spring than the contest, weather may have influenced the results. Whatever the case, the experiment does illustrate some very interesting possibilities for developing cost-effective reinforcement procedures for reducing vmt. This avenue of research certainly ought to be pursued.

Another result of the Reichel and Geller (1980) study was the verification of the leader effect found in the Hake and Foxx (1978) study. The students' professor was a subject in one of the contest treatment groups. This group's vmt reduction was almost three times that of the other groups! Since the professor's vmt did not vary from baseline to treatment, this difference was entirely due to changes in the car usage of the students and reflected the effect of a leader variable. As in the case for the lottery versus contest findings, the leader variable finding is of the greatest interest. However, it certainly deserved more detailed research in order to understand conclusively its effects. Indeed, if contests (group contingencies) and leader variables are as influential as this original work has demonstrated, significant improvements can be made in the impact and cost-effectiveness of programs designed to reduce vmt.

As pointed out in the discussion of the model of energy-related travel behaviors (Table 6.1), the consequences that should suppress car driving are usually delayed (such as the purchasing of fuel with a credit card), while the immediate consequences of car driving are usually quite reinforcing (e.g., speed, prestige, privacy). On the other hand, many immediate consequences of bus riding are often aversive (e.g., payment of fare, crowding) and the reinforcing consequences delayed (e.g., reduction of energy consumption). To reiterate, delayed consequences of behavior have much less probability of modifying behavior than do more immediate events. Thus, the task of reducing car driving might be partially accomplished by making some of the delayed consequences more immediate. One suggestion would be a "pay-as-you-go" procedure similar to those found in taxi cabs.

Such an experiment was attempted by Hayward and Everett (1975). These researchers planned to have taxi meters, indicating costs per mile of operation, mounted in several passenger cars. This was not technically possible so the following procedure was instituted. Ninety people that commuted to a large state university by themselves in cars were selected and agreed to participate in an experiment designed to determine how much it cost them to commute to work. These subjects were randomly divided into four groups, (1) mileage feedback only—a control; (2) operating cost feedback—7 cents per mile; (3) operating and depreciation cost feedback—15 cents per mile; (4) operating, depreciation and social cost feedback—25 cents per mile. (Note that these are the 1975 costs for operating a passenger car. Estimates at the time of this writing clearly double these costs.) The social costs were arbitrarily determined in an attempt to represent factors induced by cars, such as the costs of air pollution, health decrements, and building facade decay. All

subjects then received daily cost feedback on his/her windshield for a period of two weeks. This feedback was determined by the number of miles
driven in the previous 24 hours and by the subject's experimental treatment
assignment. This feedback was received in the form of 5 inch by 8 inch cards
as illustrated in Figure 6.1. The dependent variable was miles driven per
treatment condition. Different treatment groups were compared against each
other and with themselves. Pre- and post-manipulation baseline mileages
were collected for each of the treatment groups, and showed absolutely no
mileage changes induced by the experimental treatments. There were, however, significant changes in attitudes toward satisfaction with the car as a
viable mode of transportation (i.e., stronger changes for higher magnitude
feedback groups). Many pre-treatment positive attitudes toward the car
moved to the negative end of the scale after the experimental treatment (such
as an atitude about the cost of commuting to work).

This experiment demonstrated the common discrepancy between attitudes
and behavior and points out again the fallacy of assuming a good correlation
between the two. The failure to obtain a change in mileage is most likely due
to two factors. First, real response consequences were not altered. Subjects
still paid for their operating and depreciation costs primarily through a
credit system. In other words, this experiment did not manipulate actual
response consequences from a delayed temporal position to an immediate

---

YOUR CAR COSTS YOU .... ¢
FOR EVERY MILE YOU DRIVE,
AS CALCULATED BY THE
FEDERAL HIGHWAY ADMINISTRATION

SO FAR THIS WEEK YOUR
CAR HAS BEEN DRIVEN
A TOTAL OF .... MILES,
AT A TOTAL COST TO YOU
OF $..........

You may keep
this card and
show it to
others who
drive your car.

IN THE PAST _____ HOURS, YOUR CAR HAS BEEN DRIVEN _____ MILES AT A TOTAL COST TO YOU OF: $_____.

REMEMBER:

This card is intended to show you, the driver, how much your car costs you to
drive. The figure shown above represents what you have actually paid, whether
by cash or credit, to drive your car the distance indicated. This sum covers the
costs of: depreciation, maintenance, accessories, parts, tires, gas, oil, garage,
parking, tolls, insurance and State and Federal taxes.

Fig. 6.1. Sample of the cost feedback cards placed on the windshields of subject cars in a
study by Hayward and Everett (1975). Such feedback influenced relevant attitudes but not
driving behaviors.

one. It would be interesting to run this experiment via manipulation of actual consequences of mileage driven. This could be carried out by the installation of a mechanism similar to those found on an automatic washer in a laundromat. Would mileage be altered if a car driver were required to drop a quarter into the slot every two miles in order to maintain operation, even though the quarter was no more expensive than his/her current mileage costs paid for by credit?

Second, it is likely that this experiment did not influence vmt because of its attempt to alter mandatory trips (i.e., the work trip). In a setting where no other viable transportation alternatives were available, it would be difficult for an individual to modulate mileage regardless of the desire to do so. This speculation suggests that future research on this topic ought to deal with situations where trip decisions have some degree of flexibility in transportation alternatives and/or trip requirements.

In contrast to these negative findings is a study by Rothstein (1980). Feedback on a Texas community's overall gasoline consumption was provided each day during televised news broadcasts. Implementation of the television feedback was associated with decreases in consumption relative to baseline, and discontinuation of feedback resulted in a return to baseline consumption levels. Alternative explanations for the effect (e.g., increase in price, inconvenience in gas purchasing and perceived crisis situation) were found to be untenable. Also, it was noted in Chapter 3 that communitywide feedback procedure was effective in reducing environmental litter (Schnelle et al., 1980). In light of the failure of individual feedback in the Hayward and Everett study, these results for an entire community are certainly surprising. The procedures need to be replicated in other transportation settings and for other aspects of environment preservation.

Increasing Mileage-per-Gallon (mpg). Increasing mpg is another major way of saving transportation energy. Indeed, the major strategy of U.S. auto manufacturers is to develop more fuel efficient engines. It is estimated that very shortly (mid-1980s) passenger cars will be able to obtain 75 mpg. These goals will be attained through several physical-technical endeavors, ranging from engine modifications and tire design to vehicle body weight and configuration. However, little attention has been given to strategies which attempt to modify driver behaviors so that fuel savings are promoted through mpg changes. Although several oil companies publish "driving guides" on how to save fuel, these have not been evaluated, although their effect on behavior is probably negligible. However, two reinforcement-based studies have demonstrated successful strategies for modifying driving behaviors that result in improved mpg.

Lauridsen (1977) reported a successful effort to reduce gasoline consumption in automobiles through feedback and lottery interventions. Four em-

ployees of a utility company who typically drove over 50 miles a day, and
often more than 100 miles a day, served as subjects. A fuel flow meter was
installed in each of the four company vehicles driven by each of the four
subjects. In two of the automobiles (Drivers 1 and 2), the meter provided
continuous *miles-per-gallon* feedback. In the other two vehicles (Drivers 3
and 4), the meter provided continuous *gallons-per-hour* feedback. Prior to
initial baseline, the meters were installed and the drivers were informed of
the meter and its feedback function.

During initial baseline (which varied from 8 to 17 days among individuals), the meters were covered and rigged so that removal of the cover could
be detected. The drivers were asked to drive as they normally did. Mean
mpg was recorded daily for all four vehicles by one observer and at least
once a week by a second observer. During initial feedback (2 to 20 days) the
meter was uncovered so that the drivers could receive feedback. Mean mpg
was again recorded daily. Drivers 1, 2, and 3 were then returned to baseline
conditions (6 to 17 days), followed by two days of second feedback. Following the two days of initial feedback for Driver 4 and the two days of second
feedback for Drivers 1, 2, and 3, a five-day Feedback-plus-Lottery (FL)
condition was implemented. In addition to the feedback from the meters,
each driver earned one chance for each one-tenth of a gallon increase over
his individual median mpg for the last five days of the immediately preceding
baseline (i.e., second baseline for Drivers 1, 2, and 3, and initial baseline for
Driver 4). Additionally, a driver lost one chance for each one-tenth of a
gallon decrease in mpg. At the end of each day the driver was informed of his
mpg for the day, his number of chances earned or lost for the day, and his
cumulative number of chances earned or lost. The lottery winner received
the total estimated savings (based on projected gasoline saved) by all four
drivers (i.e., $20.49). Following the FL condition all drivers were returned to
baseline conditions (7 to 12 days). A second, five day FL condition was then
implemented in which only Driver 1 and 3 participated. The winner received
$8.07.

Table 6.2 shows the median mpg for each driver for the various experimental conditions. Lauridsen (1977) suggested that the failure to increase
mpg for Driver 3 during initial feedback might have been due to unrepresen-
tative data during initial baseline, which for 11 days of baseline varied daily
from 40 to 338 vmt and 9.7 to 14.9 mpg. The consistent increases obtained by
Drivers 1 and 2 when feedback was available suggests that mpg feedback
might have been more effective than gallons-per-hour feedback. Both Drivers 1 and 2 performed equally better under both feedback and FL conditions, whereas Driver 3 performed better under initial FL and Driver 4
performed better under feedback. Thus the relative efficiency of feedback
and FL was not clarified. Interviews with the drivers indicated that when
feedback was available, they tended to accelerate more slowly, maintain

Table 6.2. Median Miles-per-Gallon for each Driver.

Condition	Driver 1	Driver 2	Driver 3	Driver 4
Baseline	10.1	7.5	12.4	15.8
Feedback	10.9	8.0	11.2	18.2
Baseline	9.0	5.9	11.3	—
Feedback	11.2	7.7	11.3	—
Feedback-plus-Lottery	10.9	8.0	13.1	16.6
Baseline	10.3	6.5	8.6	16.6
Feedback-plus-Lottery	10.8	—	11.5	—

Note. Adapted from Lauridsen (1977, Table 1, pp. 12-13). Feedback was miles-per-gallon for Drivers 1 and 2 and gallons-per-hour for Drivers 3 and 4.

constant speeds, avoid streets with frequent stops, release the accelerator when going downhill, and reduce idling time. All of these techniques are considered to increase fuel efficiency (see American Automobile Association, 1975; Federal Energy Administration, 1977).

Several comments should be made concerning the Lauridsen (1977) study. First, a separate lottery condition without feedback would have served to identify the relative efficacy of the lottery contingency independent of feedback. Secondly, an interesting question is raised in that the drivers adopted well-established fuel-conserving behaviors when feedback was available. It is not clear whether these behaviors arose from the feedback itself or from previous knowledge about fuel-conserving driving behaviors that the drivers may have possessed but did not employ. A suggestion that the change in driving habits may not have been due entirely to the feedback meters is that due to the nature of the internal combustion engine, there may a temporal delay between any given driving behavior, its effect on the engine, and its effect being manifested on a feedback meter (Hurley, 1978). A major contribution of the Lauridsen (1977) study is that it demonstrated that driving behaviors can change average mpg. However, more well-designed research is needed to evaluate the influence of lottery contingencies on driving behavior and increased mpg, as well as the more general issue of the reliability and validity of feedback meters. Additionally, subjects' prior knowledge of fuel-conserving driving behaviors should be assessed. Further research is indicated, since increasing fuel economy may be a viable alternative to reducing miles traveled (see Hake & Foxx, 1978), especially for mandatory trips such as commuting to and from work.

Research on a larger scale was accomplished by Runnion et al. (1978) who reduced the amount of fuel consumed by a textile company's distribution fleet by using feedback, social recognition, and a lottery. The participants were 195 long-line and intermill drivers. Long-line drivers delivered freight throughout a 32-state region; intermill drivers operated among 58 terminals in three states. Over six million miles were driven by the 195 drivers in one year.

Both Experiments 1 and 2 evaluated mpg as the dependent measure, calculated daily for intermill drivers (Experiment 1), and on a per-trip basis for long-line drivers (Experiment 2). Data was collected from fuel-purchase tickets and odometer readings. Initial baseline lasted one week for Experiment 1. During this time the intermill drivers received no encouragement to increase mpg. The first intervention lasted one year and consisted of: (1) antecedent instructions concerning ways to increase mpg and announcement of a program to increase mpg among the drivers; (2) personal recognition on a random basis, and in the form of letters commending the driver's improved performance; (3) feedback of mpg for the fleet and for each individual, graphed and posted daily in the drivers' room at each of the 58 terminals; (4) social reinforcement from company officials in the form of nonsystematic and unstructured praise for improved performance; and (5) peer competition prompted by public display of individual performance.

During the first two weeks of the second year, the second intervention of Experiment 1 was implemented and consisted of: (1) publicly displayed feedback of fleet performance; (2) the social reinforcers obtained during the first year; (3) a personal letter to each driver informing him of his past performance; and (4) a weekly lottery for pen sets, key chains, and so forth with the company logo. For the lottery, a driver's name was added to the pool for each day of the week he obtained above 6 mpg. The lottery and personal letters were implemented on an unspecified intermittent schedule.

The average mpg for the intermill drivers was 5.73 during baseline. For the first year, the average was 6.02 mpg, a 5.06 percent increase above baseline. The average for the second year was 5.97 mpg, a 4.18 percent increase above baseline.

In Experiment 2 the same contingencies implemented during the first year of Experiment 1 were applied to the long-line drivers. The second year consisted of the second-year contingencies used in Experiment 1 plus public feedback for each long-line driver team graphed by category. The long-line fleet averaged 4.80 mpg. during baseline. The first year average was 4.90 mpg, a 2.08 percent increase above baseline. The average for the second year was 5.23 mpg, a 8.96 percent increase above baseline.

Though these changes seem small in terms of energy savings, the textile company saved enough fuel to run its entire fleet for one month at no cost. Three design limitations of the Runnion et al. research were (1) a short baseline period; (2) no comparison groups; and (3) no reversal or a multiple-baseline condition. These limitations were largely the result of the company's desire to institute money-saving procedures immediately. In addition to these design limitations, the procedures were sometimes unclear. For example, in Experiment 1 the second year lottery was implemented intermittently "on a leaner schedule as the year progressed (Runnion et al., 1978, p. 184)"; the exact schedule, or even the number of times a lottery was held were not specified. It is not clear whether the lotteries were dense (e.g., once a week) early in the year and very lean later in the year, or whether they were relatively lean at the start. Fading from once a week to once a month at one rate is quite different from fading from once every three weeks to once every two months as some other rate.

The Runnion et al. study extends the findings of Hake and Foxx (1978) by using a noncollege-student population and by applying seemingly low-cost, perhaps even cost-efficient contingencies. No cost-benefit analysis comparing the dollars saved in gasoline not purchased to the cost of implementing the contingencies was reported. Finally, the Runnion et al. investigation demonstrated long-term and large-scale effectiveness of behavioral technology to increase fuel economy.

Increasing the Use of Energy Efficient Modes of Travel

In addition to reducing the vehicle miles traveled and increasing the mpg obtained in passenger cars, a major reduction in energy consumption would result from the use of travel modes which are more energy efficient than the single occupancy passenger car. Such modes include car pools, van pools, mass transit, hitchhiking, walking, and bicycle riding. It is the intent of this section to discuss the applications of reinforcement principles for increasing three of these travel modes: van pooling, car pooling, and transit use. Unfortunately, no good examples of behavior principles applied to hitchhiking, walking, or bicycle riding have been found.

Ride sharing (through car and van pooling) has tremendous potential for energy savings. A typical eight-passenger van pool saves approximately 5,000 gallons of gasoline a year (Pratsch, 1977). Bent (1977) estimated that if 3,100 van pools were in operation by 1985, 1,218 million vmt would be saved, representing an annual savings of 19 million gallons of gasoline. Furthermore, car pooling could result in an annual savings of from one to three billion gallons of gasoline (United States Department of Transportation, 1975).

Many forms of mass transit are very energy efficient if the transit vehicle is fully occupied. Van pools are the most energy efficient, using 2,410 Btu per passenger mile traveled (pmt), express buses are second, using 3,820 Btu per pmt, and older subways are third, using 3,990 Btu per pmt. Conventional urban buses use 4,130 Btu per pmt. By comparison, the single occupancy passenger car uses 14,190 Btu per pmt (Congressional Budget Office, 1977).

Car Pooling.   Attempts to increase car pooling have employed two basic strategies: (1) preferential treatment of car poolers (Letzkus & Scharfe, 1975;

MacCalden & Davis, 1972; Rose & Hinds, 1976); and (2) efforts to organize car pools (Andrle & Dueker, 1974; Jones & Derby, 1976; Scheiner & Keiper, 1976). A number of employers have used both of these approaches (see Pratsch, 1975; United States Department of Transportation, 1975). Other researchers have evaluated the influence of attitudes and psycho-social factors on the formation and maintenance of car pools (Barkow, 1975; Dueker & Levin, 1976; Horowitz & Sheth, 1977).

Physical interventions such as priority lanes for car poolers are one of the more common techniques used to promote car pooling. Priority lanes offer the incentives of decreased travel time and avoidance of traffic congestion for users. A number of communities have implemented priority lanes for car pools, including Dade County, Florida (Rose & Hinds, 1976), Boston, Massachusetts (Miller & Deuser, 1976), Fairfax County, Virginia (Fleishman, 1975), and San Francisco, California (MacCalden & Davis, 1972).

MacCalden and Davis (1972) reported an attempt to increase car pooling in the San Francisco Bay area. Commuters who car pooled to San Francisco (i.e., at least two riders per car) received reductions in monthly fares and the use of a faster priority lane on the San Francisco-Oakland Bay Bridge. There was some increase in the use of car pools. However, there were two major problems associated with this program. First, the priority lane was located in the center of the bridge, making virtually impossible the apprehension of lane users who were not car pooling. Second, some people tried to undermine such contingencies by placing mannequins in the car to give the appearance of extra riders (Reichel & Geller, 1981).

The problem of enforcement is critical to the success of priority-lane incentives. Miller and Deuser (1976) noted that priority lanes which are physically separated from general-use lanes by safety cones or barrier walls do not pose a substantial enforcement problem. On the other hand, priority lanes that are not physically separated from general-use lanes, such as those in Dade County, Florida, have posed substantial enforcement problems. The principal problem has been that of lane use by non-car poolers (Miller & Deuser, 1976). Conventional patrol techniques such as high visibility (i.e., presence of many patrol cars) and apprehension of violators have been almost singly relied upon to enforce priority lane restrictions. For example, in Dade County, six police officers patrolled the 5.5 mile priority lane when the restrictions were in force (Rose & Hinds, 1976). However, six police officers per 5.5 miles of highway does not seem cost effective, especially when there was still an 8 percent violation rate (Rose & Hinds, 1976). Innovations in enforcement techniques for priority lanes are certainly needed (Miller & Deuser, 1976).

In addition to the enforcement problem accompanying priority lanes, the undermining procedures which some solo drivers have employed to meet the contingencies could actually reduce the overall energy conservation potential of a community transportation program. Specifically, Brasted (1978) observed that on the Shirley Highway, in Fairfax, Virginia, which has priority lanes for both buses and car poolers, drivers pick up riders at bus stops so as to qualify for the car pool lane. Such practices reduce the number of passengers carried by a bus, thereby increasing the energy intensiveness of the bus system (i.e., the ratio of fuel used to passenger miles).

Rose and Hinds (1976) reported on the Dade County priority lane project. A contraflow bus lane and a car pool lane were designated for 5.5 miles of the South Dixie Highway which links Suburban South Dade County with the Miami central business district. From 7 to 9 a.m. and 4 to 6 p.m. the two inside lanes were reserved for buses or cars with two or more occupants. Figure 6.2 shows the location of the priority lanes relative to the general use lanes. Note that the bus lane provides for movement in the direction opposite to the general flow lanes that are on the same side of the median as the bus lane; thus the bus lane is a contraflow lane. In Figure 6.2 the arrows pointing left represent the dominant flow of traffic for the morning hours. In the afternoon hours the direction and placement of the car pool and bus lanes are reversed. Overhead message boards above the lanes notify drivers of the lane restrictions.

Evaluation of the project was based on vehicle and vehicle occupancy counts made once a month for one week during eight of the first 12 months of the project. Baseline data was available from data collected six, three, and one month(s) prior to implementation of the priority lanes. Mail and telephone surveys were also conducted during the first 12 months of operation.

Results showed a five-fold increase in bus ridership levels over the level that existed before the project was implemented. However, at the time of the implementation the number of peak-period bus trips was increased from 10

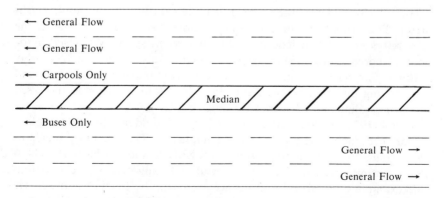

Fig. 6.2. Relative location of priority lanes on the South Dixie Highway. Source: adapted from Rose and Hinds (1976), Figure 2, p. 20.

to 84, making it difficult to specify the separate impact of the priority lane on bus ridership. Survey results showed that 65.1% of the bus riders were former solo drivers, and 12.5% had previously participated in a car pool. Of the 740 bus riders surveyed, 94% verbalized that they used the bus to get to and from work; 49.1% reported that one reason for changing to the bus was low cost (50 to 60 cents); 47.4% reported improved work-trip travel time (a 15 to 20 minute decrease) as a reason for changing, and 77.4% reported convenience as a reason.

Vehicle and vehicle-occupancy counts showed that the car pool priority lane, along with a car pooling parking lot in the central business district, increased the average occupancy per vehicle for all general use lanes from 1.30 to 1.45 persons per vehicle during the initial six months of the project. The car pool lane accounted for 40% of the rush hour person-trips during the project hours (i.e., 7 to 9 a.m. and 4 to 6 p.m.). Saving fuel was reported as a reason for changing to a car pool by 62.6% of surveyed car poolers, time advantage by 58.7%, and companionship by 37.4%. Unfortunately, Rose and Hinds (1976) did not report previous transportation mode used by car poolers nor percentage increases in car pooling.

Preferential parking incentives are perhaps the most frequently used technique to encourage car pooling. For example, the National Aeronautics and Space Administration (NASA) in Houston, Texas, initiated a car pool program in 1964. Presently, 90% of the parking permits at NASA are allocated to car pools and a mean of 3.85 employees ride to work in one car (Pratsch, 1975). Employees from both Jantzen, Inc. and Baltimore Federal agencies were matched for car pools and the lists were distributed to the employees. The matching efforts increased car pooling by 30% and 7%, respectively. Hallmark Cards and McDonnell Douglas Corporation employed both matching techniques and parking incentives, and increased car pooling by approximately 50% (Pratsch, 1975).

Hirst (1976) reviewed the energy impact of car pooling policies in Washington, D.C. Table 6.3 summarizes his findings. "Parking incentives" in the table refers to the contingency that close-in parking spaces were reserved for only car poolers. "Parking incentives plus costs" also includes a $2-per-day parking charge for solo drivers. It is clear that car pooling incentives and solo driving disincentives substantially reduce solo driving and increased both car pooling and mass transit riding.

Bryant (1974) summarized the incentives that could be offered by employers for encouraging car pooling among employees. These included preferential parking, financial bonuses, social recognition, and flexible work schedules to optimize pick up and delivery while avoiding rush-hour congestion. One example of financial rewards was reported by Letzkus and Scharfe (1975). Monetary rewards were effective in increasing car pooling among employees of the United Gas Pipeline Company in Houston, Texas. Em-

Table 6.3. Impact of Car Pooling Incentives in Washington, D.C.

	Solo Drivers	Car Pool Participants	Mass Transit Riders
Baseline	52.9%	25.4%	14.5%
Car Pool Parking Incentives	−10.69%*	22.05%	0.4%
Car Pool Parking Incentives plus Parking Costs for Solo Drivers	−22.27%*	43.82%	4.55%

* Percent change from baseline.
Source: Adapted from Hirst (1976, Table 4, p. 192).

ployees were paid up to 90 cents a day for using the public bus to commute to work. Employees who participated in car pool with four or more passengers were allowed free parking at the company's parking garage. Additionally, the company paid two-thirds of the parking fee for three-passenger car pools and one-third of the fee for two-passenger car pools. Thus the incentives not only encouraged car pooling, but large car pools as well. Participation during the first year included 508 of the 685 company employees. The total cost to the company was $105,900: $74,300 paid to the employees who rode the bus and $28,080 to the 158 employees who participated in car pools of four or more. Also, there were 15 three-passenger car pools and 12 two-passenger car pools. Unfortunately, no baseline data was reported, nor was a cost-benefit analysis reported in order to evaluate the excessive cost of this program.

A second strategy for increasing car pooling has involved company organizational efforts. Under one program information pertaining to the employees' work schedule, address, and willingness to participate in a car pool is collected and usually fed into a computer. The computer program then matches employees for car pools, and a list of potential car pools is returned to the employees. Andrle and Dueker (1974) studied car pool organizational efforts with minimal employer incentives. Three work places in Iowa City, Iowa were studied: a white collar firm, a blue collar firm, and the faculty/staff of the University of Iowa. Survey questionnaires, including attitudinal and work trip items, were administered to employees. Potential car pools were compiled on the basis of responses to the questionnaire and made available to the employees. Three months after the car pool information had been distributed, a follow-up survey was given to the employees in order to determine the efficiency of the efforts to organize the car pools.

At the University of Iowa car poolers were offered second priority parking (i.e., behind handicapped employees), where no incentives were offered by the white or blue collar firms. Since the study was conducted during the

1973-74 energy crisis, rising gasoline prices and gas station lines probably provided incentives to car pool. At the white collar firm, 111 employees indicated a willingness to car pool, but at the three-month follow-up only four had actually formed new car pools, and of these four three had given them up. Similarly, no new car pools were formed at the blue collar firm. No follow-up survey was conducted for the university employees, although car pool parking permit applications showed *no* appreciable increase. Thus, without extrinsic employer incentives and an organizational effort that goes beyond the mere distribution of information concerning potential car pools, gasoline prices do not apppear to provide an incentive for car pooling.

It again appears that cost may not be a salient contingency in one's selection of transportation mode. Indeed the reliance of the Federal Government on aversive consequences to reduce automobile usage (i.e., higher gasoline prices) has not been observed to be a viable method of reducing automobile usage. A gradual price increase in gasoline would actually allow adaptation to increasing prices. The findings of Andrle and Dueker (1974) suggest that a large and sudden increase in gasoline price may be required if aversive consequences are to be effective.

The results of the attitudinal items in the Andrle and Dueker study reflect the problem of attitude-behavior discrepancies (previously raised by Hayward & Everett, 1975). Across the three firms surveyed, 51.2% of the employees reported a willingness to car pool, yet only four car pools were actually formed! Andrle and Dueker concluded that the potential car pooler must have a fairly regular work schedule, live relatively far away from work, and want to save money. Initially, all potential car poolers will object to taking more than fifteen additional minutes to get to work, and will be concerned with the inconvenience of car pooling and the independence sacrificed by joining a car pool. The major reasons for not car pooling given in the follow-up evaluation (which consisted of a checklist) were: (1) variable work schedule; (2) no interest, and (3) too much time spent waiting and traveling. The inconvenience associated with the car pool is clearly a major deterrent. In the initial survey to determine willingness to car pool, 61% of the respondents reported inconvenience as either important or very important.

Scheiner and Keiper (1976) reported a car-pool matching effort in the Wilkes-Barre, Pennsylvania area that aimed at three markets: (1) the general public; (2) employers; and (3) labor unions. The general public was approached through media advertising of the car-pool matching effort. Employers were requested to distribute car-pool matching questionnaires to employees with a memorandum explaining the project and endorsing energy conservation. Labor unions were asked to provide names and other information necessary for the matching program. Through these efforts two people were matched for car pools through the area-wide approach, 699 employees were matched through the employer approach, and 954 were matched through the labor union approach. This matching occurred in late 1974. In early 1975, 5% of those who had been matched were interviewed over the telephone. Of those surveyed, 5.9% had formed car pools. Thus, it was estimated that only 20 car pools were formed out of the 1,655 people who had been matched by the car pool service. Scheiner and Keiper (1976) did not provide an analysis of the number of car pools formed by the market approach. Similar to the findings of Andrle and Dueker (1974), matching efforts alone did not result in a substantial increase in car pooling. It appears that without special incentives to car pool, car pool matching and organization efforts are relatively ineffective.

On the other hand, Jones and Derby (1976) presented evidence contradictory to the notion that organizational efforts (without explicit incentives) are relatively ineffective. The city of Sacramento, California provided a dial-in service designed to provide car pool matching services for the entire community. This dial-in service was promoted through media advertising and was similar to the area-wide approach reported by Scheiner and Keiper (1976). Further, employees were contacted through their employers and requested to complete and return a car-pool matching questionnaire if they were interested in car pooling. After six month, 5,083 names had been collected. Approximately 634 of these people were contacted for a follow-up interview. Of those interviewed, 21.8% had been placed in car pools (37% from the dial-in service and 19.3% from the employer service). Of those placed) 15.2% had dropped out (10.9% from the dial-in service and 19.5% from the organizational service). Of those interviewed, 92 people from the dial-in service had been placed in a car pool and 10 had dropped out and 119 people from the employer service had been placed in a car pool and 22 had dropped out.

Overall, the car-pool matching services reported by Jones and Derby were markedly more effective than the Wilkes-Barre and Iowa City efforts. As in the Wilkes-Barre and Iowa City efforts, the only general incentive to car pool was the gasoline savings which the individual could realize. Since the times at which the projects were implemented did not differ, the most obvious explanation for the differences in these efforts to form car pools is the different populations represented or the nature of the trips made. Iowa City is a relatively small college town. Wilkes-Barre is a medium-sized urban area where approximately 40 percent of the work force is employed in manufacturing (Scheiner & Keiper, 1976). Sacramento is a large city with many state and federal employers, and has presumably longer commuting distances and greater economic advantages for car pooling.

Table 6.4 summarizes the effectiveness of selected employer-sponsored efforts to increase car pooling. The results tentatively suggest that incentives may have more impact than matching efforts, but that both together may be optimal. This notion is partially supported by the increased car pooling

Table 6.4. Effectiveness of Selected Employer-Sponsored Car Pooling.

Employer	Initial percentage of car pooling employees*	Additional percentage of car pooling employees
Matching Service Only		
Air Force Accounting and Finance Center	25	20
Baltimore Federal agencies	—	7
Bell Helicopter	20	20
Boeing Aircraft	29	8
Jantzen, Inc.	—	30
Northern Natural Gas	32	27
Tennessee Valley Authority	33	14
Texaco	8	14
Mean	24.5%	17.5%
Matching Service and/or Priority Parking		
Federal Highway Administration	—	55
Hallmark Cards	—	50
McDonnell Douglas	—	50
The Pentagon	71	—
Washington, D. C. area	—	22
Mean		44.25%

* —indicates no initial data reported.
Source: Adapted from Pratsch (1975); United States Department of Transportation (1975, Table 5, p. 23).

obtained where no matching efforts had occurred (i.e., Rose & Hinds, 1976). However, Bryant (1974) noted that even though there is no known correlation between being matched for a car pool and subsequent participation in a car pool, inadequate and insufficient research may be responsible for this observation. The typical problems of field research and case-study evaluations suggest only cautious acceptance of this conclusion. For example, the lack of control groups, the inability to control other variables such as increasing gasoline prices, and the frequent failures to report baseline car pooling, limits most research on the effectiveness of employer-sponsored car pool programs.

However, a recent study by Jacobs, Fairbanks, Poche, and Bailey (1981) did combine a matching program with incentives for car pooling while simultaneously carrying out a detailed assessment of the program. On a major university campus, commuters to large parking lots were individually monitored on a daily basis by noting their car license plate numbers. After a baseline period the commuters were apprised of a car-pool matching program and then given the incentives of a reserved parking space and coupons (worth 25 cents at participating merchants) for each occupant of a car pool (i.e., two or more people per car). These coupons were given out daily to those in the car pools. These procedures increased new car pools from 10 to 20 percent, depending on what parking lot was monitored. The daily monitoring of individual car license plates allowed a detailed accounting of new car pools formed in addition to the existing car pools and the migration of other existing car pools from other lots to the parking lots with incentives. The detailed accounting of individual cars also permitted an analysis of car pool frequency for those cars in the program. The most common number of trips made by the newly formed car pools was eight or less for three months of the program. This low number of car pool trips reflects the university setting. Commuters did not have to come to the university on a daily basis as they typically had only two or three class days per week.

Jacobs et al. (1981) also carried out a detailed cost-benefit analysis of their program. When they compared the university's cost of building and maintaining a single parking space ($3,600), the benefits of the incentive program were clearly justified. Indeed, the authors noted that $3,600 is quite inexpensive compared to major central-business-district parking lot costs. Accordingly, an incentive program would look even better in a cost-benefit analysis under more common parking lot construction conditions.

Finally, Jacobs et al. (1981) noted that a post-treatment survey of the users of the parking lots showed that the availability of the car pool matching program was rather insignificant in creating car pools. The drivers noted that the incentives were the important variables, and of the two incentives, the reserved parking was the most significant. Indeed, in one treatment condition, the 25-cent coupon was dropped and the rate of car pooling was maintained by the incentive of reserved parking alone.

The Jacobs et al. study is significant as it presents a detailed analysis of individual car pooling behavior under various treatment conditions (i.e., matching programs and different incentives). As these authors noted, this research direction will truly contribute to an understanding of the salient variables for car pool inducement. As they further noted, these variables will be many and varied for different individuals. It is time to begin to understand the breadth of car pool incentives and apply the relevant ones to given individuals and population segments.

Social psychological influences on car pooling have been examined by a number of researchers. Barkow (1974) pointed out that car pooling is a social arrangement, and to better understand the contingencies involved in promoting car pooling it is necessary to develop an understanding of the psycho-social nature of car pooling. For example, Dueker and Levin (1976) compared the attractiveness of hypothetical car pools by having college students rate the relative desirability of hypothetical car pools that varied in number of riders, sex of each rider, and whether or not each rider was an acquaintance. For one-rider car pools, both males and females rated car pools with an acquaintance and car pools with a female rider as more attractive than car pools with a male rider. The results also yielded a significant interaction between sex of the rider and rider acquaintance. That is, if the rider was an acquaintance then the sex of the rider had little consequence on the attractiveness ratings, whereas if the rider was not an acquaintance then both males and females preferred female riders. Similar trends were obtained for two- and three-rider car pools.

Barkow (1974) concluded from interviews with car poolers working in the Canadian Ministry of Transportation and Communication that car pooling is for mature people, and that the success of a car pool rests on flexibility and mutual accommodation. Resistance to car pooling was seen as stemming from people's hesitancy to encounter and negotiate with strangers. This is not surprising in light of Dueker and Levin's (1976) finding that acquaintances were preferred to nonacquaintances. In the Barkow (1974) study the most frequently mentioned advantages of car pooling were money savings and relief from the tensions of driving, while the most frequently mentioned disadvantages were hypothetical constraints on freedom (e.g., obligations to be punctual, reliable, and civil to fellow riders).

Horowitz and Sheth (1977) proposed a mathematical model of ride sharing based on socioeconomic level, travel characteristics, and attitudes. The data was collected from questionnaires administered to Chicago-area residents who were contacted through employers. Among the principal conclusions were: (1) demographic and travel characteristics were poor predictors of driving alone or car pooling; (2) appeals to the issues of energy, traffic congestion, and air pollution had little influence on attitudes toward ride sharing, although respondents with a high socioeconomic level were more sensitive to such public-cost appeals; (3) perceptions toward lost time and inconvenience need to change before travel behavior will change; and (4) in general, solo drivers have a neutral attitude toward ride sharing. These conclusions suggest that certain promotional campaigns based on ride-sharing benefits to the general public (i.e., reduced energy consumption, reduced traffic congestion, and reduced air and noise pollution) will generally be ineffective. On the other hand, it may be effective to aim at alleviating concerns about the loss of independence, loss of time, and loss of convenience associated with ride sharing. For example, time can be gained (not lost) through ride sharing by allowing additional time to read the morning paper, plan the daily agenda, or socialize with fellow riders (i.e., immediate pleasant consequences).

Margolin, Misch, and Dobson (1976) employed a panel discussion technique to generate hypotheses about the incentives and disincentives of ride sharing. Homogeneous consumer groups were used, including groups of (1) central business district, blue-collar commuters, (2) suburban, white-collar commuters, (3) suburban executive and professional commuters, and (4) high-school drivers. Discussions began with open-ended and general questions and ended with discussion of transportation problems and potential solutions. The results suggested that "driving" connotes different things to different people, and incentives and disincentives vary accordingly. For example, teenagers stated that they experience pleasure and satisfaction from driving as well as a sense of freedom from parents, while laborers were apparently much less dependent on driving for satisfaction and pleasure but expressed the need for job-related driving. Thus, to provide incentives for transportation modes other than solo driving it may be necessary to establish an incentive package that offers a variety of rewards, each geared to some specific, homogeneous population.

The following points summarize the research on car pooling reviewed in this section:

1. Community interventions, such as the designation of priority lanes for car pools have been effective in increasing the average occupancy per automobile during peak-period commuter traffic (Rose & Hinds, 1976).

2. The critical issue of enforcement of priority lane restriction must be resolved more cost efficiently.

3. The effectiveness of car pool formation efforts is equivocal. Andrle and Dueker (1974) and Scheiner and Keiper (1976) found car pooling matching services to be relatively ineffective in initiating car pools, whereas Jones and Derby (1976) reported similar organizational efforts to be relatively effective. Demographic and sociological factors (including residential location and trip length requirements) may account for the discrepancy between investigations. Further, it is not clear if additional incentives such as priority lanes are needed to increase the effectiveness of organizational efforts, although incentives alone, without organizational efforts, have facilitated car pool formation (Rose & Hinds, 1976).

4. Some perceptions about car pooling are not influential in the initiation of a car pool, but may become rewards for maintenance of one. For example, reduced personal and public costs were not found to be sufficient incentives for initiation of a car pool (Andrle & Dueker, 1974; Horowitz & Sheth, 1977), but may serve as rewards for the maintenance of already established car pools (Barkow, 1974).

5. The initiation and maintenance of car pooling is mediated by social factors such as sex, prior acquaintance with riders (Dueker & Levin, 1976), and social skills (Barkow, 1974), as well as demographic and reference-group factors (Margolin et al., 1976).

This final point has important ramifications. Nietzel et al. (1977) recommended the use of computer matching to form car pools. Indeed, the car pool formation projects reported by Scheiner and Keiper (1976) and Jones and Derby (1976) used computerized matching services. However, computer-formed car pools are impersonal and do not overcome the reservation people feel when negotiating with strangers (Barkow, 1974). Furthermore, the information needed for computerized formation of car pools runs counter to current concerns about privacy (Margolin et al., 1976).

If prior acquaintance (Dueker & Levin, 1976) and social skills (Barkow, 1974) are determining factors in car pool formation and maintenance, then a more personalized approach is necessary. Such an approach could take the form of an employee "car pool contest," whereby employees from specific neighborhoods or work sections compete for prizes awarded by the employer to those groups with the highest percentage of car poolers. Alternatively, company-time "car pool parties" could be organized where employers give their employees the opportunity to meet and become acquainted with others interested in forming a car pool. Such a procedure was employed by the Hewlett Packard company in Colorado Springs, Colorado (Pratsch, 1975). Computer-matching services could not be practically employed because of variable work schedules. Extended "coffee breaks" were arranged for employees from predetermined residential locations. During these "coffee breaks" employees discussed possible arrival times and routes and were able to negotiate and compromise, overcoming the limitations of a computer-based matching effort. As a result, 40% of the employees participated in car pools. Such techniques afforded the opportunity to develop acquaintances, generate group cohesiveness, indicate company commitment to car pooling, and facilitate a social attention phenomenon similar to that identified by Hake and Foxx (1978) as a determinant of energy-conserving automobile usage.

In addition to techniques aimed at lessening the aversive social factors involved in organizing car pools, the additional time spent traveling in a car pool could be offset with additional time at coffee breaks and lunch, and/or company car use for car pooling employees when emergencies arise. Additional time allowed at coffee breaks and lunch could serve as an incentive for car pooling. Again, the use of techniques that demonstrate company commitment will take advantage of the social attention or leader phenomenon (Hake & Foxx, 1978; Reichel & Geller, 1980).

Van Pools. A second major form of ride sharing is the van pool. The 3M Commute-A-Van system (CAV) reported by Owens and Sever (1977) provides a cost-efficient model for increasing ride-sharing behavior. With continued growth and hiring at the 3M corporate headquarters in St. Paul, Minnesota, the need for additional parking space in a limited area posed a substantial problem in the early 1970s. To avoid investment in a costly new parking facility and to reduce traffic congestion, 3M developed the CAV. The program began in 1973 with six, 12-passenger vans and presently consists of a fleet of 86 vans with more being added. The CAV avoids a major problem of car pooling, i.e., the requirement of at least one person willing to use his or her own car with compensation barely adequate to meet operating expenses (Owens & Sever, 1977). The following more detailed description of the CAV shows its additional benefits and its potential as a model for both large and small organizations.

For specific residential areas in the St. Paul vicinity, a van-pool coordinator was selected. Selection was based on special interviews with employees at 3M who had indicated an interest in becoming van-pool coordinators. The coordinator for a selected residential area was charged with driving the van, picking up and returning passengers, arriving for service, maintaining the van, training backup drivers, billing riders, keeping records, and parking overnight. An innovative system of contingencies was arranged in order to encourage participation as a coordinator, including a free ride to and from work, personal use of the van at 7 cents per mile, the receipt of all passenger fares over the minimum required of eight, and convenient parking at 3M. The coordinator filed an expense voucher once a month to determine the amount due 3M for personal and business use and the amount due the coordinator for maintenance expenses. Comments from riders surveyed revealed a diverse set of positive consequences for riders, ranging from reduced gasoline and insurance bills and lack of tension from driving, to socializing with fellow riders and "sitting next to Mary (Owens & Sever, 1977, p. 79)."

The CAV program currently operates on a self-amortizing basis (i.e., the income generated by the program pays for the cost of the program). Fares are based on operating costs (gasoline and maintenance) and on fixed costs (initial cost, depreciation over four years, insurance and licensing). Initially the monthly fares ranged from $19.50 to $29.50 per passenger depending upon the residential area from which the van operated. Fares collected from passengers in excess of eight were given directly to the pool coordinator, providing an incentive for the coordinator to enlist the maximum number of riders (i.e., 11). Van pool programs are especially appealing from a reinforcement perspective because all the parties involved (3M, the van drivers, and the passengers) receive pleasant consequences, thus promoting the maintenance of the program.

A CAV rider survey conducted in 1976 revealed that 49% of the riders were former solo drivers. Further, there had been no significant decline in car pooling even though 22% of CAV riders formerly participated in a rotating car pool, and 16% were former car-pool riders. Thus employees (presumably solo drivers) not participating in the CAV program began to car pool. This could be the result of increased awareness of car pooling as a transportation alternative and/or an effort to demonstrate potential for a successful van pool in an area not presently served by the CAV.

A survey was made in 1974 to compare mode of transportation to work among 3M employees with a similar survey conducted in 1970. In 1970, prior to the CAV there were 7,731 employees at the 3M corporate headquarters.

Of the employees, 80.5% were solo work-trip drivers, 13% rode in car pools, and .5% rode mass transit. In 1974 with 9,486 employees, 64.5% were solo drivers, 20% were car pool riders, 1.2% rode mass transit, and nearly 6% participated in CAV. The average gross occupancy per vehicle increased from 1.24 in 1970 to 1.55 in 1974, a 25% increase. It is apparent that the CAV directly reduced automobile usage. Specifically, from 1970 to 1974 there were 1,755 more employees (a 22% increase from 1970) and 98 fewer solo drivers (a 1.6% decrease from 1970). Perhaps even more encouraging is that 97% of the CAV riders reported an intention to use the van as their permanent means of getting to and from work (Owens & Sever, 1977).

The CAV is presently operating at the 3M plants in St. Paul, Los Angeles, and New Jersey. Owens and Sever (1977) reported that the program saves more than 2.25 million vehicle miles per year, 190,000 gallons of gasoline per year, and more than 735 parking spaces at 3M corporate headquarters in St. Paul.

Transit Use. Transit use is the third type of energy efficient travel behavior to be discussed. The majority of the work in this area has focused on encouraging bus ridership—one of several modes of mass transit. These examples fall in cells 3 and 4 of Table 6.1, a Reinforcement Model of Energy Related Travel Behaviors. In other words, some of the studies attempted to alter ridership by offering riders pleasant consequences or positive reinforcers (cell 3 manipulations), while others removed unpleasant events or punishers for bus riding (cell 4 manipulations). Under each of these strategies for changing ridership (i.e., positive reinforcement or punishment removal for riding) there are case studies and experiments. Case studies are those programs that manipulated consequence variables, yet did not evolve directly from experimental behavioral analysis. For example, marketing theory and practice, economic perspectives, and just plain old brainstorming have generated programs which manipulated variables according to reinforcement principles. The second classification (i.e., experiments), are those programs that evolved directly from behavioral investigations and principles.

Table 6.5 presents an overview of several case studies. The table is divided into case studies that reinforced bus riding on a continuous schedule of reinforcement, those that reinforced bus riding on a variable schedule of reinforcement, and those that attempted to encourage ridership by removing the punishment of fare payment. Fare payment for a transit trip and/or the requirement of "exact fare" could be viewed as punishers for transit use. Many systems have reduced fares for short periods of time (e.g., a "Nickel Day") in order to promote transit, and other systems have eliminated the fare altogether. Many of these case studies are reviewed in the booklet *Low Fare, Free Fare Transit* by Goodman and Green (1977).

Table 6.5. Examples of Manipulations Made by Transit Systems That Follow Certain Principles of Reinforcement Theory. These are Termed "Case Studies."

Continuous Reinforcement Examples

City	Program Description
Minneapolis, MN	Coupon for sundae for rider of new minibus service.
Minneapolis, MN	Free zoo tickets when advance fare is purchased.
Denver, CO	Fast-food coupons distributed at promotional talks.
Indianapolis, IN	Fast-food coupons distributed to purchaser of advance bulk fares.
Worcester, MA	Free passes and savings bonds as prizes to color scheme designer of bus.
Syracuse, NY	Free hamburger coupon to bulk pass purchasers.
Iowa City, IA	Novelty items to children who ride buses.
St. Louis, MO	Free bus tokens to those who patronize banks.

Schedule of Reinforcement Examples

City	Program Description
Portland, OR	Bus riders draw for car and cash prizes.
Dallas, TX	Bingo contest with major prizes. Playing cards available on bus, games played on bus during off-peak hours.
Buffalo, NY	Major cash and travel prizes by drawings. Entries available on buses and from merchants.

Punishment Removal via Free and Reduced Fare Examples

City	Program Description
Salem, OR	Cherriot Commuter Club. Frequent riders permitted free fares.
Pittsburgh, PA	Free transit on buses with novelty markings.
Rockford, IL	Free transit tickets to new residents.
Boise, ID	Home Free Program. Merchants provide shoppers with transit tokens to return home for free.
St. Louis, MO	Free transit tokens to those who patronize banks.
Seattle, WA	Magic Carpet Ride. Free transit when within the central business district.
Madison, WI	Fare reduction during weekends. Fare removal during mid-day.
Denver, CO	System-wide off-peak free transit.
Trenton, NJ	System-wide off-peak free transit.
Dallas, TX	Free transit when within central business district.

It is difficult to evaluate many of the case studies, since evaluation data have usually not been systematically collected. Even if data were recorded, objective reports of the findings are hard to find and/or obtain. However, the transit system implementing these programs deserve credit for innovation. Indeed, there are reports of very successful programs. For example, the hamburger coupons distributed to purchasers of monthly bus passes in Syracuse increased pass sales to 86% above previous sales (American Public Transit Association, 1975a). Dallas reported an 80% increase in downtown ridership when their program was instituted (American Public Transit Association, 1975b). Moreover, preliminary documents report a 45% to 50% ridership increase in Trenton during the off-peak hours (Connor, 1979) and a 90% increase in Denver during the off-peak hours (Swan & Knight, 1979).

One major criticism of several case studies is the lack of attention to the concept of target behavior and response contingency. It is often difficult to determine what behavior the transit system was trying to strengthen. For example, in Denver food coupons were given to individuals for attending a transit promotional talk rather than riding the bus. Similarly, in St. Louis individuals received bus tokens for patronizing certain banks. These programs seem better suited for increasing bank patronage or attendance at promotional talks rather than increasing bus ridership. Clearly more effective programs for increasing transit ridership could have been designed had the issues of target behavior and response contingency been carefully addressed (as detailed in Chapter 2). We now turn to the experiments that evolved specifically from reinforcement principles and were designed to encourage bus ridership. These constitute the work of Peter Everett and his colleagues.

Reinforcing Bus Ridership. Several experiments designed to change transit ridership by reinforcing riders have evolved directly from reinforcement principles (Everett, 1973; Everett et al., 1974). The Deslauriers and Everett (1977) study is representative of this work. These researchers established a token reinforcement procedure on a campus bus system that served 30,000 students and 6,000 faculty and staff. Tokens were given to passengers immediately upon boarding a bus. The tokens could be traded in varying quantities at local business establishments for a variety of goods and services. Several area merchants agreed to accept tokens in exchange for goods ranging from candy bars to draft beer, hamburgers, and record albums, (see Figure 6.3 for a sample token). The researchers reimbursed the merchants at a predetermined rate for each token collected. However, several merchants allowed the researchers to purchase the tokens at a discounted rate because of the advertising benefits of involvement in the program and the increased store traffic generated by token possessors. This arrangement demonstrates the large-scale, economic viability of this approach.

THANK YOU FOR RIDING ON THE RED STAR BUS

 # ONE TOKEN

THESE TOKENS ARE REDEEMABLE FOR ICE CREAM, BEER, PIZZA, COFFEE, CIGARETTES, MOVIES, FLOWERS, RECORDS, ETC. CONSULT THE "BUS TOKEN EXCHANGE SHEET" (AVAILABLE ON THE RED STAR BUS) FOR A COMPLETE LIST OF AVAILABLE GOODIES AND EXCHANGE RATES. TOKENS ARE VALUABLE AND EASILY EXCHANGED AT STORES LISTED ON THE "BUS TOKEN EXCHANGE SHEET."

— THANK YOU FOR BEING ECOLOGICAL —

GOOD UNTIL END OF TERM

Fig. 6.3. A sample token (from Everett, Hayward, & Meyers, 1974).

In this experiment, two schedules of token reinforcement were tested, a continuous schedule of reinforcement (i.e., all the riders were reinforced) and a variable schedule of reinforcement (i.e., a certain proportion of the riders received tokens for boarding the bus).

Three campus buses on the same route were used, one for the experimental bus and two controls. Several weeks of baseline data were collected on all the buses. After this period and with appropriate media announcements, large red stars (used to discriminate the reinforcement bus from control buses) were placed on one of the buses and all passengers boarding during the next several days paid a 10 cent fare and then had a one out of three odds of receiving a token (a variable person ratio of three or VPR 3). After 15 days of VPR 3, the odds of token receipt for riding the bus were altered to 100% (i.e., continuous reinforcement). This condition continued for several days, and then with the appropriate media announcements the treatment was reversed to the VPR 3 schedule. After several days in this last condition, the red stars were taken off the bus and baseline conditions repeated (i.e., no tokens on any of the three buses).

Figure 6.4 depicts the results of the experiment. Of most importance, both of the reinforcement inverventions increased ridership to levels significantly greater than controls. Furthermore, there were no significant differences between ridership levels obtained under the variable person ratio schedule and the continuous reinforcement schedule. Such a finding is particularly encouraging in light of the mission of this study to develop a more econom-

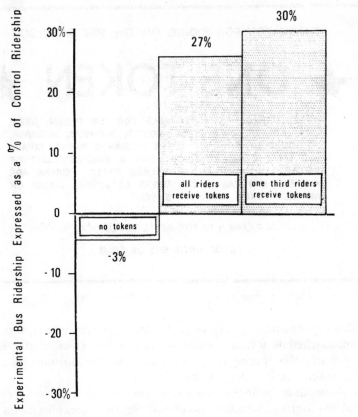

Fig. 6.4. Ridership on the experimental bus as a function of no token reinforcement, continuous token reinforcement, and variable token reinforcement. Source: Adapted from Deslauriers and Everett, 1977.

ical method of using a reinforcement procedure in a transit setting. Similar ridership increases were attained under intermittent reinforcement as under continuous reinforcement, yet at one-third the cost (i.e., only one-third the number of tokens were distributed). This savings combined with the discount the merchants normally passed onto the researchers yielded a relatively inexpensive positive reinforcement program. Restricting a cost-benefit analysis of the Deslauriers and Everett experiment to a consideration of fare revenue and the direct cost of backup reinforcers (i.e., merchant reimbursement), the variable reinforcement intervention yielded a net loss in revenue of only 5%. A similar economic analysis for continuous reinforcement indicated a 75% net loss in revenue. In an applied setting, a 5% loss in revenue could easily be overcome by arranging for local merchants to minimally increase their discount of the face value of the tokens exchanged at their establishments.

Removal of Punishers for Transit Use. While the cities mentioned in Table 6.5 should be congratulated on their innovations, only the surface has been scratched with regard to the effect of punishment removal or reduction on transit use. Many punishers (such as transit crowding, wait time, trip time) other than fare payment could be reduced or removed (see Table 6.1). Furthermore, many additional parameters of fare reduction or removal could be explored. It was the intent of two experiments to do just that—to explore additional parameters of fare removal. These experiments attempted to encourage bus ridership by removing the transit fare (i.e., a punisher for bus riding). The experiment by Everett, Gurtler, and Hildebrand (1981) was designed to assess the effects of various amounts of free transit and time parameters for free transit validity. In order to factor out these variables, the following procedure was implemented. Twenty-six hundred households within two blocks of a new urban transit route (serving a university, a downtown business district, and suburban middle income private homes and apartments) were randomly divided into four groups. Each group received a letter with a written announcement of the new route, a route map and timetable, and a packet of coupons good for free bus rides on the new route. Group 5/5 received five coupons for the next five consecutive days, Group 5/15 received five coupons good for the next fifteen days, Group 15/5 received fifteen coupons good for the next five days, and Group 15/15 received fifteen tokens for the next fifteen days. The dependent variables were ridership increases on the new bus route and the differential rate of coupon return from each experimental condition.

Independent of the type of coupon received, ridership increased 58% above baseline levels during the intervention. This compares to a range of ridership increases of 8% to 19% for the four control routes. The average of ridership increases was 16% for the control buses.

Figure 6.5 illustrates the differential impact of the various treatment conditions. The condition leading to the highest proportion of bus rides to coupons distributed was five coupons for fifteen days. The group of households receiving fifteen coupons good for five days exhibited the least transit use in proportion to the number of coupons they received. Results such as these are important since they give insight to the most salient free ride program to implement. If a transit system is concerned with the greatest impact per free ride, then according to this study, the distribution of a smaller number of coupons good for a longer time period is most appropriate. However, on an absolute basis (independent of how many coupons were distributed), the greatest number of rides was generated by the group holding the fifteen coupons good for fifteen days.

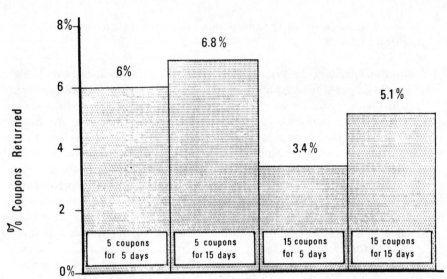

Fig. 6.5. The percent of the coupons returned for bus rides for the various treatment conditions of the Free Transit Magnitude and Expiration Date experiment. Source: Adapted from Everett, Gurtler, and Hildebrand, 1981.

A second punishment removal experiment was carried out by Everett, Deslauriers, Newsom, and Anderson (1978), a variant of the free transit study just discussed. As in the previous study, potential riders (i.e., individuals living along a bus route) were mailed coupons which were exchangeable for free bus rides. The uniqueness of this experiment was that more free-ride coupons were given to individuals *contingent* upon their using the initial coupons.

The study was carried out in the following manner. Each subject in two treatment groups (200 subjects each) was mailed 12 coupons good for free rides on any bus of a campus transit system. These coupons were good for the next nine consecutive days. The two groups differed in the following fashion. For one group, the 12 initial coupons each stated that after the nine-day expiration time, each subject would receive 12 more coupons in the mail regardless of how many times they rode the bus during the initial nine days (i.e., the Control Group or Non-Contingent Free Transit Group). For the next group, each coupon stated that for every coupon of the initial 12 *used*, each subject would receive in the mail *one* additional coupon at the end of the nine days (i.e., One-for-One Response-Contingent Free Transit Group).

Figure 6.6 presents the results of this experiment. The Contingent Free Transit Condition yielded a significantly greater ridership than did the Non-Contingent Free Transit Condition.

The findings of this study have practical significance, indicating not only that free transit increases ridership, but that the method of free transit distribution can substantially modify ridership levels. These findings can be directly applicable to the operation of a free transit program on a much larger scale. As opposed to a mail distribution program, it would be quite feasible to distribute free transit coupons to passengers immediately upon boarding a bus in a fashion similar to distributing a transfer. Furthermore, it would be quite interesting to explore in detail the effects of various ratios of additional coupons received per initial coupon distributed (i.e., effects of scheduling).

Several comments are appropriate relative to the future of applied behavior analysis strategies for encouraging transit ridership. First, a continued effort to develop cost-effective applications of reinforcement techniques must be pursued. Three immediate suggestions for this endeavor would be to

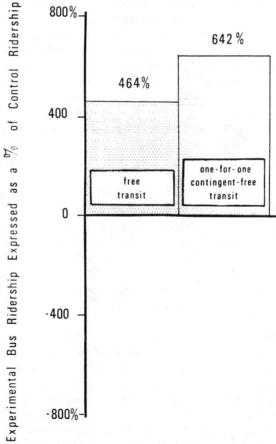

Fig. 6.6. The percent ridership increases as a function of free transit and one-for-one contingent free transit. Source: Adapted from Everett, Deslauriers, Newsom, and Anderson, 1978.

research further the reinforcement schedule control of bus riding, to involve merchant support of token exchange procedures to a greater degree, and to assess the costs of accommodating more and more cars in major urban areas. Through a more comprehensive analysis of scheduling control impacts upon bus riding, a relationship between maximal riding levels under conditions of minimal reinforcement could be determined. The economic benefits are obvious. Further merchant involvement would clearly help defray the costs of a token reinforcement procedure. Through innovative marketing analyses, it is possible that much of the cost of a token reinforcement procedure could be borne by merchants because of the increased store traffic and patronage generated by involvement in such a program. Furthermore, it is possible that a merchant could partially support a system which brings customers to his/her store, while obviating some of the tremendous costs of providing adequate parking spaces. Finally, a significant economic gain may be realized by a major urban area by keeping passenger cars out of the central city. Lee (1972) found that the presence of private automobiles in the city of San Francisco required a 50% subsidy from non-automobile related revenues. Lee obtained this figure by calculating only direct costs of accommodating the car (e.g., road maintenance and traffic control). If it were possible to calculate the many other costs (e.g., pollution, emphysema, building facade decay, and noise induced stress) incurred by permitting automobiles access to congested urban areas, the 50% subsidy would certainly grow. In the long run a comprehensive analysis might demonstrate that a city may indeed save money if every bus rider were paid cash upon boarding a bus and leaving the car at home.

Second, it is important to study the cost effectiveness of other reinforcers for bus riding. The token reinforcement system worked well with a certain subject population in the campus setting and a university town. However, other settings may require other reinforcers, especially when given the task of trying to attract the"hard core"middle to upper-middle class car driver to a bus system. To these individuals one of the most salient reinforcers for choice of transportation mode may be prestige, and riding a bus certainly does not yield prestige! Indeed, the automobile and the airplane, the most popular modes of transportation today, filtered down from the rich to the middle and lower classes. The policy of first establishing a transportation system for the transportation deprived must be closely analyzed. Will it "filter up" to the middle class and the rich? The modeling and social diffusion literature (see Chapter 8) suggests that the answer is no. If not, how many years has the public transportation movement been set back? This is a critical question that must be looked at. On the other hand, larger reinforcers may simply be needed for people of better economic means. This could be accommodated by allowing the tokens to be lottery tickets for higher cash payoffs (e.g., $100). Additionally, non-fare reinforcers should be investigated, including service-related consequences such as ride quality, service frequency and trip flexibility.

Third, it is critical to develop maintenance procedures for travel-change interventions. A reinforcement procedure will change bus riding behavior, but it is often impractical to maintain this procedure over a long period. Even under continual maintenance of a reinforcement procedure, behaviors may adapt and decrease in frequency. Research is needed to determine the duration of a behavior change under a continuance of reinforcement procedures and to define strategies for withdrawing a reinforcement procedure while still maintaining a ridership increase. There are some documented techniques of withdrawing reinforcement (e.g., in a slow phased fashion) that tend to favor response maintenance. Ideally, it is hoped that a positive reinforcement strategy will induce a behavior change (riding the bus) and then natural reinforcers of that new behavior (e.g., reducing transportation expenses, making friends on the bus) will maintain the travel behavior when the reinforcers that initially induced the change are withdrawn.

Fourth, it is necessary to test positive reinforcement procedures in more normal urban settings than a campus bus system and university town. This is mandatory if these procedures are to have an impact on urban transportation. Experiments in a "laboratory setting" are important, since they allow large degrees of freedom to test unknown parameters at a realistic cost. Laboratory research is the model used in basic science, and it has stimulated a broad range of successful applications at a cost much more reasonable than if the applied problem were dealt with in vivo. As successful parameters are determined in controlled settings, the research should be extended to natural settings. Indeed, projects sponsored by the U.S. Department of Transportation are now under way that intend to expand these applications to major urban areas. A token reinforcement procedure to encourage bus ridership will be tested in a city of 350,000 for a period of two years, and various parameters of free transit (i.e., punishment removal) will be tested in a metropolitan area of two million residents for two years.

SUMMARY AND CONCLUSIONS

Several reinforcement-based studies have been discussed that have attempted to increase the rate of energy efficient travel behaviors. These studies are summarized in Table 6.6. This area of application seems to be a very promising one for applied behavior analysis. Clearly, the contingencies for travel behavior will be changed regardless of planning. Our society will continue to have fuel shortages throughout the foreseeable future. The choice is to plan

Table 6.6. An Overview of Reinforcement Based Studies of Energy Related Travel Behaviors.

Transportation Research	Antecedents			Consequences		
	Target	Strategy	Outcome	Target	Strategy	Outcome
Foxx & Hake (1977) [college campus]	reduced vmt	goal-setting pamphlet	combined with consequences (cwc)	reduced vmt	monetary reward, car servicing, tours[1]	20% reduction
Hake & Foxx (1978) [college campus]	reduced vmt	goal-setting pamphlet	cwc	reduced vmt	monetary reward[1]	22.5% reduction
					self-monitoring and monetary reward[2]	12.6%
Reichel & Geller (1980) [college campus]	reduced vmt	verbal instructions, flyers	cwc	reduced vmt	group competition & public feedback[1]	22% reduction/ 62% reduction
Everett & Hayward (1975) [university employees]				reduced vmt	cost feedback as to daily commuting cost based on car mileage	0% vmt reduction, subjects concerned over car costs.
Lauridsen (1977) [organization]				increased mpg	mpg feedback meter	+.65 mpg
					mpg feedback meter, lottery	+.65 mpg

Table 6.6. (Continued)

Study						Results
Runnion et al. (1978) [organization]	increased mpg	written instructions	cwc	increased mpg (1st year)	public feedback, personal recognition, social reinforcement, peer competition	+5.06% (short-haul)[3] +2.08% (long-haul)[3]
	increased mpg	written instructions	cwc	increased mpg (2nd year)	public & personal feedback, social reinforcement, lotteries	+4.18% (short-haul)[3] +8.96% (long-haul)[3]
Letzkus & Scharfe (1975) [organization with 685 employees]	?	?	?	car pooling	reduced parking fee 4+ = free parking 3 = 1/3 fee 2 = 2/3 fee	participation rates were: 23.1% 6.6% 3.5%
Rose & Hinds (1976) [interstate highway]	carpooling bus ridership	lane designation sign	cwc	car pooling bus ridership	priority lane[4] priority lane[5]	500% increase +11% in persons/vehicle
Pratsch (1975) [various organizations]	?	?	?	car pooling	preferential parking	44% increase
Hirst (1976) [Washington, D.C., parking lots]	?	?	?	car pooling	preferential parking	22.1% increase
					preferential parking & $2 daily cost to solo drivers	43.8% increase

Table 6.6. (Continued).

Transportation Research	Antecedents			Consequences		
	Target	Strategy	Outcome	Target	Strategy	Outcome
Jacobs et al. (1981) [college campus]	car pooling	flyer, computer match list	cwc	car pooling	token reinforcement & reserved parking	+8% (lot A) +3% (lot B)
					reserved parking	+10% (lot A)
Deslauriers & Everett (1977) [college campus]	bus ridership	newspaper ad	cwc	bus ridership	token economy (CRF sched) (VR3 sched)	+27%[6] +30%
Everett, et al. (1981) [2,600 households in a college town]	bus ridership	advertisement flyer	cwc	bus ridership	free fare coupon distributed, good for various different days and number of rides	+58% 5 coupons good for 15 days most effective
Everett, et al. (1978) [college campus]	bus ridership	advertisement flyer	cwc	bus ridership	free fare coupons distributed and noncontingent additional coupon; additional coupon contingent on use of original	+ 464% + 642%

[1] Confounded by "leader variable"—subjects associated with investigator.
[2] Monetary reward for calculating average daily vmt.
[3] Only one week of initial baseline.
[4] Accompanied by 740% increase in number of bus trips during rush hour.
[5] Enforcement problems—six police officers for 5.5 miles.
[6] Questionnaire results revealed that most new bus riders would have walked; car drivers were not modified.

or not to plan contingencies for travel behavior. Behaviors can slowly be changed to energy efficient ones by good planning—or society will get there by many crises and shocks of an unplanned reality.

As this area of research and application grows, it would be most appropriate to explore joint implementations of actions from all the cells of the reinforcement model of energy-related travel behaviors (presented in Table 6.1). For example, what would be the joint effect of simultaneously removing reinforcers for car use, punishing car use, removing punishers for transit use, and reinforcing transit patronage? This is a provocative question to pursue and is consistent with the systematic approach to environment preservation (see Chapter 8 for more on this subject). Additionally, it would be of benefit to demonstrate the actions that are most synergistic and those that have the highest payoff in a cost-effective manner.

Table 6.7 presents an analysis of the types of reinforcement theory techniques that have been applied to the target behaviors of interest to this chapter (reducing vmt, increasing mpg, and increasing the use of travel modes other than the single-occupancy passenger car). The numbers in the cells of the table represent the number of studies found that dealt with the respective transportation behavior by a given reinforcement technique. Although one could debate the labeling of the margins in the table (i.e., the categorization of the behavioral strategies), the table does convey an important message—reinforcement applications have been minimal to date, as evidenced by the low numbers in the cells and by the many empty cells of the table. There is a breadth of reinforcement strategies that could yet be applied to the target behaviors of concern.

For example, in the category of stimulus control much work could be carried out. An interesting question raised by Deslauriers and Everett concerns the effects of prompting alone. In their study, prompting (i.e., advertisements and red stars) was always associated with token reinforcement. A study to evaluate the effectiveness of prompting alone is indicated. Perhaps merely making a bus more attractive, by painting a mural on the sides for example, could increase bus ridership.

Stimulus control research is also needed with regard to transit information aids. Lack of effective communication as to bus routes and schedules may leave an individual in the wrong part of town and without an easy return route. This is in addition to the embarrassment of making a mistake in public (i.e., in front of other riders). Thus, a host of punishing consequences can result from poor transit information. Indeed, Everett, Anderson, and Makranczy (1977) found that when college seniors were given typical transit maps, only 41% of the objective trip-related questions were answered correctly (see Table 6.8).

Research designed to determine the attributes of information systems that truly communicate to individuals how to navigate in a transit environment is

Table 6.7. An Analysis of the Types of Strategies Evolving from Experimental Behavior Analysis and Their Application to Various Transportation Target Behaviors.

	TRANSPORTATION TARGET				ENERGY EFFICIENT TRAVEL			
BEHAVIORAL TECHNIQUE	REDUCE vmt	INCREASE mpg	Car Pool	Van Pool	Transit Use	Hitchhiking	Bicycling	Walking
REINFORCEMENT (positive or negative)	3	2	4	1	1			
PUNISHMENT					2			
EXTINCTION (includes punishment removal)								
REINFORCEMENT DELAY								
PUNISHMENT DELAY	1							
STIMULUS CONTROL[1]								
MODELING								

[1] Antecedent manipulations applied in conjunction with consequences are not put in this category as it is reserved for stimulus control manipulations only.
Note: The numbers in each cell of the table represent the number of studies that were found that deal with the respective transportation behavior by a given behavioral strategies.

Table 6.8. Percent Correct Responses for Each of the Seven Objective
Performance Questions for all 19 Pamphlets.

Question	Percent Correct
What is the name (or number) of the bus you take?	39
What time will you board the bus?	45
How much will the trip cost?	44
Will you travel on ____ Street for part of the trip?	49
What is the name of the bus stop where you will get off the bus?	53
How long will the trip take?	24
Which bus would you take for a return trip?	29
Overall performance	41

Source: Adapted from Everett, Anderson, and Makranczy (1977).

scarce and would certainly be an appropriate endeavor. An additional and allied focus would be to research the relationship between transit geographic structure (e.g., linear, circular, balloon) and user knowledge of the system. Transit routes are often determined by rider origin-destination studies, labor contracts, fleet size, and one-way street configurations. Little if any concern is given to the users' perceptions of urban geography. Attention to users' urban "cognitive maps" when designing transit routes might well enhance their ability to understand and, in turn, use mass transit.

Much investigation regarding the effect of punishment removal (other than fare payment) for transit use is also needed. Initial work by Lundberg (1976) and Slater and Watson (1980) has shown that transit vehicle conditions (e.g., crowding and trip unpredictability) are stressful. Would usage increase following the removal or partial removal of these punishers contingent on transit use?

In addition to investigating the salience of other reinforcement strategies on the energy-related target behaviors, many subcategories of the target behaviors could be studied. For example, the ultimate reduction in vmt would be to stay at home. An alternative approach to the general target behavior of reduced automobile usage combined with increased usage of other modes of transportation is to decrease the need for mobility by making the home environment more reinforcing and efficient in meeting family needs (see Skinner, 1975).

In an attempt to modify travel behavior, Gurin (1976) investigated several strategies to effect changes in the home environment. The eight strategies investigated were: (1) substitute phone calls for trips (indeed, in the future the use of new telecommunication systems for different kinds of work may result in more work simply being done at home); (2) reduce household and personal stress; (3) improve dwelling designs to lessen family conflicts, thereby reducing the need for "get away from it all and escape trips"; (4)

increase home-centered recreational activities; (5) facilitate home delivery of goods and services; (6) locate desired destination activities near to home; (7) improve household location decisions; and (8) reduce peak-hour travel.

Social science literature and information from a comprehensive case study of male high school students from the Boston working class were used to forecast behavioral responses to these eight strategies. Gurin (1976) found substantial institutional cultural barriers to the implementation of these strategies as well as psycho-social barriers. Much like Margolin et al. (1976), Gurin demonstrated the need to consider subgroup characteristics before implementing specific interventions. For example, Gurin considered substituting telephone calls for travel. He noted the following barriers to such an intervention applied to working-class teenagers: (1) parental reluctance to install telephones in rooms where teenagers could hold private conversations; (2) teenagers value face-to-face interactions in order to develop and strengthen friendships; (3) teenager interactions are felt to be more effective in person; (4) teenager social conversations often take place in groups; and (5) teenage panelists expressed distrust of the telephone company. None of these barriers specifically preclude the application of contingency management of teenage populations in order to encourage telephone calls in place of automobile usage. Rather these barriers present specific factors that require the development of incentives to counter. Indeed, a market segmentation approach (i.e., the determination of individual preferences for reinforcers) should be embraced whenever dealing with behavior change strategies.

Two subcategories of the target behavior "transit use" could also be investigated. The first involves the host of behaviors leading up to transit use. Primary among these would be "waiting behaviors." Attention has been given to the reinforcers and punishers contingent on being in a transit vehicle (e.g., fare, crowding, ride quality). Yet the wait for a trip is often significantly greater in time than the trip itself. Concern over the inherent reinforcers and punishers in the waiting situation is very important, and the potential payoff could be greater than simply focusing only on the events paired with actual vehicle entry and use. The second subcategory involves the behaviors of transit drivers. Drivers are traditionally paid for effective vehicle operation and not customer relations. The majority of management control techniques involve punitive actions. Drivers could act as public relations people, sources of information, and general promoters of a transit system. Which of these driver behaviors would encourage transit use and what types of reinforcement strategies would increase and maintain these driver behaviors?

In summary, reinforcement techniques to promote energy efficient travel behavior show much promise. Yet many of the target behaviors listed in Table 6.7 (bicycling , walking, and hitchhiking) have not beeen investigated. Furthermore, many reinforcement techniques (punishment, extinction, reinforcement delay, stimulus control, modeling) or combinations of techniques have not been tried. Indeed, this area of application is new and the agenda promises to be a rich one. The challenge is to develop salient strategies for changing energy consumptive travel behaviors while remaining within the bounds of political, ethical, practical, and economic reality.

Chapter 7
Water Conservation
Robin C. Winkler

Water is a prime necessity for life. It is one resource which makes possible the development of all others. It is the first requirement in homes and is essential for maintaining the health of a community.

In absolute terms, water is abundant, but about 97% occurs as salt water. Of the remaining 3% that is low in dissolved salts, a large proportion is in glaciers, ice caps and ground water; only 0.365% of all fresh water is found at any one time on land surfaces or in the atmosphere. Assuming world consumption of water at the present rate and assuming current rates of population growth, it has been estimated that there will be a global water resource problem around the beginning of the next century (Kalinin & Bykov, 1969; Simmons, 1974).

At the regional level, uneven spatial distribution of rainfall, evaporation, groundwater resources, and storage sites make water a contemporary resource problem. In high technology societies, water resource problems take three major forms: insufficient or high-cost water retarding industrial development; damage to ecology through the use of dams, pipes, and underground water to overcome threats to supply; and reduction in water quality with effects on health.

Aston (1976), in analyzing water resources and consumption in Hong Kong, a city with major water resource problems, noted that water is one of the most important resources in natural biological ecosystems. Such ecosystems serve as a useful analogy to the urban ecosystem. Faced with limiting water resources, biological organisms and urban ecosystems have essentially three overlapping options in order to ensure their growth, development and ultimate persistence:

The first of these is one that places maximum demand on other resources of the system, such as materials, nutrients, energy and finances in the case of the urban ecosystem. This option, which by its very nature has to be a short-term measure, entails traveling further afield to collect water or, in the case of plants, increased development of the root system to extend to soil areas with larger reserves of available water. Given this extended water absorption network of the plant or of a city, water can be withdrawn provided that there is water present and that other resources are not limiting. As water becomes less and less available by being more strongly adsorbed onto soil particles or combined with other nutrients, salts or contaminants, then the demand for these resources will become greater and greater and it may well be the limit of resources that restricts the availability of water [Aston, 1976, p. 348].

A second option Aston (1976) describes:

entails some form of adaptation as either a structural, biochemical or cultural change . . . in contrast to the first option it is a very long-term measure. Generally successful desert occupants have developed efficient strategies for coping with their water deficient environment. Some common ephemeral annuals will only germinate if there is sufficient water available to carry them through to seed set and maturity. . . . The siesta is a form of cultural adaptation to hot climates with low water availability [p. 349].

The third option for dealing with water shortages is the topic of this chapter: conservation. Plants have an inherent ability to conserve water by reducing water loss through transpiration when there is less water available from the atmosphere or soil. Such inherent controls to modulate domestic and commercial need for water are not available to humans, but behavioral systems can be developed for similar ends.

Another crucial aspect of water resource management is that energy is consumed in all phases of the water system: procuring and storing, treating and pumping, and heating, treating and disposing of waste water. The U.S. Department of Energy has estimated that residential water heating is the second largest energy user, accounting for 17% of household energy expenditure and taking up 4% of the total national energy budget. In Waterloo, Canada, the Regional Water Department accounts for 34% of all the energy used by the region, only 3% less than that used for transportation (Bond, 1979). Water-related energy costs for the same region are actually higher than for transportation (45% Water Department, 34% Transportation) because of the higher cost of the type of energy needed for water services. The relationship between water and energy consumption is closer still for electricity. The Waterloo Water Department consumes over 85% of all electricity in the region. A further illustration of the link between energy and water consumption is nicely shown by a simple domestic example. It takes as much energy to shave with hot water once as it does to shave for an entire year with an electric razor (Bond, 1979)!

The present chapter, therefore, is closely related to the preceding discussion of energy conservation. The linkage between water and energy conservation is not only in terms of using potentially similar procedures to save water or energy, but in the fact that successful water conservation is accompanied by energy conservation. However, if behavioral approaches toward water conservation are to be successful, they must be embedded in the particular history and circumstances of water resource management.

Behavioral approaches to water conservation are still very early in their development, compared to other areas of behavioral intervention concerned with environment preservation. This chapter focuses primarily on residential water consumption and is designed to:

1. analyze the factors affecting water consumption and outline major issues in water resource management;
2. review the prominent approaches to water conservation found in the field of water resource management;
3. develop a systemic view of behavioral interventions for water conservation that integrates disciplines at a theoretical and practical level; and
4. review research in water conservation with a systemic behavioral framework, paying particular attention to concepts and procedures that will be needed for further research.

PATTERNS OF DOMESTIC WATER CONSUMPTION

As in clinical behavior modification, a careful assessment of the behavior to be changed is necessary before intervening. Water consumption is not a simple phenomenon definable by a single measure. Total water consumption recorded on the household meter reflects a wide range of behaviors performed by the residents. These multiple behaviors performed by different household members actually define the targets of intervention. Total recorded consumption is not only an artifact of those behaviors. (Recall the distinction between outcome-based and response-based contingencies discussed in Chapter 2.)

The first assessment task, therefore, is to break down total domestic consumption into its component parts. This breakdown varies regionally according to climate, type of residence, and town planning. Table 7.1 provides a set of descriptions of where water is typically used *inside* private dwellings in different countries and regions. These figures provide one basis for formulating priority targets for a water conservation program. Typically, water supply authorities can provide breakdowns of total consumption for their own area.

An important distinction is between water used inside the dwelling and water used outside the dwelling. Behaviors involved in these two types of usage are markedly different and the household members engaging in them may be different. In regions where single-family houses are the predominant type of dwelling, external usage may be more important. For example, Weeks

Table 7.1. Approximate Components of Interior Household Water
Use by Percent in Three Countries.

Components of use	Durfor and Becker[1] (United States)	Howe, Russel and Young[2] (United States)	Sharp (Britain)	Pilbeam (Australia)	Winkler (Australia)
Toilet flushing	41	45	41	27	31
Washing, bathing	37	30	37	22	38
Kitchen use (dish washing)	6		11	13	9
Household cleaning	3	20			
Clothes washing	4		11	13	16
Drinking, cooking	5	5			6
Sundries	4			25	

[1] As given by Fair, Geyer, and Okun (1966).
[2] As given by Whitford (1970).
Source: Adapted from Weeks and McMahon (1974), p. 63.

and McMahon (1973) estimated that 50 to 70% of total summer domestic consumption is spent on the garden in Australian cities (where there is a very high proportion of private dwellings on quarter-acre lots).

Having categorized the behavioral components of water consumption somewhat, the factors that might be controlling such behaviors can be considered. The research on factors controlling residential water consumption is extensive, scattered, and incomplete. Table 7.2 summarizes factors controlling water consumption and refers to hypothesized consequences rather than actual research outcome because of the incompleteness of the data. Thus, Table 7.2 offers a comprehensive picture of variables which behavior scientists need to include in research studies, either as variables to study or to control. It also provides a beginning for any attempt to develop a behavioral analysis of water consumption that is both practical and comprehensive.

Five factors deserve particular attention: income, climate, dwelling, price, and rate structure. Income is of major importance. Defined in various ways, income relates positively to consumption levels and is likely to moderate most intervention attempts. Rises in the cost of water affect low income users most, but it is high income users who can cut back the most, since they use the most. Because high income users are likely to be of higher education, and they are more responsive to conservation inputs but less responsive to economic incentives, because they spend less of their income on water (Winkler & Winett, 1981). Climate is second in importance. Summer is obviously the time of peak use, and this peak determines the cost of supply. Interventions are best directed at summer use. The third factor is type of dwelling. Residents of apartments without gardens who do not pay directly for water,

Table 7.2. Factors That May Affect the Level of Residential
Water Use Per Dwelling*

Factor	Hypothesized Usage Effects
A. *Physical Factors*	
1. Temperature during growing season	Amount of water for lawn watering
2. Amount and frequency of precipitation during growing season	
3. Length of growing season	Rate and frequency of watering, but not the amount required
4. Water-retaining characteristics of soil	
B. *Family Income*	
1. Level of disposable income in household	Number of types of water-complementary activities
2. Level of disposable income per capita	Indoor and outdoor uses of water, particularly during summer
3. Frequency of use and efficiency of water-using equipment (e.g. sprinklers, baths, toilets)	
4. Size of lot	Amount of water for watering in summer
5. Area in lawn or shrubs	
6. Sale value of residence	Serves as a measure of income and of water-using equipment (e.g., lawn, bathrooms, etc.)
7. Assessed sale value of residence	
8. Connection to public sewer	If drainage is not good, less water is used for lawn watering
9. Type of housing (i.e. single-unit, townhouse, high rise)	Townhouse, high-rise apartments are not metered individually; less water for lawn watering
10. Density of Housing	

Table 7.2. (Continued).

Factor	Hypothesized Usage Effects
C. Other Household Characteristics	
1. Number of persons in residence	Increased requirements for indoor use
2. Number of working adults	Indoor requirements affected inversely
3. Number of children	Indoor and outdoor uses
4. Number of days the family is not in residence	Requirements affected inversely
D. Type of Service: Accessibility and Quality of Supply	
1. Number of taps: single or multiple	Residence with multiple taps use more water
2. Pressure of water supply	Loss from faulty equipment varies directly
3. Quality of water (e.g. color, hardness, odor, cleanness, taste, temperature)	Some indoor uses may decline when quality is not high
E. Management	
1. Metering	Reduced use due to more careful use and repair of equipment
2. Size of minimum bill	Water use varies directly
3. Amount of water allowed with minimum bill	Water use varies directly
4. Frequency of billing	If bill is small, water use varies directly; if bill is large, water use varies inversely
5. Commodity charge (price)	Water use varies inversely
6. Summer charges	Summer water use varies inversely
7. Effluent charges (as a commodity charge)	Same effect as price
8. Exhortation and restriction	Water use reduced at peak-usage periods
F. Cultural	
1. Religion	Probably affects indoor uses
2. Habits	Possibly affects all uses

Source: adapted from Grima (1972) pp. 34-36.

consume less of it externally and may consume more internally than those
who have a detached house and garden.

The final two factors are price and rate structure. Price is the cost of a
given amount of water to the consumer, whereas rate structure refers to the
way in which prices are charged. The way in which prices are charged varies
considerably, from flat rates to contingent charging in either direction (higher
or lower price for using more water), with some rate structures based on a
mixture of the two. Indeed, behavioral interventions have been shown to
have different effects in the presence of different price and rate structures
(Winkler & Winett, 1982). Hence, analyses of water conservation will differ
by country, region, season, and historical period, and caution is advised
when generalizing between studies.

MEETING VERSUS MANAGING DEMAND

Two strategies for supplying water to consumers may be distinguished. One
is simply concerned with supplying the demand for water that exists at a
given time and place; a second is concerned with managing demand so that
water may be used more efficiently or more appropriately according to
certain planning criteria. The first approach takes demand for granted and
endeavors to create a supply system that *meets demand* now and in the
future. The second approach regards demand as something to be *controlled
or managed*. Where water is cheap and easily available, a policy of meeting
demand is the overriding concern of suppliers. However, where water is less
readily available and more costly, a policy of managing demand becomes
more important to suppliers.

The transition from meeting demand to managing demand is difficult.
Policies which aim at meeting demand pay little attention to people and their
behavior and pay most attention to balancing expenditure with income. The
expertise required in such an enterprise involves engineering, economics, and
administration. People are considered important primarily as paying customers who are to be served. The idiosyncrasies of human beings are something
of a nuisance, threatening to complicate the clearcut worlds of engineering,
economics, and flow charts.

Some policies aim at managing demand. Demand management means
influencing consumption patterns that reflect idiosyncrasies of human behavior. For this approach, different skills are required—communications,
media, behavior analysis, attitude surveys—and involve the expertise of
different professional groups. This shift coincides with increases in political complexity. Where a resource is cheap and readily available, it is
less contentious; where there is not enough of it to go around cheaply, it
is fought over.

The history of many cities throughout the world is illustrative of movement from a policy of meeting to managing demand (Winkler, Syme, & Thomas, 1979). Demand obviously grows as a city grows, and as previously noted, grows as incomes increase. Easily exploitable water resources are committed first, but as demands increase the real cost of supply in economic, social, and ecological terms increases as less attractive resources have to be tapped. The need for including expertise about people and their behavior grows accordingly. But old habits die hard, and institutions are more apt to remain the same than change. The U.S. Office of Water Resources doubled the number of projects they funded from 1966 to 1972, but their support for social science projects remained constant over the same period, at a low 16% (James, 1974). In Australia, the Water Research Foundation funded only five social science projects between 1956 and 1975—5% of all research programs (Winkler et al., 1979). Of the social science projects funded by the U.S. Office of Water Resources between 1966 and 1972, half were conducted by economists, 24% by people from planning and management disciplines, with the remaining 26% shared among anthropology, geography, political science, and sociology. No psychology-based research was funded. However, it can be expected that greater input will come from behavioral science disciplines as the shift from meeting to managing demand continues. Behavioral science should offer critical input to the development of water policy.

The major problem with a policy of meeting demand is that taking demand for granted contributes to growth in demand. Overspending results, and the cost of water increases to cover increased expenditure. The flooding of lands and rivers by dams, the construction of pipe systems over long distances, the pollution of underground water, and the lowering quality of drinking water, all suggest that demand for water must be reduced.

Expansion of the objectives of water resource development was reflected in the 1971 report of the Special Task Force of the U.S. Water Resources Council (James, 1974). Prior to this report, water resource projects were assessed primarily in economic terms, with a secondary assessment of more intangible social and ecological criteria. However, in this report the Task Force called for multi-objective planning, with projects being assessed in terms of four criteria: national economic development (monetary assessment including distal effects); environmental quality; social well-being; and regional development (equitable distribution).

However, recommendations to assess projects in these four areas are not necessarily followed, nor is equal emphasis given to each criteria. Part of the problem lies in the absence of adequate theory and measures to study the more complex processes involved in environmental quality, social well-being, and regional development. Part of the problem also lies in political processes which influence differential emphasis given to each area. For example, the problems of narrowly defined economic and technical project assessments can be briefly illustrated with the assessment of dam construction in Africa and Asia. Bennett (1974) summarized a series of studies on the effects of dams in Zambia, Egypt,and Vietnam on cultural ecology and health. Three dams on the African continent resulted in forced relocation of 275,000 people, with destructive effects on economies and cultures that had been closely tied to the flooded land. The dams also sufficiently disturbed the ecology so that once innocuous diseases became major health problems. Fertilizer pollution, fishery problems, nutritional changes, tropical diseases, and resettlement resulted from damming in the Mekong River Delta. In each of these cases, preliminary multipurpose assessment using the above four criteria may have been able to minimize the cost of focusing too intensively on economic/engineering criteria.

DEMAND MANAGEMENT

The rate structures used by many supply authorities reflect a policy of meeting rather than managing demand. Charging-systems within such policies are primarily geared toward providing sufficient revenue to the supply authority so that it has enough income to meet the cost of supplying water to its consumers. A demand management policy adds a further criterion in formulating rate structures—encouragement of conservation. One major approach to demand management is therefore economic—what rate structures will encourage conservation while satisfying revenue, equity, and acceptability criteria? A second major approach to demand management is behavioral. A major thrust of this approach is to focus directly on consumption behavior and attitudes in order to encourage water conservation. A third approach, environmental design, addresses itself to modification of the environment inside and outside the home in order to reduce consumption. The major strategies here are: (1) low cost retrofits that reduce water used by toilets, showers, and faucets; (2) the design of new toilets, showers, and faucets that use less water; (3) the redesign of the garden so it needs less water; and (4) the design of systems to use recycled water.

A fourth approach to demand management is legislative. Both economic and social approaches shape the environment in which people consume water. The legislative approach requires people to change behavior. It is a harder option but more direct and influential. Demand management of water by legislation is usually used in crisis situations to restrict uses of water that are deemed unnecessary (e.g., restricting external use to hand-held hoses and designing building codes that reduce the size of a toilet flush).

A fifth approach applies engineering technology and has two major targets in the present context: metering and system loss. In many parts of the world, meters are not used to record domestic water use. Rate structures in the absence of meters are fixed at a level typically based on housing values (see below) and are necessarily independent of consumption levels. Meters are rarely designed to provide salient feedback to users, and there had been some disagreement regarding the influence of meters on water consumption (e.g., Fair, Geyer, & Okun, 1966 contrasted with Risbridger, 1952). Usage-based rate structures usually accompany metering, thus confounding the effects of feedback and rate structure. However, installation of meters is one step toward demand management through its influence on economic factors.

The other main target of an engineering approach to demand management is system loss. Total usage in a region, as calculated by summing meter readings at consumption sites, is less than total use recorded from measures of water transferred from dams, mains, etc., to consumers. This discrepancy, termed system loss, is a function of a number of factors. The two most important are slow leaks (not recorded on household meters) and meter inaccuracy or failure. The former wastes water; the latter loses revenue that must be recovered in higher water rates.

Effective management of demand for water requires action at all five fronts: economic, behavioral, environmental design, legislative, and engineering. Each has a particular contribution to make. Local conditions will determine the nature of the mix for a combined program, but the behavioral approach is relevant to each of the other approaches. That is, the effectiveness of each approach is dependent on the water consumption behavior of people involved and their attitudes regarding the policies each approach adopts. Failure to come to grips with these behaviors and attitudes will reduce the effectiveness of any conservation strategy.

Behavior scientists should not wait for experts in other disciplines to recognize the fundamental role of behavior. Rather, they need to: (1) familiarize themselves at least at an introductory level with the other approaches to demand management; (2) work in association with members of other disciplines who are applying their approaches to demand management (e.g., economists, engineers, lawyers, planners); and (3) develop theory and research that attempts to integrate behavioral science with other related disciplines. The following sections of this chapter are organized around these goals.

Interdisciplinary integration is needed at both theoretical and practical levels. At the theoretical level, linkages between data and theory in different disciplines are needed; at the practical level, integrated multi-objective conservation programs need to be developed. Of the social sciences, economics has the longest and most extensive involvement in water resource planning. Therefore, integration of behavioral approaches with economics may be particularly productive.

BEHAVIORAL ECONOMICS

Economics and psychology have developed separately, with some notable exceptions (Strumpel, Morgan, & Zahn, 1972). There has been little interaction between the two disciplines, yet both are fundamentally concerned with human behavior (Kagel & Winkler, 1972). The potential overlap between economics and applied behavior analysis is particularly obvious with regard to reinforcement principles. Both economic and reinforcement theory are essentially hedonic theories; both are concerned with choice under constraint (Rachlin, 1980). Indeed, contemporary reinforcement theory has advanced from the old Thorndikean notion of reinforcers "stamping in" behavior to the notion that organisms allocate their behavior according to environmental and biological constraints (Staddon, 1980).

An economic analysis places central importance on the fact that any change in a system is accompanied by changes elsewhere in the system. Although an intervention may focus on a specific target behavior, it is still systemic in its effect. Therefore, a theoretical framework is needed that conceptualizes systems of behavior and predicts effects of changes in these systems. Behavioral economics provides such a framework (Winkler & Winett, 1982).

Once the relevant system of behaviors and influential factors is described, the next task is to develop a model that depicts how these behaviors and factors interact. In fact, econometric models of demand for water have been developed for this purpose (Howe & Linaweaver, 1967). Econometric models illustrate the need for describing how the components of the systems affecting water consumption interact to influence consumption, but they are too removed from direct reliable observation of individual behaviors. The data base on which these models are formulated is often subject to considerable error and is in aggregate rather than individual form, as is the data by which the models are tested (Kagel & Winkler, 1972).

Experimental analysis of behavior provides a research strategy for linking the systemic models of econometrics to individual behavior in an empirically sound fashion. Initial extensions of behavior analysis for environment preservation were accomplished as demonstration projects. Consequently, these early studies have been poorly integrated with the theory, research, and practice already existing in the various problem areas of environment preservation. For example, Krantz (1971) noted the tendency for operant-based psychology to isolate itself from the rest of psychology, as well as from other disciplines.

The research reported in the following section illustrates a movement toward the kind of systemic approach implied by behavioral economics. It is necessarily only a beginning; the major thrust is to demonstrate how concepts in economic and behavioral science can be linked with the various approaches to demand management. Systemic and theoretical interpretation of these data are yet to come.

Economic Approaches to Water Demand Management

There are two major targets of an economic approach to demand for water. The first concerns price; the second is tariff rate structure. These two variables are of direct relevance to a behavioral approach, because the monetary cost of water to the consumer is easily conceptualized within reinforcement theory. For example, price may be viewed in terms of reinforcement magnitude and rate structure in terms of reinforcement scheduling.

Price. Water is an essential good and therefore it less responsive to price changes than nonessential goods. Econometric studies of the relationship between changes in price and changes in consumption show that price generally has a limited effect on water consumption. In economic terms, the price elasticity of domestic demand for water (i.e., the percent change in consumption divided by percent change in price) is low (less than 1); put another way, domestic demand for water is inelastic.

Howe and Linaweaver (1967) reported a price elasticity for internal residential water demand of −0.23. In this case, a 10% increase in the price of water would result in a 2.3% drop in water consumption. These authors suggested that summer external demand is more price elastic and reported higher regional elasticities for the drier, western areas of the U.S. (−0.70) and for humid, eastern areas (−1.57). From Canadian data, Grima (1972) calculated an elasticity of −1.07 for external summer demand. Gallagher and Robinson (1977) suggested similar price elasticities for Australia. However, in another report from Canada, a 60% price rise produced no noticeable change in consumption (Gold, 1979). These elasticities were obtained from analyzing the relationships between "naturally occurring" rate changes and consumption data from supply authority records and from studying usage in areas that differ in water prices.

Econometric estimates of price elasticity (and income elasticity) of water used inside and outside the house typically indicate that water used outside the house is more responsive to price changes than water used inside (Howe & Linaweaver, 1967). These estimates are based on records obtained from regional water supply authorities, which do not differentiate internal from external use. In fact, only total use is recorded. How is it then that different elasticities are calculated from such data? The standard approach is to use total winter consumption as a "proxy" for, or estimate of, internal consumption. External consumption is estimated by subtracting total winter usage from the calculation of total summer usage. The effect of price variation on these estimates is then used to calculate the internal and external elasticities.

A behavioral approach to water conservation should also separate internal and external consumption, since such consumption data represent quite different behaviors. However, a behavioral approach emphasizes direct observation of individual households by the investigator, and direct recording of internal and external usages (Kagel & Winkler, 1972). The value of this behavioral orientation for economic analysis of demand for water can be illustrated through an investigation of the assumptions made in calculating differential estimates of elasticities of demand for water used inside and outside the home. These estimates are crucial to the models of demand developed by economists for use in water resource management by policy makers (Winkler et al., 1979). As such, behavioral analysis can provide important observational data for use in policy and planning.

Two assumptions underlie the estimation procedure used by economists. The first is that all winter consumption is internal. The second is that internal consumption is constant from winter to summer. These are plausible assumptions in regions with severe winters. However, in temperate regions with mild winters these assumptions may not hold. For example, Australia has hot, dry summers and temperate winters relative to North America. Yet these same two assumptions are made both in U.S. and Australian policy research (Gallagher & Robinson, 1977).

To test these two assumptions (i.e., that total winter consumption is internal, and that internal consumption is the same in winter and summer), water consumption data were obtained from 400 representative households in the Perth metropolitan area (Western Australia). The target households were selected to be representative of income (although a slight underrepresentation occurred at low income levels). Standard water-board meters were installed by a plumber in the external area of each house in such a way as to record all water used from outside faucets. This required from two to five meters per house, depending on the pipe system. Records from each meter were totalled to provide a record of external usage, and this total was subtracted from the standard water meter which recorded total consumption. The difference provided a record of internal consumption. In this way, it was possible to record directly external, total, and internal water consumption. Meters were left in the ground for two summers and one winter (1978 to 1979). During the first summer and winter (1978), there was a drought and restrictions were in force limiting external water use to hand-held hoses. Restrictions had been lifted by summer, 1979. All meters were read a minimum of four times each season by a trained meter reader. Interreader agreement was close to perfect on two samples of ten households, one in 1978 and one in 1979.

Neither hypothesis could be confirmed. Although total winter use was considerably lower than total summer use, total winter use was significantly higher than internal use (Winkler et al., 1979). This difference occurred despite restrictions on external use. However, although restrictions would have lowered external use because watering by hand is less convenient than leaving sprinklers on, the restrictions were introduced because of drought conditions and therefore householders may have wanted to water their gardens more. The second hypothesis that internal consumption in winter is the same as summer internal consumption was also not supported. Comparisons with both 1978 and 1979 summer data showed significantly higher internal consumption during the summer (Winkler et al., 1979).

Therefore, direct observation of individual household data suggests that the assumptions underlying economic estimates of differential price and income elasticities for internal and external water use have been in error. Two implications follow from these results. The first is that direct observational data should be used to calculate an error term for estimates used in economic models of internal, external, and total demand. In other words, existing economic estimation procedures should be continued (since there is a great deal of easily available data on total consumption), but direct observation data should be used to estimate the inaccuracy in such estimations. The second implication of the Perth study is that economic estimation procedures which are purely correlational should be supplemented with direct behavioral observation of demand as a function of price variation.

The behavioral approach, using field experiments with volunteer samples and direct observation rather than post-hoc records, is discussed further in the next section. As has been shown in Chapter 5 (on residential energy conservation), monetary rebates used as incentives for conservation may be regarded as experimental manipulations of resource price. To the extent that resource consumption remains unchanged, rebates essentially increase the cost of the resource, since failure to conserve means a loss of a rebate or procurement of the resource at a higher price. As was noted in Chapter 5, behavioral analysis of resource consumption using monetary rebates represents empirical determinations of the price elasticity of resource demand.

Tariff Rate Structures. Tariff rate structures are the schedules by which the supply authorities charge customers for the water they use. In behavioral terms, tariff rate structures are analogous to reinforcement schedules with the charges made to customers acting as negative reinforcers or punishers. Viewed in this way behavioral and economic approaches have a common concern: the design of acceptable tariff rate structures or monetary incentive systems that promote maximum water conservation.

Conservation, although important, is not the only criterion relevant to the design of tariff-rate structures. According to Gold (1979), six criteria for evaluating rate structures may actually be distinguished:

1. Total costs should be recovered.
2. Excess profits should not be produced.
3. No sector should be charged less than the cost of service.
4. Conservation should be considered.
5. Degree of equity, or the degree that all social sectors are affected equally by the tariff structure should be considered.
6. Also considered is the difficulty of implementation in the present utility system, (e.g., the need for extra monitoring or billing systems).

Five commonly used rate structures may be distinguished: (1) decreasing block rate, where water is cheaper as more is used (this reflects economies of scale in supplying water); (2) flat rates regardless of usage with an excess charge (i.e., flat rate to a point plus charge proportional to excess use beyond this point); (3) increasing block pricing or pay as you use (i.e., price increases with rises in use); (4) peak load pricing (a form of marginal cost pricing designed to penalize peak users); and (5) uniform rate structure where excess capacity users are subsidized by average users. It is also important to note that water is not metered in 10% of the municipalities in the United States, and all customers are charged on a set-price basis. Such lack of metering has been shown to be related to increased consumption (Cone & Hayes, 1980). Table 7.3 provides a brief summary of these rate structures, assessing them against the six criteria listed above.

With regard to incentives only, increasing price with increased usage and peak load pricing are most likely to be effective in reducing consumption, since these schedules make costs to the consumer most directly contingent on consumption. The excess charge would rank next, followed by flat rate and decreasing block rate. This ranking is based on the reasonable assumption that making price contingent on consumption, so that cost to the consumer drops with reduced consumption, will result in reduced consumption. However, the actual impact of these different systems is difficult to compare. The different rate schedules have not been subjected to experimental analysis. Consumption data before and after schedule changes have been confounded with other factors, particularly increased publicity about shortages. Also, change in rate structure may coincide with average price increases.

McGarry (1978) reviewed the effects on demand of changing from a uniform rate structure to an increasing block rate, and concluded that consumption was significantly reduced. In Washington, D.C., the short-term effects of introducing an increasing block rate were striking. Residential consumers reduced their consumption an average of 13%, and total consumption dropped well below the previous five-year average (McGarry, 1978).

A behavioral approach to water conservation emphasizes not only the role

Table 7.3. Summary of Rate Structures and Predicted Outcomes.

Types of Outcomes	Decreasing Block Rates	Peak-Load Pricing	Uniform Rates	Excess-Use Charge	Increasing Block Rates
Total Costs Recovered?	Yes	No	Yes	Yes	Yes
Excess Prices?	No	No	No	No	No
Cost of Service Recovered?	Yes	No	Yes	Yes	Yes
Environment Preserving?	No	Yes	Sometimes	Yes	Yes
Equity Considerations	Low users subsidize large users and may pay more than average cost; disincentive for conservation.	May discriminate against efficient users.	Average users subsidize excess capacity users.	Low winter users may be overcharged.	Large users may subsidize low users and pay more than average cost.
Ease of Implementation	Some alterations needed, but not difficult with computer billing.	Difficult—must change pricing and metering systems	Easy to understand and administer.	Some modifications are needed, but can be done with computer billing.	Some alterations needed, but not difficult with computer billing.
Comments	Inequity and negative conservation effect are prime features.	Modifying metering system may limit use.	Good for small cities where computer billing is not available.	Can establish an absolute limit for low winter users to overcome equity problems.	Price discrimination can be used to overcome equity problems.

Source: Adapted from Gold (1979, p. 7).

of incentives in designing rate structures, but also the use of field testing to assess effects of specific rate structures. The studies reviewed by McGarry (1978) were unable to attribute changes in consumption to pure changes in rate structure because of confounds in the average cost of water and publicity about water problems. These confounds resulted from reliance on pre-post (AB) comparisons to assess effects. A behavioral approach would include rigorous evaluation of the impact of different rate structures on small samples from relevant communities before large-scale application. Such evaluations would be accomplished as single-subject experimental designs, where a small sample of volunteers are exposed in different sequences to the rate structures being compared, or where volunteers are randomly allocated to groups exposed to different rate structures. There are obvious practical limitations to this approach (e.g., legal problems of varying rates, and volunteer effects), but the next section shows that such field experiments are possible and useful.

However, a purely economic approach may be insufficient to modulate demand. The problem may be illustrated by a regional model of water demand developed for Perth, Western Australia (Thomas, 1979; Winkler et al., 1979). The model was designed to investigate the ability of price changes to moderate growth in consumption. The model combined information about the relationship between current consumption and price variation (i.e., price elasticity). With a constant price, consumption was predicted to increase at an annual rate of 2.4% per year over the 50-year period considered. A price increase of 32% (as imposed in 1978) was predicted to reduce consumption by 6% in the first year. In four years, however, the initial level of consumption would be restored, and thereafter the annual growth rate would be similar to the historic trend. In order to halve the increase in water consumption for the 50-year period and thus maintain constant per capita consumption, price would have to be increased initially by 5% every year and gradually reduced to 2% by year 50. These substantial and continuous price changes would be necessary to offset the effects of population and income increases. Thus, it seems that a purely economic approach to management of water demand is insufficient and needs to be supplemented by other strategies. Behavioral strategies can be particularly compatible with an economic approach.

BEHAVIORAL APPROACH TO WATER DEMAND MANAGEMENT

Because self-report is often a poor predictor of behavior (as discussed in Chapter 2), behavioral approaches to conservation have played down the role of self-report data and have focused directly on consumption behavior.

However, a stratified random sample of 400 households in Perth, Australia, showed that self-report data can predict water consumption and suggest strategies for encouraging water conservation (Syme et al., 1979). Six factors were obtained from survey data which accounted for 93% of the measurement variance. When these six factors were used to predict high and low consuming households (i.e., the top and bottom quartiles) in a discriminant function analysis, a highly significant discriminant function was obtained (Wilks' Lambda = 0.72, $p < 0.001$), and 74% of the cases could be appropriately classified as high or low consumers. Compared with low consumers, high consumers were less likely to think that water supply problems were going to be solved by technological means and ranked water as a less important social issue. The groups did not differ in their intentions to save. As a whole, people believed 26% of the city's water was wasted but thought they could save only 13% of their usage. Clearly, there was a strong belief that it was others who wasted the most water. Consumers had very little idea whether they used more or less water than others. In response to the statement "Compared to others I don't use very much water," only 10% strongly agreed or disagreed, and 26% were undecided. Forty-eight percent agreed, again suggesting that people tend to blame the problem on others. However, there was general agreement that a water shortage problem did exist, 92% agreeing that Perth citizens use too much water.

From this self-report research emerge two relevant conclusions for the design of behavior management programs:
1. Consumers must be led to believe that they (rather than others) have a responsibility for water conservation.
2. Consumers must receive feedback to show them the amount of water they use relative to comparable others.

The failure to find a difference between high and low consumers, with regard to intentions to save water, indicates that conservation efforts should target specific water conserving behaviors rather than general willingness to conserve. This conclusion is consistent with energy conservation data (Verhallen & Van Raaij, 1980), and with applied behavior analysis (see Chapter 2). The strategies used to promote domestic electricity conservation within a behavioral approach (e.g., rebates, feedback, and various forms of written or media communications) should be quite appropriate for motivating water conservation. To the author's knowledge, the first study of this kind was completed by the Australian group in Perth, as described below.

The study was not designed to show how well a mixed package of behavioral interventions could modify consumption but rather to investigate the impact of a realistic monetary rebate on consumption. Rebates have two effects: motivational and informational. The first is a function of the money earned through the rebate. The rebate provides information that the household has conserved water, and the size of the rebate gives feedback as to how much water has been conserved. To separate the motivational and informational effects of the rebate, a Feedback group received the same informational feedback as the Rebate group but was given no rebate. Thus, this feedback system was designed to control for informational effects of the rebate rather than as an optimal feedback system aimed at maximizing conservation. During the experimental period, the water records of the city were studied as a noncontact control comparison.

Two further questions were asked in this research. One concerned the differential effect of rebates on high and low income consumers. Compared to high income consumers, low income consumers are likely to be more responsive to a given monetary rebate but have less room to save (i.e., a floor effect). High income consumers who use more water may be less responsive to a monetary rebate but have more potential for saving. A second question concerned the effect of rebates on different types of water use. Previous data gathered from baseline studies of the experimental samples indicated that a high proportion of water is used outside the home during the summer, presumably on gardens. Econometric data noted above suggest that external usage is more price elastic (i.e., more responsive to changes in price) than internal usage (Howe & Linaweaver, 1967). The hypothesis generated from the second question was that external usage during the summer would be more responsive to a rebate than internal usage (or total usage).

The 47 households in the study were divided at the median into high and low income groups, and each was randomly allocated to a weekly Rebate (n = 24) or weekly Feedback condition (n = 23). Subjects in the Feedback condition received the same information as subjects in the Rebate condition. Weather and city water consumption were monitored throughout the study period. Rebates were determined on a rational basis in order to be relevant to local water supply policy considerations. Winkler and Winett (1982) have pointed out the danger of using large rebates (with respect to normal price of the resource) which provoke conservation but also show low price elasticity, i.e., a large rebate may produce a behaviorally significant effect but represent little benefit due to the large (infeasible) price change produced by the rebate.

The economic viability of the rebate scheme, developed in collaboration with two economists (J. F. Thomas and D. Ditwyler), was determined by the estimated range of water conservation that consumers might achieve and the reduction in costs that the water authority would experience as a result of reductions in consumption. Cost reductions to the water authority could occur mainly through capital savings if the yearly increase in consumption was curtailed. This would reduce the need for new water facilities.

For the purpose of setting the rebates, it was assumed that behavior changes could bring about at least a 10% reduction in domestic water consumption. An economic analysis of urban management showed that a 10% reduction would be sufficient to stabilize per capita domestic consumption in the Perth metropolitan region. In other words, a 10% reduction would compensate for the predicted yearly increase in demand, excluding increased demand due to population growth.

The predicted savings by the Water Board to result from a 10% per capita reduction in domestic usage was estimated to be $8.36 $\times$ 10^6 per year (Field, 1979). This estimate was calculated from the amount of money the Water Board predicted they would have to spend on building dams and trunk mains to cope with the yearly increase in demand for water. The estimated number of domestic services in Perth is approximately 225,000. Thus, the approximate savings by the Water Board was estimated to be $37.00 per household per year ($8.36 $\times$ 10^6 $\div$ 2.25 $\times$ 10^5).

The above figure of $37.00 was an estimated savings based on annual water consumption. However, water consumption is not stable throughout a year. Hence, it was considered important to establish a rebate relevant to the time of year during which the intervention period occurred. Thus the ratio of water consumption in March to the total yearly consumption for Perth was used to calculate the savings to the Water Board for a 10% reduction of consumption during March, i.e., 140 $\div$ 1,194 (Weeks & McMahon, 1974). The estimated savings for March = $37.00 $\times$ (140 $\div$ 1194) = $4.30 per household per month or $1.08 per household, each week. The average consumption of the households in this study was 11.88 kiloliter per week in February. A weighted average was calculated to approximate March consumption, i.e., 11.88 $\times$ (140 $\div$ 154) = 10.8 kiloliter per March week.

From the assumption that a 10% decrease in domestic consumption would equate to the Water Board's estimated savings of $8.36 $\times$ 10^6, a reduction of approximately 1.08 kiloliter (10% of 10.8 kl) per week in March for households would be necessary. A reduction of 1.08 kiloliter would result in a savings for each household of $1.08 in March. Thus, a rebate of $1.00 was offered for each kiloliter that the households reduced their consumption below their weighted weekly average.

This rebate was provided weekly for four weeks. The Feedback group received weekly information on the total used in the previous week and the amount of increase or decrease from their baseline average total consumption. As the Rebate group also received this feedback, it was predicted that the added rebate would produce greater conservation than the Feedback group. Meters were read weekly (99% agreement between meter readings). Internal usage was calculated by adding together the data from additional meters installed outside the house to record external usage and subtracting this from the standard household meter which recorded total use. A four-week baseline was recorded (in addition to the one year already recorded for most households), and a two-week follow-up was carried one week after the intervention period. Each week subjects filled out special data cards providing information on any family absences, visitors, and social gatherings.

Analysis of variance of baseline total consumption showed no difference due to income level or intervention group; nor were any interactions significant. Neither total nor external consumption-change over baseline (mean baseline minus mean intervention period) showed a significant effect for income level or intervention group, indicating a similar pattern for internal consumption. However, total and external consumption dropped an average of 27.9% and 33.2%, respectively, for the two treatment groups, from pre- to post-intervention.

The rebate apparently added nothing to weekly feedback. This could be either because both rebate and feedback were equally effective in producing conservation or because neither was effective in overcoming other factors such as seasonal variation. Total metropolitan consumption and weather data were used to solve this dilemma; that is, the city as a whole was used as a no-intervention control. During baseline, average daily urban consumption was 516 megaliters and during the intervention period it was 430 megaliters. Nondomestic water use in Perth is 46% of Perth's consumption and is relatively static over the year. Therefore, the non-domestic usage was estimated to be 221 megaliters per day, giving a domestic change for the city of 33% from baseline to intervention periods (313 to 209 megaliters per day). This figure approximates the change in the study period, and suggests that neither rebate and weekly feedback nor weekly feedback alone could be regarded as responsible for the drop in consumption observed during the intervention period.

The drop in consumption from baseline to intervention was largely due to climatic variables, particularly mean maximum temperature. Mean maximum temperature and total consumption were highly correlated ($r = .85$, $p < .01$), a relationship almost entirely due to external consumption. Rainfall was associated with a decrease in consumption.

Asked to comment on the study in a post-experiment interview, 68% indicated weekly feedback was not an incentive to reduce consumption. Furthermore, 57% believed the rebate to be unrealistically high, whereas only 5% thought it was unrealistically low. All but four said they had read the weekly statements left for them, but only five reported an organized plan to save (three Rebate and two Feedback subjects). Thirteen of the 47 subjects indicated that a rebate strategy was a good idea, saying that it would work for others who used too much water. The eight subjects who were explicitly negative about a rebate strategy made the following comments (which serve as possible explanations for the lack of a rebate effect):

1. Rebates would not work because water is so cheap.
2. Their lawns and gardens are more valuable than money earned from rebates.
3. Rebates might have worked when it was hotter, and water shortages were obvious.

Only five participants in the Feedback group said they would have saved water if offered the rebate schedule used. Analysis of the twelve subjects who said they had tried to save showed they came equally from both intervention conditions and did not in fact reduce more than the others in the study.

Finally, water consumption and survey responses were compared between those who had volunteered to be in the experimental sample and the sample of 400 surveyed from which the participants had been drawn. The sample of 400 was a stratified random sample of the city metropolitan area. No difference was found between the volunteers and the larger sample in terms of total annual consumption ($\overline{X}$ = 506 kiloliter per volunteer versus 415 kiloliter per resident in the control sample of 400; t (258) = 1.17, p > .05). However, the volunteers scored significantly higher on the Watkins Water Concern Scale (Watkins, 1974) which assessed the seriousness with which respondents perceived water conservation and other water issues ($\overline{X}$ = 15.41 vs. 14.02; t (258) = 3.55, p < .001).

Why were rebates ineffective? The data on internal and external consumption in terms of climatic effects and householders' estimates of their relative importance indicated that if consumption were to have decreased, it would have dropped most easily for external uses. It would seem that the rebate was not large enough to offset the contingencies sustaining external usage behaviors. Some subjects did perceive the rebate as large but regarded their gardens and lawns as more valuable. Subjects reported that they spent an average of 17 hours per week in their gardens, spent $50–100 each year on their gardens, and considered that a well-kept garden increased the value of a house by $1,000–2,000. It was apparent that these benefits of water consumption (leisure value, monetary value, and presumably aesthetic value) outweighed any impact of rebate or weekly feedback.

This interpretation is a direct outcome of the systemic behavioral economics approach outlined above and articulated in Winkler (1980a, b). Conservation interventions present consumers with choices between reducing usage and competing alternatives. If there are behaviors other than water usage which will maintain the leisure, economic, and aesthetic values of the garden, then these will be adopted if the "cost" of water usage increases. For example, if the value of the garden is threatened (or perceived to be threatened) by reduced water consumption, then the "cost" of water usage will need to go higher before water conservation occurs. It is therefore important to specify and then investigate what these competing behaviors are and how householders perceive them. Syme, Kantola, and Thomas (1980) have initiated this type of investigation, focusing on the value of gardens in terms of investment, perceived added value to one's house, and leisure.

Because of higher concern about water, it is possible that the sample had already conserved as much as they could. Their projected amount of savings (between 0 to 5% for most uses) was lower than the representative sample as a whole (13%). They also scored higher on the Watkins Water Concern Scale. However, that scale does not reliably predict consumption (Watkins, 1974), and the consumption of the experimental sample was in fact no different from the survey sample and the average for the metropolitan area.

CONCLUSIONS AND FUTURE DIRECTIONS FOR WATER CONSERVATION

In the Perth project, an economic variable (i.e., monetary rebates) was unsuccessful in modifying the water use of residential consumers. The results indicated that the price elasticity of water is low, at least under the conditions of this study. Further, the interview data of the Perth study suggested that an approach based solely on financial incentives will probably be insufficient to modify water consumption. This finding is relatively consistent with the behavioral approach to other environmental problems. That is, a multifaceted, multidisciplinary approach is often needed to promote behavior change for environment preservation. In this section, a comprehensive approach to water management is outlined which draws on data and conclusions from other problem areas (discussed earlier in this text). Finally, some of the dangers involved in solely promulgating pure behavior control strategies for resource management are noted.

Throughout this text, a multidisciplinary, multicomponent approach has been advocated, with the behavior scientist playing a key role in program development and evaluation. A first step in designing an effective water management program is to assess appropriate targets for conservation and the potential for change in the designated targets. Recall, for example, that in the residential sector, space heating and cooling and water heating were defined as the most appropriate targets for energy conservation, since these practices accounted for 79% of energy use in the home. For water conservation we must consider that the toilet, shower, and sink account for about 75% of interior water consumption (see Table 7.1). Therefore, a water conservation program should focus on those practices. Moreover, as for residential energy conservation, low-cost devices are readily available to modify water consumption at the target locations. More specifically, various devices are available to decrease the required water for a toilet, a shower, and a sink faucet. Indeed, it has been estimated that toilet dams, shower flow restrictors, and faucet aerators can reduce daily water consumption by 35%, i.e., from 70 gallons to 45 gallons per resident (Milne, 1976).

Additional data indicate that overall use may be much more malleable than expected from the research discussed above. For example, Agras, Jacob, and Lebedeck (1980) documented savings of 30% during the California drought of 1976 to 1978, although the exact mechanisms for promotion of water conservation were unclear. Most likely, consumers in California used a variety of strategies to modify their internal and external consumption. Further, since water conservation has generally not been a focus of national or state policy, it is highly likely that many of the simplest, least costly, and effective procedures have not yet been adopted (Cone & Hayes, 1980).

A comprehensive approach to water conservation in the residential sector should include these components:

1. *Information* in the news media, including; (a) the rationale for saving water (e.g., the diminishing supply of clean, cheap water); (b) explanation of the low cost and simplicity involved in saving water; (c) demonstration of specific target practices (e.g., appropriate use of faucets and exterior hoses); (d) information on the non-risk to health or comfort of specific conservation behaviors; and (e) techniques for saving water during gardening and plant care.

2. Provisions for the *dispensing of low-cost devices* such as shower-flow restricters, either at frequented public places (shopping malls) or on a door-to-door basis (U.S. Department of Energy, 1980). However, recent research suggests that this strategy can be made more effective if devices are not just given to consumers but actually installed for them (Buttram & Geller, 1981; Erickson & Geller, 1981). This can be a task given to scouting groups and other community organizations.

3. Appropriate *economic incentives* need to be instituted that include increasing block-rate pricing (the rate increases per block of consumption) and peak-period pricing (i.e., during summer months). As with energy conservation, tax credits could be given for water conservation retrofits.

4. *Laws* and *building codes* need to be revised so that appliances, toilets, and plumbing fixtures that use excessive water are banned, while appliances and fixtures that use minimal water are mandated.

5. Manufacturers need to be encouraged to *develop* and *market* equipment and plumbing fixtures that reduce water consumption (e.g., through consumer initiative, changes in laws and ordinances, and even tax incentives).

6. Consumer billing practices should be changed so that consumers: (a) are billed more frequently; (b) are given realistic conservation goals; (c) can observe their daily conservation goals; and (d) are shown their water consumption in relation to a prior period and their conservation goal. In other words, *feedback* strategies need to be introduced to promote water conservation, as described in Chapter 5 for residential energy conservation.

7. The various components and overall approach to water conservation need to be continuously *evaluated*. For example, the effects of different rate structures, media appeals, and indeed the actual savings through physical interventions are still unclear.

Recent water consumption research by Scott Geller and his students exemplifies several of the principles which we suggest for a comprehensive approach to environmental protection (Buttram & Geller, 1981; Erickson & Geller, 1981). For this study the water meters of 134 residences were read daily for ten weeks: five consecutive weeks of baseline and five weeks of a treatment phase which contrasted behavioral, engineering and educational approaches to promote residential water conservation. The behavioral approach consisted of two components. One was a daily feedback card which conveyed: (1) gallons of water used the previous day; (2) the percent increase or decrease from median baseline consumption; (3) the percent increase or decrease from average consumption during the treatment phase; (4) smiling or frowning faces corresponding to decreases or increases in water consumption, respectively. The second component was a weekly summary graph which included: (1) a line representing median baseline water consumption; (2) a line representing average consumption since the treatment phase began; and (3) a day-by-day plotting of water consumption.

The engineering approach consisted of installing a set of low-cost water conservation devices in the participants' homes. Four different types of devices were chosen: toilet dams; shower-flow limiters; shower shut-off controls; and flow-reducing aerators for the kitchen faucet.

The educational approach involved the door-to-door distribution of a handbook describing: the problems resulting from wasteful water use, how water and energy use are related, and specific techniques for saving water in the home.

Using a factorial design during the treatment phase, the impact of each intervention approach was examined separately and in all possible combinations. This factorial design resulted in seven treatment groups and a no-intervention control. The participants were divided into experimental groups using a matching procedure that controlled for residence location, baseline consumption, and family size. For a five-day period after baseline, devices were installed in half of the residences. It was requested that the subjects not remove any of the devices until the treatment phase was completed. After the devices were installed, the education packets were distributed to the appropriate participants, and the feedback procedure began. Feedback cards were delivered each afternoon and were attached in an obtrusive location on the residents' front doors. Weekly summary graphs were delivered in the same manner each Wednesday afternoon.

The analysis of variance of water consumption was consistent with the results of Winkler et al. (1979). That is, neither the feedback nor education interventions was sufficient in promoting reduced water consumption. Attitude surveys conducted during baseline and treatment demonstrated increased concern for water conservation as a result of education and feedback and showed minimal inconvenience due to the installed water saving devices. This latter result is especially notable, because the 67 homes with devices installed averaged a 17 gallon per day reduction in water use from baseline to treatment, compared to a mean daily reduction of four gallons for the 67 homes without these devices (p < .01).

A third phase of this study involved the distribution of the water conservation devices to the 67 no-device homes, along with installation instructions and an appeal to help conserve water by following the installation instructions. Follow-up home visits (two months later) indicated that 44% of the residents had installed the aerator, 38% had installed a toilet dam, and 29% had installed the shower shut-off control. These installation percentages are not inconsistent with the telephone-interview evaluation of the 1979 fall program of the U.S. Department of Energy, which suggested that 27% of the shower-flow limiters distributed to 4.5 million residents were installed (U.S. Department of Energy, 1980). Thus, this rather comprehensive research by Geller et al. demonstrated limitations of feedback and educational strategies (as shown earlier in this chapter and in prior chapters), showed cost effectiveness for certain water conservation devices when installed appropriately, and suggested that the next challenge is to derive strategies for motivating the purchase and installation of low-cost water saving devices. But meeting this challenge on a large scale will require interdisciplinary input from at least behavior scientists, media experts, engineers, manufacturers, lawyers, economists, legislators, and public administrators.

A sole reliance on economic policy or just behavioral or media strategies for promoting environment preservation will probably result in ineffective programs. Although the potential of a behavioral economics perspective is restated in the next chapter, the current chapter ends on a cautionary note regarding the application of only simple pricing strategies for solving complex, multifaceted problems. One reason for issuing this warning is that at the time of this writing (summer, 1981), marketplace solutions are being advocated as the panacea for problems of productivity and resource management. In the *New York Times*, Professor Leonard Rapping of the University of Massachusetts recently commented on the problems of supply-side economics and pricing strategies:

It is inadequate, indeed even dangerous, to force Americans into conservation by simply raising prices, thereby making corporations like the energy conglomerates as rich as Croesus, and then watching a scared and demoralized public scurry to survive. People must be organized, educated and trained in effective means of restructuring their patterns of consumption and investment.

Any student of organizational and informational theory knows that, while the market is a useful social arrangement, it connects institutions and individuals only imperfectly. It does not replace the need for information, planning, requalification and cooperation [Rappling, 1981, p. 2].

Chapter 8
The Future of Behavioral Technology for Environment Preservation

This final chapter focuses on changes that need to occur in the conceptualizations, strategies, and roles of the behavior scientist in order to achieve more effective impact on environment problem solving. While the emphasis in this chapter is on change among behavior scientists, behavior change is an interactive, reciprocal process between people and the environment. In the present case, this means that the points and suggestions in this chapter can only come to fruition if policies in environment preservation are at least somewhat favorable toward attempts at behavioral intervention. As also expressed in Chapter 1, our hope is that some favorable outcomes in behavioral projects will help to accelerate policy changes which facilitate environment preservation.

CONCEPTUALIZATION

The framework for this text as described in Chapter 2 and throughout the chapters was based on the principles of applied behavior analysis and social learning theory. One of the hallmarks of recent formulations of social learning theory is the extension of that framework beyond the original boundaries outlined by learning theories and principles dominant in the 1950s and 1960s (Bandura, 1977). In many instances, principles derived from animal laboratory work have been "stretched" to fit human situations. Likewise, contemporary social learning theory considers cognitive processes and includes a systems or ecological perspective for analyzing problems and designing interventions. In addition, a striking aspect of Bandura's (1977) reformulation of the social learning position was his attempt to consider theory and data from related fields, such as communications and social diffusion theory.

In this text we have emphasized the need for interdisciplinary interaction, most notably among behavior scientists, engineers, architects, economists, and communications professionals. The point we wish to emphasize here, and as evidenced in Bandura's work, is that behavior scientists not only have to work with professionals in other disciplines, but they also have to expand their conceptualizations so that a "behavioral framework" includes theory from other fields. Two examples are provided to illustrate this position.

Discussions of the management of water resources in Chapter 7 include a strong case for a behavioral economics approach (see also Chapter 5). As has been discussed in detail elsewhere (Kagel & Winkler, 1972), many of the concepts and phenomena studied in psychology, and particularly in resource conservation, are markedly similar to topics in economics. In fact, behavioral evaluations can provide economics with a more empirical base and improve the predictions of econometric modeling which is frequently used in policy development. Further, the work detailed in Chapter 7 on monetary rebates for water conservation and in Chapter 5 on rebates for energy conservation illustrates an example of a direct, potential contribution of behavioral science to economic policy. Rebates investigated within field studies provide an empirical basis for predicting elasticity functions.

More extensive incorporation of economic concepts in behavior change strategies for environment preservation should improve their effectiveness. In Chapter 7, for example, economic considerations were the basis for deciding the amount of rebate to be used for promoting water conservation, and throughout the text we have alluded to or shown cost-benefit and cost-effectiveness data. While the allocation of funds and cost effectiveness are important aspects in planning and evaluating environment preservation programs, a greater integration of economics and behavioral principles seems needed. We offer the following example as a case in point.

Frequent feedback and monetary rebates have often been used to try to reduce energy consumption (Chapter 5). However, an examination of the studies described in Chapter 5 suggested that consumers' responsiveness to these procedures as measured by percent reduction in consumption was variable. Thus, there have been instances of minimal or no impact of frequent feedback. An overview of these studies suggests that economic factors play a critical role in consumer responsiveness. For example, the cost of energy has changed over time and is also variable across regions of the country. Different households also allocate different amounts of their budget ("budget share") for energy expenditures based on consumption patterns, utility rates, and income. Using these factors and others, a meta-analysis was performed on the residential energy conservation studies from 1973 to 1980 that focused on heating or cooling and used frequent feedback or rebate strategies. It was found that the cost of energy was predictive of responsiveness ($r = .50$, $p < .01$), but that budget share was the best predictor of responsiveness ($r = .62$, $p < .01$; see Winkler & Winett, 1982).

Generally, this analysis suggested that behavior scientists need to examine factors and systems external to target behaviors that may influence individual responsiveness. More specifically, the analysis suggested that when budget share for energy expenditures was low, behavioral procedures were much less likely to be effective. Indeed, recent work by Geller and his students has shown daily, state-of-the-art feedback techniques to have no effect on water consumption (Buttram & Geller, 1981; Erickson & Geller, 1981). Water is simply too cheap at the present time.

The foregoing discussion primarily indicated that behavior scientists need to apply economic principles in their conceptualizations. However, consistent with this interactive perspective, we suggest that beyond experimental methodologies for predicting elasticity functions, economics have much to gain from psychological concepts and procedures. For example, virtually all resource conservation policy has addressed only economic factors, because there is apparently limited knowledge or appreciation by economists of other variables that may affect consumer behavior (Kagel, 1981). In a summer project on comfort and energy conservation described in Chapter 5, economic factors such as cost of energy and budget share would have predicted minimal responsiveness. However, a combination of behavioral and communications strategies produced reductions of electricity used for cooling as much as 45%. That is, economic factors were overpowered by a well-planned program which offered consumers alternative ways to remain comfortable with minimal air conditioning and supported the plan and information by video-media and feedback procedures.

These examples suggest that an integration of behavioral and economic principles is likely to yield beneficial outcomes in environment preservation. Another potentially efficacious cross-fertilization of concepts and techniques involves behavioral principles and communications theory. The effective use of media for prompting attitudinal and behavioral change should be a primary consideration in the development of large-scale intervention strategies. For example, what is the best way to present information on mass transit systems (Chapter 6)? How can the media be effectively used to model energy and water conservation strategies (Chapters 5 and 7)? What would be the impact of television or newspaper feedback regarding a community's progress in reducing litter (Chapter 3) and recovering resources (Chapter 4)? There are well known, field-tested principles of information, attitudes, and behavior change in communications theory (Maccoby & Alexander, 1980). The behavior scientist needs to incorporate these principles into his/her marketing and intervention plans. Likewise, it seems to us that communication policy and diffusion theory can profit from behavioral science concepts. For example, video-media should use modeling principles; and diffusion theory (Rogers & Shoemaker, 1971) could profit from the inclusion of modeling, reinforcement, and feedback principles, a point considered below in the description of a comprehensive community model for environment preservation. Then too, media professionals are becoming increasingly interested in merging their technology with community organization principles (McAlister, Puska, Koskela, Pallonen, & Maccoby, 1980). Thus, the integration of behavioral principles with economic and communications concepts are two examples of the potential benefits from interdisciplinary collaboration with other professionals. The following discussion introduces additional considerations for maximizing the environmental benefits of behavior change strategies.

DIRECTIONS AND STRATEGIES

Within behavioral environmental problem solving, new directions and strategies are needed. Attention must focus on procedures that have potential for cost-effective, large-scale application. However, an overemphasis on cost effectiveness when procedures are first developed and tested can be detrimental in the long run. Within environment preservation, one works within a changing context. For example, many of the procedures, including home visits for energy audits used in the Residential Conservation Service (RCS) program (Federal Register, 1979), are far more time-consuming and costly than virtually any of the behavioral strategies. Further, as shown in Chapter 5, procedures that are not cost effective under one utility rate structure may be strikingly cost effective under higher rates which currently exist in certain parts of the country and probably will exist in other parts in the near future. Thus, while behavior scientists must be cognizant of cost and dissemination factors, a promising procedure or technique should not be scrapped in the development stage only because it does not appear cost effective under present conditions.

In addition, decisions regarding cost effectiveness are often somewhat subjective and value biased. For example, consider that cost-effectiveness evaluations were conducted on the policy of closing off city streets on weekends to automobiles (e.g., environmental gain versus loss in revenue for commercial sales, restaurants, taxis, etc.). In the end, the policy may be implemented because (besides political considerations) there is a consensus that a city without cars is more aesthetically pleasing and improves the quality of life. Thus, while cost factors must be a primary consideration, attention should not be directed solely to monetary cost, particularly in the early developmental stage of environment preservation procedures.

Diffusion theory also can be used to provide ideas on how techniques or programs can be formulated so that they have the best chance of actual adoption on a large scale (Rogers & Shoemaker, 1971). For example, techniques, procedures, products, or programs that are more likely to be adopted by consumers should be: (1) able to show their "relative advantage" in solving a problem (suggesting the role of feedback); (2) compatible with current norms; (3) relatively simple; and perhaps (4) "triable" before the consumer makes a final commitment to the innovation (Fawcett et al., 1980; Rogers & Shoemaker, 1971).

Returning to behavior change procedures and programs, we must readily acknowledge a weakness of the work presented in this book and in applications of behavioral principles to other problems (Wilson & O'Leary, 1980). Most projects described here have been short-term demonstration studies with minimal attempts to demonstrate long-term behavior change. Surely the goal should not be to simply promote recycling, bus-ridership, or water conservation for two months, but permanently. At this point in time, the technology of behavior change for "maintenance" has been widely discussed, but it is not until recently that more active efforts have focused on program, person, and system factors related to long-term change (Karoly & Steffens, 1980). If a behavioral approach to solving environmental problems is to be seriously considered by policy makers, then in most instances long-term change must be demonstrated. Such effects might be achieved by the successful marketing of environment preservation products and by the implementation of strategies designed to promote maintenance of behavior change. However, an interactive perspective suggests that the enactment of environment preserving policies can help promote more permanent behavior change, even as the result of short-term behavioral programs. For example, if the current procedures for the RCS program were bolstered so as to include feedback on energy savings and some continual personal contact with auditors, some initial retrofitting steps taken by consumers as a result of a home audit may then actually be implemented and energy efficient practices continued.

One broad-scale approach for the development, evaluation, and dissemination of environment preservation programs is the "experimental social innovation" approach demonstrated for mental health problems (e.g., Fairweather et al., 1974). This approach is highly compatible with the empirical position of this text. The first stage in experimental social innovation involves the development and field evaluation of a model program to solve a particular set of problems. For example, a number of the techniques described throughout this book could be used in a coherent and comprehensive way to promote "energy efficient communities." Indeed, Geller (1982) has proposed such a model that would use physical and behavioral strategies and would focus on the residential/consumer, commercial/industrial, and governmental/institutional sectors and on five basic targets for conservation: heating/cooling, transportation, solid waste management, equipment efficiency, and water consumption. The model is partially based on current efforts by Keep America Beautiful, Inc., as applied only to solid waste management (see Chapter 3) but would go far beyond those efforts in terms of scope of targets, procedures to be implemented, and resources and agencies that would need to be coordinated. A complete description of this model is given later in this chapter, but for the purpose of the present discussion, several key points are: (1) the model attempts to organize most facets of energy conservation and efficiency in a community under a single program; (2) the model contrasts with current environment preservation programs which are fragmented and have limited centralization of effort; and (3) the multifaceted program consists of multiple stages with a community working toward becoming certified as an "energy efficient community."

The first part of the experimental social innovation approach involves the comparison of the new model with existing approaches to the problem. In the present example, the comprehensive energy efficient community model can be implemented in several communities with results compared to the current array of programs attempting to solve the same problems in comparable communities. Outcome measures would include costs, energy savings, gain or loss of jobs and revenue, as well as subjective evaluations by community residents (Wolf, 1978). It is likely that several studies would be needed to develop the program properly. However, for the model to enter the next stage of the experimental social innovation approach, it must show superiority to current practices across significant outcome measures.

The second stage in the experimental social innovation approach involves active dissemination of the successful model. This is necessary because it has been frequently shown (Fairweather et al., 1979) that simply conducting studies and having the results circulated in the media and professional journals in no way assures that the program will be widely adopted. Unfortunately, while much has been written about marketing and dissemination, there is actually very little empirical data that clearly show the most effective ways to promote adoption of a program.

Fairweather et al. endorse an experimental approach to dissemination rather than stop at the stage in which the success of a model program has been demonstrated, behavior scientists should also become involved in experimental studies on the dissemination of that model. For example, with any program, experiments can investigate the best way to attempt aspects of a program, and to help people actually implement a particular program. It is very important throughout such field experiments that the integrity of the model is not threatened (Fairweather et al., 1974). For example, if in the first stage of experimentation an "energy efficient community model A" was carefully developed and evaluated, it must be assured that the model will not change during the dissemination process so that it is now "model B." The programs and outcomes for new communities adopting the model must mirror the procedures and results of the original experiments. This is a difficult point to adhere to on several accounts. On the one hand, it is undoubtedly true that altering the model in any way will reduce the predictability of successful outcomes. On the other hand, the original Fairweather et al. work showed very limited adoption of a highly cost-effective model. Diffusion theory also suggests the need to design an innovation so that it is compatible with current circumstances (Rogers & Shoemaker, 1971). Therefore, it is recommended that considerable prior assessments, ongoing consumer feedback, and local evaluations be used to fine tune a model. In this way, the innovation can be made more acceptable to the community, yet still retain efficacious components.

The principle of *participatory planning* is relevant here. That is, it is important that local citizens (i.e., the potential participants) play a major role in defining behavioral goals and programs, in order to increase community acceptance and involvement. Indeed, the people should set their own behavioral goals; behavior scientists are the technocrats who can lay out the behavior change strategies for reaching those goals and can recommend appropriate techniques for evaluating the efficacy of certain program strategies in reaching those goals. Proper program evaluations can then lead to *participatory refining* of programs and goals.

Thus, when involved in efforts to develop programs with large-scale applicability, behavior scientists should work closely with, but not be confined by, principles of cost effectiveness; pay particular attention to strategies for long-term response maintenance; become well versed in diffusion theory; should consider the experimental social innovation approach of Fairweather et al. from initial model development to dissemination of successful models; and should enlist citizen participation throughout all aspects of program planning, implementation, evaluation, and refinement.

A COMPREHENSIVE APPROACH

One of the problems alluded to in the brief discussion of the energy efficient community model and represented in this book by separate chapters for different categories of environmental problems, is that each problem has its own bureaucracy, traditions, procedures, and constituency. There have been minimal comprehensive, coordinated attempts to solve environmental problems and *improve quality of life.*

From experience on interdisciplinary and large-scale community projects, Geller (1982) has developed the model shown in Figure 8.1 for organizing an entire community around environment preservation. The plan, an "energy conserving community" (ECC) system, is not offered as a panacea, but as a model that will require adaptation to particular locales and systematic evaluation regarding: (1) its acceptability to community leaders and consumers, (2) the amount of actual participation in the program, and (3) the actual savings made in energy by sector, target, and strategy. The model employs the $2 \times 3 \times 5$ factorial introduced in Chapter 1: two general approaches (physical and behavioral), three sectors (residential/consumer, commercial/ industrial, and government/institutional), and five conservation targets (heating/cooling, transportation, solid waste management, equipment efficiency, and water consumption).

What is particularly intriguing about this model is the meshing of reinforcement and community organization principles. For example, throughout the process (see Figure 8.1), Geller recommends the use of local and national commendation as a communty first earns eligibility as a "certified energy conserving community" and then reaches certain criteria toward becoming a "certified energy efficient community." Financial assistance from state and federal sources would be made contingent upon reaching specified criteria, with subsequent funding contingent in turn on maintenance of certain levels of energy efficiency. However, since it is well known that the immediacy of reinforcement is an important parameter in motivating behavior change, local incentives would be developed to promote accomplishment of successive approximations toward reaching specified criteria.

Considerable community organization is necessary in order to develop plans for the program, implement and evaluate strategies, and provide local reinforcement. An initial commitment is needed to start the program and involves a letter of endorsement from the mayor of a community, allocation of start-up funds for the first year of operation by the community, and an agreement to send a ten-member team (one representative for each of the two general strategies and five targets) to a training conference. It is proposed that the training conferences be organized under state extension and/ or energy offices which are in turn accountable to a national coordinating agency.

At the training conference, the work teams from particular communities learn the plan for coordinating, motivating, and evaluating a community-wide program for energy conservation. Some workshop presentations are specialized according to the five conservation targets and two basic approaches, and on these occasions the work teams split up according to individual areas of expertise. The teams are given as a group the background, techniques, and materials for presenting local workshops to the three community sectors. These local workshops are designed to inform individuals of cost-effective conservation strategies for their particular situations and to collaborate with the work teams on the design of local incentive programs for stimulating and maintaining conservation activities in five target areas of three community sectors.

After the training conference, the ten-member work teams return home to initiate conservation programs under the overall 2 (Approach) × 3 (Sector) × 5 (Target) factorial. Major initial tasks of the work team include: (1) establishment of a local headquarters; (2) allocation of financial support; (3) administration of workshops to key leaders in government institutions, com-

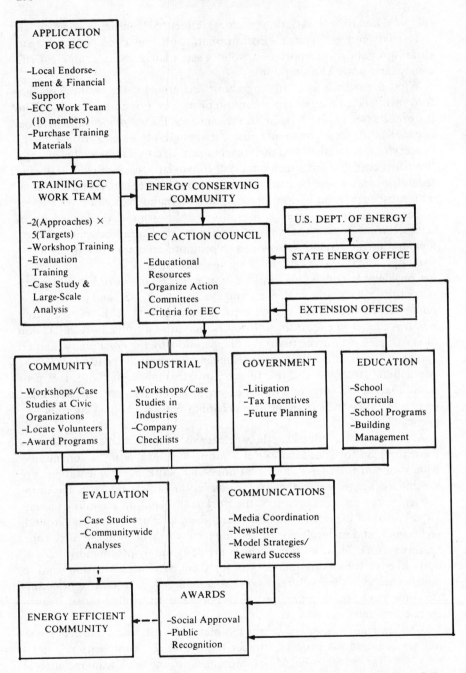

Fig. 8.1. Organization plan for an energy conserving community. Adapted from Geller (1982).

mercial enterprises, industrial complexes, and community agencies; (4) implementation of an overall community analysis of resource consumption in the five target areas of the three major community sectors; (5) selection of demonstration projects representative of each target area within each sector; and (6) organization of a local Action Council.

The Action Council is the key organizational component and work force of the plan. This proposed 30-member council includes influential leaders from the three community sectors, experts in the five target areas, and professionals from disciplines related to the physical and psychological approaches to energy conservation (e.g., architecture, economics, education, engineering, physics, psychology, and sociology). Important responsibilities of this committee include: (1) maintaining an up-to-date library of resources relevant to energy conservation; (2) maintaining communications with local extension agents and with the energy conservation specialists who ran the training conference, certified the community as energy *conserving*, and are responsible for certifying communities as energy *efficient*; (3) organizing and monitoring the five action teams (described below) that carry out energy conservation education, promotion, and demonstration projects; (4) evaluating progress of the action teams, including comparisons of baseline, treatment, and follow-up data; and (5) developing criteria for an energy efficient community.

The real success of a local program is determined by the activities of five action teams which are coordinated and monitored by the Action Council. The following five components of this comprehensive plan outline briefly the primary responsibilities of the five concomitant action teams.

1. The *Communications Team* is responsible for communicating the activities of an energy conserving community, thereby publicly commending individual and group efforts toward energy conservation and showing other people strategies for reducing energy consumption. All communication media are used (television, radio, newspaper), and an in-house newsletter is developed.

2. The *Education Team* is responsible for keeping all other teams informed of relevant techniques for conserving energy and for promoting increases in energy education in public schools. This committee may sponsor public education programs for teaching energy concepts or special school projects which demonstrate principles of energy use and energy savings.

3. The *Community Team* is responsible for locating and coordinating local civic organizations for energy conservation activities. Volunteer groups are taught to administer mini-workshops, implement neighborhood conservation projects, assist in communitywide analyses of energy use, and run special award programs among individuals and groups for motivating action toward conservation goals.

4. The *Government Team* is responsible for applying governmental policy

to encouraging energy conservation and for planning strategies to meet long-range energy needs. For example, such a team might be able to formulate policies, ordinances, and tax-rebate programs for motivating energy education and conservation. Government agencies and institutions could establish simple conservation programs in any of the five target areas and thus establish themselves as public models of the appropriate application of conservation strategies. These teams also sponsor the administration of energy workshops to government personnel.

5. The *Industrial Team* is responsible for promoting energy conservation in the commercial/industrial sector of the community and establishing visible examples of the successful application of energy conserving procedures in commerical and industrial enterprises. An attempt is made to demonstrate publicly the application of conservation strategies in all four target areas. This committee promoted the plan by administering energy conservation workshops to special work groups in commercial and industrial settings.

Geller (1982) has developed this reinforcement, community-organization model as a general framework. Other problems in environment preservation discussed in this text can be incorporated into this model. In addition, the actual strategies for environment preservation must be developed locally and tailored to local needs and concerns, so that they can help assure optimal problem solving and community acceptance. For example, van pooling and promotion of solar energy may be important components of a program in Southern California, while repair of mass transit and retrofitting of buildings may be more important targets in the Northeast. However, by far the most important aspect of this plan is the attempt at coordinating the numerous and relatively piecemeal efforts to various environment preservation agencies in one concerted and cohesive program. The fact that more than 229 American communities and six other countries are involved in a similar Clean Community System developed by Keep America Beautiful, Inc. for solving waste management problems suggests the viability of this more elaborate plan for energy conservation and environmental protection (Pendley, 1981).

Note also that the development and implementation of this model is consistent with our emphasis on interdisciplinary efforts and broader conceptualization by behavior scientists. For example, the model relies on both psychological and physical technology and can employ principles from behavioral science, economics, communications, political science, diffusion theory, and urban systems analysis.

ROLE DEVELOPMENT

For the behavior scientist reading this text who is not currently involved in environment problem solving, it is hoped that you have been inspired to ask the question: "How can I get involved?" The purpose of this section is to delineate a number of points that may be helpful in such an endeavor. These same points should be useful for undergraduate behavior science majors and graduate students in the behavioral and social sciences who are considering a career related to environment preservation. Represented in these points are some of the present strengths and limitations of the behavioral approach to solving environmental problems, the types of roles that need to be assumed by the behavior scientist, the knowledge bases that must be mastered, as well as advice on working with other disciplines.

Language. Probably the best way to assure one's *non*involvement in environment preservation is to enter agencies and/or talk with other professionals traditionally engaged in the particular field and use exclusively the language of behavioral science. This approach implies a lack of understanding or respect for other people and disciplines. It is more appropriate to use lay language or the language of the other profession. For example, do not say "reinforcement contingencies" when the term "incentive conditions" would convey the same meaning. And when addressing economists, for example, knowledge of how incentive conditions relate to "elasticity functions" is important. It is also necessary to be well versed in the language of a particular environment preservation problem. For example, when talking with energy professionals, familiarity with terms such as "retrofitting," "load management," "peak load," and "load shedding" seem crucial. This leads to our second point.

Expertise in a Specific Area. Professionals engaged in solving a particular environmental problem will most likely be unimpressed by an array of eclectic interests by the behavior scientist seeking to work with them. Rather, professionals in environmental problem solving would most likely want to consult with a person who was an expert in a specific area. This is exemplified by Peter Everett who does not define himself as a psychologist working on environmental protection and transportation but as a "transportation management expert." While one can debate the merits and drawbacks of defining one's expertise by a problem area instead of a discipline or argue about the ease of transferring behavioral methodologies and techniques from one problem to another, the basic point remains the same—one must become an expert in a problem area to maximize personal impact on environment preservation. This is true not only to market personal worth to other professionals, but also to design realistic and effective programs. For example, the days of simply demonstrating the applicability of a behavioral technique to residential energy conservation are past. In residential energy conservation, it has been noted that behavior scientists need to have knowledge of human comfort, low-cost, no-cost conservation techniques, high-cost retrofitting, rate structure, and economic factors. On the other hand, it is conceivable that if a model such as the comprehensive community program described in the prior section is adopted by some communities, there may actually be a role for a behavior scientist who is a generalist in environmental topics.

On Not Being a Radical Behaviorist. In some ways this point is redundant with points 1 and 2, but the message is worth reiterating. "Radical behaviorist" does not mean a person who is politically radical, but one who conceptually and procedurally always adheres to the strictures of operant methodology or experimental behavior analysis. This would include conceptualizing problems in a certain way and only using particular terminology, evaluation designs, and measures. We have already discussed problems in limiting oneself to professional jargon and only being knowledgeable in a single discipline. While in no way downplaying the need for good measurement and evaluation (see Chapter 2), reasonable flexibility is necessary when working in the "real world." Being adamant on some issues that are easily compromisable, such as a specific research design or intervention strategy, is another sure way *not* to become involved in designing and evaluating actual programs for environment preservation.

Balance in Presentation. Each of the authors has been trained as a research scientist and is committed to the scientific method. Certainly, one facet of this type of career training is the insistence on basing decisions on data ("Let's look at the data"; "What do the data indicate?"). Further, each of the authors works in a "stream of research" or systematic replication mode of research, where one study builds on and follows another. A conflict occurs when addressing a problem for which there are limited research data. In that situation, many behavior scientists would prefer to say, "I don't know if 'x' could solve the problem. We need to do about five or six studies to find out." Although this is a scientifically laudable position, such a stance will decrease the perceived value of behavioral science to an environment preservation practitioner who wants help *now* in solving a problem. In this situation, we advocate that a balance be struck. It is not ethical to say, "I have just the strategy that will work," and it is not effective to say, "I really don't know; I need four years to find out." A reasonable and ethical balance can be found in a statement such as this one: "I think I know something that might work and why don't we try it?" This statement represents a reasonable hunch, based on research in other areas on procedures that may be effective, but at the same time offers no absolute promise of a cost-effective solution.

Preliminary Work. There is no substitute for experience, but at first glance an old and familiar problem emerges: "I have no credentials in the field so I can't get any funding and/or cooperation, but without funding or cooperation I can't develop any credentials." The answer to this dilemma is relatively simple. The authors of this text accomplished their initial work in environment preservation (i.e., for five or more years) on "shoe-string" and, at times, "out-of-pocket" budgets. There is nothing wrong with this practice. It represents one's confidence and commitment. Besides building credentials and knowledge in the field, there are also some advantages to this approach. For example, it is possible to literally respond overnight to an opportunity and do a focused project with little, if any, agency or institutional restrictions.

This approach can certainly be followed by students. Students generally have in their possession the highest cost item on any behavioral science project—"personpower." There are a number of working models for effectively applying undergraduate and graduate students in a range of capacities for community problem solving (see Geller, 1972; Jason, 1981; Rappaport, 1977) that can be adapted to problems in environment preservation.

Clientele. To acquire financial support, it is important to pick a problem area where there is a large potential pool of clients. For example, energy-related work in the public sector is somewhat limited in terms of clients. There is the federal government, state government, extension systems, and utility companies which generally are large regional corporations. Since these energy agencies and companies have not had a history of supporting behavioral research, the likelihood of support from this limited number of clients for behavioral environment work is not good. However, this situation may change. For example, the promotion of solar energy and the use of other renewable sources of energy represent a potentially diverse and decentralized set of companies.

Services for managing water resources and solid waste disposal tend to be more decentralized than energy systems. For example, many communities have their own transportation, water, recycling, or waste disposal systems, suggesting again a diversified set of potential clients. For some environmental problems there may be more opportunities to find agencies and companies interested in behavioral science proposals. And this situation could be augmented in the future by decentralized, but more comprehensive programs as discussed previously in this chapter.

Diffusion Potential. As stated earlier, diffusion theory—the processes involved in communication about the adoption of an innovation—has much to offer behavior scientists (Rogers & Shoemaker, 1971). One aspect of diffusion theory consistent with a social learning position is that other respected individuals can have important influences on our behavior. For example, if for a variety of reasons a number of highly respected and influential people in a community started to commute to work by bicycle, it would not be surprising to observe a sudden increase in other citizens using bicycles for commuting purposes. However, the same prediction would not be made if the initial bike riders were less respected members of the community. Many different innovations in our society that are related to environment preservation (e.g., automobiles, large detached homes, a range of appliances) were first used by the wealthy and were filtered down and emulated by the less wealthy.

One of the conflicts in policy is that much federal and state funding in environment preservation is earmarked for the poor, and many proenvironmental practices such as using mass transit are still somewhat associated with being poor. Thus, such policies may help the poor but hinder wider-scale adoption of environment preserving practices. While in no way suggesting that the federal and state governments should abdicate responsibilities to the poor, we do feel that agencies and behavior scientists need to be cognizant of factors associated with the large-scale adoption of innovations and practices. For example, Everett (1980) proposed that "luxury buses" be established (e.g., comfortable Mercedes buses with food and beverage service and so on). Such buses would require a high price for this special service but would still be likely to induce wealthier people to ride the bus. Bus ridership would then become a status symbol, with this practice modeled by less wealthy citizens on perhaps less luxurious and expensive buses. Although the social equity and procedures involved in such an approach can be debated, the point we wish to stress here is that by focusing only on certain target groups, our impact may be quite limited.

Reallocation of Time. Behavior scientists involved in environmental problem solving (and other applied and public problems) have to be prepared to make some reallocations of their professional time. For example, while many professionals may prefer to conduct laboratory or small-scale field projects and publish results in professional journals, strict adherence to this academic tradition will not assure maximal impact on environment preservation problems. We have already indicated that the mere publication of findings in no way results in the dissemination (adoption) of the procedures, practices, or products of a research project (Fairweather et al., 1974). Further, it is quite obvious that in an era of diminished resources and opportunities, acquiring support and developing collaborative agreements is a highly competitive and political process. If one is not willing to spend time developing relationships with other professionals, becoming part of a particular environment preservation network, and engaging in other promotional activities, then one's impact on this field will probably be limited.

However, here it is possible to distinguish between personal success and impact on the field. For example, within a behavioral science academic discipline, success is mostly determined by quality publications in discipline journals. Such work may or may not have an impact on environmental policy and problems.

Given this situation, it is important to become proficient at publication within a discipline and also to allocate time to disseminating findings through channels other than the professional publications in one's discipline. For example, the authors have extensive experience working with news services to develop articles on their work. One of the authors has done innumerable workshops, is a frequent guest (indeed, at this point, a local celebrity) on local television shows in the role of an expert in environmental preservation, and received national television and newspaper coverage of his work. These activities must be recognized and respected as part of the job—as activities that require professional expertise and that represent valuable ways to disseminate research findings. If done extensively and accurately, these activities take considerable time and should be recognized and rewarded by universities and other institutions. For example, at Virginia Polytechnic Institute and State University, some of these activities are regarded as invaluable extension work.

Perseverance. There are very few professionals who can make an immediate and significant impact on a field so that their perspective and agenda is respected and supported. As we have noted repeatedly in this text, the behavioral scientist is a newcomer to the environment preservation domain, and it is only in very recent years that there has been any significant interest or support for a behavioral approach. For example, it took each of the authors about five to seven years of continual research and publication to receive any visibility outside of the behavioral science profession and to have any impact on other professionals in the field. As in many other endeavors, one can expect that initially the the reinforcement schedule will be very lean and that there is simply no substitute for perseverance and a willingness to put in the time and effort to reach long-term goals.

At the same time, realistic assessments have to be made regarding the type of efforts that result in professional success within a discipline and those that impact on a societal problem. As has been pointed out here, such efforts may at times be quite different from each other. Upon entry into the field, it is important that professional goals be specified. The initial period in the field is also of obvious importance in learning the language, concepts, and "nuts and bolts" of a problem area; in learning how to present oneself to different professionals and join an interdisciplinary network; and in becoming facile in disseminating behavioral principles, research procedures, and effective strategies through news media.

Thus, we hope in the future that the behavior scientist working in the field will be knowledgeable in specific problem areas, but will perhaps work at developing and evaluating more comprehensive programs, be effective in collaborating with the media and other disciplines, have a rich conceptual framework, and will focus on the development of strategies to promote long-term and large-scale behavioral innovation.

POSTSCRIPT

Drastic and in many cases irrevocable energy and environmental policies will be enacted in the 1980s. We say irrevocable since once a "path" is chosen, as has been pointed out before (Lovins, 1977), it will be most difficult, if not impossible, to change directions at this late hour. In this text, we have repeatedly emphasized that conservation and efficiency offer a viable alternative to the singular reliance on an uncertain high-technology energy path. To paraphrase Stobaugh and Yergin (1979), conservation can provide the cheapest, most abundant energy source that is currently available, providing a way to bring us safely to the time when diverse energy sources will most likely be available.

One of the unfortunate results of attempts to promote conservation during the last five years has been the association of conservation with sacrifice and discomfort, a diminished quality of life, and hard economic times. The lack of a concerted conservation effort in this country probably has had much to do with our unstable economy (e.g., a result of the tremendous amount of assets leaving this country to pay for foreign oil). Further, contrary to what has been indicated by some policymakers and politicians, there is little evidence to suggest that conservation will necessarily diminish employment or productivity (Purcell, 1981; Stobaugh & Yergin, 1979). We have also suggested repeatedly throughout this book that there is virtually nothing aversive about adopting more energy efficient, environment preserving policies.

Recall the vignettes at the beginning of Chapter 1 that first depict the more typical American energy and environmental behaviors and then illustrate more efficient and preserving behaviors. The authors of this book argue that the efficient and preserving behaviors comprise a more functional and aesthetic life style. What is particularly desirable about high energy bills, overheated buildings, polluted air, water shortages, littered streets, or roads snarled with cars? None of us is romanticizing "the good old days," or longing to return to the pastoral past. Indeed, that is just the point! There is nothing about cleaning our environments, finding alternatives to the automobile, or making our homes and buildings energy efficient that implies returning to some undesirable point in history. On the contrary, it seems to us that if our energy and environmental practices were modified, we would be considerably enhancing the quality of life in this country.

Do these statements mean that we do not endorse exploration of new energy sources or increased productivity from contemporary sources? No. We do endorse such efforts where they are safe and do not damage the environment. But let us use a not too distant analogy to clarify our position. Suppose we were still drawing our water by bucket from a well. However, our bucket had a large hole in the bottom so that about a third of the water always flowed out as we drew it up, and once we got the bucket to the top, we were careless so that another third of the water splashed out. We then concluded from this experience that our only hope was to dig yet another well!

New energy explorations and developments are fine, if we first examine, assess, and modify our inefficient technology and wasteful behaviors. To simply try to continue to fuel existing policies and practices is a mistake. We hope this text prompts the development of viable alternatives.

References

Agras, W. S., Jacob, R. G., & Lebedeck, M. The California drought: A quasi-experimental analysis of social policy. *Journal of Applied Behavior Analysis*, 1980, **13**, 561-570.

American Automobile Association, *Gas watcher's guide*. Falls Church, Virginia: Author, 1975.

American Public Transit Association. State funds flowing to R-GRTA. *Passenger Transport*, May 16, 1975, **33**, 20. (a)

American Public Transit Association. BART offers cut-rate tickets. *Passenger Transport*, July 11, 1975, **33**, 2. (b)

Andrle, S., & Dueker, K. J. *Attitude toward and evaluation of carpooling* (Technical Report No. 32). Iowa City, Iowa: University of Iowa, Center for Urban Transportation Studies, 1974.

Appelhof, M. Worms—A safe, effective garbage disposal. *Organic Gardening and Farming Magazine*. August, 1974, pp. 65-69.

Appelhof, M. *Composting your garbage with worms*. Unpublished manuscript, Kalamazoo Nature Center, 7000 N. Westnedge, Kalamazoo, Michigan, 49007, 1979.

Appelhof, M. *Energy considerations: Resource recycling and energy recovery*. Presentation before the Resource Recovery Advisory Committee, South Central Michigan Planning Council, July 1980.

Appelhof, M. Worms vs. high technology. *The Creative Woman*. Summer, 1980, **4**, 23-28.

Applehof, M. Personal communication with E. Scott Geller, February 7, 1981.

Applied Decision Systems, Inc. *Transportation planning simulation*. Paper presented at Environmental and Urban Systems Research Conference, U.S. Department of Transportation, Washington, D.C., September 21, 1970.

Arbuthnot, J. The roles of attitudinal and personality variables in the prediction of environmental behavior and knowledge. *Environment and Behavior*, 1977, **9**, 217-232.

Arbuthnot, J., Tedeschi, R., Wayner, M., Turner, J., Kressel, S., & Rush, R. The induction of sustained recycling behavior through the foot-in-the door technique. *Journal of Environmental Systems*, 1977, **6**, 353-366.

ASHRAE Handbook of Fundamentals. New York: American Society of Heating, Refrigerating and Air Conditioning Engineers, Inc., 1972.

Ashton, W., Howard-Ferreira, S., & Bond, L. *An incomplete guide to water conservation: Residential water conservation*, Vol. 2. Waterloo, Ontario, Canada: Regional Municipality of Waterloo, 1979.

Aston, A. Water resources and consumption in Hong Kong. *Urban Ecology*, 1976, **2**, 327-353.

Ayllon, T., & Azrin, N. *The token economy: A motivational system for therapy and rehabilitation*. New York: Appleton Century Crofts, 1968.

Bacon-Prue, A., Blount, R., Pickering, D., & Drabman, R. An evaluation of three litter control procedures—trash receptacles, paid workers, and the marked item technique. *Journal of Applied Behavior Analysis*, 1980, **13**, 165-170.

Baer, D. M., Wolf, M. M., & Risley, T. R. Some current dimensions of behavior analysis. *Journal of Applied Behavior Analysis*, 1968, **1**, 91-97.

Baltes, M. M., & Haywood, S. C. Application and evaluation of strategies to reduce pollution: Behavioral control of littering in the football stadium. *Journal of Applied Psychology*, 1976, **61**, 501-506.

Bandura, A. *Principles of behavior modification*. New York: Holt, Rinehart & Winston, 1969.

Bandura, A. Self-efficiency: Toward a unifying theory of behavioral change. *Psychological Review*, 1977, **84**, 191-215. (a)

Bandura, A. *Social learning theory*. Englewood Cliffs, New Jersey: Prentice-Hall, 1977. (b)

Bandura, A., & Walters, R. H. *Social learning and personality development*. New York: Holt, Rinehart & Winston, 1967.

Barkow, B. *The psychology of car pooling*. Ontario, Canada: Ministry of Transportation and Communication, 1974.

Battalio, R. C., Kagel, J. H., & Winkler, R. C. "Analyses of individual behavior in a token economic system: An economist's perspective." In *Experimentation in controlled environments and its implications for economic behavior and social policy making*. C. G. Miles, Ed. Toronto, Canada: A. R. F., 1975.

Battalio, R. C., Kagel, J. H., Winkler, R. C., Fisher, E. G., Jr., Basmann, R. L., & Krasner, L. A. test of consumer demand theory using observations of individual consumer purchases. *Western Economic Theory*, 1973, **11**, 411-428.

Battalio, R. C., Kagel, J. H., Winkler, R. C., & Winett, R. A. Residential electricity demand: An experimental study. *The Review of Economics and Statistics*, 1979, **61**, 180-189.

Becker, L. J. The joint effect of feedback and goal setting on performance: A field study of residential energy conservation. *Journal of Applied Psychology*, 1978, **63**, 228-233.

Becker, L. J., & Seligman, C. *Preliminary evaluation of an energy feedback conservation program*. Symposium presentation at Eastern Psychological Association meeting, Washington, D.C., 1978.

Becker, L. J., & Seligman, C. Reducing air-conditioning waste by signaling it is cool outside. *Personality and Social Psychology Bulletin*, 1978, **4**, 412-415.

Becker, L. J., & Seligman, C. Welcome to the energy crisis. *Journal of Social Issues*, 1981, **37**, 1-7.

Becker, L. J., Seligman, C., & Darley, J. M. *Psychological strategies to reduce energy consumption* (Project summary report). Princeton, New Jersey: Princeton University, Center for Energy and Environmental Studies, 1980.

Becker, L. J., Seligman, C., Fazio, R. H., & Darley, J. M. Relationship between attitudes and residential energy consumption. *Environment and Behavior*, 1981, in press.

Beckey, T., & Nelson, L. W. Field test of energy savings with thermostat setback. *ASHRAE Journal*, January 1981, pp. 67-70.

Bell, P. A., Fisher, J. D., & Loomis, R. J. *Environmental psychology*. Philadelphia: W. B. Saunders, 1978.

Bennett, J. W. "Anthropological contributions to the cultural ecology and management of water resources." In *Man and water: The social sciences in management of water resources*. L. D. James, Ed. Lexington, Kentucky: University Press of Kentucky, 1974.

Bent, M. D. *Vanpooling: A technique for estimating impacts* (Technical Memorandum 34). Baltimore, Maryland: Regional Planning Council, June 1977.

Bickman, L. Environmental attitudes and action. *The Journal of Social Psychology*, 1972, **87**, 323-324.

Bittle, R. G., Valesano, R., & Thaler, G. The effects of daily cost feedback on residential electricity consumption. *Behavior Modification*, 1979, **3**, 187-202.

Bittle, R.G., Valesano, R. M., & Thaler, G. M. The effects of daily feedback on residential electricity usage as a function of usage level and type of feedback information. *Journal of Environmental Systems*, 1980, **9**, 275-287.

Blakely, E. Q., Lloyd, K. E., & Alferink, L. A. *The effects of feedback on residential electrical peaking and hourly kilowatt consumption*. Unpublished manuscript, Department of Psychology, Drake University, 1977.

Bond, L. "Energy-water conservation relationship." In *An incomplete guide to water conserva-*

tion: Residential water conservation, Vol. 2. W. Ashton, S. Howard-Ferreira, & L. Bond, Eds. Waterloo, Ontario, Canada: Regional Municipality of Waterloo, 1979.

Brasted, W. Personal communication with E. Scott Geller, July 25, 1978.

Brasted, W., Mann, M., & Geller, E. S. Behavioral interventions for litter control: A critical review. *Cornell Journal of Social Relations*, Summer 1979, **14**, 75-90.

Bree, W. R. *Antilittering and recycling research.* Symposium presentation at the American Psychological Association meeting, San Francisco, California, 1977.

Brehm, J. W. *A theory of psychological reactance.* New York: Academic Press, 1966.

Brehm, J. *Responses to loss of freedom: A theory of psychological reactance.* New York: General Learning Press, 1972.

Brown, L. R., Flavin, C., & Norman, C. *Running on empty.* New York: W. W. Norton and Company, 1979.

Bruce-Briggs, B. *The war against the automobile.* New York: E. P. Dutton, 1977.

Bryant, D. A. *Study and evaluation of commuter carpool programs in certain metropolitan areas* (Technical Report No. GCA-TR-74-S-G). Bedford, Massachusetts: GCA Corporation, Technology Division, April 1974.

Buel, M. H. Local trashmen agree to collect recyclables. *Willamette Week*, August 29, 1977, pp. 1; 3.

Burgess, R. L., Clark, R. N., & Hendee, J.C. An experimental analysis of anti-littering procedures. *Journal of Applied Behavior Analysis*, 1971, **4**, 71-75.

Buttram, B. A., & Geller, E. S. *Analyses of behavioral, educational, and engineering strategies for motivating residential water conservation.* Unpublished manuscript, Department of Psychology, Virginia Polytechnic Institute and State University, 1981.

Carlyle, J. T. *Attempts to promote residential energy and water conservation.* Unpublished masters thesis, Department of Psychology, Virginia Polytechnic University and State University, 1980.

Carter, President Jimmy. *The national energy plan.* Televised speech to the nation, April 29, 1977.

Chapman, C., & Risley, T. R. Anti-litter procedures in an urban high-density area. *Journal of Applied Behavior Analysis*, 1974, **7**, 377-384.

Clark, R. N., Burgess, R. L., & Hendee, J. C. The development of anti-litter behavior in a forest campground. *Journal of Applied Behavior Analysis*, 1972, **5**, 1-5.

Cone, J. D., & Hayes, S. C. *Environmental problems: Behavioral solutions.* Monterey, California: Brooks/Cole Publishing Company, 1980.

Congressional Budget Office. *Urban transportation and energy: The potential savings of different modes.* Washington, D.C., Author, September 1977.

Connor, D. L. *Findings of preliminary analyses of the Trenton, New Jersey, off-peak fare-free transit demonstration.* Trenton, New Jersey: U.S. Department of Transportation, January 1979. (NTIS 52-0001-79-1)

Controller General of the U.S. *Residential energy conservation outreach activities—A new federal approach needed.* Report to the Congress of the United States, Washington, D.C., February 11, 1981.

Cope, J. G., & Geller, E. S. *Promoting the use of automobile litter bags in community settings.* Unpublished manuscript, Department of Psychology, Virginia Polytechnic Institute and State University, 1981.

Corey, J. Personal communication to E. Scott Geller, March 30, 1977.

Couch, J. V., Garber, T., & Karpus, L. Response maintenance and paper recycling. *Journal of Environmental Systems*, 1979, **8**, 127-137.

Craig, C. S., & McCann, J. M. Developing strategies for influencing residential consumption of electricity. *Journal of Environmental Systems*, 1980, **9**, 175-188.

Cruickshank, R., Standard, K. L., & Russell, H. B. L. *Epidemiology and community health in warm climate countries*. New York: Churchill Livingstone, 1976.

Crump, S. L., Nunes, D. L., & Crossman, E. K. The effects of litter on littering behavior in a forest environment. *Environment and Behavior*, 1977, **9**, 137-146.

Dallmeyer, K. E. *Hitchhiking—A viable addition to a multimodel transportation system*. Boulder, Colorado: Center of Transportation Studies, University of Colorado, March 1975. (NTIS No. PB-242 203)

Darley, J. M. Energy conservation techniques as innovations, and their diffusion. *Energy and Building*, 1978, **1**, 339-343.

Delprata, D. J. Prompting electrical energy conservation in commercial users. *Environment and Behavior*, 1977, **9**, 433-440.

Denver Research Institute. *Litter in Colorado, 1971-1972* (Technical report). Denver, Colorado: University of Denver, Denver Research Institute, 1973.

Dernbach, J. Michigan's bottle bill gives new momentum to national campaign. *Environment Action Bulletin*, April 30, 1977, pp. 3-5.

Deslauriers, B. C. A behavioral analysis of transportation: Some suggestions for mass transit. *High Speed Ground Transportation Journal*, 1975, **9**, 13-19.

Deslauriers, B. C., & Everett, P. B. Effects of intermittent and continuous token reinforcement on bus ridership. *Journal of Applied Psychology*, 1977, **62**, 369-375.

Deutscher, I. Words and deeds: Social science and social policy. *Social Problems*, 1966, **13**, 235-254.

Deutscher, I. *What we say/what we do: Sentiments and acts*. Glenview, Illinois: Scott, Foresman and Company, 1973.

Dodge, M. C. *Modification of littering behavior: An exploratory study*. Unpublished masters thesis manuscript, Department of Psychology, Utah State University, 1972. (Reprinted by the Institute for the Study of Outdoor Recreation and Tourism, Logan, Utah.)

Dorf, R. C. *Technology and society*. San Francisco: Boyd and Fraser Publishing Company, 1974.

Dueker, K. J., & Levin, I. P. *Carpooling: Attitudes and participation* (Technical Report No. 81). Iowa City, Iowa: University of Iowa, Center for Urban Transportation Studies, 1976.

Duncan, R. C. The "ORE plan" for recycling household solid waste: An alternative garbage collection system. *Compost Science*, January-February 1975, pp. 24-32.

Duncan, R. C. An economic garbage collection and recycling service. *Compost Science*, January-February 1976, pp. 12-25. (a)

Duncan, R. C. The role of the ORE plan in developing a nationwide recycling network. *Compost Science*, Summer 1976, pp. 25-32. (b)

Environmental Action Foundation. Solid waste bill becomes law. *Memo*, Solid Waste Project, Washington, D.C., December 1976, pp. 1-2. (a)

Environmental Action Foundation. Voters ban throwaways in Michigan, Maine. *Memo*, Solid Waste Project, Washington, D.C., December 1976, p. 1. (b)

Environmental Action Foundation. Paper profits. *Garbage Guide*, No. 9, Washington, D.C., 1977. (a)

Environmental Action Foundation. Resource recovery. *Garbage Guide*, Washington, D.C., 1977. (b)

Environmetrics, Inc. *The urban systems model* (Technical Report). Washington, D.C.: U.S. Department of Transportation, Office of The Secretary, Assistant Secretary for Environment and Urban Systems, 1972.

Erickson, J., & Geller, E. S. *Applications of educational versus engineering strategies to promote residential water conservation*. Final Report for Grant #NSF SPI-8003981 from the National Science Foundation, March 1981.

Everett, P. B. The use of the reinforcement procedure to increase bus ridership. *Proceedings of the 81st Annual Convention of the American Psychological Association*, 1973, **8**, 891-892.

Everett, P. B. "A behavioral approach to transportation systems management." In *Behavioral community psychology: Progress and Prospects*. D. Glenwick & L. Jason, Eds. New York: Praeger, 1980.

Everett, P. B. "Reinforcement theory strategies for modifying transit ridership." In *Human behavior and the environment: Transportation*. I. Altman, J. Wohlwill, & P. Everett, Eds. New York: Plenum Press, 1982, in press.

Everett, P. B., Anderson, V. B., & Makranczy, V. Transit route pamphlets: Do they work? *Transit Journal*, 1977, **3**, 59-70.

Everett, P. B., Deslauriers, B. C., Newson, T., & Anderson, V. B. The differential effects of two free ride dissemination procedures on bus ridership. *Transportation Research*, 1978, **12**, 1-6.

Everett, P. B., Gurtler, M. D., & Hildebrand, M. G. Free transit: How much—How long? *Transportation Research*, 1981, in press.

Everett, P. B., & Haywood, S. C. Behavioral technology—An essential design component of transportation systems. *High Speed Ground Transportation Journal*, 1974, **8**, 139-143.

Everett, P. B., Haywood, S. C., & Meyers, A. W. Effects of a token reinforcement procedure on bus ridership. *Journal of Applied Behavior Analysis*, 1974, **7**, 1-9.

Everett, P. B., Studer, R. B., & Douglas, T. J. Gaming simulation to pretest operant-based community interventions: An urban transportation example. *American Journal of Community Psychology*, 1981, in press.

Fair, G. M., Geyer, J. C., & Okun, D. A. *Water and waste water engineering*. Vols. 1 and 2. New York: Wiley, 1966.

Fairweather, G. W., Sanders, D. H., & Tornatzky, L. G. *Creating change in mental health organizations*. New York: Pergamon Press, 1974.

Fawcett, S. B., Mathews, R. M., & Fletcher, R. K. Some promising dimensions for behavioral community technology. *Journal of Applied Behavior Analysis*, 1980, **13**, 505-518.

Federal Energy Administration. *Tips for energy savers*. Washington, D.C.: U.S. Government Printing Office, 1977.

Ferster, C. B., & Skinner, B. F. *Schedules of reinforcement*. New York: Appleton-Century-Crofts, 1957.

Field, J. Chief Engineer of Metropolitan Water and Sewage Supply Board, Perth, Australia. Personal communication with Robin A. Winkler, February, 1979.

Finnie, W. C. Field experiments in litter control. *Environment and Behavior*, 1973, **5**, 123-144.

Fleischman, E. Public incentives. *Proceedings of the 1975 National Conference on Areawide Carpooling*, Houston, Texas, December 8-10, 1975. Washington, D.C.: Federal Highway Administration, Urban Planning Division, 1975.

Forstater, I., & Twomey, E. *Vanpooling: A summary and description of existing vanpool programs*. Washington, D.C.: U.S. Environmental Protection Agency, January 1976.

Fowler, S. Irony department: Capitol Hill switching to deposit containers. *Environment Action Bulletin*, September 4, 1976, pp. 7-8.

Foxx, R. M., & Hake, D. F. Gasoline conservation: A procedure for measuring and reducing the driving of college students. *Journal of Applied Behavior Analysis*, 1977, **10**, 61-74.

Frankena, F., Buttel, F. H., & Morrison, D. E. *Energy/society annotations*. Unpublished manuscript, Department of Sociology, Michigan State University, 1977.

Franz, M. This town accepts the composting challenge. *Compost Science*, May-June 1971, **12**, No. 3.

Freeman Associates, Inc. *Public service advertising for the division of litter control*. Presentation to the Virginia Litter Control Board, Richmond, Virginia, 1977.

Freedman, J. L., & Fraser, S. C. Compliance without pressure: The foot-in-the-door technique. *Journal of Personality and Social Psychology*, 1977, **4**, 195-202.

Gallagher, D. R., & Robinson, R. W. *Influence of metering, pricing policies and incentives on water use efficiency* (Technical Paper No. 19). Australian Water Resources Council, Australian Government Publishing Service, 1977.

Geller, E. S. A training program in behavioral modification: Design, outcome, and implication. JSAS *Catalog of Selected Documents in Psychology*, 1972, **2**, 28. (Ms. No. 95)

Geller, E. S. Prompting anti-litter behaviors. *Proceedings of the 81st Annual Convention of the American Psychological Association*, 1973, **8**, 901-902.

Geller, E. S. Increasing desired waste disposals with instructions. *Man-Environment Systems*, 1975, **5**, 125-128.

Geller, E. S. *Behavioral approaches to environmental problem solving: Littering and recycling.* Symposium presentation at the Association for the Advancement of Behavior Therapy meeting, New York, 1976.

Geller, E. S. *Proenvironmental behavior: Policy implications of applied behavior analysis.* Symposium presentation at the American Psychological Association meeting, Toronto, Canada, 1978.

Geller, E. S. "Applications of behavioral analysis for litter control." In *Behavioral community psychology: Progress and prospects.* D. Glenwick & L. Jason, Eds. New York: Praeger, 1980. (a)

Geller, E. S. "Saving environmental resources through waste reduction and recycling: How the behavioral community psychologist can help." In *Helping in the community: Behavioral applications.* G. L. Martin & J. G. Osborne, Eds. New York: Plenum Press, 1980. (b)

Geller, E. S. Evaluating energy conservation programs: Is verbal report enough? *Journal of Consumer Research*, 1981, in press. (a)

Geller, E. S. "Waste reduction and resource recovery: Strategies for energy conservation." In *Advances in environmental psychology, Vol. 3. Energy conservation: Psychological perspectives.* A. Baum & J. E. Singer, Eds. Hillside, N.J.: Lawrence Erlbaum Associates, 1981. (b)

Geller, E. S. "The energy crisis and behavioral science: A conceptual framework for large scale intervention." In *Rural psychology.* A. W. Childs & G. B. Melton, Eds. New York: Plenum Press, 1982.

Geller, E. S., Bowen, S. P., & Chiang, R. N. S. *A community-based approach to promoting energy conservation.* Symposium presentation at the American Psychological Association meeting, Toronto, Canada, 1978.

Geller, E. S., Brasted, W. S., & Augustine, M. N. *A community education model for energy conservation: Implementation, evaluation, and implication.* Symposium presentation at the Eastern Psychological Association meeting, Washington, D.C., 1978.

Geller, E. S., Brasted, W., & Mann, M. Waste receptacle designs as interventions for litter control. *Journal of Environmental Systems*, 1980, **9**, 145-160.

Geller, E. S., Casali, J. G., & Johnson, R. P. Seat belt usage: A potential target for applied behavior analysis. *Journal of Applied Behavior Analysis*, 1980, **13**, 669-675.

Geller, E. S., Chaffee, J. L., & Ingram, R. E. Promoting paper recycling on a university campus. *Journal of Environmental Systems*, 1975, **5**, 39-57.

Geller, E. S., Farris, J. C., & Post, D. S. Promoting a consumer behavior for pollution control. *Journal of Applied Behavior Analysis*, 1973, **6**, 367-376.

Geller, E. S., Ferguson, J. F., & Brasted, W. S. *Attempts to promote residential energy conservation: Attitudinal versus behavioral outcome* (Technical Report for Title 1 Grant, 1978). Blacksburg, Virginia: Virginia Polytechnic Institute and State University, Department of Psychology, 1978.

Geller, E. S., Johnson, R. P., & Pelton, S. L. Community-based interventions for encouraging safety belt use. *American Journal of Community Psychology*, 1981, in press.

Geller, E. S., Koltuniak, T. A., & Shilling, J. S. *Response avoidance prompting: A cost-effective strategy for theft deterrence.* Manuscript submitted for publication, 1981.

Geller, E. S., Mann, M., & Brasted, W. *Trash can design: A determinant of litter-related behavior.* Paper presented at the American Psychological Association meeting, San Francisco, California, 1977.

Geller, E. S., Talbott, E., & Paterson, L. *A cost-effective incentive strategy for motivating seat belt usage.* Manuscript submitted for publication, 1981.

Geller, E. S., Witmer, J. F., & Orebaugh, A. L. Instructions as a determinant of paper-disposal behaviors. *Environment and Behavior*, 1976, **8,** 417-438.

Geller, E. S., Witmer, J. F., & Tuso, M. E. Environmental interventions for litter control. *Journal of Applied Psychology*, 1977, **62,** 344-351.

Geller, E. S., Wylie, R. C., & Farris, J. C. An attempt at applying prompting and reinforcement toward pollution control. *Proceedings of the 79th Annual Convention of the American Psychological Association*, 1971, **6,** 701-702.

Gold, J. *The effect of water rate structure on water conservation* (Technical Report). Waterloo, Ontario, Canada: University of Waterloo, Department of Man-Environment Studies, 1979.

Goldstein, A. P., Heller, K., & Sechrest, L. B. *Psychotherapy and the psychology of behavior change.* New York: Wiley, 1966.

Golob, T. F., Canty, E. T., Gustafson, R. L., & Vitt, J. E. An analysis of consumer preferences for a public transportation system. *Transportation Research*, 1972, **6,** 81-102.

Goodman, K. M., & Green, M. A. *Low fare, free fare transit.* Washington, D.C.: UMTA, February, 1977. (NTIS No. 52-0002-77-1)

Gravino, M. "Highgrading: A development plan for LEDC Rural Recycling Project." In *Highgrading: A demonstration of the feasibility of recovering resources from solid waste at rural sites in Lane County.* Eugene, Oregon: Lane Economic Development Council, 1981.

Greene, A. K. Bring 'em back, repack and save. *Proceedings, 1975 Conference on Waste Reduction.* Washington, D.C.: U.S. Environmental Protection Agency, 1975, pp. 105-112.

Grima, A. P. *Residential water demand.* Toronto: University of Toronto Press, 1972.

Gurin, D. B. Pragmatic evaluation of telephones, activity scheduling, and other strategies to modify travel behavior of population sub-groups. *Transportation Research Record*, 1976, No. 583, 29-35.

Hake, D. F., & Foxx, R. M. Promoting gasoline conservation: The effects of reinforcement schedules, a leader and self-recording. *Behavior Modification*, 1978, **2,** 339-369.

Hamad, C. D., Bettinger, R., Cooper, D., & Semb, G. *Using behavioral procedures to establish an elementary school paper recycling program.* Unpublished manuscript, Department of Psychology, University of Kansas, 1979.

Hamad, C.D., Cooper, D., & Semb, G. *Resource recovery: The use of a group contingency to increase paper recycling in an elementary school.* Unpublished manuscript, University of Kansas, 1977.

Hannon, B. *System energy and recycling.* March 1973. (NTIS No. PB-233-183)

Hargroves, B. T., & McGray, M. *TRANSPON (transportation policy negotiation).* Unpublished manuscript, The Pennsylvania Transportation Institute, The Pennsylvania State University, 1973.

Hayes, S. C., & Cone, J. D. Reducing residential electrical use: Payments, information, and feedback. *Journal of Applied Behavior Analysis*, 1977, **10,** 425-435.

Hayes, S. C., & Cone, J. D. Reduction of residential consumption of electricity through simple monthly feedback. *Journal of Applied Behavior Analysis*, 1981, **14,** 81-88.

Hayes, S. C., Johnson, V. S., & Cone, J. D. The marked item technique: A practical procedure for litter control. *Journal of Applied Behavior Analysis*, 1975, **8,** 381-386.

Hayward, S. C., & Everett, P. B. *A failure of response cost feedback to modify car driving behavior.* Paper presented at the Midwestern Association of Behavior Analysis meeting, Chicago, Illinois, 1975.

Heberlein, T. A. Moral norms, threatened sanctions, and littering behavior. (Doctoral dissertation, University of Wisconsin, 1971). *Dissertation Abstracts International*, 1972, **32,** 5906A. (University Microfilms No. 72-2639).

Heberlein, T. A. *Beliefs about sanctions, norm activation and violation of the anti-littering norm.* Paper presented at the Rural Sociological Society meeting, Montreal, Canada, 1974.

Heberlein, T. A. Conservation information: The energy crisis and electricity consumption in an apartment complex. *Energy Systems and Policy*, 1975, **1**, 105-117.

Hendee, J. C. No, to attitudes to evaluate environmental education. *The Journal of Environmental Education*, 1971, **3**, 65.

Hersen, M., & Barlow, D. H. *Single case experimental designs: Strategies for studying behavioral change.* New York: Pergamon Press, 1976.

Hirst, E. Transportation energy conservation policies. *Science*, 1976, **192**, 15-20.

Hirst, E. Understanding energy conservation. *Science*, 1979, **206**, 427.

Horowitz, A. D., & Sheth, J. N. *Ridesharing to work: A psychosocial analysis.* Warren, Michigan: General Motors Corporation, 1977.

Howard-Ferreira, S., & Robinson, J. E. *Community-information programs* (Municipal Working Group on Water Conservation Alternatives, Working Paper No. 2). Waterloo, Ontario, Canada: University of Waterloo, March 1980.

Howe, C. W., & Linaweaver, F. P. The impact of price on residential water demand and its relation to system design and price structures. *Water Resources Research*, 1967, **3**, 13.

Humber, N. Waste reduction and resource recovery—there's room for both. *Waste Age*, November 1975.

Humphrey, C. R., Bord, R. J., Hammond, M. M., & Mann, S. Attitudes and conditions for cooperation in a paper recycling program. *Environment and Behavior*, 1977, **9**, 107-124.

Hurley, J. Personal communication with E. Scott Geller, July 11, 1978.

Ingram, R. E., & Geller, E. S. A community integrated, behavior modification approach to facilitating paper recycling. JSAS *Catalog of Selected Documents in Psychology*, 1975, **5**, 327. (Ms. No. 1097)

Institute for Local Self-Reliance. *Composting in the city.* Washington, D.C.: Community Self-Reliance Series, Author, 1975.

Institute for Local Self-Reliance. *National recycling research agenda project for the National Science Foundation: Final report* (Technical Report for Grant OPA 79-19013 from the National Science Foundation). Washington, D.C.: Waste Utilization Division, Author, March 1980.

Jacobs, H. E. *An analysis of motivational effects in encouraging participation in a residential recycling program.* Unpublished masters thesis, Department of Psychology, Florida State University, 1978.

Jacobs, H. E., & Bailey, J. S. *A preliminary analysis of motivational factors in a residential recycling program.* Symposium presentation at the Southeastern Psychological Association meeting, New Orleans, Louisiana, 1979. (a)

Jacobs, H. E., & Bailey, J. S. *The Leon County recycling program: The development of an empirically derived communitywide resource recovery program.* Symposium presentation at the Association for Behavior Analysis meeting, Dearborn, Michigan, 1979. (b)

Jacobs, H., Fairbanks, D., Poche, C., & Bailey, J. S. Behavioral community psychology: Multiple incentives in encouraging carpool formation on a university campus. *Journal of Applied Behavior Analysis*, 1981, in press.

James, L. D. "The challenge to the social sciences." In *Man and water: The social sciences in management of water resources.* L. D. James, Ed. Lexington, Kentucky: University Press of Kentucky, 1974.

Jason, L. A. Training undergraduates in behavior therapy and behavior community psychology. *Behaviorists for Social Action Journal*, 1981, **3**, 1-8.

Jason, L. A., & Figueroa, Y. *Fences as a stimulus control strategy: Reducing dog litter in an urban area.* Paper presented at the Association for Behavior Analysis meeting, Dearborn, Michigan, 1980.

Jason, L. A., McCoy, K., Blanco, D., & Zolik, E. S. Decreasing dog litter: To help a community group. *Evaluation Review*, 1980, **4**, 355-369.

Jason, L. A., Zolik, E. S., & Matese, F. Prompting dog owners to pick up dog droppings. *American Journal of Community Psychology*, 1979, **7**, 339-351.

Johnson, M. H., & Leonard, E. *Prevention is better than pickup.* Paper presented at the 59th Annual Meeting of State Highway Officials, Los Angeles, California, 1973.

Johnson, R. P., & Geller, E. S. Engineering technology and behavior analysis for interdisciplinary environmental protection. *Behavior Analyst*, 1980, **3**, 23-29.

Johnson, R. P., & Geller, E. S. *Contingent versus noncontingent rewards for promoting seat belt usage.* Manuscript submitted for publication, 1981.

Jones, B., & Derby, J. Sacramento car-pool projects: Interim evaluation report. *Transportation Research Record*, 1976, No. 619, 38-42.

Kagel, J. H. Personal communication with Richard A. Winett, January 1981.

Kagel, J. H., Battalio, R. C., & Walker, J. M. "Volunteer artifacts and experiments in economics: Specification of the problem and some initial data from small-scale field experiments." In *Research in experimental economics.* V. L. Smith, Ed. Greenwich, Connecticut: JAI Press, 1980.

Kagel, J. H., & Winkler, R. C. Behavioral economics: Areas of cooperative research between economics and applied behavior analysis. *Journal of Applied Behavior Analysis*, 1972, **5**, 335-342.

Kalinin, G. P., & Bykov, V. C. The world's water resources present and future. *Impact of Science on Society*, 1969, **19**, 135-150.

Karoly, P., & Steffens, J. J. *Improving the long-term effects of psychotherapy.* New York: Gardner Press, 1980.

Kazdin, A. E. *Behavior modification in applied settings.* Homewood, Illinois: Dorsey, 1975.

Keep America Beautiful, Inc. *Fact sheet: Litter is a national disgrace.* New York: Author, 1970.

———. *Annual Review.* New York: Author, 1976.

———. *Clean community system: Application for certification.* New York: Author, 1977. (a)

———. *Clean community system: Business & industry sub-committee guide.* New York: Author, 1977. (b)

———. *Clean community system: Communication sub-committee guide.* New York: Author, 1977. (c)

———. *Clean community system: Community survey guide.* New York: Author, 1977. (d)

———. *Clean community system: Community organizations sub-committee guide.* New York: Author, 1977. (e)

———. *Clean community system: Glossary & index.* New York: Author, 1977. (f)

———. *Clean community system: Litter/solid waste analysis guide.* New York: Author, 1977. (g)

———. *Clean community system: Municipal organizations sub-committee guide.* New York: Author, 1977. (h)

———. *Clean community system: Organizing the community.* New York: Author, 1977. (i)

———. *Clean community system: Photometric index instructions.* New York: Author, 1977. (j)

———. *Clean community system: Schools sub-committee guide.* New York: Author, 1977. (k)

———. *Clean community system: Slide presentation script-information workshop version.* New York: Author, 1977. (l)

———. *Clean community system: Slide presentation script-training workshop version.* New York: Author, 1977. (m)

———. *Clean community system: Trainer's manual.* New York: Author, 1977. (n)

———. *Clean Community System Bulletin*, No. 2. New York: Author, 1977. (o)

———. *Clean Community System Bulletin*, No. 3. New York: Author, 1977. (p)

———. *Initiating the clean community system.* New York: Author, 1977. (q)

———. *News from Keep America Beautiful, Inc.*, New York: Author, 1977. (r)

———. *The clean community system works.* New York: Author, 1977. (s)

———. Canada seventh country to implement CCS. *Clean Community System Bulletin*, August

1979, pp. 1-2. (a)

———. Photometric index. *Clean Community System Bulletin*, August 1979, pp. 2; 4. (b)

———. Macon starts action in model energy program. *Clean Community System Bulletin*, November-December 1980, p. 1

Kehoe, J. F., & Geller, E. S. *An evaluation of the 1978-1979 Virginia Division of Energy Home Package distribution program: Final report* (Technical Report for Grant 848030-1 from the Viriginia Department of Energy). Blacksburg, Virginia: Virginia Polytechnic Institute and State University, Department of Psychology, 1980.

Kiefer, I. *Incentives for tire recycling and reuse.* Washington, D.C.: U.S. Environmental Protection Agency, 1974.

King, H. D. A more positive strategy. *Proceedings, 1975 Conference on Waste Reduction.* Washington, D.C.: U.S. Environmental Protection Agency, 1975, pp. 129-135.

Knapp, D. *Case studies in resource recovery: Highgrading in Lane County, Oregon.* Invited address at Recycling Research Agenda Conference for the National Science Foundation, Washington, D.C., 1979.

Knapp, D. "Making highgrading work: An evaluation of the LEDC Rural Recycling Project." In *Highgrading: A demonstration of the feasibility of recovering from solid waste at rural sites in Lane County.* Eugene, Oregon: Lane Economic Development Council, 1981.

Kohlenberg, R. J., & Anschell, S. *Conclusions and recommendations for electrical energy conservation based on the Washington rate demonstrations project* (Technical Report). Seattle, Washington: University of Washington, Institute of Governmental Research, 1980.

Kohlenberg, R. J., Barach, R., Martin, C., & Anschell, S. *Experimental analysis of the effects of price and feedback on residential energy conservation.* Unpublished manuscript, Department of Psychology, University of Washington, 1976.

Kohlenberg, R. J., & Phillips, T. Reinforcement and rate of litter depositing. *Journal of Applied Behavior Analysis*, 1973, **6**, 391-396.

Kohlenberg, R. J., Phillips, T., & Proctor, W. A behavioral analysis of peaking in residential electricity energy consumption. *Journal of Applied Behavior Analysis*, 1976, **9**, 13-18.

Krantz, D. L. The separate worlds of operant and non-operant psychology. *Journal of Applied Behavior Analysis*, 1971, **4**, 61-70.

LaBreque, M. Garbage—Refuse or resource? *Popular Science*, June 1977, pp. 95-98; 166.

LaHart, D., & Bailey, J. S. Reducing children's littering on a nature trail. *Journal of Environmental Education*, 1975, **7**, 37-45.

Lane Economic Development Council. *Highgrading: A demonstration of the feasibility of recovering resources from solid waste at rural sites in Lane County.* Eugene, Oregon: Lane Economic Development Council, 1981.

Lauridsen, P. K. *Decreasing gasoline consumption in fleet-owned automobiles through feedback and feedback-plus lottery.* Unpublished masters thesis, Department of Psychology, Drake University, 1977.

League of Women Voters of the U.S. *Recycle: In search of new policies for resource recovery.* (Pub. No. 132). Washington, D.C.: League of Women Voters Education Fund, 1972.

Lee, D. B. *A cost-oriented methodology for short-range transportation planning* (Technical Report No. 66). Iowa City, Iowa: University of Iowa, Center for Urban Transportation Studies, 1976.

Letzkus, T., & Scharfe, V. Employer incentive programs. *Proceedings of the 1975 National Conference on Areawide Carpooling.* Houston, Texas, 1975. Washington, D.C.: Federal Highway Administration, Urban Planning Division, 1975.

Levenson, H. Perception of environmental modifiability and involvement in antipollution activities. *The Journal of Psychology*, 1973, **84**, 237-239.

Levenson, H. Involvement in antipollution activities and perceived negative consequences from pollution. *Perceptual and Motor Skills*, 1974, **38**, 1105-1106.

Lloyd, K. E. "Reactions to a forthcoming energy shortage: A topic in behavioral ecology." In *Helping in the community: Behavioral applications*. G. L. Martin & J. G. Osborne, Eds. New York: Plenum Press, 1980.

Loube, M. *Beverage containers: The Vermont experience*. Washington, D.C.: U.S. Environmental Protection Agency, 1975.

Lovins, A. B. *Soft energy paths*. San Francisco, California: Friends of the Earth, 1977.

Lovins, A. B., & Lovins, L. H. Reagan's energy policy: Conservative or ultra-liberal? *The Washington Post*, November 22, 1980, p. 23.

Lundberg, V. Urban commuting crowdedness and catecholamine secretion. *Journal of Human Stress*, 1976, **2**, 26-32.

Luyben, P. D. Effects of informational prompts on energy conservation in college classrooms. *Journal of Applied Behavior Analysis*, 1980, **13**, 611-617.

Luyben, P. D., & Bailey, J. S. Newspaper recycling: The effects of rewards and proximity of containers. *Environment and Behavior*, 1979, **11**, 539-557.

Luyben, P. D., Warren, S. B., & Tallman, R. A. Recycling beverage containers on a college campus. *Journal of Environmental Systems*, 1980, **9**, 189-202.

Lynn, L. F. "A decade of policy developments in the income maintenance system." In *Evaluation studies: Review annual, Vol. 3*. T. D. Cook, Ed. Beverly Hills, California: Sage Publications, 1978.

MacCalden, M., & Davis, C. *Report on priority lane experiment on the San Francisco - Oakland Bay Bridge* (Technical Report). San Francisco, California: Department of Public Works, 1972.

Maccoby, N., & Alexander, J. "Use of media in life style programs." In *Behavioral medicine: Changing health life styles*. S. M. Davidson, Ed. New York: Brunner/Mazel, Inc., 1980.

Maccoby, N., Farquhar, J. W., Wood, P., & Alexander, J. K. Reducing the risk of cardiovascular disease: Effects of a community-based campaign on knowledge and behavior. *Journal of Community Health*, 1977, **3**, 100-114.

Margolin, J. B., Misch, M. R., & Dobson, R. D. Incentives and disincentives to ride-sharing behaviors: A progam report. *Transportation Research Record*, 1976, No. 592, 41-44.

Margulies, W. P. Steel and paper industries look at recycling as an answer to pollution. *Advertising Age*, 1970, **41**, 63.

Mayer, J. A., & Geller, E. S. *Prompting and incentive strategies for promoting bike path usage*. Unpublished manuscript, Department of Psychology, Virginia Polytechnic Institute and State University, 1981.

McAlister, A., Puska, P., Koskela, K., Pallonen, U., & Macoby, N. Mass communication and community organization for public health education. *American Psychologist*, 1980, **35**, 375-379.

McClelland, L., & Belsten, L. Prompting energy conservation in university dormitories by physical, policy, and resident behavior changes. *Journal of Environmental Systems*, 1979-1980, **9**, 29-38.

McClelland, L., & Cook, S. W. Energy conservation effects of continuous in-home feedback in all-electric homes. *Journal of Environmental Systems*, 1980, **9**, 169-173.

McDermott, J. Recycling: New answers to NYC's big problem. *Journal of Appropriate Technology*, Spring, 1980, **1**, 9-10.

McGarry, R. S. *Water and sewer conservation oriented rate structure*. Paper presented at the National Conference on Water Conservation and Municipal Wastewater Flow Reduction, Chicago, Illinois, 1978.

McLaughlin, E. *A recycle system for conservation of water in residences* (Technical Report). University Park, Pennsylvania: Pennsylvania State University, 1975.

Michael, J. *Defective contingencies are the rule rather than the exception*. Invited address at the Association for Advancement of Behavior Therapy meeting, New York, 1980.

Miller, C., & Deuser, R. Issues in enforcement of busway and bus and carpool lane restrictions. *Transportation Research Record*, 1976, No. 606, 12-17.

Milne, M. *Residential water conservation* (Technical Report No. 35). Davis, California: California Water Resources Center, 1976.

Mitchell, J. G. Keeping America bottled (and canned). *Audubon*, 1976, **78**, 106-113.

NARI. *Recycling resources: A guide to effective solid waste utilization.* National Association of Recycling Industries, 1973.

National Cooperative Highway Research Program. *Energy effects, efficiencies and prospects for various modes of transportation* (Technical Report NCHRP Synthesis 43). Washington, D.C.: Transportation Research Board, 1977.

Newsom, T. J., & Makranczy, U. J. Reducing electricity consumption of residents living in mass-metered dormitory complexes. *Journal of Environmental Systems*, 1978, **1**, 215-236.

Nicol, M., Winkler, R. C., Syme, G. J., & Haggard, A. *Analysis and modification of domestic water consumption.* Unpublished mansucript, Department of Psychology, University of Western Australia, 1981.

Nietzel, M. T., Winett, R. A., MacDonald, M. L., & Davidson, W. S. *Behavioral approaches to community psychology.* New York: Pergamon Press, 1977.

Office of Solid Waste Management Programs. *Proceedings, 1975 Conference on Waste Reduction.* Washington, D.C.: U.S. Environmental Protection Agency, 1975.

O'Neill, G. W., Blanck, L. S., & Joyner, M. A. The use of stimulus control over littering in a natural setting. *Journal of Applied Behavior Analysis*, 1980, **13**, 379-381.

Osborne, J. G., & Powers, R. B. "Controlling the litter problem." In *Helping in the community: Behavioral applications.* G. L. Martin & J. G. Osborne, Eds. New York: Plenum Press, 1980.

Owens, R. D., & Sever, H. L. *The 3M commute-a-van program* (Progress Report 2). St. Paul, Minnesota: 3M Company, 1977.

Palmer, M. H., Lloyd, M. E., & Lloyd, K. E. An experimental analysis of electricity conservation procedures. *Journal of Applied Behavior Analysis*, 1978, **10**, 665-672.

Pendley, D. L. Staff Vice President for Communications and Program Development, Keep America Beautiful, Inc. Personal communication with E. Scott Geller, October 16, 1981.

Peterson, J. R. Environmental protection and productivity. *Proceedings, 1975 Conference on Waste Reduction.* Washington, D.C.: U.S. Environmental Protection Agency, 1975, pp. 41-44.

Powers, R. B., Osborne, J. G., & Anderson, E. G. Positive reinforcement of litter removal in the natural environment. *Journal of Applied Behavior Analysis*, 1973, **6**, 579-586.

Pratsch, L. *Carpool and buspool matching guide* (4th ed.). Washington, D.C.: U.S. Department of Transportation, Federal Highway Administration, January 1975.

Pratsch, L. *Vanpooling discussion paper.* Unpublished manuscript, Federal Highway Administration, Washington, D.C., April 1975.

Public Opinion Surveys, Inc. *Who litters—And why.* Prepared for Keep America Beautiful, Inc. Princeton, New Jersey: Author, 1968.

Purcell, A. H. *The waste watchers: A citizen's handbook for conserving energy*, New York: Anchor Press/Doubleday, 1980.

Purcell, A. H. The world's trashiest people: Will they clean up their act or throw away their future? *The Futurist*, February 1981, pp. 51-59.

Purdom, P. W., & Anderson, S. H. *Environmental science: Managing the environment.* Columbus, Ohio: Charles E. Merrill Publishing Company, 1980.

Quarles, J. R. Jr., The need for action grows. *Proceedings, 1975 Conference on Waste Reduction.* Washington, D.C.: U.S. Environmental Protection Agency, 1975, pp. 21-26.

Rachlin, H. "Economics and behavioral psychology." In *Limits to action: Allocation of individual behavior.* J. E. R. Staddon, Ed. New York: Academic Press, 1980.

Rachlin, H., & Burkhard, B. The temporal triangle: Response distribution in instrumental conditioning. *Psychological Review*, 1978, **85**, 22-47.

Rachlin, H., Kagel, J. H., & Battalio, R. C. Substitutability in time allocation. *Psychological Review*, 1980, **87**, 355-374.

Rappaport, J. *Community psychology: Values, research and action.* New York: Holt, Rinehart, & Winston, 1977.

Rapping, L. A. Comment: Supply side's bad side. OP-CIT article, Business Section, *New York Times,* March 15, 1981, p. 3.

Recker, W. W., & Stevens, R. F. Attitudinal models of modal choice: The multinomial case for selecting network trips. *Transportation,* 1976, **5,** 355-375.

Reich, J. W., & Robertson, J. L. Reactance and norm appeal in antilittering messages. *Journal of Applied Social Psychology,* 1979, **9,** 91-101.

Reichel, D. A., & Geller, E. S. *Group versus individual contingencies to conserve transportation energy.* Paper presented at the Southeastern Psychological Association meeting, Washington, D.C., 1980.

Reichel, D. A., & Geller, E. S. "Applications of behavioral analysis for conserving transportation energy." In *Advances in environmental psychology, Vol. 3. Energy conservation: Psychological perspectives.* A. Baum & J. E. Singer, Eds. Hillsdale, New Jersey: Lawrence Erlbaum Associates, 1981.

Reid, D. H., Luyben, P. L., Rawers, R. J., & Bailey, J. S. The effects of prompting and proximity of containers on newspaper recycling behavior. *Environment and Behavior,* 1979, **8,** 471-483.

Resource Technology, Inc. *Ten steps for changing your oil and recycling your used oil.* Kansas City, Kansas: Resource Technology, Inc., 1981.

Resources Agency. *A pilot water conservation program bulletin 191.* State of California: Department of Water Resources, 1978.

Rhotton, W. W. *Systems level consulting.* Paper presented at workshop on behavioral consultation with the mining industry, Department of Psychology, Virginia Polytechnic Institute and State University, Blacksburg, Virginia, 1980.

Rice, B. Fighting inflation with buttons and slogans. *Psychology Today,* 1975, **7,** 49-52.

Richards, C. S. Assessment and behavior modification via self-monitoring: An overview and bibliography. JSAS *Catalog of Selected Documents in Psychology,* 1977, **27,** 298-313 (Ms. No. 214)

Risbridger, C. A. *Survey of supply and delivery systems.* International Water Supply Association, Second Congress, 1952.

Roberts, F. J. *The domestic use of water in Perth—An overview.* Paper presented at the Water Research Foundation Seminar, Perth, Australia, 1975.

Robinson, J. P. *How Americans use time: A social-psychological analysis of everyday behavior.* New York: Praeger, 1977.

Robinson, S. N. Littering behavior in public places. *Environment and Behavior,* 1976, **8,** 363-384.

Robinson, S. N., & Frisch, M. H. *Social-environmental influences on littering in a post office.* Paper presented at the Eastern Psychological Association meeting, New York, April 1975.

Rodale Press, Inc. The bottle bill struggles ahead. *Environmental Action Bulletin,* September 1976, **7,** 1.

Rogers, E. M., & Shoemaker, F. F. *Communication of innovations.* New York: Free Press, 1971.

Rohles, F. H. Conserving energy by expanding the thermal comfort envelope. *Proceedings of the Human Factors Society Annual Meeting,* 1978, pp. 533-536.

Rohles, F. H. Thermal comfort and strategies for energy conservation. *Journal of Social Issues,* 1981, **37,** 132-149.

Rose, H. S., & Hinds, D. H. South Dixie Highway contraflow bus and car-pool lane demonstration project. *Transportation Research Record,* 1976, No. 606, 18-22.

Rosenthal, R. *Experimenter effects in behavioral research.* New York: Appleton-Century-Crofts, 1966.

Rosenthal, R., & Rosnow, R. L. (Eds.) *Artifact in behavior research.* New York: Academic Press, 1969.

Ross, M. H., & Williams, R. H. *Our energy: Regaining control.* New York: McGraw-Hill, 1981.

Rothstein, R. N. Television feedback used to modify gasoline consumption. *Behavior Therapy*, 1980, **11**, 683-688.

Runnion, A., Watson, J. D., & McWhorter, J. Energy savings in interstate transportation through feedback and reinforcement. *Journal of Organizational Behavior Management*, 1978, **1**, 180-191.

Ruvin, H. Beverage container legislation: The referendum in Dade county. *Proceedings, 1975 Conference on Waste Reduction.* Washington, D.C.: U.S.Environmental Protection Agency, 1975, pp. 124-128.

Ryan, W. *Blaming the victim.* New York: Random House, 1971.

Samtur, H. *Litter control strategies: An analysis of litter, littering behavior, and litter control programs* (Technical Report). Washington, D.C.: Office of Solid Waste Mangement Programs, U.S. Environmental Protection Agency, 1979.

Savage, J. F., & Richmond, H. R. III. Oregon's bottle bill: A riproaring success. *OSPIRG Reports.* Portland, Oregon: Oregon Student Public Interest Research Group, 1974.

Sazima, H., Johnson, R. P., Carlyle, J., & Geller, E. S. *Attempts to encourage large-scale water and energy conservation.* Paper presented at the American Psychological Association meeting, New York, 1979.

Scheiner, J. L., & Keiper, S. A. Car-pool information project: Innovative approaches improve results. *Transportation Research Record*, 1976, No. 619, 16-18.

Schnelle, J. F., Gendrich, J. G., Beegle, G. P., Thomas, M. M., & McNess, M. P. Mass media techniques for prompting behavior change in the community. *Environment and Behavior*, 1980, **12**, 157-166.

Seaver, W. B., & Patterson, A. H. Decreasing fuel oil consumption through feedback and social consumption. *Journal of Applied Behavior Analysis*, 1976, **9**, 147-152.

Seed, A. H., Jr. Who litters—And why? *Environmental Education*, 1970, **1**, 93-94.

Seldman, N. *Garbage in America: Approaches to recycling.* Washington, D.C.: Institute for Local Self-Reliance, 1975.

Seldman, N. Collection/recycling systems challenge resource recovery. *Environmental Action Bulletin*, October 1976, pp. 1-2 (a)

Seldman, N. Waste utilization—The trouble with high technology. *Self-Reliance*, September 1976, pp. 11-16. (b)

Seldman, N. *New directions in solid waste planning.* Washington, D.C.: Institute for Local Self-Reliance, April 1977.

Seligman, C., Becker, L. J., & Darley, J. M. "Encouraging residential energy conservation through feedback." In *Advances in environmental psychology, Vol. 3. Energy conservation: Psychological perspectives.* A. Baum & J. E. Singer, Eds. Hillsdale, New Jersey: Erlbaum Associates, 1981.

Seligman, C., & Darley, J. M. Feedback as a means of decreasing residential energy consumption. *Journal of Applied Psychology*, 1977, **62**, 363-368.

Seligman, C., & Hutton, R. B. Evaluating energy conservation programs. *Journal of Social Issues*, 1981, **37**, 51-72.

Seligman, C., Kriss, M., Darley, J. M., Fazio, R. H., Becker, L. J., & Pryor, J. B. Predicting residential energy consumption from homeowners' attitudes. *Journal of Applied Social Psychology*, 1981, in press.

Serrin, W. The Michigan bottle law: Model for a federal ban? *The New York Times*, June 1979, p. 3.

Sharpe, W. *Selection of water conservation devices for installation in new or existing dwellings.* Unpublished manuscript, Institute for Research on Land and Water Resources, Pennsylvania State University, 1978.

Sharpe, W. E., & Fletcher, P. W. *The impact of water saving device installation on resource conservation* (Research Publication 98). University Park, Pennsylvania: Pennsylvania State University, Institute for Research on Land and Water Resources, 1977.

Shelby, B. B. *The relation of sex roles to neatness socialization: Normative orientation and littering.* Unpublished masters thesis, Department of Sociology, University of Wisconsin, 1973.

Shippee, G. Energy consumption and conservation psychology: A review and conceptual analysis. *Environmental Management,* 1980, **4,** 297-314.

Sidman, M. *Tactics of scientific research: Evaluating experimental data in psychology.* New York: Basic Books, 1960.

Silver, R. R. Arthur, Talking Ashcan, "Eats" C. W. Post Trash. *New York Times,* March 17, 1974.

Simmons, I. G. *The ecology of natural resources.* London, England: Edward Arnold, 1974, p. 424.

Skinner, B. F. *The behavior of organisms.* New York: Appleton-Century-Crofts, 1938.

Skinner, B. F. *Beyond freedom and dignity.* New York: Knopf, 1971.

Skinner, B. F. *Walden two revisited.* Invited address as the American Psychological Association meeting, Chicago, Illinois, September 1975.

Skinner, J. H. Effects of reuse and recycling of beverage containers. *Proceedings, 1975 Conference on Waste Reduction.* Washington, D.C.: U.S. Environmental Protection Agency, 1975, pp. 136-139.

Slater, J. S., & Watson, B. G. *Psychological and physiological indicators of stress in various travel and commuting modes.* Unpublished masters thesis, Department of Psychology, The Pennsylvania State University, 1980.

Slavin, R. E., & Wodarski, J. S. *Using group contingencies to reduce natural gas consumption in master-metered apartments* (Technical Report No. 232). Baltimore, Maryland: Johns Hopkins University, Center for Social Organization of Schools, 1977.

Slavin, R. E., Wodarksi, J. S., & Blackburn, B. L. A group contingency for electricity conservation in master-metered apartments. *Journal of Applied Behavior Analysis,* 1981, **14,** 357-363.

Smith, F. L., Jr. Waste paper recycling: Review of recent market demand and supply. *Pulp & Paper,* September 1975.

Smith, V. L. "Relevance of laboratory experiments to testing resource allocation theory." In *Evaluation of econometric models.* J. Kmenta & J. B. Ramsey, Eds. New York: Academic Press, 1980.

Socolow, R. H. *Saving energy in the home.* Cambridge, Massachusetts: Ballinger Publishing Company, 1978.

Sokolosky, S. "Energy: Case studies." In *Public transportation: Planning, operations, and management.* G. E. Grey & L. A. Hoel, Eds. Englewood Cliffs, New Jersey: Prentice-Hall, 1979.

SRI International. *Evaluation of the federal energy administration vanpool marketing and implementation demonstration program.* Washington, D.C.: U.S. Government Printing Office, 1978.

Staddon, J. E. R., Ed. *Limits to action: Allocation of individual behavior.* New York: Academic Press, 1981.

Steininger, M., & Voegtlin, K. Attitudinal bases of recycling. *The Journal of Social Psychology,* 1976, **100,** 155-156.

Stern, P. C. The car-pool game: How to mobilize group spirit. *Psychology Today,* 1979, **12,** pp. 16; 26.

Stern, P. C., & Gardner, G. T. *The place of behavior change in the management of environmental problems.* Unpublished manuscript, Institution for Social and Policy Studies, Yale University, 1980.

Stern, P. C., & Gardner, G. T. Psychological research and energy policy. *American Psychologist,* 1981, **4,** 329-342.

Stern, P. C., & Kirkpatrick, E. M. Energy behavior. *Environment,* 1977, **19,** 10-15.

Stevens, W., Kushler, M., Jeppesen, J., & Leedom, N. *Youth energy education strategies: A statistical evaluation.* Lansing, Michigan: Energy Extension Service, Michigan Department of Commerce, 1979.

Stobaugh, R. & Yergin, D. *Energy future: Report of the energy project of the Harvard Business School.* New York: Random House, 1979.

Strumpel, B., Morgan, J. N., & Zahn, E., Eds. *Human behavior in economic affairs.* Amsterdam: Elsevier, 1972.

Swan, S., & Knight, R. *Denver off-peak free fare public transit experiment.* Washington, D.C.: UMTA, 1979. (NTIS No. 06-0010-79-1)

Syme, G. J., Kantola, S. J., Reed, T. R., & Winkler, R. C. "Psychological studies of water consumption." In *Hydrology and Water Resources Symposium.* Perth, Australia: Institute of Engineers, 1979.

Syme, G. J., Kantola, S. J., & Thomas, J. F. "Water resources and the quarter acre block." In *People and the man-made environment.* R. Thorne & S. Arden, Eds. Sydney, Australia: School of Architecture, University of Sydney, 1980.

Syrek, D. B. *California litter—A comprehensive analysis and plan for abatement* (Technical Report prepared for the California State Assembly Committee on Resources and Land Use). Sacramento, California: Institute for Applied Research, 1975.

Syrek, D. B. *Litter reduction effectiveness, Volume one: The clean community system in Tampa, Macon, and Charlotte* (Technical Report). Sacramento, California: Institute for Applied Research, 1977. (a)

Syrek, D. B. *Litter reduction effectiveness, Volume two: Washington's litter control program and Oregon's container deposit legislation* (Technical Report). Sacramento, California: Institute for Applied Research, 1977. (b)

Thomas, J. F. Economic aspects of land use policies in a saline catchment. *Proceedings of the National Environmental Economic Conference.* Canberra, Australia: The Australian Government Publishing Service, 1979.

Tietzen, C., & Hart, S. S. Compost for agricultural land? *Journal of the Sanitary Engineering Division,* 1969, **95,** 269-287.

Tillman, R., & Kirkpatrick, C. A. *Promotion: Persuasive communication in marketing.* Homewood, Illinois: Richard D. Irwin, Inc., 1972.

Tuso, M., & Geller, E. S. Behavior analysis applied to environmental/ecological problems: A review. *Journal of Applied Behavior Analysis,* 1976, **9,** 526.

Ullmann, L. P., & Krasner, L., Eds. *Case studies in behavior modification.* New York: Holt, Rinehart & Winston, 1965.

United States Department of Energy. Residential conservation service program. *Federal Register.* Washington, D.C.: U.S. Government Printing Office, November 7, 1979.

United States Department of Energy. *The low cost/no cost energy conservation program in New England: An evaluation* (Technical Report for Contract DE-AM0180CS21366). Washington, D.C.: Office of Buildings and Community Systems, Market Development Branch, 1980.

United States Department of Energy. Residential efficiency program. *Federal Register.* Washington, D.C.: U.S. Government Printing Office, January 26, 1981.

United States Department of Transportation. *Carpool incentives and opportunities.* Washington, D.C.: U.S. Government Printing Office, February, 1975.

United States Environmental Protection Agency. *The urban noise survey* (EPA Report No. 550/9-77-100). Washington, D.C.: Author, 1977.

Van Liere, K. D., & Dunlap, R. E. The social bases of environmental concern: A review of hypotheses, explanations and empirical evidence. *Public Opinion Quarterly,* 1980, **44,** 181-197.

Van Liere, K.D., & Dunlap, R. E. Environmental concerns: Does it make a difference how it's measured? *Environment and Behavior,* 1981, in press.

Van Tine, D. G. For a total systems approach. *Proceedings, 1975 Conference on Waste Reduction.* Washington, D.C.: U.S. Environmental Protection Agency, 1975, pp. 113-118.

Verhallen, T. M. M., & Van Raaij, W. F. *Household behavior and energy use, No. 7.* Rotterdam, The Netherlands: Erasmus University, Papers on Economic Psychology, May 1980.

Waggoner, D. The Oregon bottle bill—Facts and fantasies. *Environment Action Bulletin,* September 1976, pp. 2-3.

Wahl, D., & Allison, G. *Reduce: Targets, means and impacts of source reduction.* Washington, D.C.: League of Women Voters Education Fund, 1975.

Wahl, D., & Bancroft, R. L. Solid waste management today . . . Bring about municipal change. *Nation's Cities,* August 1975, pp. 17-32.

Walker, E. A. Industry's commitment to waste reduction. *Proceedings, 1975 Conference on Waste Reduction.* Washington, D.C.: U.S. Environmental Protection Agency, 1975, pp. 119-123.

Walker, J. M. Energy demand behavior in a master-meter apartment complex: An experimental analysis. *Journal of Applied Psychology,* 1979, **64,** 190-196.

Ward, P. Deadly throwaways: Plastic six-pack binders and metal pull-tabs doom wildlife. *Defenders,* 1975.

Watkins, G. A. Developing a 'water concern' scale. *Journal of Environmental Education,* 1974, **5**(4), 54-58.

Waverman, L. Estimating the demand for energy: Heat without light. *Energy Policy,* 1977, **5,** 2-11.

Weeks, C. R., & McMahon, T. A. A comparison of water use in Australia and the USA. *Journal of American Water Works Association,* April 1973, pp. 232-237.

Weeks, C. R., & McMahon, T. A. Urban water use in Australia. *Civil Engineering Transactions,* 1974, **16,** 58-66.

Weigel, R. H. Environmental concern: The development of a measure. *Environment and Behavior,* 1978, **10,** 3-15.

Weigel, R. H., & Newman, L. S. Increasing attitude–behavior correspondence by broadening the scope of the behavioral measure. *Journal of Personality and Social Psychology,* 1976, **33,** 793-802.

Weigel, R. H., Woolston, V. L., & Gendelman, D. S. *Psychological studies of pollution control: An annotated bibliography.* Unpublished manuscript, Department of Psychology, Amherst College, 1979.

Weiglin, P. C. Marketing and the management attitude. *Transit Journal,* 1975, **2,** 35-44.

Wendt, K. A. Approaches to source reduction. *Proceedings, 1975 Conference on Waste Reduction.* Washington, D.C.: U.S. Environmental Protection Agency, 1975, pp. 66-77.

Westerman, R. R. Waste management through product design: The case of automobile tires. *Proceedings, 1975 Conference on Waste Reduction.* Washington, D.C.: U.S. Environmental Protection Agency, 1975.

Whitford, P. W. *Forecasting demand for urban water supply* (Standford Report EEP-36). Project on Engineering Economic Planning, 1970.

Wicker, A. W. Attitudes vs. action: The relationship of verbal and overt responses to attitude objects. *Journal of Social Issues,* 1969, **25,** 41-78.

Wicker, A. W. An examination of the "other variables" explanation of attitude-behavior inconsistency. *Journal of Personality and Social Psychology,* 1971, **19,** 18-30.

Williamson, D. R. *Statistics of water use.* Paper presented at the Water Research Foundation Seminar, Perth, Australia, 1975.

Wilson, G. T., & O'Leary, K. D. *Principles of behavior therapy.* Englewood Cliffs, N.J.: Prentice-Hall, 1980.

Winett, R. A. Efforts to disseminate a behavioral approach to energy conservation. *Professional Psychology,* 1976, **7,** 631-636.

Winett, R. A. Prompting turning-out lights in unoccupied rooms. *Journal of Environmental Systems,* 1978, **6,** 237-241.

Winett, R. A. "An emerging approach to energy conservation." In *Behavioral community psychology*. D. Glenwick & L. Jason, Eds. New York: Praeger, 1980.

Winett, R. A. *Energy conservation in the residential sector: A broad behavioral approach to high priority programs*. Unpublished manuscript, Department of Psychology, Virginia Polytechnic Institute and State University, 1981.

Winett, R. A., & Geller, E. S. Comment on psychological research and energy policy. *American Psychologist*, 1981, **36**, 425-426.

Winett, R. A., Hatcher, J., Leckliter, I., Fort, T. R., Fishback, J. F., & Riley, A. Modifying perception of comfort and electricity used for heating by social learning strategies: Residential field experiments. *ASHRAE Transactions*, 1981, **87**, 555-565.

Winett, R. A., Hatcher, J., Leckliter, I., Fort, T. R., Fishback, J. F., Riley, A. W., & Love, S. *The effects of videotape modeling and feedback on residential comfort, the thermal environment, and electricity consumption: Winter and summer studies*. Unpublished manuscript, Department of Psychology, Virginia Polytechnic Institute and State University, 1981.

Winett, R. A., Kagel, J. H., Battalio, R. C., & Winkler, R.C. Effects of monetary rebates, feedback and information on residential electricity conservation. *Journal of Applied Psychology*, 1978, **63**, 73-78.

Winett, R. A., Kaiser, S., & Haberkorn, E. The effects of monetary rebates and daily feedback on electricity conservation. *Journal of Environmental Systems*, 1977, **5**, 327-338.

Winett, R. A., & Neale, M. S. Psychological framework for energy conservation in buildings: Strategies, outcomes, directions. *Energy and Buildings*, 1979, **2**, 101-116.

Winett, R. A., & Neale, M. S. Results of experiments on flexitime and family life. *Monthly Labor Review*, November 1980, pp. 29-32.

Winett, R. A., & Neale, M. S. Flexible work schedules and family time allocation: Assessment of a system change on individual behavior using self-report logs. *Journal of Applied Behavior Analysis*, 1981, **14**, 39-46.

Winett, R. A., & Neale, M. S. "Modifying settings as a strategy for permanent, preventive behavior change: Flexible work schedules and family life as a case in point." In *Improving the long-term effects of psychotherapy*. P. Karoly & J. J. Steffen, Eds. New York: Gardner Press, 1981.

Winett, R. A., Neale, M. S., & Grier, H. C. The effects of self-monitoring and feedback on residential electricity consumption. *Journal of Applied Behavior Analysis*, 1979, **12**, 173-184.

Winett, R. A., Neale, M. S., Williams, K. R., Yokley, J., & Kauder, H. The effects of individual and group feedback on residential electricity consumption: Three replications. *Journal of Environmental Systems*, 1979, **8**, 217-233.

Winett, R. A., & Nietzel, M. Behavioral ecology, : Contingency management of residential use. *American Journal of Community Psychology*, 1975, **3**, 123-133.

Winkler, R. C. The relevance of economic theory and technology to token reinforcement systems. *Behavior Research and Therapy*, 1971, **9**, 81-88.

Winkler, R. C. "Behavioral economics, token economics and applied behavior analysis." In *Limits to action: The allocation of individual behavior*. J. E. R. Staddon, Ed. New York: Academic Press, 1981. (a)

Winkler, R. C. "Target behavior changes in behavioral economics." In *Current developments in the quantification of steady-state operant behavior*. C. M. Bradshaw, Ed. Amsterdam: Elsevier, 1981. (b)

Winkler, R. C., & Burkhard, B. *Towards a holistic analysis of behavior modification through behavioral economics*. Unpublished mansucript, Department of Psychology, University of Western Australia, 1981.

Winkler, R. C., Syme, G. J., & Thomas, J. F. "Social factors and water consumption." In *Hydrology and Water Resources Symposium*, Perth, Australia: Institute of Engineers, 1979.

Winkler, R. C., & Winett, R. A. Behavioral interventions in resource management: A systems approach based on behavioral economics. *American Psychologist*, 1982, in press.

Witmer, J. F., & Geller, E. S. Facilitating paper recycling: Effects of prompts, raffles, and contests. *Journal of Applied Behavior Analysis*, 1976, **9**, 315-322.

Wodarski, J. S. The reduction of electrical energy consumption: The application of behavior analysis. *Behavior Therapy*, 1976, **8**, 347-353.

Wolf, M. M. Social validity: The cure for subjective measurement or how applied behavior analysis is finding its heart. *Journal of Applied Behavior Analysis*, 1978, **11**, 203-214.

Yukobousky, R., & Fichter, P. Mobility club: A grassroots smalltown transport concept. *Transportation Research Record*, 1976, No. 559, 89-100.

Zerega, A. M. Transportation energy conservation policy: Implications for social science research. *Journal of Social Issues*, 1981, **37**, 31-50.

Author Index

Subject Index

About the Authors

E. Scott Geller received his Ph.D. in Experimental Psychology in 1969 from Southern Illinois University and is currently Professor in the Department of Psychology at Virginia Polytechnic Institute and State University. He is a member of the American Psychological Association, the Association for Behavior Analysis, the International Association of Applied Psychologists, and Psychonomic Society. He has published more than 80 articles in professional journals and has given over 100 presentations at professional conventions. About half of his professional efforts have been in behavioral community psychology (i.e., the application of behavioral analysis to the solution of community problems), and he has recently written seven book chapters in this area. Since 1973, Dr. Geller has been a principal investigator on 17 research grants, amounting to more than $500,000 of financial support from a variety of agencies, including the National Science Foundation; the U.S. Department of Health, Education, and Welfare; the U.S. Department of Energy; the U.S. Department of Transportation; General Motors Research Laboratories; and the Virginia Departments of Agriculture and Commerce, Welfare and Institutions, Energy, and Litter Control. He is on the Editorial Board of *Journal of Applied Behavior Analysis* and *Population and Environment: Behavioral and Social Issues* and serves as guest reviewer for numerous other journals in experimental and applied psychology.

Richard A. Winett earned his Ph.D. in 1971 in Clinical Psychology from the State University of New York at Stony Brook. From 1971 to 1976, he was an assistant professor of psychology at the University of Kentucky; from 1976 to 1979, he was senior research associate at the Institute for Behavioral Research in Silver Spring, Maryland; and since 1979, he has been Associate Professor in the Department of Psychology at Virginia Polytechnic Institute and State University. Dr. Winett's main interests have been in applying behavioral technology in educational settings and for environmental protection, particularly energy conservation. More recently, his work has included issues and standards in comfort and conservation in residential settings, alternative work patterns and community life, media approaches to behavior change, behavioral economics as applied to resource management, and health promotion. He is the author or coauthor of over 60 articles.

Peter B. Everett received his Ph.D. in Experimental Psychology and city and regional planning from the University of North Carolina at Chapel Hill in 1970. He is currently Asssociate Professor of Man-Environment Relations (an interdisciplinary environmental planning program emphasizing a social behavior approach to planning) and a faculty associate of The Pennsylvania Transportation Institute at The Pennsylvania State University. Dr. Everett's research has focused on transportation consumer information systems, travel behavior and energy, and the social impact of transportation innovations. He has worked with several agencies, including the U.S. Department of Transportation; the U.S. Department of Energy; the Pennsylvania, Washington, and North Carolina Departments of Transportation; and transportation systems in the following cities: Denver, Seattle, Spokane, State College, Bridgeport, Minneapolis-St. Paul, Toronto, Portland, Knoxville, Vancouver, and Vail. He is a past board member of the Centre Area Transportation Authority in State College, Pennsylvania, a member of the Transportation Research Board of the National Academy of Science committees on transit service characteristics, transit consumer concerns, transit marketing, transit performance characteristics, and marketing evaluation. He is also a member of the American Psychological Association and The Environmental Design Research Association.

Robin C. Winkler obtained his Ph.D. in Clinical Psychology from the University of South Wales in 1970 and is currently Associate Professor and Director of Clinical Training in the Department of Psychology of the University of Western Australia, Perth, Australia. He is a frequent visitor to the United States, with visiting professorships in the psychology departments at the State University of New York at Stony Brook (1970-71), Stanford University (1980), and in the economics department at Texas A & M (1975). He has pioneered research in the integration of economics and behavior modification and has received two research awards for his work in this area. Currently, his professional interests include behavioral economics and the application of behavioral technology to a range of social action concerns, including rights of mental clients, homosexuals, and patients in the health-care system.